EXPLORING UNITED STATES HISTORY

A READER

Volume II: 1865 to the Present

Second Edition

Edited by

Thomas M. Camfield

Joseph M. Rowe, Jr.

Sam Houston State University

KENDALL/HUNT PUBLISHING COMPANY
2460 Kerper Boulevard P.O. Box 539 Dubuque, Iowa 52004-0539

The following articles are reprinted from *American Heritage Magazine* by special permission of American Heritage, a division of Forbes, Inc.:

Bliven, Bruce, "Tempest Over Teapot," August, 1965, pp. 20–23, 100–105.
Braden, Tom, "The Birth of the CIA," February, 1977, pp. 4–13.
Carson, Gerald H., "Who put the borax in Dr. Wiley's butter?", August, 1956, pp. 58–63 and 95.
Cawthon, Charles, "July, 1944: St. Lô," June, 1974, pp. 4–11, 82–88.
Damon, Allan L., "The Great Red Scare," February, 1968, pp. 22–27, 75–77.
Davis, Kenneth S., "The Deadly Dust," February, 1971, pp. 44–47, 92–93.
Garraty, John A., "Bryan," December, 1961, pp. 4–11, 108–115.
Hale, William Harlan, "The Road to Yalta," June, 1961, pp. 34–40, 82–85.
Hamilton, Virginia Van Der Veer, "The Gentlewoman and the Robber Baron," April, 1970, pp. 78–86.
Honan, William H., "Japan Strikes: 1941," December, 1970, pp. 12–15, 91–95.
Jacob, Kathryn Allamong, "The Mosher Report," June/July, 1981, pp. 57–64.
Karp, Walter, "The Hour of the Founders," June/July, 1984, pp. 24–31.
Leuchtenburg, William E., "The Needless War with Spain," February, 1957, pp. 33–44 and 95.
O'Connor, Richard, "Mr. Coolidge's Jungle War," December, 1967, pp. 36–39, 89–93.
Sears, Stephen W., "Shut the Goddam Plant!," April/May, 1982, pp. 49–64.
Stevenson, Janet, "Rosa Parks Wouldn't Budge," February, 1972, pp. 56–64 and 85.
Tarr, Joel A., "Urban Pollution—Many Long Years Ago," October, 1971, pp. 65–69 and 106.
Weaver, John D., "Bonus March," June, 1963, pp. 18–23, 92–97.
Weisberger, Bernard A., "The Strange Affair of the Taking of the Panama Canal Zone," October, 1976, pp. 6–11, 68–77.
Westin, Alan F., "Ride-in," August, 1962, pp. 57–64.

Contents

Preface

Although largely an acquired taste, interest in history is also an inherent trait of human beings, developing with self-consciousness and out of curiosity about one's self and others, about time and events. For those of us enamored with the study of the past, it seems a natural, meaningful and important activity.

For human history to be fully appreciated, it needs to be studied in its grand sweep over the centuries and, at the same time, in its minute detail. History survey courses at the university level are primarily intended to introduce students to the major themes, trends and developments of peoples and nations. Such courses, and the textbooks used in them, necessarily focus on the sweep of events at the expense of detailed examinations of particular persons or topics.

This volume and its companion are intended to supplement a survey course textbook for United States history. They have been prepared in an effort to assure that our survey course students are exposed to detailed treatments of selected people and events, thereby perhaps acquiring an appreciation of this aspect of historical study. The articles we have chosen come from among the many superb pieces of scholarship which have appeared over the past forty-odd years in *American Heritage,* one of the nation's finest popular history journals. We think they offer the student an excellent sampling of the varied, rich and exciting history of the United States and its people.

April, 1990

Thomas M. Camfield
Joseph M. Rowe, Jr.

Preface to the Second Edition

Like most authors and editors, we welcome the opportunity to issue a second edition of this reader. It has permitted us to correct typographical errors which found their way into the first edition. It also offered us a chance to alter content and emphasis on the basis of actual classroom experience with the initial volume, and to introduce a few excellent articles which only the restrictions of space prevented inclusion the first time around.

November, 1991

Thomas M. Camfield
Joseph M. Rowe, Jr.

Part One

Emergence of Modern America

Industrialization, Urban Development, Protest and Reform

The period from the end of the Civil War to World War I was one of the most diverse in our nation's history. While the people continued to seize and settle the wilderness areas and to wage the last of the Indian wars, they also proceeded to transform the nation's economy into the urban industrial capitalist society which was to characterize the United States in the twentieth century. Developments of the late 19th and early 20th centuries shaped the significant features of modern America. The articles which follow have been selected with this theme in mind.

Alan Westin's account of the Afro-American struggle for civil rights in the 1870's and 1880's provides a fitting introduction to the modern period of United States history. It is a poignant reminder that protest and litigation by racial (and ethnic and religious) groups in pursuit of the ideals of liberty and equality—so much a part of our recent history—spans the entire period since the Civil War.

The rapid and extensive industrial developments of this period not only transformed the nation's economy, they also gave rise to immense concentrations of population, cities teeming with citizens drawn from virtually every quarter of the globe. These cities experienced numerous problems—problems of growth exceeding expansion of services, of an impoverished immigrant laboring class, of political corruption, of inadequate provision for health, education and welfare. Joel Tarr's discussion of pollution helps to convey a sense of the urban America of a century ago. He, too, reveals that still other problems of contemporary America are not unique to our times but have roots in a more distant past.

By the same token, Virginia Van Der Veer Hamilton's article reminds us that Americans of the early twentieth century rose to protest the unsavory practices and abuses of giant industrial corporations as have others ever since. Her account of Ida Tarbell's muckraking *History of the Standard Oil Company* helps illuminate both late nineteenth century industrialization and early twentieth century reform efforts.

The articles by Gerald Carson, John Garraty and Kathryn Jacob also reveal how developments eighty to a hundred years ago bear a similarity to those of our own time. The quest for governmental action arose as issues of health and welfare became matters of public concern for citizens of the United States. When the products of unregulated food and drug industries came under scrutiny, as Carson informs us, there was an understandable outcry of protest and subsequent enactment of the first federal laws to protect the public from the unscrupulous practices exposed.

Major features of this period were reflected in the life and career of William Jennings Bryan, as Garraty effectively demonstrates. A leader of agrarian protest, Bryan gave voice to the complaints of rural Americans for half a century. His views on reform represented the reactions of a substantial body of Americans to the transformations of their lives and of their nation wrought by industrialization.

The life and career of Clelia Mosher, like Bryan's, encompassed a broad swath of modern United States history. The struggle of American women for freedom and equality of opportunity, a century ago, is superbly revealed in Kathryn Jacob's biographical sketch of this fascinating and remarkable physician.

Ride-in!

Alan F. Westin

It began one day early in January when a Negro named Robert Fox boarded a streetcar in Louisville, Kentucky, dropped his coin into the fare box, and sat down in the white section of the car. Ordered to move, he refused, and the driver threw him off the car. Shortly after, Fox filed a charge of assault and battery against the streetcar company in the federal district court, claiming that separate seating policies were illegal and the driver's actions were therefore improper. The district judge instructed the jury that under federal law common carriers must serve all passengers equally without regard to race. So instructed, the jury found the company rules to be invalid and awarded damages of fifteen dollars (plus $72.80 in legal costs) to Mr. Fox.

Immediately there was sharp criticism of the Fox decision from the city and state administrations, both Democratic; the company defied the court's ruling and continued segregated seating. After several meetings with local federal officials and white attorneys co-operating with them, Louisville Negro leaders decided to launch a full-scale "ride-in." At 7 P.M. on May 12, a young Negro boy boarded a streetcar near the Willard Hotel, walked past the driver, and took a seat among the white passengers. the driver, under new company regulations, did not attempt to throw him off but simply stopped the car, lit a cigar, and refused to proceed until the Negro moved to "his place." While the governor, the Louisville chief of police, and other prominent citizens looked on from the sidewalks, a large crowd which included an increasingly noisy mob of jeering white teen-agers gathered around the streetcar.

Before long, there were shouts of "Put him out!" "Hit him!" "Kick him!" "Hang him!" Several white youths climbed into the car and began yelling insults in the face of the young Negro rider. He refused to answer—or to move. The youths dragged him from his seat, pulled him off the car, and began to beat him. Only when the Negro started to defend himself did the city police intervene: they arrested him for disturbing the peace and took him to jail.

This time the trial was held in Louisville city court, not the federal court. The magistrate ruled that streetcar companies were not under any obligation to treat Negroes exactly as they treated whites, and that any federal measures purporting to create such obligations would be "clearly invalid" under the constitutions of Kentucky and the United States. The defendant was fined, and the judge delivered a warning to Louisville Negroes that further ride-ins would be punished.

But the ride-in campaign was not halted that easily. In the following days, streetcar after streetcar was entered by Negroes who took seats in the white section. Now the drivers got off the cars entirely. On several occasions, the Negro riders drove the cars themselves, to the sound of cheers from Negro spectators. Then violence erupted. Bands of white youths and men began to throw Negro riders off the cars; windows were broken, cars were overturned, and for a time a general race riot threatened. Moderate Kentucky newspapers and many community leaders deplored the fighting; the Republican candidate for governor denounced the streetcar company's segregation policies and blamed the violence on Democratic encouragement of white extremists.

By this time, newspapers across the country were carrying reports of the conflict, and many editorials denounced the seating regulations. In Louisville, federal marshals and the United States attorney backed the rights of the Negro riders and stated that federal court action would be taken if necessary. There were even rumors that the President might send troops.

Under these threats, the streetcar company capitulated. Soon, all the city transit companies declared that "it was useless to try to resist or evade the enforcement by the United States authorities of the claim of Negroes to ride in the cars." To "avoid serious collisions," the company would thereafter allow all passengers to sit where they chose. Although a few disturbances took place in the following months, and some white intransigents boycotted the streetcars, mixed seating became a common practice. The Kentucky press soon pointed with pride to the spirit of conciliation and harmony which prevailed in travel facilities within the city, calling it a model for good race relations. Never again would Louisville streetcars be segregated.

The event may have the familiar ring of recent history, but it is not, for it occurred ninety-one years ago, in 1871. The streetcars were horse-drawn. The President who considered ordering troops to Louisville was ex-General Grant, not ex-General Eisenhower. The Republican gubernatorial candidate who supported the Negro riders, John Marshall Harlan, was not a post-World War II leader of the G.

O. P. but a former slaveholder from one of Kentucky's oldest and most famous
political families. And the "new" Negroes who waged this ride-in were not members of the Congress of Racial Equality and the National Association for the Advancement of Colored People, or followers of Dr. Martin Luther King, but former
slaves who were fighting for civil rights in their own time, and with widespread
success.

And yet those dramatic sit-ins, ride-ins, and walk-ins of the 1870's are almost
unknown to the American public today. The standard American histories do not
mention them, providing only thumbnail references to "bayonet-enforced" racial
contacts during Reconstruction. Most commentators view the Negro's resort to direct action as an invention of the last decade. Clearly, then, it is time that the
civil-rights struggle of the 1870's and 1880's was rescued from newspaper files
and court archives, not only because it is historically important but also because it
has compelling relevance for our own era.

Contrary to common assumptions today, no state in the Union during the
1870's, including those south of the Mason-Dixon line, required separation of
whites and Negroes in places of public accommodation. Admission and arrangement policies were up to individual owners. In the North and West, many theatres,
hotels, restaurants, and public carriers served Negro patrons without hesitation or
discrimination. Some accepted Negroes only in second-class accommodations, such
as smoking cars on railroads or balconies in theatres, where they sat among whites
who did not have first-class tickets. Other northern and western establishments, especially the more exclusive ones, refused Negro patronage entirely.

The situation was similar in the larger cities of the southern and border states.
Many establishments admitted Negroes to second-class facilities. Some gave first-
class service to those of privileged social status—government officials, army officers, newspapermen, and clergymen. On the other hand, many places of public
accommodation, particularly in the rural areas and smaller cities of the South, were
closed to Negroes whatever their wealth or status.

From 1865 through the early 1880's, the general trend in the nation was toward wider acceptance of Negro patronage. The federal Civil Rights Act of 1866,
with its guarantee to Negroes of "equal benefit of the laws," had set off a flurry
of enforcement suits—for denying berths to Negroes on a Washington-New York
train; for refusing to sell theatre tickets to Negroes in Boston; and for barring
Negro women from the waiting rooms and parlor cars of railroads in Virginia, Illinois, and California. Ratification of the Fourteenth Amendment in 1868 had
spurred more challenges. Three northern states, and two southern states under Reconstruction regimes, passed laws making it a crime for owners of public-accom-
modation businesses to discriminate. Most state and federal court rulings on these
laws between 1865 and 1880 held in favor of Negro rights, and the rulings built up
a steady pressure on owners to relax racial bars.

Nevertheless, instances of exclusion and segregation continued throughout the 1870's. To settle the issue once and for all (thereby reaping the lasting appreciation of the Negro voters), congressional Republicans led by Senator Charles Sumner pressed for a federal statute making discrimination in public accommodations a crime. Democrats and conservative Republicans warned in the congressional debates that such a law would trespass on the reserve powers of the states and reminded the Sumner supporters that recent Supreme Court decisions had taken a narrow view of federal power under the Civil War amendments.

After a series of legislative compromises, however, Sumner's forces were able to enact the statute; on March 1, 1875, "An Act to Protect all Citizens in their Civil and Legal Rights" went into effect. "It is essential to just government," the preamble stated, that the nation "recognize the equality of all men before the law, and . . . it is the duty of the government in its dealings with the people to mete out equal and exact justice to all, of whatever nativity, race, color, or persuasion, religious or political . . ."

Section 1 of the act declared that "All persons within the jurisdiction of the United States shall be entitled to the full and equal enjoyment of the accommodations . . . of inns, public conveyances on land or water, theaters and other places of public amusement; subject only to the conditions and limitations established by law, and applicable alike to citizens of every race or color. . . ." Section 2 provided that any person violating the act could be sued in federal district court for a penalty of $500, could be fined $500 to $1,000, or could be imprisoned from thirty days to one year. (A separate section forbade racial discrimination in the selection of juries.)

Reaction to the law was swift. Two Negro men were admitted to the dress circle of Macauley's Theatre in Louisville and sat through the performance without incident. In Washington, Negroes were served for the first time at the bar of the Willard Hotel, and a Negro broke the color line when he was seated at McVicker's Theatre In Chicago. But in other instances, Negroes were rejected despite "Sumner's law." Several hotels in Chattanooga turned in their licenses, became private boardinghouses, and accepted whites only. Restaurants and barber shops in Richmond turned away Negro customers.

Suits challenging refusals were filed en masse throughout the country. Perhaps a hundred were decided in the federal district courts during the late 1870's and early 1880's. Federal judges in Pennsylvania, Texas, Maryland, and Kentucky, among others, held the law to be constitutional and ruled in favor of Negro complainants. In North Carolina, New Jersey, and California, however, district judges held the law invalid. And when other courts in New York, Tennessee, Missouri, and Kansas put the issue to the federal circuit judges, the judges divided on the question, and the matter was certified to the United States Supreme Court.

But the Supreme Court did not exactly rush to make its ruling. Though two cases testing the 1875 act reached it in 1876 and a third in 1877, the Justices simply held them on their docket. In 1879, the Attorney General filed a brief defending the constitutionality of the law, but still the Court reached no decisions. In 1880, three additional cases were filed, but two years elapsed before the Solicitor General presented a fresh brief supporting the statute. It was not until late in 1883 that the Supreme Court passed upon the 1875 act, in what became famous as the *Civil Rights Cases* ruling. True, the Court was badly behind in its work in this period, but clearly the Justices chose to let the civil-rights cases "ripen" for almost eight years.

When they finally came to grips with the issue, six separate test suits were involved. The most celebrated had arisen in New York City in November of 1879. Edwin Booth, the famous tragedian and brother of John Wilkes Booth, had opened a special Thanksgiving week engagement at the Grand Opera House. After playing *Hamlet, Othello,* and *Richelieu* to packed houses, he was scheduled to perform Victor Hugo's *Ruy Blas* at the Saturday matinee on November 22.

One person who had decided to see Booth that Saturday was William R. Davis, Jr., who was later described in the press as a tall, handsome, and well-spoken Negro of twenty-six. He was the business agent of the *Progressive-American,* a Negro weekly published in New York City. At 10 o'clock Saturday morning, Davis' girl friend ("a bright octoroon, almost white," as the press put it), purchased two reserved seats at the box office of the Grand Opera House. At 1:30 P.M., Davis and his lady presented themselves at the theatre, only to be told by the doorkeeper, Samuel Singleton, that "these tickets are no good." If he would step out to the box office, Singleton told Davis, his money would be refunded.

It is unlikely that Davis was surprised by Singleton's action, for this was not the first time he had encountered such difficulties. Shortly after the passage of the 1875 act, Davis had been refused a ticket to the dress circle of Booth's Theatre in New York. He had sworn out a warrant against the ticket seller, but the failure of his witnesses to appear at the grand jury proceedings had led to a dismissal of the complaint. This earlier episode, as well as Davis' activity as a Negro journalist, made it probable that this appearance at the Opera House in 1879 was a deliberate test of the management's discriminatory policies.

Though Davis walked out of the lobby at Singleton's request, he did not turn in his tickets for a refund. Instead, he summoned a young white boy standing near the theatre, gave him a dollar (plus a dime for his trouble), and had him purchase two more tickets. When Davis and his companion presented these to Singleton, only the lady was allowed to pass. Again Davis was told that his ticket was "no good." When he now refused to move out of the doorway, Singleton called a policeman and asked that Davis be escorted off the theatre property. The officer told Davis that the Messrs. Poole and Donnelly, the managers of the Opera House, did not admit colored persons. "Perhaps the managers do not," Davis retorted, "but the laws of the country [do]."

The following Monday, November 24, Davis filed a criminal complaint; on December 9, this time with witnesses in abundance, Singleton was indicted in what the press described as the first criminal proceeding under the 1875 act to go to trial in New York. When the case opened on January 14, 1880, Singleton's counsel argued that the 1875 law was unconstitutional. "It interferes," he said, "with the right of the State of New York to provide the means under which citizens of the State have the power to control and protect their rights in respect to their private property." The assistant United States attorney replied that such a conception of states' rights had been "exploded and superseded long ago." It was unthinkable, he declared, that "the United States could not extend to one citizen of New York a right which the State itself gave to others of its citizens—the right of admission to places of public amusement."

The presiding judge decided to take the constitutional challenge under advisement and referred it to the circuit court, for consideration at its February term. This left the decision up to Justice Samuel Blatchford of the Supreme Court, who was assigned to the circuit court for New York, and District Judge William Choate. The two judges reached opposite conclusions and certified the questions to the United States Supreme Court.

Davis' case, under the title of *United States v. Singleton,* reached the Supreme Court in 1880. Already lodged on the Court's docket were four similar criminal prosecutions under the act of 1875. *U.S. v. Stanley* involved the refusal of Murray Stanley in 1875 to serve a meal at his hotel in Topeka, Kansas, to a Negro, Bird Gee. *U.S. v. Nichols* presented the refusal in 1876 of Samuel Nichols, owner of the Nichols House in Jefferson City, Missouri, to accept a Negro named W. H. R. Agee as a guest. *U.S. v. Ryan* involved the conduct of Michael Ryan, doorkeeper of Maguire's Theatre in San Francisco, in denying a Negro named George M. Tyler entry to the dress circle on January 4, 1876. In *U.S. v. Hamilton,* James Hamilton, a conductor on the Nashville, Chattanooga, and St. Louis Railroad, had on April 21, 1879, denied a Negro woman with a first-class ticket access to the ladies' car.

There was a fifth case, with a somewhat different setting. On the evening of May 22, 1879, Mrs. Sallie J. Robinson, a twenty-eight-year-old Negro, purchased two first-class tickets at Grand Junction, Tennessee, for a trip to Lynchburg, Virginia, on the Memphis and Charleston Railroad. Shortly after midnight she and her nephew, Joseph C. Robinson, described as a young Negro "of light complexion, light hair, and light blue eyes," boarded the train and started into the parlor car. The conductor, C. W. Reagin, held Mrs. Robinson back ("bruising her arm and jerking her roughly around," she alleged) and pushed her into the smoker.

A few minutes later, when Joseph informed the conductor that he was Mrs. Robinson's nephew and was a Negro, the conductor looked surprised. In that case, he said, they could go into the parlor car at the next stop. The Robinsons finished the ride in the parlor car but filed complaints with the railroad about their treatment and then sued for $500 under the 1875 act. At the trial, Reagin testified that he had thought Joseph to be a white man with a colored woman, and his experience was that such associations were "for illicit purposes."

Counsel for the Robinsons objected to Reagin's testimony, on the ground that his actions were based on race and constituted no defense. Admitting the constitutionality of the 1875 law for purposes of the trial, the railroad contended that the action of its conductor did not fall within the statute. The district judge ruled that the motive for excluding persons was the decisive issue under the act: if the jury believed that the conductor had acted because he thought Mrs. Robinson "a prostitute travelling with her paramour," whether "well or ill-founded" in that assumption, the exclusion was not because of race and the railroad was not liable. The jury found for the railroad, and the Robinsons appealed.

These, with William Davis' suit against the doorkeeper of New York's Grand Opera House, were the six cases to which the Supreme Court finally turned in 1882. The Justices were presented with a learned and eloquent brief for the United States submitted by Solicitor General Samuel F. Phillips, who reviewed the leading cases, described the history of the Civil War amendments to the Constitution, and stressed the importance to the rights of citizens of equal access to public accommodation. Four times since 1865, Phillips noted, civil-rights legislation had been enacted by a Congress filled with men who had fought in the Civil War and had written the war amendments. These men understood that "every rootlet of slavery has an individual vitality, and, to its minutest hair, should be anxiously followed and plucked up. . . ." They also knew that if the federal government allowed Negroes to be denied accommodation "by persons who notably were sensitive registers of local public opinion," then "what upon yesterday was only 'fact' will become 'doctrine' tomorrow."

The Supreme Court Justices who considered Phillips' brief and the six test cases were uncommonly talented, among them being Chief Justice Morrison R. Waite, a man underrated today; Joseph P. Bradley, that Court's most powerful intellect; and Stephen J. Field, a *laissez-faire* interpreter of American constitutional law. John Marshall Harlan, the youngest man on the Court, had already started on the course which was to mark him as the most frequent and passionate dissenter in the Gilded Age.

As a whole, the Court might have appeared to be one Act. All were Republicans except Justice Field, and he was a Democrat appointed by Abraham Lincoln. All except Justice Harlan, who was the Court's only southerner, had made their careers primarily in the northern and western states. Without exception, all had supported the Northern cause in the war, and none had any hostility toward Negroes as a class.

Yet on the afternoon of October 15, 1883, Justice Bradley announced that the Court found Sections 1 and 2 of the Civil Rights Act of 1875 to be unconstitutional. (This disposed of five of the cases; the sixth, *U.S. v. Hamilton,* was denied review on a procedural point.) There was added irony in the fact that Bradley delivered the majority opinion for eight of the Justices. A one-time Whig, Bradley had struggled for a North-South compromise in the darkening months of 1860–61, then had swung to a strong Unionist position after the firing on Fort Sumter. He had run for Congress on the Lincoln ticket in 1862 and in 1868 headed the New Jersey electors for Grant. When the Thirteenth and Fourteenth Amendments were adopted, he had given them firm support, and his appointment to the Supreme Court by Grant in 1870 had drawn no criticism from friends of the Negro, as had the appointment of John Marshall Harlan seven years later.

Bradley's opinion had a tightly reasoned simplicity. The Thirteenth Amendment forbade slavery and involuntary servitude, he noted, but protection against the restoration of bondage could not be stretched to cover federal regulation of "social" discriminations such as those dealt with in the 1875 statue. As for the Fourteenth Amendment, that was addressed only to deprivations of rights by the *states;* it did not encompass *private* acts of discrimination. Thus there was no source of constitutional authority for "Sumner's law"; it had to be regarded as an unwarranted invasion of an area under state jurisdiction. Even as a matter of policy, Bradley argued, the intention of the war amendments to aid the newly freed Negro had to have some limits. At some point, the Negro must cease to be "the special favorite of the law" and take on "the rank of a mere citizen."

At the Atlanta Opera House on the evening of the Court's decision, the end man of Haverly's Minstrels interrupted the performance to announce the ruling. The entire orchestra and dress circle audience rose and cheered. Negroes sitting in the balcony kept their seats, "stunned," according to one newspaper account. A short time earlier, a Negro denied entrance to the dress circle had filed charges against the Opera House management under the 1875 Act. Now his case—their case—was dead.

Of all the nine Justices, only John Marshall Harlan, a Kentuckian and a former slave-holder, announced that he dissented from the ruling. He promised to give a full opinion soon.

Justice Harlan's progress from a supporter of slavery to a civil-rights dissenter makes a fascinating chronicle. Like Bradley, he had entered politics as a Whig and had tried to find a middle road between secessionist Democrats and anti-slavery Republicans. Like Bradley, he became a Unionist after the firing on Fort Sumter. But there the parallels ended. Although Harlan entered the Union Army, he was totally opposed to freeing the slaves, and his distaste for Lincoln and the Radicals was complete. Between 1863 and 1868, he led the Conservative party in Kentucky, a third-party movement which supported the war but opposed pro-Negro and civil-rights measures as "flagrant invasions of property rights and local government."

By 1868, however, Harlan had become a Republican. The resounding defeat of the Conservatives in the 1867 state elections convinced him that a third party had no future in Kentucky. His antimonopoly views and his general ideas about economic progress conflicted directly with state Democratic policies, and when the Republicans nominated his former field commander, Ulysses S. Grant, for President, in 1868, Harlan was one of the substantial number of Conservatives who joined the G.O. P.

His views on Negro rights also changed at this time. The wave of vigilante activities against white Republicans and Negroes that swept Kentucky in 1868–70, with whippings and murders by the scores, convinced Harlan that federal guarantees were essential. He watched Negroes in Kentucky moving with dignity and skill toward useful citizenship, and his devout Presbyterianism led him to adopt a "brotherhood-of-man" outlook in keeping with his church's national position. Perhaps he may have been influenced by his wife, Mallie, whose parents were New England abolitionists. As a realistic Republican politician, he was also aware that 60,000 Kentucky Negroes would become voters in 1870.

Thus a "new" John Harlan took the stump as Republican gubernatorial candidate in 1871, the year of the Louisville streetcar ride-ins. He opened his rallies by confessing that he had formerly been anti-Negro. But "I have lived long enough," he said, "to feel that the most perfect despotism that ever existed on this earth was the institution of African slavery." The war amendments were necessary "to place it beyond the power of any State to interfere with . . . the results of the war. . . ." The South should stop agitating the race issue, and should turn to rebuilding itself on progressive lines. When the Democrats laughed at "Harlan the Chameleon" and read quotations from his earlier anti-Negro speeches, Harlan replied: "Let it be said that I am right rather than consistent."

Harlan soon became an influential figure in the Republican party and, when President Rutherford B. Hayes decided to appoint a southern Republican to the Supreme Court in 1877, he was a logical choice. Even then, the Negro issue rose to shake Harlan's life again. His confirmation was held up because of doubts by some senators as to his "real" civil-rights views. Only after Harlan produced his speeches between 1871 and 1877 and party leaders supported his firmness on the question was he approved.

Once on the Supreme Court, Harlan could have swung back to a conservative position on civil rights. Instead, he became one of his generation's most intense and uncompromising defenders of the Negro. Perhaps his was the psychology of the convert who defends his hew faith more passionately, even more combatively, than the born believer. Harlan liked to think that he had changed because he knew the South and realized that any relaxation of federal protection of the rights Negroes would encourage the "white irreconcilables" first to acts of discrimination and then to violence, which would destroy all hope of accommodation between the races.

When Harlan sat down in October of 1883 to write his dissent in the *Civil Rights Cases,* he hoped to set off a cannon of protest. But he simply could not get his thoughts on paper. He worked late into the night, and even rose from half-sleep to write down ideas that he was afraid would elude him in the morning. "It was a trying time for him," his wife observed. "In point of years, he was much the youngest man on the Bench; and standing alone, as he did in regard to a decision which the whole nation was anxiously awaiting, he felt that . . . he must speak not only forcibly but wisely."

After weeks of drafting and discarding, Harlan seemed to reach a dead end. The dissent would not "write." It was at this point that Mrs. Harlan contributed a dramatic touch to the history of the *Civil Rights Cases*.

When the Harlans had moved to Washington in 1877, the Justice had acquired from a collector the inkstand which Chief Justice Roger Taney had used in writing all his opinions. Harlan was fond of showing this to guests and remarking that "it was the very inkstand from which the infamous *Dred Scott* opinion was written." Early in the 1880's, however, a niece of Taney's, who was engaged in collecting her uncle's effects, visited the Harlans. When she saw the inkstand she asked Harlan for it, and the Justice agreed. The next morning Mrs. Harlan, noting her husband's reluctance to part with his most prized possession, quietly arranged to have the inkstand "lost." She hid it away, and Harlan was forced to make an embarrassed excuse to Taney's niece.

Now, on the Sunday morning, probably early in November of 1883, after Harlan had spent a sleepless night working on his dissent, Mallie Harlan remembered the inkstand. While the Justice was at church, she retrieved it from its hiding place, filled it with a fresh supply of ink and pen points, and placed it on the blotter of his desk. When her husband returned from church, she told him, with an air of mystery, that he would find something special in his study. Harlan was overjoyed to recover his symbolic antique. Mrs. Harlan's gesture was successful, for as she relates:

> The memory of the historic part that Taney's inkstand had played in the Dred Scott decision, in temporarily tightening the shackles of slavery upon the negro race in those antebellum days, seemed, that morning, to act like magic in clarifying my husband's thoughts in regard to the law . . . intended by Sumner to protect the recently emancipated slaves in the enjoyment of equal 'civil rights.' His pen fairly flew on that day and, with the running start he then got, he soon finished his dissent.

How directly the recollection of Dred Scott pervaded Harlan's dissent is apparent to anyone who reads the opinion. He began by noting that the pre-Civil War Supreme Court had upheld congressional laws forbidding individuals to interfere with recovery of fugitive slaves. To strike down the Act of 1875 meant that "the rights of freedom and American citizenship cannot receive from the Nation that efficient protection which heretofore was unhesitatingly accorded to slavery and the rights of masters."

Harlan argued that the Civil Rights Act of 1875 was constitutional on any one of several grounds. The Thirteenth Amendment had already been held to guarantee "universal civil freedom"; Harlan stated that barring Negroes from facilities licensed by the state and under legal obligation to serve all persons without discrimination restored a major disability of slavery days and violated that civil freedom. As for the Fourteenth Amendment, its central purpose had been to extend national citizenship to the Negro, reversing the precedent upheld in the Dred Scott decision; its final section gave Congress power to pass appropriate legislation to enforce that affirmative grant as well as to enforce the section barring any state action which might deny liberty or equality. Now, the Supreme Court was deciding what legislation was appropriate and necessary for those purposes, although that decision properly belonged to Congress.

Even under the "State action" clause of the Fourteenth Amendment, Harlan continued, the 1875 act was constitutional; it was well established that "railroad corporations, keepers of inns and managers of places of public accommodation are agents or instrumentalities of the State." Finally, Harlan attacked the unwillingness of the Court's majority to uphold the public-carrier section of the act under Congress' power to regulate interstate trips. That was exactly what was involved in Mrs. Robinson's case against the Memphis and Charleston Railroad, he reminded his colleagues; it had not been true before the Congress had had to cite the section of the Constitution on which it relied.

In his peroration, Harlan replied to Bradley's comment that Negroes had been made "a special favorite of the law." The war amendments had been passed not to "favor" the Negro, he declared, but to include him as "part of the people for whose welfare and happiness government is ordained."

> Today, it is the colored race which is denied, by corporations and individuals wielding public authority, rights fundamental in their freedom and citizenship. At some future time, it may be that some other race will fall under the ban of race discrimination. If the constitutional amendments be enforced, according to the intent with which, as I conceived, they were adopted, there cannot be in this republic, any class of human beings in practical subjection to another class. . . .

The *Civil Rights Cases* ruling did two things. First, it destroyed the delicate balance of federal guarantee, Negro protest, and private enlightenment which was producing a steadily widening area of peacefully integrated public facilities in the North and South during the 1870's and early 1880's. Second, it had an immediate and profound effect on national and state politics as they related to the Negro. By denying Congress power to protect the Negro's rights to equal treatment, the Supreme Court wiped the issue of civil rights from the Republican party's agenda of national responsibility. At the same time, those southern political leaders who saw anti-Negro politics as the most promising avenue to power could now rally the "poor whites" to the banner of segregation.

If the Supreme Court had stopped with the *Civil Rights Cases* of 1883, the situation of Negroes would have been bad but not impossible. Even in the South, there was no immediate imposition of segregation in public facilities. During the late 1880's, Negroes could be found sharing places with whites in many southern restaurants, streetcars, and theatres. But increasingly, Democratic and Populist politicians found the Negro an irresistible target. As Solicitor General Phillips had warned the Supreme Court, what had been tolerated as the "fact" of discrimination was now being translated into "doctrine": between 1887 and 1891, eight southern states passed laws requiring railroads to separate all white and Negro passengers. The Supreme Court upheld these laws in the 1896 case of *Plessy v. Ferguson*. Then in the Berea College case of 1906, it upheld laws forbidding private schools to educate Negro and white children together. Both decisions aroused Harlan's bitter dissent. In the next fifteen or twenty years, the chalk line of Jim Crow was drawn across virtually every area of public contact in the South.

Today, as this line is slowly and painfully being erased, we may do well to reflect on what might have been in the South if the Civil Rights Act of 1875 had been upheld, in whole or in part. Perhaps everything would have been the same. Perhaps forces at work between 1883 and 1940 were too powerful for a Supreme Court to hold in check. Perhaps "Sumner's law" was greatly premature. Yet it is difficult to believe that total, state-enforced segregation was inevitable in the South after the 1880's. If in these decades the Supreme Court had taken the same *laissez-faire* attitude toward race relations as it took toward economic affairs, voluntary integration would have survived as a counter-tradition to Jim Crow and might have made the transition of the 1950's less painful than it was. At the very least, one cannot help thinking that Harlan was a better sociologist than his colleagues and a better southerner than the "irreconcilables." American constitutional history has a richer ring to it because of the protest that John Marshall Harlan finally put down on paper from Roger Taney's inkwell in 1883.

Alan F. Westin is an associate professor of public law and government at Columbia University. He is at present working on a biography of Justice John Marshall Harlan—who, incidentally, was the grandfather of a present Supreme Court Justice who bears the same name.

For further reading: The Constitutional Doctrines of Justice Harlan, *by Floyd Barzillia Clark (Johns Hopkins, 1915);* The Supreme Court in United States History, *Vol. II: 1836–1918, by Charles Warren (Little, Brown, 1960);* The Strange Career of Jim Crow, *by C. Vann Woodward (Oxford University Press, 1958).*

Urban Pollution—Many Long Years Ago

Joel A. Tarr

To many urban Americans in the 1970's, fighting their way through the traffic's din and gagging on air heavy with exhaust fumes, the automobile is a major villain in the sad tale of atmospheric pollution. Yet they have forgotten, or rather never knew, that the predecessor of the auto was also a major polluter. The faithful, friendly horse was charged with creating the very problems today attributed to the automobile: air contaminants harmful to health, noxious odors, and noise. At the beginning of the twentieth century, in fact, writers in popular and scientific periodicals were decrying the pollution of the public streets and demanding ''the banishment of the horse from American cities'' in vigorous terms. The presence of 120,000 horses in New York City, wrote one 1908 authority for example, is ''an economic burden, an affront to cleanliness, and a terrible tax upon human life.'' The solution to the problem, agreed the critics, was the adoption of the ''horseless carriage.''

A concern with clean streets and with the horse as a principal obstacle to them was nothing new. European cities had shown concern for the problem as early as the fourteenth century, as had American cities from their beginnings. But it required a more statistically minded age to measure the actual amount of manure produced by the horse. Sanitary experts in the early part of the twentieth century agreed that the normal city horse produced between fifteen and thirty pounds of manure a day, with the average being something like twenty-two pounds. In a city like Milwaukee in 1907, for instance, with a human population of 350,000 and a horse population of 12,500, this meant 133 tons of manure a day, for a daily average of nearly three-quarters of a pound of manure for each resident. Or, as health officials in Rochester, New York, calculated in 1900, the fifteen thousand horses in that city produced enough manure in a year to make a pile 175 feet high covering an acre of ground and breeding sixteen billion flies, each one a potential spreader of germs.

Milwaukee and Rochester resembled other American cities in 1900 in having thousands of horses at work in their streets even after the automobile and electric streetcar had been introduced. Chicago had 83,330, Detroit 12,000, and Columbus 5,000. Overall, there were probably between three and three and a half million horses in American cities as the century opened, compared with about seventeen million living in more bucolic environments. (Today, at a time when horseback riding for pleasure is on the rise, the total number of horses in the United States is somewhat over seven million.) The ratio of horses to people was much higher in cities where traction lines were not yet completely electrified. In 1890, even after electrification had already begun, twenty-two thousand horses and mules were still required simply for pulling street cars in New York City and in Brooklyn, with a total of ten thousand performing similarly in Philadelphia and Chicago. Ten years earlier, when New York and Brooklyn had counted no electric railways and 1,764,168 souls, they had a total equine population of 150,000 to 175,000.

To a great extent nineteenth-century urban life moved at the pace of horse-drawn transportation, and the evidence of the horse was everywhere—in the piles of manure that littered the streets attracting swarms of flies and creating stench, in the iron rings and hitching posts sunk into the pavements for fastening horses' reins, and in the numerous livery stables that gave off a mingled smell of horse urine and manure, harness oil and hay. In 1880 New York and Brooklyn were served by 427 blacksmith shops, 249 carriage and wagon enterprises, 262 wheelwright shops, and 290 establishments dealing in saddles and harnesses. They were eminently necessary. On a typical day in 1885 an engineer, Francis V. Greene, making a study of urban traffic conditions, counted 7,811 horse-drawn vehicles, many with teams of two or more horses, passing the busy corner of Broadway and Pine Street.

While some of these conveyances were fine carriages drawn by spirited teams, the most common city horses were commercial or work animals. City streets were crowded with large team-pulled drays guided by husky and colorfully profane drivers and piled high with heavy freight. Among these, single-horse spring wagons twisted their way, making deliveries of ice, milk, and goods of every kind to residential areas. Their sides were often brightly decorated with advertisements, catching the eyes of passers-by and of the riders in the many omnibuses and hacks plying their routes. The horse remained essential in urban civilization, even after the development of the steam engine. As the *Nation* noted in 1872, though great improvements had been made in the development of such "agents of progress" as the railroad, the steamboat, and the telegraph, modern society's dependence on the horse had "grown almost *pari passu* with our dependence on steam." For it was the horse who fed the railroads and steamboats with passengers and freight, and who provided transportation within the cities.

Yet this hard-working animal, so vital to the functioning of urban society, posed problems that were recognized by even the earliest American city dwellers. The question of clean streets was most obvious. In eighteenth-century Boston and New York, money was allocated by the city fathers for street cleaning, and householders were required to sweep the road in front of their doorways. Cities made sporadic attempts during the mid-nineteenth century to mechanize the tasks of sanitation. In 1855 New York introduced street-sweeping machines and self-loading carts, and in 1865 urban entrepreneurs formed the New York Sanitary and Chemical Compost Manufacturing Company for the purpose of "cleansing cities, towns, and villages in the United States" with several varieties of mechanical devices adapted to the task. By 1880 almost all cities over thirty thousand in population employed street-cleaners.

American cities made their most sustained efforts to clean the streets under the stimulus of the fear induced by epidemics of cholera, smallpox, yellow fever, or typhoid. Many eighteenth- and nineteenth-century medical authorities believed that such diseases were caused by "a combination of certain atmospheric conditions and putrefying filth," among which horse manure was a chief offender. In 1752 Boston selectmen allocated extra funds to clean the streets because of the fear that street dirt might contain smallpox infection, and in 1795, during the yellow-fever season, town officials invited neighboring farmers to collect the manure from the streets free of charge. The city fathers of New York, faced by the threat of cholera in 1832, made special efforts to cleanse the cobblestones, thereby divesting the city "of that foul aliment on which the pestilence delights to feed."

But unless jolted by rampant disease, city authorities and citizens tolerated a great deal of "that foul aliment" in their streets. One reason, perhaps, was a reluctance to spend money on such an unsatisfying, if crucial, municipal effort. Some cities tried to cover the cost of street cleaning by selling the manure for fertilizer. In 1803 the New York superintendent of scavengers expended about twenty-six thousand dollars for street cleaning and realized over twenty-nine thousand dollars from the sale of the manure collected. Despite this instance of profitable purifying, however, paid scavenging did not generally achieve great results. In those cases where private contractors were responsible for cleaning the streets, citizens often complained that they neglected other forms of rubbish and only collected the salable manure. Nor did a shift to public sanitation service improve things. Officials of post-Civil War years often reported that street dirt was becoming too mixed with other forms of litter to be sold as fertilizer. Moreover, whatever the salable quality of the street refuse, urban sanitation departments during the nineteenth century were notoriously inefficient. Vexed by graft and corruption, they were staffed by "old and indigent men," "prisoners who don't like to work," and "persons on relief."

Street cleaning, therefore, remained largely inadequate, and one is thus not surprised to discover that newspapers, diaries, and governmental reports abound with complaints about the problems created in the city by horse manure left in the public thoroughfares. Manure collected into unattended piles by the street cleaners bred huge numbers of flies and created "pestilential vapors." Offal was sometimes carried from wealthy residential neighborhoods and dumped in poor neighborhoods, where it was left to rot. Streets turned into virtual cesspools when it rained, and long-skirted ladies suffered the indignity of trailing their hems in liquefied manure. In London, ladies and gentlemen were aided in their navigation through a sea of horse droppings by "crossing-sweepers," but no such group appeared in more democratic American cities. Yet dry weather was not great improvement, for then there were complaints of the "pulverized horse dung" that blew into people's faces and the windows of their homes, and over the outdoor displays of merchants' wares. The coming of paved streets accelerated this problem, as wheels and hoofs ground the sun-dried manure against the hard surfaces and amplified the amount of dust.

And then there was noise. In many American cities, early paving consisted largely of cobblestones, on which the clopping and clanking of horses' iron shoes and the iron-tired wheels of carts and wagons created an immense din. Benjamin Franklin complained in the late eighteenth century of the "thundering of coaches, chariots, chaises, waggons, drays and whole fraternity of noise" that assailed the ears of Philadelphians. Similar comments about urban noise were made by travellers in other cities. Attempts were made quite early to quiet the clamor. In 1747, in Boston, the town council banned traffic from King Street so that the noise would not distract the deliberations of the General Court. In 1785 New York City passed an ordinance forbidding teams and wagons with iron-shod wheels from the streets. In London good medical management required the putting of straw on the pavement outside sick people's houses to muffle the sounds of traffic, a practice undoubtedly followed in America. Yet the problem grew with the growing nation. As late as the 1890's a writer in *Scientific American* noted that the sounds of traffic on busy New York streets made conversation nearly impossible, while the author William Dean Howells complained that "the sharp clatter of the horses' iron shoes" on the pavement tormented his ear.

If the horse, by his biological necessities, created problems for the city, the city, in turn, was a harsh environment for the animals whose possession had once been the mark and privilege of nobility. The horse belonged to the open spaces and the battlefield. In an urban setting he was, with rare exception, a drudge. City horses were notoriously overworked. The average streetcar nag had a life expectancy of barely two years, and it was a common sight to see drivers and teamsters savagely lashing their overburdened animals. The mistreatment of city horses was a key factor in moving Henry Bergh to found the American Society for the Prevention of Cruelty to Animals in 1866. When released from harness, the working steed usually was led to a crowded and unsanitary stable without adequate light or air. Only the pleasure horses kept by the city's "swells" to drive handsome rigs in the park had access to the green fields enjoyed by their country cousins.

Many overworked, mistreated urban horses simply died in the city streets. Moreover, since asphalt-paved or cobbled streets were slipperier than dirt roads, horses often stumbled and fell. An unfortunate beast who broke a leg in this way was destroyed where it lay. (In order to minimize the risk of stumbles, some veterinarians recommended that city draft horses be shod with rubber-padded horseshoes, but few owners followed this advice.) A description of Broadway appearing in the *Atlantic Monthly* in 1866 spoke of the street as being clogged with "dead horses and vehicular entanglements." The equine carcasses added fearsomely to the smells and flies already rising in clouds from stables and manure piles. In 1880 New York City removed fifteen thousand dead horses from its streets, and as late as 1912 Chicago carted away nearly ten thousand horse carcasses. A contemporary book on the collection of municipal refuse advised that, since the average weight of a dead horse was thirteen hundred pounds, "trucks for the removal of dead horses should be hung low, to avoid an excessive lift." The complaint of one horse lover that "in the city the working horse is treated worse than a steam-engine or sewing machine," was well justified.

By the 1880's and 90's the immense population growth of American cities, the need for improved urban transportation to keep up with the geographic spread of communities, and a growing awareness of the need for better sanitation in the interest of public health, all emphasized the drawbacks of the horse as the chief form of urban locomotion and spurred a search for alternatives. The first major breakthrough came with the development of the cable car and the electric trolley car in the late 1880's. Traction companies were quick to substitute mechanical power for animal power on their streetcar lines. Writing in *Popular Science Monthly* in 1892, United States Commissioner of Labor Carroll D. Wright maintained that electric power was not only cheaper than horsepower, but also far more beneficial to the city from the perspective of health and safety. "The presence of so many horses constantly moving through the streets," wrote Wright somewhat ponderously, "is a very serious matter. The vitiation of the air by the presence of so many animals is alone a sufficient reason for their removal, while the clogged condition of the streets impedes business, and involves the safety of life and limb." While electric-powered transportation began to make inroads on the horse's domain, improvements in the gasoline engine made it clear that the automobile would soon be a viable alternative. Even the bicycle craze of the nineties reminded many that horseless commuting was possible over reasonable distances.

Horse lovers became defensive about the future of that quadruped. Writing in the *Chautauquan* in 1895, Robert L. Seymour maintained that while the "cheap horse" might be doomed, the "costly, good-looking horse, the horse of history, the heroic horse in action, will probably last long." Can you imagine, asked Seymour, "Napoleon crossing the Alps in a blinding snow storm on a bicycle or Alexander riding heroically at the head of his armies in a horseless carriage?" It is hard to blame Seymour for not having the prophetic gift to foresee tank commanders dashing ahead of their squadrons. A more fundamental error seems to have been made by a writer in *Lippincott's Magazine* who insisted that since "Americans are a horse-loving nation . . . the wide-spread adoption of the motor-driven vehicle in this country is open to serious doubt." Less romantic observers, however, embraced the possibility of the elimination of the horse with enthusiasm. When William Dean Howells' fictional traveller from the nonexistent, utopian land of Altruria visited Chicago's World's Fair of 1893, he noted with pleasure that this metropolis of the future had "little of the filth resulting in all other American cities from the use of the horse."

During the opening years of the twentieth century the movement toward salvation by internal combustion continued to gather headway. Such popular journals as *Harper's Weekly, Lippincott's Magazine,* and the *Forum,* as well as more specialized periodicals like *American City, Horseless Age, Motor,* and *Scientific American,* were filled with articles extolling the automobile and the motor truck and disparaging the horse. One of the most common was economic analysis, which argued, as did one writer in *Munsey's Magazine,* that "the horse has become unprofitable. He is too costly to buy and too costly to keep." Articles such as these computed the expense of the "horse cost of living" and compared it unfavorably to the expense of automobile upkeep. Other articles pointed out the advantages the motor truck had over the horse in hauling freight and in preventing traffic tie-ups by moving faster. One writer in *American City* noted that the good motor truck, which was immune to fatigue and to weather, did on the average of two and a half times as much work in the same time as the horse and with one-quarter the amount of street congestion. "It is all a question of dollars and cents, this gasoline or oats proposition. The automobile is no longer classed as a luxury. It is acknowledged to be one of the great time-savers in the world."

But a second and equally—if not more—convincing argument for the superiority of the motor vehicle over the horse rested on the testimony that the automobile was a better bet from the perspective of public medicine. "The horse in the city is bound to be a menace to a condition of perfect health," warned Dr. Arthur R. Reynolds, superintendent of the Chicago health department in 1901. Public health officials in various cities charged that windblown dust from ground-up manure damaged eyes and irritated respiratory organs, while the "noise and clatter" of city traffic aggravated nervous diseases. Since, noted *Scientific American*, the motor vehicle left no litter and was "always noiseless or nearly so" (a judgment hard to understand if one has heard a primitive auto engine), the exit of the horse would "benefit the public health to an almost incalculable degree."

Also blamed on the horse were such familiar plagues as cholera and typhoid fever and intestinal diseases like dysentery and infant diarrhea. The reason why faithful dobbin was adjudged guilty was that such diseases were often transmitted by the housefly, and the favorite breeding place of the fly was the manure heap. In the late 1890's insurance company actuaries discovered that employees in livery stables and those living near stables had a higher rate of infectious diseases, such as typhoid fever, than the general public. Sanitation specialists pursued the question, and the first decade of the twentieth century saw a large out-pouring of material warning of the danger of the infection-carrying "queen of the dung-heap," *Musca domestica*. The most obvious way to eradicate the "typhoid fly," as the carrier was called by L. O. Howard, chief of the Bureau of Entomology of the Department of Agriculture and a leader of a campaign to stamp out flies, was to eliminate the horse.

Writing in *Appleton's Magazine* in 1908, Harold Bolce, entitled his article "The Horse Vs. Health." In a thoroughgoing assault he blamed most of the sanitary and economic problems of the modern city on the horse and essayed to calculate the savings if all horses were replaced by automobiles and motor trucks. His figures were arrived at by an intriguing formula. According to Bolce, twenty thousand New Yorkers died each year from "maladies that fly in the dust" created mainly by horse manure. He estimated the monetary value to the community of these people's lives, plus the cost of maintaining hospitals to treat them, and laid the entire bill on the withers of the inoffensive horse. To this sum he added the cost of street cleaning and rubbish disposal. He also attributed a higher urban cost of living to the failure to use speedy motor trucks, instead of horses, in transporting goods. Finally he computed and added the costs of traffic congestion and reached a total of approximately one hundred million dollars as the price that New York City paid for not banning the horse from its streets. What fed Bolce's indignation was not so much hate of horses, perhaps, as dedication to progress. The horse, he maintained, represented one of the last stands of brute animal strength over applied science and, as such, had to go—Americans could no longer afford "the absurdities of an horse-infected city."

While no city ever took such drastic actions as banning horses completely from its boundaries, many cities did eventually forbid them the use of certain streets and highways. But in the long run the horse's opponents triumphed without recourse to legislation. The number of horses in cities dropped sharply as the automobile and the motor truck rapidly gained popularity, although the number of horses in the nation stayed high until the 1920's (there were 20,091,000 horses reported in the 1920 census). As this happened, the benefits promised by motor-vehicle enthusiasts seemed to be initially realized. Streets were cleaner, particle pollution resulting from ground-up manure and the diseases thereby produced were diminished, the number of flies was greatly reduced, goods were transported more cheaply and efficiently, traffic travelled at a faster rate, and the movement of people from crowded cities to suburbs was accelerated by the automobile. Events appeared to justify the spokesmen for the advantages of the motor vehicle over the horse.

And yet, as current difficulties resulting from the massive use of the automobile attest, the motor vehicle's proponents were extremely short-sighted in their optimistic faith that their innovation would not only eradicate the urban health problems created by the horse but would also avoid the formation of new ones. As the number of automobiles proliferated and such cities as New York and Los Angeles experienced smog conditions that were a serious hazard to public comfort and health, it became apparent that the automobile, too, was a major obstacle to humane metropolitan existence.

Are the problems of noise and air pollution created by thousands of cars and trucks ''worse'' than those for which the horse was responsible? It is impossible to answer flatly. Altered environmental and demographic conditions in the city today, when judged beside those of a century or so ago, make specific comparisons between the horse and the automobile as polluters difficult at best. Aside from the disagreeable aesthetic effect created by horse manure, its chief impact upon public health seemed to come from wind-blown manure particles that irritated respiratory organs; from the reservoir furnished by the manure for disease spores, such as those of tetanus; and, most critically, from the fact that horse dung provided a breeding ground for the fly, proven by medical science to be the carrier of thirty different diseases, many of them acute. The pollution created by the automobile, on the other hand, is also aesthetically displeasing; and while it has not yet been firmly linked to any specific disease, it has primarily a chronic effect on health. The pollutants released by the internal-combustion engine irritate people's eyes and lungs, weakening their resistance to disease and worsening already present health problems. The immense number of automobiles in cities today has produced environmental difficulties that, unless soon dealt with, will generate problems that will dwarf those produced by horses in the cities of the past.

But the narrowness of vision of the early automobile advocates and their conviction that their machines would make urban life more tolerable, can be understood not as their failing alone. Most Americans, when informed of some technological advance that promises to alter their lives for the better without social cost, rush to embrace it. Second thoughts come later. Witness the apprehensions voiced presently over nuclear power plants after an initial flush of enthusiasm

based on the hope that this cleaner and more efficient method of generating elec-
tricity would free us from dependence on dirty fossil fuels. We are only now learning to weigh the biological and other costs of new inventions with some caution.
The career of the automobile has been one element in our education. Horses may
be gone from city streets, but the unforeseen problems created by their successors
still beset us.

Professor Joel Tarr, of Carnegie-Mellon University, is an expert on the problems of America's emerging urban centers in the early 1900's.

The Gentlewoman and the Robber Baron

Virginia Van der Veer Hamilton

One wintry morning in 1902 a prim, resolute spinster presented herself at 26 Broadway in New York City, bastion of the power Standard Oil organization. Promptly she was ushered through a maze of empty corridors to a reception room facing an open courtyard. As she waited, she became aware that a man in a nearby window was observing her stealthily.

Over the next two years this unlikely visitor paid many calls to one of the most awesome addresses in the American financial world. Each time she saw only the clerks who guided her, a secretary, and Henry H. Rogers, vice president of Standard Oil. But always she noticed the same shadowy figure watching her from the window. Was John D. Rockefeller, master of the oil industry, peeping at Ida Minerva Tarbell, lady journalist?

If so, Ida's turn to peep came one Sunday in 1903 when she visited the Euclid Avenue Baptist Church in Cleveland. Feeling a little guilty about it, she had invaded Rockefeller's church for a firsthand look at the man whose business practices she dared to castigate. Her quarry soon appeared. At sixty-four Rockefeller exuded power, but Ida observed that his big head had a wet look, his nose resembled a sharp thorn, and his lips were thin slits. Constantly, uneasily, Rockefeller peered around the familiar congregation, but if he recognized the stranger in its midst, he gave no sign.

Although the nation's richest man and his most persistent critic never met, their confrontation in the pages of *McClure's Magazine* enthralled thousands of Americans. Safe within their Victorian mansions, well-bred ladies shuddered at the audacity of one of their sex who had the spunk to describe the legendary Rockefeller as cold, ruthless, and unethical.

For eighteen installments—from November, 1902, to April, 1904—Ida's monumental "History of the Standard Oil Company" fired the indignation of middle-aged and middle-class citizens caught up in the rebellious mood of Progressivism. Politicians from statehouse legislators to Teddy Roosevelt at the White House took note of the furor. Its echoes eventually penetrated even the remote chambers of the Supreme Court.

Readers of *McClure's,* turning their October, 1902, issue, were introduced to the sensational serial by a full-page photograph of Ida. The magazine's star writer wore a severe, high-collared white dress adorned with tucks and embroidery, and her dark hair was piled high on her head. She looked away from the camera with an air of cool detachment. Miss Tarbell, *McClure's* announced, had completed her long study of "the most perfectly developed trust in existence." Her account would begin the following month.

S. S. McClure, impulsive and mercurial, boasted that the founding of *McClure's* and the discovery of Ida Tarbell were his proudest achievements. In Paris in 1892 he had bounded up four flights of steps to an apartment to meet the little-known American writer. After pouring out his plans for *McClure's,* S.S. borrowed forty dollars and left. "I'll never see that money," Ida lamented, but to her relief the forty dollars was promptly repaid. Two years later Ida, serious, purposeful, and thirty-seven, joined the staff of *McClure's* in New York.

S. S. soon had reason to congratulate himself. Ida was an immediate hit with readers, who paid ten cents a copy for his lively magazine. They liked her biography of Napoleon, produced "on the gallop" in six weeks. They followed with avid interest her series on Abraham Lincoln, written after four years of painstaking research in Kentucky, Indiana, and Illinois.

As thousands of new subscribers joined his circulation lists, McClure gave Ida most of the credit. The life of Lincoln, he said, "told on our circulation as nothing ever had before." By 1900 *McClure's* was reaching 350,000 homes and was second in circulation only to its bitter rival, *Munsey's.* If McClure liked an idea, he bragged, then millions of readers would like it, too. "There's only one better editor than I am," he admitted, "and that's Frank Munsey. If he likes a thing, then everybody will like it."

Alert to the mood of his readers, McClure sensed their concern about social and political reform. Lincoln Steffens, therefore, must check into corruption in the big cities. Ray Stannard Baker must investigate labor unions and the coal strike then going on in the anthracite fields of Pennsylvania (see "The Coal Kings Come to Judgement" in the April, 1960, AMERICAN HERITAGE). As for Ida, why not a study of one of the monopolies that frightened small businessman? Why not, in fact, the prototype of them all? "Out with you!" S. S. commanded his talented staff. "Look, see, report."

"Don't do it, Ida," her father pleaded. "They will ruin the magazine." Others warned her of the "all-seeing eye and the all-powerful reach" of Standard Oil. If *McClure's* persisted, friends predicted, "they'll get you in the end."

Standard Oil was well aware that a popular journalist—and a female at that—was prying into its past. Executives of the corporation asked no less a public figure than Mark Twain to inquire what *McClure's* planned to publish. "You will have to ask Miss Tarbell," S. S. replied. "Would Miss Tarbell see Mr. Rogers?" Twain inquired. When her supporters heard that Ida was visiting 26 Broadway to get the company's side of its history, they were instantly suspicious. "You'll become their apologist before you get through," many prophesied.

At their first meeting Ida and Henry Rogers discovered that they had been neighbors years before in the booming oil regions of Pennsylvania, where Ida's father had made tanks and Rogers had been an independent refiner. They even recalled the beauty of a wooded ravine separating their homes. Although she decided that Henry Rogers was "as fine a pirate as ever flew his flag in Wall Street," Ida was not beguiled by nostalgic memories. She alone, she told the Standard Oil executive, would be the judge of what she wrote.

Diligent and methodical, Ida studied musty records of the many lawsuits brought against Standard Oil in the thirty years since its incorporation. Every pertinent document must be located: "somewhere, some time," Ida insisted, "a copy turns up." Rogers once suggested that Ida should meet Rockefeller himself, and somewhat apprehensively she agreed. But their meeting was never arranged.

Seeking firsthand knowledge of Standard's methods, Ida interviewed other businessmen. Reluctant though they might be, they usually responded to her firm, dignified manner. One eccentric Cleveland millionaire received her with his hat on, his feet propped on his desk, and his face buried in a newspaper. As Ida quietly began to ask questions, he placed his feet on the floor, put down the newspaper, removed his hat, and gave her his respectful attention.

Her first installment was a vivid account of the brawling, gambling spirit of pioneer days in the Pennsylvania oil country. In 1859, when they heard the exhilarating news that oil was gushing out of a well near Titusville, thousands of adventurous Americans poured into the area, and a whole series of boom towns—with names like Pit Hole, Oil City, Petroleum Center, and Rouseville—hastily sprang up. "On every rocky farm," Ida wrote, "in every poor settlement of the region, was some man whose ear was attuned to Fortune's call, and who had the daring and the energy to risk everything he possessed in an oil lease." Saloons, brothels, and dance halls catered to a drifting population of fortune seekers.

Recalling the atmosphere of her youth, Ida praised the efforts of many citizens of this rough frontier to create schools, churches, and a proper environment. Her own parents, Esther and Franklin Tarbell, had shepherded their children into respectable middle-class ways, highlighted by family picnics on Chautauqua Lake or an occasional trip to Cleveland. Crusading suffragettes visited the Tarbell home, and young Ida fell under the spell of the fervent talk. "I must be free," she vowed, "and to be free I must be a spinster." At fourteen she prayed on her knees that God would keep her from marriage.

To prepare for a career, Ida entered Allegheny College at Meadville, the lone girl in a freshman class of forty "hostile or indifferent" boys. After graduation she hoped to become a biologist, but fate and S. S. McClure decided otherwise. Now, twenty-two years later, this child of the oil regions who elected spinsterhood and freedom was challenging the ruler of the oil industry himself.

At the close of the first chapter Ida offered her readers an enticing glimpse of the drama to come. Praising the independent oil producers, who gambled their lives and money in an uncertain new industry she wrote:

> Life ran swift and ruddy and joyous in these men. They were still young, most of them under forty, and looked forward with all the eagerness of the young who have just learned their powers, to years of struggle and development. . . . There was nothing too good for them, nothing they did not hope and dare. But suddenly, at the very heyday of this confidence, a big hand reached out from nobody knew where, to steal their conquest and throttle their future.

The "big hand," she revealed in her next installment, was an enterprising young man with "remarkable commercial vision, a genius for seeing the possibilities in material things." As a boy of thirteen John Rockefeller discovered that lending money at 7 per cent interest was more profitable than his earlier job of digging potatoes: "It was a good thing," the boy reasoned, "to let the money be my slave." This principle, Ida told her readers, was the foundation of a great financial career.

During the Civil War, Rockefeller chose to sell produce to the Union army rather than to serve in its ranks. Before the war ended, the twenty-three-year-old merchant had foreseen greater potential in refining a new product, oil, to light the homes and lubricate the machines of America. Under his shrewd and frugal leadership his first refinery prospered. There must be no waste, Rockefeller decreed. He found a market even for the residuum that other refineries allowed to flow away into the ground. "It hurt him to see it unused," Ida wrote, "and no man had a heartier welcome from the president of the Standard Oil Company than he who would show him how to utilize any proportion of his residuum." Rather than pay a barrelmaker, Rockefeller set up his own barrel factory.

The youthful refiner got his greatest joy from a good bargain. One of those whom Ida interviewed told her that the only time he had ever seen Rockefeller enthusiastic was at the news that his firm had bought a cargo of oil much below the market price. "He bounded from his chair with a shout of joy," the man recollected, "danced up and down, hugged me, threw up his hat, acted so like a madman that I have never forgotten it."

On the basis of the large amount of oil he shipped eastward, Rockefeller began to receive the railroad rebates that Ida charged were the keystone of his future empire. She described how he and other large refiners conspired to force railroads to grant them "drawbacks," additional rebates on the shipments of their competitors. Members of this clandestine combination, known as the South Improvement Company, received a rebate of $1.06 a barrel on crude oil shipped from Cleveland to New York, plus a drawback of $1.06 on each barrel shipped by their rivals. When an independent refiner paid eighty cents a barrel to ship oil from Pennsylvania fields to Cleveland, the South Improvement Company received a forty-cent-per-barrel drawback on the shipment.

This advantage, Ida charged, was used as a club over the heads of other refiners in Cleveland, forcing them to "sell or perish." His competitors wanted to keep their own businesses, Ida said, but "Mr. Rockefeller was regretful but firm. It was useless to resist, he told the hesitating; they would certainly be crushed if they did not accept his offer." When twenty-one of the twenty-six firms sold out to Rockefeller, he controlled one fifth of the nation's oil refining; "almost the entire independent oil interests of Cleveland collapsed in three months' time," Ida informed her readers. Privately an indignant Rockefeller denied Ida's version. Standard had been an angel of mercy to the Cleveland firms in distress, he told friends. "They didn't collapse," he insisted. "They had collapsed before! That's the reason they were so glad to combine their interest with ours, or take the money we offered." However, Rockefeller, who had always met criticism with lofty silence, refused to reply publicly to the articles in *McClure's*. "Not a word," he insisted. "Not a word about that misguided woman!"

But the heir to Standard Oil, John D. Rockefeller, Jr., was stung to a veiled defense of his father's business creation. In a speech entitled "Christianity and Business" he told members of the Y.M.C.A. at his alma mater, Brown University: "The American Beauty rose can be produced in its splendor and fragrance only by sacrificing the early buds which grow up around it." Critics of Standard Oil never let John D., Jr., forget this unfortunate metaphor. Recalling it several years later, a bishop declared from the pulpit: "A rose by any other name will smell as sweet, but the odor of that rose to me smacks strongly of crude petroleum."

If the creation of a perfect rose justified the sacrifice of other buds, could the same rationale be applied to the Standard Oil Trust? Ida's answer was a vehement No. The heroes of her serial were the independent oil "farmers" and refiners whose livelihood was threatened by Rockefeller's growing consolidation. "They believed," Ida wrote, "in independent effort—every man for himself and fair play for all. They wanted competition, loved open fight. They considered that all business should be done openly; that the railways were bound as public carriers to give equal rates; that any combination which favored one firm or one locality at the expense of another was unjust and illegal."

The producers rose in united revolt against the South Improvement Company and the man whom they believed to be its Mephistopheles, refusing to sell oil until railroads agreed not to grant rebates, drawbacks, or any other special privileges.

Ida remembered vividly that her own father, by then a producer himself, was one of those who had pledged not to sell.

The South Improvement Company scheme was defeated, but Rockefeller, Ida said, "had a mind which stopped by a wall, burrows under or creeps around." He next negotiated a new rebate arrangement between Standard Oil and the New York Central Railroad. In a burst of indignant prose Ida berated her protagonist:

> There was no more faithful Baptist in Cleveland than he. Every enterprise of that church he had supported liberally from his youth. He gave to the poor. He visited its sick. He wept with its suffering. Moreover, he gave unostentatiously to many outside charities of whose worthiness he was satisfied. He was simple and frugal in his habits. He never went to the theatre, never drank wine. He gave much time to the training of his children, seeking to develop in them his own habits of economy and charity. Yet he was willing to strain every nerve to obtain for himself special and unjust privileges from the railroads which were bound to ruin every man in the oil business not sharing them with him.

Rockefeller's next tactic, Ida explained, was to form a national Refiner's Association to force oil producers to sell their output to a united front of refiners. To offset the power of the refiners, drillers organized a Producers' Association. The producers realized that overproduction was their curse. If they agreed to stop drilling new wells for six months and shut down their pumps for thirty days, supplies of crude oil would dwindle, and prices would rise. To the producers' surprise, Rockefeller and his fellow refiners offered them a contract for 200,000 barrels of oil at $3.25 a barrel. They signed. But when 50,000 of the 200,000 barrels had been shipped, the refiners' association broke its contract, declaring that the producers had failed to limit production and that plenty of oil was available at $2.50 a barrel. Ida placed the blame on Rockefeller for "leading them into an alliance, and at the psychological moment throwing up his contract."

One producer told Ida what it had been like to negotiate with Rockefeller, who during one meeting sat and rocked with his hands covering his eyes.

> I made a speech which I guess was pretty warlike. Well, right in the middle of it, John Rockefeller stopped rocking and took down his hands and looked at me. You never saw such eyes. He took me all in, saw just how much fight he could expect from me, and I knew it, and then up went his hands and back and forth went his chair.

Month by month Ida pressed her indictment, picturing Rockefeller as a sinister conspirator obsessed with a passion to control the entire oil industry for the "holy blue barrel," as his competitors called it, of Standard Oil. He arranged for Standard to receive even more favorable rebates from major railroads. When independent operators developed a revolutionary new means of transporting oil by pipelines, the canny Rockefeller realized that this method was the shipping trend of the future. He moved into the pipeline business, driving out rivals until he controlled the entire pipeline system of the oil regions. He set up a nationwide network, paying spies to report on rival shipments, deliberately underselling his competitors, and then, having driven his rivals out of a territory, set any price he pleased.

Summarizing Rockefeller's goal, Ida wrote:

Briefly stated, his argument was this: "Controlling all refineries, I shall be the only shipper of oil. Being the only shipper, I can obtain special rates of transportation which will drive out and keep out competitors; controlling all refineries, I shall be the only buyer, and can regulate the price of crude (oil) as I can the price of refined."

The charge of spying, published in a chapter titled "Cutting to Kill," abruptly ended Ida's harmonious interviews with Henry Rogers. To substantiate her charges, *McClure's* reproduced records sent to Ida secretly by a young shipping clerk in a Standard plant. They were undercover reports from railroad agents, listing oil shipments by rival producers. On her next visit to 26 Broadway, Ida found Rogers "by no means cordial." When he asked where she got "the stuff," she replied boldly: "You know very well that I could not tell you where I got that stuff, but you know very well that it is authentic." It was their last interview.

Although the doors of Standard Oil closed to Ida, she was invited to meet an even more unexpected source of information. Frank Rockefeller summoned her secretly to Cleveland to hear his grievances against his successful brother. To help finance a shipping business, Frank had borrowed money from John D. and put up his Standard Oil stock as collateral. During the Panic of '93, when Frank was unable to meet his obligations, John D. foreclosed and took over the stock. Frank, observed Ida, was more frivolous than his brother, more generous, "not a safe man to handle money. . . . So it was a kind of obligation to the sacredness of money," she wrote, "that John Rockefeller had foreclosed on his own brother."

After chastising Rockefeller for many months, Ida produced an installment called "The Legitimate Greatness of the Standard Oil Company" in which she freely acknowledged its leader's business efficiency. Rockefeller's passion for detail and for plowing profits back into the company, she said, had resulted in a masterpiece of organization. Even the dust on the floors of his tin factories was sifted to save filings and bits of solder.

While granting Rockefeller his due, Ida could not forgive practices she considered illegitimate and debasing to business morality. His success, she feared, would tempt thousands of others to "Commercial Machiavellianism." In the wake of his company monopoly, Ida said, Rockefeller left a trail of devastated small businesses:

Why one should love an oil refinery the outsider may not see, but to the man who had begun one still and had seen it grow by his own energy and intelligence to ten, who now sold 500 barrels a day where he once sold five, the refinery was the dearest spot on earth save his home. . . . To ask such a man to give up his refinery was to ask him to give up the thing which, after his family, meant most in life to him.

But faced with the growing power of Standard Oil, the independents did give up. Describing one who sold out, Ida wrote that "he realized that something . . . was at work in the oil business—something resistless, silent, perfect in its might—and he sold out to that something." Along Oil Creek, she said, "the little refineries which for years had faced every difficulty with stout hearts collapsed. 'Sold out,' 'dismantled,' 'shut down,' is the melancholy record."

As dramatic proof of the fierceness of the conflict Ida devoted an entire installment to "The Buffalo Case," in which managers of a Standard affiliate in New York were convicted of conspiring to blow up a rival refinery to force it out of business. In another chapter she shocked her public by repeating the tale of Widow Backus, who declared in an affidavit that Rockefeller had fleeced her of a fair price when she sold her husband's refinery to Standard Oil. Ida said of the widow:

> She had seen every effort to preserve an independent business thwarted. Rightly or wrongly, she had come to believe that a refusal to sell meant a fight with Mr. Rockefeller, that a fight meant ultimately defeat, and she gave up her business to avoid ruin.

Historians later criticized Ida for repeating the widow's tale, which was of questionable accuracy, but true or exaggerated, it made a sensational installment. Victorian ladies of comfortable means could identify with the plight of Widow Backus.

Acknowledged as "Lord of the Oil Regions" by 1879, Rockefeller controlled 90 per cent of the oil business of the nation, dominating refining, transporting, and marketing. The entire pipeline system of the Pennsylvania fields belonged to Standard. Rockefeller had achieved his goal, Ida wrote, "because he had the essential element to all great achievement, a steadfastness to purpose once conceived which nothing can crush."

To handle the affairs of his giant monopoly, Rockefeller created a new type of business organization, the trust, whereby he and eight other trustees managed the entire structure. But public resentment against the monopoly began to be reflected in a rush of legal suits. Ida reminded her readers of the 1892 ruling by the supreme court of Ohio that had resulted in dissolution of the Standard Oil Trust. It was replaced by the Standard Oil Company of New Jersey, which functioned as holding company for the Rockefeller interests.

After eighteen chapters and almost four years of research and writings Ida and *McClure's* rested their case against John D. Rockefeller. Summing it all up, Ida told her faithful readers that they were paying more for oil under monopoly conditions than they would pay under free competition. Business opportunity in the oil industry, she said, was now limited to a few hundred men.

But there was a more serious side to it, she concluded. The ethical cost of all this should be a deep concern. "Canonize 'business success,' and men who make a success like that of the Standard Oil Trust become national heroes!" Defenders of Rockefeller might justify his methods by saying, "It's business" or "All humans are erring mortals," but Ida would not accept a moral code that "would leave our business men weeping on one another's shoulders over human frailty, while they picked one another's pockets."

In a last plea to her readers she urged them to ostracize monopolists who used unethical practices as they would ostracize unethical doctors, lawyers, or athletes, for "a thing won by breaking the rules of the game," she moralized, "is not worth the winning."

As her public exploded with warmth, *McClure's* was deluged with angry letters. Ida, readers said, was a modern Joan of Arc and "the Terror of the Trusts." Her study reminded one man of "the clarion notes of the old prophets of Israel." Another called it "the *Uncle Tom's Cabin* of today." A letter addressed to "Ida M. Tarbell, Rockefeller Station, Hades," reached her promptly.

McClure's, packed with articles by Steffens and Baker as well as with Ida's literary dynamite, thrived on its crusading zeal. But Ida was even more of a celebrity than her colleagues, and they joined in the general admiration for her work. "Ida Tarbell was the best of us," Baker admitted. In a western city a newspaper hailed the arrival of William Allen White and Ida with the headline "Celebrated Writers Here." S. S. wrote his protégée: "You are today the most generally famous woman in America."

Ida's "History" evoked even more praise when it was published as a two-volume book in 1904. "Miss Tarbell," said the Cleveland *Leader,* "has done more to dethrone Rockefeller in public esteem than all the preachers in the land." The New York *News* declared that "Rockefeller's very conscience is exposed by her search for truth." The Norfolk *Dispatch* and the Washington *News* proclaimed Ida "a great woman historian" and "probably the most talented woman writer of history that this country has produced."

Standard, however, was not without its defenders. In Pennsylvania the Oil City *Derrick,* subsidized by the company, headlined its review: "Hysterical Woman Versus Historical Facts." A Harvard economist, Gilbert Montague, who wrote a sympathetic history of Standard's operations, termed Ida "a mere gatherer of folklore." The popular essayist Elbert Hubbard said Standard Oil was an example of "survival of the fittest" and called Ida a "literary bushwhacker" who "shot from cover and . . . shot to kill." The nickname Miss Tarbarrel was coined by Standard supporters. Even Rockefeller himself, not a notably humorous man, adopted the pun with glee.

While interest in Ida's history was at its height, new oil discoveries by wildcatters drilling deep in the Kansas plains caused a fresh boom. Standard Oil moved quickly into the new fields, threading its pipelines across prairie and farmland. But

McClure's had reached even the remote farmers of Kansas. Populists, women's clubs, and independent oilmen vowed to keep Standard out of their fields even if they had to set up a state-owned refinery in the penitentiary. At the urging of the oilmen Ida visited the new arena. To her dismay she was received as a prophet and serenaded by oil boomers. "But here I was," she wrote later, "fifty, fagged, wanting to be let alone while I collected trustworthy information for my articles—dragged to the front as an apostle."

The news from Kansas, added to the cumulative effect of the Tarbell series, helped stir Congress to action. In February, 1905, it authorized the Bureau of Corporations to investigate the low price of crude oil, particularly in Kansas. Could the wide margin between the prices of crude and refined, a Kansas congressman asked, be attributed to the operations of a trust or conspiracy?

Enthusiastically the Bureau of Corporations dug into its assignment. In the first of three lengthy reports to Congress, it concluded that Standard "habitually" received and was still receiving secret rebates and other "unjust and illegal discriminations" from railroads. The second report charged that Standard controlled the only major pipeline serving the oil industry and that it fought would-be competitors with lawsuits, right-of-way disputes, aid to railroads, and price wars. The final report accused Standard of keeping oil prices artificially high at the expense of the American consumer. Commissioner Herbert Knox Smith called for prosecution of Standard under the Sherman Antitrust Act.

The bureau's findings were not news to Ida's readers. One cartoonist pictured President Roosevelt receiving the reports on a slate bearing these words: "Standard Oil is just as naughty as Ida said it was." In the background of the cartoon was Henry Rogers, muttering to Rockefeller: "And I had my fingers crossed too."

But Roosevelt, who had originally encouraged federal legal action against Standard, became exasperated at the public vogue for the literature of exposure as other magazines and writers rushed to copy *McClure's* successful formula. Shortly after the appearance of an article in *Cosmopolitan* titled "The Treason of the Senate" an angry Roosevelt applied the term "muckrakers" to responsible and irresponsible journalists alike. Pondering the President's attack years later, Ida decided that Teddy preferred to conduct trust busting on his own and resented writers "stealing his thunder."

Meanwhile, Standard's troubles were multiplying. Three antitrust suits were brought against the corporation in state courts in 1904, four in 1905, and fourteen in 1906. Many resulted in fines or the temporary ouster of Standard from a state. The most sensational fine, $29,240,000 for 1,462 violations of the Elkins Act forbidding acceptance of rebates, was handed down by Judge Kenesaw Mountain Landis in August, 1907. Although this decision was later reversed, the "Big Fine" made Judge Landis famous and added drama to the controversy.

Once when Ida was searching for material in Indiana and Ohio, an order went out from Standard headquarters: "Simply ignore her entirely." But in the face of such mounting hostility even Standard Oil could not play the sphinx forever. The company began to give out information on its operations and employed Ivy Ledbetter Lee, an early public relations counsel, to place advertisements and friendly stories in newspapers and magazines. It ordered five thousand copies of Montague's book and distributed them to employees, ministers, libraries, teachers, and prominent citizens.

Rockefeller's own image was under such attack that a group of Congregational ministers balked at accepting his gift of $100,000 to their board of missions, calling it "tainted money." Later, to their embarrassment, they found that some of their colleagues had actually requested the gift. But the term "tainted money" briefly captured many a headline. Undeterred, Rockefeller intensified his long habit of philanthropy. Two months after the final chapter of the Standard Oil history appeared in *McClure's,* he announced gifts of one million dollars to Yale University and ten times that amount to the General Education Board, a philanthropy in aid of higher education that he had helped to establish two years before. No one objected. Such sums, the New York *Sun* commented dryly, "deodorize themselves." When it was charged that Rockefeller was using philanthropy to silence criticism, Ida came to his defense, reminding critics that Rockefeller had been a steady giver to church and charity since boyhood. If his gifts were larger now, she pointed out, it was because his income was greater and perhaps because he sought to call public attention to the benefits reaped from Standard Oil.

John D. proved his own most effective advocate. In 1909 he published a slim book titled *Random Reminiscences of Men and Events.* Although he did not mention Ida or other critics by name, it was obvious the outcry was on Rockefeller's mind. "Just how far one is justified . . . in defending himself from attacks is a moot point," he wrote. *Reminiscences,* an informal account of the early career, principles, and recreations of the nation's richest man, also contained useful hints on how to give money away wisely. This little book, one Rockefeller biographer has said, "did more to make Rockefeller a human figure than tons of Sunday supplement articles."

Random Reminiscences, however, did not persuade the federal government to call off a suit charging Standard Oil with violation of the Sherman act. The case dragged through three and a half years of litigation. In 1909 a federal circuit court sustained the government's position, but Standard appealed to the Supreme Court. Many an editor invited Ida to analyze the testimony. "I could have made a good killing out of that long investigation . . ." she recalled later. "But I had no stomach for it." Weary of all the controversy, she wished only "to escape into the safe retreat of a library where I could study people long dead."

Finally, on May 15, 1911, the decision was handed down. The highest court in the land declared Standard Oil of New Jersey to be a monopoly, in restraint of trade, based on unfair practices. Charging that Standard's object was "to drive others from the field and exclude them from their right to trade,'' the court ordered the holding company dissolved. The justices, in effect, agreed with Ida.

''The History of the Standard Oil Company'' was probably the most sensational serial ever to appear in an American magazine. Allan Nevins, in his biography of Rockefeller, called it ''the most spectacular success of the muckraking school of journalism, and its most enduring achievement.'' As a historian Ida Tarbell had her flaws. She was untrained in economics. She yearned to turn back the clock to an era of individualism in business. She was obviously partial to independent oilmen, even though she scolded them for lacking the patience and fortitude to organize effectively against Rockefeller. In her indignation she sometimes exaggerated the iniquity of her archvillain.

But at a time when strong men quailed before the Rockefeller reputation, this daughter of the oil regions, fortified by her sense of righteous morality, boldly voiced their feelings. Although small operators lost their struggle for existence, Ida carried the day in the contest for public opinion. A modern-day historian of the muckraking era, David M. Chalmers, believes the image she fashioned of Rockefeller as a ''cunning, ruthless Shylock'' has not been successfully erased by a half century of Rockefeller family philanthropy. Forty years after her serial appeared, *Time* magazine credited the *McClure's* articles with bringing in a ''gusher of public resentment that flowed all the way to the U.S. Supreme Court.''

Was Ida's study an accurate work of historical research, or was it a subjective attack on practices of which she disapproved? Modern business historians, looking back on the ''History'' with the hindsight of a later era, generally substantiate her charges that Standard Oil built its monopoly upon special favors from railroads, mastery of the pipeline system, and sharp marketing practices, all of which helped force small independents out of the fields and refineries.

But Ida raised a larger question: Was it better for the American oil industry to have free, albeit cutthroat, competition, or to fall under the dominance of a monopoly with the power to maintain orderly production and a profitable, if higher, price structure? It is this aspect of her account that still arouses controversy. Social historians tend to be on Ida's side, business historians to defend Rockefeller; both schools agree, however, that Ida was a pioneer business historian and that, although she worked with the crude research tools of the early 1900's and became a special pleader for her own moralistic ideas of business ethics, she presented a remarkably clear and truthful picture of the rise of Standard Oil.

Though John D. Rockefeller never met the stern spinster who judged his business morality so harshly, she and Rockefeller's son, John D., Jr., did meet at a conference called by President Wilson after World War I. The younger Rockefeller, who had once compared Standard Oil to an American Beauty rose, had become disenchanted and had made ''one of the most important decisions of my life.'' Resigning his directorships in Standard Oil and U.S. Steel, he announced in

1910 that he would devote his life to giving away the immense sums of money that flowed from his father's business creation.

When John D., Jr., realized he was to meet Ida, he sought the advice of William Allen White. The famous Kansas editor knew the younger Rockefeller as a gentle and kindhearted person for whom Ida's book had been "an unpleasant fact which gave him something more than pause." He advised Rockefeller to meet Miss Tarbell casually and naturally; as two sensitive people they would bridge the awkward situation. After the meeting White saw John D., Jr., hurrying into the street to hail a cab for Miss Tarbell. Later he was amused to see them, placed together by some inspired host at a formal dinner, "chatting amiably . . . each trying to outdo the other in politeness."

Although Ida wrote many other books and articles, none of her later works had the impact of the Standard Oil history. In 1922 she tried to revive her interest and write a third volume on Standard. But the fire and the burning indignation that had caught a nation's attention were gone. "Repeating yourself," she decided, "is a doubtful practice."

In 1937, as Ida at eighty was writing her autobiography, John D. Rockefeller died at the age of ninety-seven. The lady who had been his nemesis lived seven more years, enjoying the tranquility of her Connecticut farm, where she made jelly and raised peonies, lettuce, and potatoes. An interviewer who sought her out in this retreat found her characteristically self-effacing: "The proof that I am able to do anything so worthwhile as raise a potato never fails to thrill me," said the Terror of the Trusts.

Dr. Virginia Van der Veer Hamilton is an assistant professor of history at the University of Alabama in Birmingham. She wrote "Hugo Black and the K.K.K." for our April, 1968, issue and is now completing a full-length biography of Mr. Justice Black.

For further reading: Success Story: The Life and Times of S. S. McClure, by Peter Lyon (Scribner, 1963); John D. Rockefeller: A Study in Power, by Allan Nevins (2 volumes, Scribner, 1940); All In the Day's Work, the autobiography of Ida M. Tarbell (Macmillan, 1939); The History of the Standard Oil Company, by Ida M. Tarbell, abridged and with an introduction by David M. Chalmers (Harper Torchbooks, 1966).

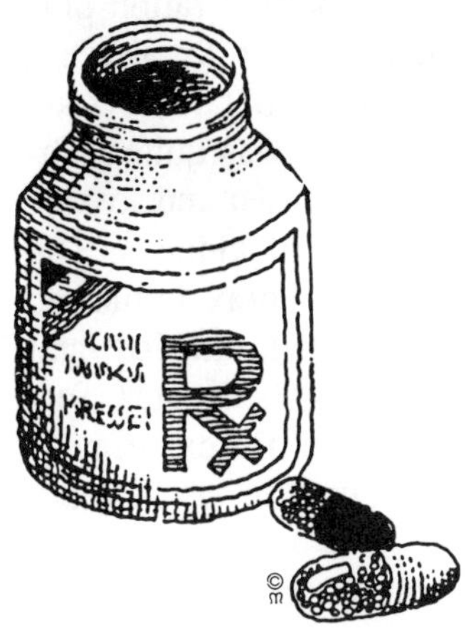

Who Put the Borax in Dr. Wiley's Butter?

Gerald H. Carson

On a hot and humid July morning in 1902, a burly, 200-pound scientist and connoisseur of good food and drink sat hunched over his desk in a red brick building in Washington and planned deliberately to feed twelve healthy young men a diet containing borax. Dr. Harvey W. Wiley, chief chemist of the Department of Agriculture, had in mind a double objective: first, to determine the effects upon human beings of certain chemicals then commonly used to preserve processed foods; and, more broadly, to educate the public in the need for federal "pure food" law. Food preparation was becoming industrialized and subject to more complicated processing; products were traveling longer distances, passing through many hands. Manufacturers, facing a novel situation, turned to dubious additives to make their products appear more appetizing or to preserve them. Borax compounds, the first object of Dr. Wiley's investigations, were used to make old butter seem like new.

Volunteers for the experiment were recruited from the Department of Agriculture. They pledged themselves to obey the rules. A small kitchen and dining room were fitted out in the basement of the Bureau of Chemistry offices with the assistant surgeon-general in attendance to see to it that the subjects of the experiment did not get too much borax, and Dr. Wiley to see that they got enough. A bright reporter, George Rothwell Brown, of the Washington *Post,* gave the volunteers an enduring handle, "the poison squad"; and before long the public began referring to Wiley, affectionately or otherwise according to the point of view, as "Old Borax."

Six of Dr. Wiley's co-operators at the hygienic table got a normal ration plus measured doses of tasteless, odorless, invisible boracic acid. The other six also enjoyed a wholesome diet, with equally tasteless, odorless, invisible borate of soda added to their menu. The resulting chemical and physiological data was quite technical. But the meaning was clear. The effects of borax included nausea and loss of appetite, symptoms resembling those of influenza and overburdened kidneys. The feeding experiments continued over a five-year period. After the borax initiation, which made a popular sensation, the squad subsequently breakfasted, lunched, and dined on dishes containing salicylates, sulfurous acid and sulfites, benzoates, formaldehyde, sulfate of copper, and saltpeter. Seldom has a scientific experiment stirred the public imagination as did Dr. Wiley's novel procedures in, as he said, "trying it on the dog."

"My poison squad laboratory," said Dr. Wiley, "became the most highly advertised boarding-house in the world."

A popular versifier wrote a poem about it, the "Song of the Pizen Squad." Lew Dockstader introduced a topical song into his minstrel show. The chorus closed with the prediction:

Next week he'll give them mothballs á la Newburgh or else plain:
O they may get over it but they'll never look the same!

The New York *Sun* sourly handed Wiley the title of "chief janitor and policeman of the people's insides," an expression of one line of attack which the opposition was to take—invasion of personal liberty.

The movement to protect the health and pocketbook of the consumer was directed no less at "the patent medicine evil" than it was at the chaotic situation in the food manufacturing field. The "cures" for cancer, tuberculosis, "female weakness," the dangerous fat reducers and "Indian" cough remedies were a bonanza for their proprietors, and many an advertising wizard who knew little enough of drugs or materia medica came to live in a jigsaw mansion and drive a spanking pair of bays because he was a skillful manipulator of hypochondria and mass psychology. Slashing exposés in the popular magazines told of babies' soothing syrups containing morphine and opium, of people who became narcotic addicts, of the use of tonics that depended upon alcohol to make the patient feel frisky.

"Gullible America," said Samuel Hopkins Adams in an angry but thoroughly documented series of articles, "will spend this year [1905] some seventy-five millions of dollars" in order to "swallow huge quantities of alcohol . . . narcotics . . . dangerous heart depressants . . . insidious liver stimulants."

The nostrum vendors at first looked upon the Food and Drugs Act as a joke. In time the manufacturers of Pink Pills for Pale People learned the hard way that they were living dangerously when they ignored the precept, "Thou shalt not lie on the label."

As public interest rose in "the food question," powerful groups took their places in the line of battle to contest the pure food and drug bills which appeared, and died, in Congress with monotonous regularity. On the one side were aligned consumer groups—the General Federation of Women's Clubs, the National Consumers' League, the Patrons of Husbandry, and the labor unions. With them stood food chemists who had had experience in state control work, the American Medical Association, important periodicals (*Collier's Weekly*, Bok's *Ladies' Home Journal, World's Work, The Independent, Cosmopolitan*), President Theodore Roosevelt, and Dr. Wiley.

In opposition were the food manufacturers and manufacturers of articles used in the adulteration of foods and drugs such as cottonseed oil, the proprietary medicine industry, the distillers, canners, *Leslie's Weekly* (to which Dr. Wiley was anathema), newspaper publishers opposed for business reasons, Chicago meat packers, and powerful lobbyists holed up at the Willard and the Raleigh Hotel; also an obdurate Senate, responsive to pressures from big business. Wiley, as the leading personality in the fight for a food bill, achieved the uncommon distinction of acquiring almost as many enemies as did President Roosevelt himself.

When the average member of Congress, newspaper publisher, or pickle manufacturer smelled socialism and deplored the effects of the proposed legislation upon business, he was only responding normally to two powerful stimuli: self-interest and the nostalgic memory of his lost youth. Most mature Americans of the 1880–1900 period were born on farms or in rural areas and knew the conditions of life of a scattered population. The close-knit farm family was the dominant economic unit. It raised, processed, cured, and stored what it ate, and there is abundant evidence that it ate more and better food than the common man of Europe had ever dreamed of tasting. There was no problem of inspection of deceptive labels. No "Short-weight Jim" invaded the home kitchen or smokehouse. If the preparation was unsanitary, it was no one else's business. What wasn't raised locally was obtained by barter. There were adequate forces of control over that simple transaction—face-to-face bargaining, community of interest, fear of what the neighbors would say.

As to drugs and medicines, grandmas could consult the "family doctor" book and compound her home remedies from roots, herbs, and barks gathered along the edge of forest, meadow, and stream: catnip for colic, mullein leaf for asthma, the dandelion for dyspepsia, and so on through the list of simples, essences, flowers, tinctures, and infusions, whose chief merit was that they did not interfere with the tendency of the living cell to recover.

When Americans were called to the cities by the factory whistle, a dramatic change took place in their food supply. No longer was there personal contact between the producer and consumer, nor could the buyer be wary even if he would. For how could a city man candle every egg, test the milk, inquire into the handling of his meat supply, analyze the canned foods which he consumed in increasing quantities?

Since foodstuffs had to stand up in their long transit from the plant to the home, it is not surprising that unhealthy practices developed. During the "embalmed beef" scandal, for example, there was a debate as to whether a little boric acid in fresh beef was after all only an excusable extension of the ancient and accepted use of saltpeter in corning beef. Analytical chemistry was called upon increasingly to make cheap foods into expensive ones, to disguise and simulate, to arrest the processes of nature. The food manufacturers raided the pharmacopoeia. But the salicylic acid that was approved in the treatment of gout or rheumatism was received with mounting indignation on the dining room table where it proved to be a depressant of the processes of metabolism. It was objectionable on another ground too—that it led to carelessness in the selection, cleansing, and processing of foodstuffs.

It is difficult to picture today the vast extent of adulteration at the beginning of this century. More than half the food samples studied in the Indiana state laboratory were sophisticated. Whole grain flour was "cut" with bran and corn meal. The food commissioner of North Dakota declared that his state alone consumed ten times as much "Vermont maple syrup" as Vermont produced. The *Grocer's Companion and Merchant's Hand-Book* (Boston, 1883), warned the food retailer, in his own interest, of the various tricks used to alter coffee and tea, bread and flour, butter and lard, mustard, spices, pepper, pickles, preserved fruits, sauces, potted meats, cocoa, vinegar, and candies. A New York sugar firm was proud to make the point in its advertising of the 1880's that its sugar contained "neither glucose, muriate of tin, muriatic acid, nor any other foreign, deleterious or fraudulent substance whatever." The canned peas looked garden-fresh after treatment with $CuSO_4$ by methods known as "copper-greening." The pork and beans contained formaldehyde, and catsup benzoic acid. As a capstone of inspired fakery, one manufacturer of flavored glucose (sold as pure honey) carefully placed a dead bee in every bottle to give verisimilitude.

The little man of 1900 found himself in a big, big world, filled with butterine and mapleine.

This is not to suggest that the pioneer food manufacturer was as rascally as his contemporaries, the swamp doctor and the lightening rod peddler. What was occurring was less a collapse of human probity than an unexpected testing of human nature in a new context. Someone has said that all morality is based upon the assumption that somebody might be watching. In the milieu of late Nineteenth-Century business, nobody seemed to be watching. Thus the food crusade became necessary as a means of redressing the balance in the market which had turned so cruelly against the ordinary American and, indeed, against the honest manufacturer.

The ensuing controversy was symptomatic of the passing—painful, nostalgic to many, including no doubt many a big business senator—of the old, simple life of village and farm which was doomed by the expanding national life. It was, one feels, not solely in defense of the hake (sold as genuine codfish with boric acid as a preservative) that Senator George Frisbie Hoar of Massachusetts rose in the Senate to exalt "the exquisite flavor of the codfish, salted, made into balls, and eaten on a Sunday morning by a person whose theology is sound, and who believes in the five points of Calvinism."

The friends of food reform needed all the courage and public discussion they could muster. Since 1879, when the first federal bill was proposed, 190 measures to protect the consumers had been introduced in Congress, of which 49 had some kind of a subsequent history, and 141 were never heard of again. Meanwhile the states did what they could. About half of them had passed pure food laws by 1895. But there was no uniformity in their regulations. Foods legal in one state might be banned in another. Some of the laws were so loosely drawn that it was quite conceivable that Beechnut Bacon might be seized by the inspectors because no beechnuts were involved in its curing. Was Grape-Nuts misbranded because the great Battle Creek "brain food" had only a fanciful connection with either grapes or nuts? One bill actually proposed a numerical count of the contents of a package— the grains of salt, the cherries in a jar or preserves. What if Mr. Kellogg had to count every corn flake which went into his millions of packages?

Conflicts and foolish regulations could be ironed out over a period of time. The fatal flaw was that individual states had no power to get at the real problem: interstate traffic in the "patented" bitters, cancer cures, and strawberry jellies made out of dyed glucose, citric acid, and timothy seed.

The act which Wiley drew up was first introduced in 1902. It was successfully sidetracked in one legislative branch or the other for four years. The provisions were simple. In essence, it was a labeling act.

"Tell the truth on the label," Dr. Wiley said, "and let the consumer judge for himself."

Some of the legislators who opposed the act were states' rights Democrats, concerned about constitutional interpretation, who in the end fortunately saw the wisdom of sacrificing principle for expediency. Others were Old Guard Republicans who were special custodians of the *status quo* and highly sensitive to the sentiments of the business community: men like Senators Aldrich of Rhode Island (wholesale groceries), Kean of New Jersey (preserving and canning), Platt of Connecticut (home of the great Kickapoo Indian remedies), Hale and Frye of Maine, along whose rock-bound coast the familiar Maine herring became "imported French sardines," packaged in boxes with French labels.

The tactic in the Senate was one of unobtrusive obstruction and lip service to the idea of regulation. Open opposition was never much of a factor. "The 'right' to use deceptive labels," observed *The Nation,* "is not one for which impassioned oratory can be readily invoked." When a serious try was made to pass a general pure food law in 1902–3, Senator Lodge was able to direct the attention of the Senate to legislation more urgently needed, such as a Philippine tariff bill. In the last session of the 59th Congress (1904–5) the food bill was considered less pressing than a proposal to award naval commissions to a couple of young men who had been expelled from the Academy for hazing but still wanted very much to become officers in the United States Navy.

President Roosevelt finally decided to push the issue. "Mr. Dooley" offered a version of how it happened. "Tiddy," he said, was reading Upton Sinclair's novel, *The Jungle,* a grisly sociological tract on "Packingtown." "Tiddy was toying with a light breakfast an' idly turnin' over th' pages iv th' new book with both hands. Suddenly he rose fr'm th' table, an' cryin': 'I'm pizened,' begun throwin' sausages out iv th' window. Th' ninth wan sthruck Sinitor Biv'ridge on th' head an' made him a blond. It bounced off, exploded, an' blew a leg of a secret-service agent, an' th' scatthred fragmints desthroyed a handsome row iv ol' oak-trees. Sinitor Biv'ridge rushed in, thinkin' that th' Prisidint was bein' assassynated be his devoted followers in th' Sinit, an' discovered Tiddy engaged in a hand-to-hand conflict with a potted ham. Th' Sinitor fr'm Injyanny, with a few well-directed wurruds, put out th' fuse an' rendered th' missile harmless. Since thin th' Prisidint, like th' rest iv us, has become a viggytaryan. . . ." At any rate, in his annual message to Congress, December 5, 1905, Roosevelt recommended in the interest of the consumer and the legitimate manufacturer "that a law be enacted to regulate interstate commerce in misbranded and adulterated foods, drinks, and drugs," and the bill was re-introduced to the Senate by Senator Weldon B. Heyburn of Idaho. Pressure from the American Medical Association, the graphic exposé of revolting conditions in the Chicago packing houses, and Roosevelt's skillful use of the report of an official commission which investigated the stockyards, finally forced a favorable vote in the Senate and then the House on the Pure Food and Drugs Bill. The meat inspection problem was, actually, a different matter. But an angry public was in no mood to make fine distinctions. Meat, processed foods, and fake medicines all tapped the family pocketbook, all went into the human stomach, and all smelled to high heaven in the spring of 1906. Roosevelt signed the bill into law on June 30, 1906.

The enforcement of the law was placed in the hands of Dr. Wiley. According to the Doctor, it was after the bill became law that the real fight began. Most food and drug manufacturers and dealers adjusted their operations to the new law, and found themselves in a better position because of it, with curtailment of the activities of fly-by-night competition in goods of known quality. But there were die-hards like the sugar and molasses refiners, the fruit driers, whisky rectifiers, and purveyors of wahoo bitters, Peruna and Indian Doctor wonder drugs.

The administration of the Food and Drugs Act involved the Bureau of Chemistry in thousands of court proceedings, *United States v. Two Barrels of Desiccated Eggs, United States v. One Hundred Barrels of Vinegar;* and one merciful judge noted that Section 6 extended the protection of the act to our four-footed friends.

Pure food inspectors had seized 620 cases of spoiled canned cat food. When the case of the smelly tuna fish turned up in the western district court of the state of Washington, the judge cited man's experience with cats throughout recorded time: ''Who will not feed cats must feed mice and rats.'' He confirmed the seizure and directed an order of condemnation.

The law was subsequently strengthened both by legal interpretations and by legislative action, as experience developed needs not met by the original act. Government technicians worked with private industry in the solution of specific problems such as refrigeration and the handling of food. When Dr. Wiley retired from public service in 1912, a revolution had occurred in food processing in only six years' time. Yet the food industry had hardly begun to grow.

''The conditions created by the passage of the act,'' said Clarence Francis, former president and chairman of the board of General Foods Corporation, ''invited responsible business men to put real money into the food business.''

The next 25 years saw the decline of the barrel as a food container and its replacement by the consumer unit package; the setting of official standards for the composition of basic food products; and the banning of quack therapeutic mechanical devices such as the electric belt, whose galvanic properties were once presented so vividly to the ''Lost Manhood'' market. We still have with us in some measure the ''horse beef'' butcher and the ''butterlegger.'' Tap water remains a tempting means of ''extending'' many foods. But there is no question about the general integrity of our food supply, the contribution to the national well-being of the original food law, as amended, and the readiness of today's food industry leaders to accept what is now called the Food, Drug, and Cosmetic Act as a proper blueprint of their obligation to the nation's consumers.

Gerald H. Carson, a retired advertising agency executive and author of The Old Country Store, *is a student of American social history. He contributed ''Holiday Time at the Old Country Store'' to the December, 1954, issue of* AMERICAN HERITAGE.

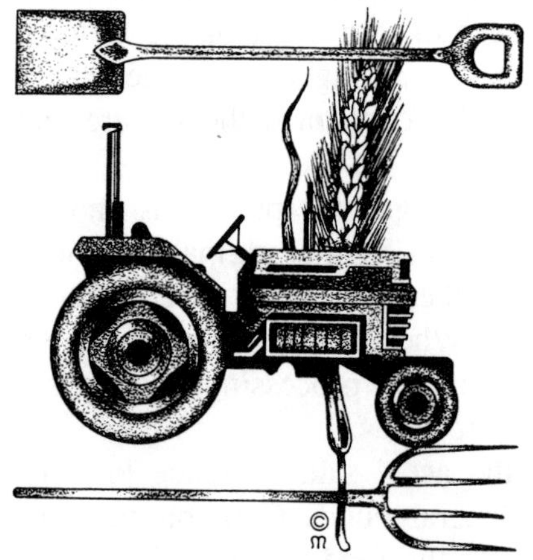

Bryan

John A. Garraty

*A*mericans are a proud, ambitious, and hopeful people; they are easily riled when life does not measure up to their expectations, and quick to express their displeasure. Only one "era of good feelings" is recorded in our history: it was short, merely superficially calm, and quickly followed by the broils and battles of the Age of Jackson. On the other hand, fundamental conflicts of interest and opinion among Americans have been extremely rare. Our Constitution, for example, has been amended only a dozen times since the Bill of Rights was added nearly two hundred years ago; it is not basically different today from what it was then.

This combination of over-all placidity and local tumult is understandable. America has been generally receptive to new ideas, but has not tended to swallow them whole. Reformers who want to make basic changes seldom get far in our system; although their reforms are often achieved, they themselves seldom achieve power. Traditionally this "law" of American politics has been explained by the tendency of the major parties to make concessions to radical ideas as soon as they show signs of becoming popular, and by the generally happy and prosperous condition of the American people, which has predisposed them toward moderation and gradualism. I would like to suggest, without fundamentally questioning that view, that reformers also defeat themselves, not through the ends they cherish but by the means they choose.

This article and two that will follow will try to demonstrate this proposition by examining the careers of three reformers of the Progressive Era, that period from the turn of the century to World War I when America was adjusting to its *rapid emergence as a great industrial nation. Our subjects are William Jennings Bryan, a Democrat: George W. Perkins, one of Theodore Roosevelt's "Bull Moosers"; and Robert M. La Follette, until the tag end of his long career always a Republican. Despite the diversity of their politics all three considered themselves "progressives," and have been accepted as such by historians. All were "good" men, utterly incorruptible, who devoted their lives to fruitful public service. All accomplished a great deal. But all, in the end, failed to achieve their chief objectives. What went right? What went wrong?*

That is our story.   *—J. A. G.*

"The President of the United States may be an ass," wrote H. L. Mencken during the reign of Calvin Coolidge, "but he at least doesn't believe that the earth is square, and that witches should be put to death, and that Jonah swallowed the whale." The man to whom the vitriolic Mencken was comparing President Coolidge was William Jennings Bryan of Nebraska, one of the dominant figures in the Progressive movement. According to Mencken, Bryan was a "peasant," a "zany without sense or dignity," a "poor clod," and, in addition, an utter fraud. "If the fellow was sincere, then so was P. T. Barnum," he sneered.

It was certainly easy enough, and tempting, for sophisticates to come to the conclusion that Bryan was a buffoon and a fake. His undignified association in his declining years with the promotion of Florida real estate and his naïve and bigoted religious views, so pitilessly exposed by Clarence Darrow during the famous "Monkey Trail" in Dayton, Tennessee, lent substance to the Mencken view of his character. So did Bryan's smug refusal, while Secretary of State under Woodrow Wilson, to serve alcoholic beverages at Department receptions and dinners because of his personal disapproval of drinking, and his objection to the appointment of ex-President Charles W. Eliot of Harvard as Ambassador to China on the ground that Eliot was a Unitarian, and therefore not a real Christian. "The new Chinese civilization," said Bryan, "was founded upon the Christian movement." Eliot's appointment might undermine the work of generations of pious missionaries, he implied. Bryan's unabashed partisanship—he talked frankly after Wilson's election of filing government positions with "deserving Democrats"—did not seem to jibe with his pretensions as a reformer. And his oratorical style, magnificent but generally more emotional than logical, was disappointing to thinking people. John Hay called him a "Baby Demosthenes" and David Houston, one of his colleagues in Wilson's Cabinet, states that "one could drive a prairie schooner through any part of his argument and never scrape against a fact." Being largely a creature of impulse, Bryan was, Houston added, "constantly on the alert to get something which has been represented to him as a fact to support or sustain his impulses."

But these flaws and blind spots were not fundamental weaknesses; they should never be allowed to overshadow Bryan's long years of devoted service to the cause of reform. If there were large areas about which he knew almost nothing, there were others where he was alert, sensible, and well-informed; certainly he was not a stupid man, nor was he easily duped or misled. Although a professional politician, as his remark about "deserving Democrats" makes clear, he was utterly honest personally and devoted to the cause of the people, as he understood it.

He was perfectly attuned to the needs and aspirations of rural America. In the early nineties he was in the forefront of the fight against high tariffs on manufactured goods. Later in the decade he battled for currency reform. At the turn of the century he was leading the assault against imperialism. During Theodore Roosevelt's primacy he was often far ahead of the intrepid Teddy, advocating a federal income tax, the eight-hour day, the control of monopoly and the strict regulation of public utilities, woman suffrage, and a large number of other startling innovations. Under Wilson he played a major part in marshaling support in Congress for the Federal Reserve Act and other New Freedom measures. Whatever his limitations, his faults, or his motives, few public men of his era left records as consistently "progressive" as Bryan's.

For years he led the Democratic party without the advantage of holding office. Three times he was a presidential candidate; although never elected, he commanded the unswerving loyalty of millions of his fellow citizens for nearly thirty years. He depended more on his intuition than on careful analysis in forming his opinions, but his intuition was usually sound; he was more a man of heart than of brain, but his heart was great.

Bryan was known as the Great Commoner, and the title was apt. He was a man of the people in origin and by instinct. He was typical of his age in rendering great respect to public opinion, whether it was informed or not. To Bryan the voice of the people was truly the voice of God. "I don't know anything about free silver," he announced while running for Congress early in the nineties. "The people of Nebraska are for free silver and I am for free silver. I will look up the arguments later." (It should be added that he did indeed "look up the arguments later." Less than a year after making this promise he arose in the House to deliver without notes a brilliant three-hour speech on the money question, a speech of great emotional power, but also fact-laden, sensible, and full of shrewd political arguments. When he sat down, the cheers rang out from both sides of the aisle.)

Bryan was born in Salem, Illinois, in 1860, a child of the great Middle West. Growing up in the heart of the valley of democracy, he absorbed its spirit and its sense of protest from his earliest years. After being graduated from Illinois College in 1881, he studied law in Chicago and for a time practiced his profession in Jacksonville, Illinois. But in 1887, stimulated by a talk with a law-school classmate from that city, he moved west to Lincoln, Nebraska. He quickly made his way in this new locale. Within a year he was active in the local Democratic organization, and in 1890, a month before his thirtieth birthday, he won his party's nomination for congressman.

Nebraska was traditionally a Republican state, its loyalty to the party of Lincoln forged in the heat of the Civil War. But by 1890 tradition was rapidly losing its hold on voters all over the Middle West. For the farmers of the American heartland were in deep trouble, and the Republican party seemed unwilling to do much to help them.

Tumultuous social and economic changes shaped the nation in the years after Appomattox. Within a single generation the United States was transformed from what was essentially a land of farmers into a modern industrial society, and in the process the Middle West was caught in a relentless economic vise. During the flush times of the sixties, when the Union Army was buying enormous amounts of food and fodder, and foreign demand was unusually high, the farmers of the region had gone into debt in order to buy more land and machinery. In the seventies and eighties, however, agricultural prices, especially those of such major staple crops as wheat and cotton, fell steeply. Wheat, which had sold as high as $2.50 a bushel in wartime, was down to fifty cents by the early nineties.

The impact of this economic decline was intensified by the changing social status of the farmer. Agriculture was losing its predominant place in American life. In the days of the Founding Fathers, about ninety per cent of the population was engaged in working the soil, and the farmer was everywhere portrayed as the symbol of American self-reliance and civic virtue. "Those who labor in the earth," Jefferson said, "are the chosen people of God." But as the factory began to outstrip the farm, the farmer lost much of his standing. While the old symbol remained—it was especially in evidence around election time—a new and disturbing image of the farmer as a hick, a rube, a hayseed—a comic mixture of cocky ignorance, shrewd self-interest, and monumental provincialism—began to challenge it.

Naturally the farmers resented their loss of both income and prestige, but there was little they could do about either. Price declines were largely a response to worldwide overproduction, resulting from improvements in transportation and the opening up of new farmlands in Australia, Argentina, Canada, Russia, and elsewhere. Nor did the farmers, who desired manufactured goods as much as everyone else, really want to reverse the trend that was making them a minority group in a great industrial nation. But as they cast about for some way out of their plight, they were profoundly disturbed by certain results of the new development which did seem amenable to reform.

Industrial growth meant the mushrooming of great cities. These gave birth to noxious slums where every kind of vice flourished, where corrupt political organizations like the venal Tweed Ring in New York were forged, and where radical political concepts like socialism and anarchism sought to undermine "the American way of life." In the words of Jefferson, the farmers' hero, cities were "ulcers and the body politic."

Giant industries also attracted hordes of immigrants; these seemed to threaten the Middle West both by their mere numbers and by their "un-American" customs and points of view. Could the American melting pot absorb such strange ingredients without losing much of its own character?

Furthermore, to the citizens of Nebraska and other agricultural states, the new industrial barons appeared bent on making vassals of every farmer in America. The evidence seemed overwhelming: Huge impersonal corporations had neither souls nor consciences; profit was their god, materialism their only creed. The "interests," a tiny group of powerful tycoons in great eastern centers like Boston, New York, and Philadelphia, were out to enslave the rest of the country. Farmers worked and sweated only to see the "interests" make off with most of the fruit of their toil. Too many useless middlemen grew fat off the mere "handling" of wheat and cotton. Monopolistic railroads overcharged for carrying crops to market, unscrupulous operators of grain elevators falsely downgraded prime crops and charged exorbitant fees. Cynical speculators drove the price of staples up and down, sometimes making and losing millions in a matter of minutes, without the slightest regard for the effect of their operations on the producers whose sweat made their deadly game possible.

Conspiring with bankers and mortgage holders, all these groups combined to dictate the federal government's money policy. Population and production were surging forward; more money was needed simply to keep up with economic growth. Yet the government was deliberately cutting down on the amount of money in circulation by retiring Civil War greenbacks. On debt-ridden farmers plagued by overproduction, the effect of this deflation was catastrophic. Or so it seemed from the perspective of rural America.

While undoubtedly exaggerated, this indictment of the "interest" was taken as gospel throughout large sectors of the South and West. As a result, demands for "reform" quickly arose. The leading reformers were for the most part sincere, but few of them were entirely altruistic and many were decidedly eccentric. Participating in the movement for a variety of motives but without coming to grips with the main problem of American agriculture—overproduction—were coarse demagogues like Senator "Pitchfork Ben" Tillman of South Carolina, and unwashed characters like the wisecracking congressman from Kansas, "Sockless Jerry" Simpson. There were professional orators like the angry Mary Ellen Lease (her detractors called her "Mary Yellin' "), and homespun economic theorists like "Coin" Harvey and "General" Jacob Coxey, who believed so strongly in paper money that he named his son Legal Tender. The excesses of such people frightened off many Americans who might otherwise have lent a sympathetic ear to the farmers' complaints; others who might have been friendly observed the antics of the reformers with contempt and wrote off the whole movement as a joke.

Since neither of the major parties espoused the farmers' cause wholeheartedly, much of the protest found its way into various third-party organizations. At first, discontented elements concentrated on opposing the government's policy of retiring the paper money put in circulation during the Civil War. To save these greenbacks from extinction a Greenback (later Greenback-Labor) party sprang up. In 1878 its candidates polled a million votes, but decline followed as currency reformers turned to other methods of inflation.

Meanwhile the Patrons of Husbandry, better known as the Grange, originally a social organization for farm families, had begun to agitate in local politics against the middlemen who were draining off such a large percentage of the farmers' profits. In the seventies the Grangers became a power in the Middle West; in state after state they obtained the passage of laws setting maximum rates for railroads and prohibiting various forms of discrimination. The operations of grain elevators were also subjected to state regulation by "Granger Laws" in states such as Illinois, Iowa, Wisconsin, and Minnesota. The Grange abandoned political activity in the eighties, but other farm organizations quickly took its place. These coalesced first into the Northern Alliance and the Souther Alliance, and around 1890 the two Alliances joined with one another to become the Populist party.

Although William Jennings Bryan was a Democrat, he had grown up amid the agitations of the Granger movement. His father had even run for Congress in the seventies with Greenback party support. The aspirations and the general point of view of the midwestern farmers were young Bryan's own. Public men, he admitted late in life to the journalist Mark Sullivan, are "the creatures of their age. . . . I lived in the very center of the country out of which the reforms grew, and was quite naturally drawn to the people's side."

And they to his, one must add. Discontented farmers in his district were on the lookout for men who understood them and their problems. In 1888 the Republicans had carried the seat by 3,000 votes; now, in 1890, Bryan swept in with a lead of 6,713.

Bryan made an excellent record in his first Congress. He was a hardworking member, studying the technicalities of the tariff question for months before making his first important speech. But he saw that the tariff was rapidly being replaced by the money question as the crucial issue of the day. When he yielded the floor after completing his tariff speech, he collared a young Texas congressman named Joseph W. Bailey, who posed as a financial expert. Sitting on a sofa in the rear of the House chamber, he quizzed Bailey about the problem of falling prices. Bailey told him the tariff had little or no effect on the plight of the farmer; the whole difficulty arose from "an appreciation in value of gold." Interested, Bryan demanded a list of books on the subject and was soon deep in a study of the money question.

To a man like Bryan, studying the money question meant searching for some means of checking the deflationary trend that was so injurious to his farmer constituents. He quickly discovered that most farmbelt financial authorities felt this could best be done by providing for the free coinage of silver. In 1873 the United States had gone on the gold standard, which meant that only gold was accepted for coinage at the mint. By going back to bimetallism, the amount of bullion being coined would be increased, and if the favorable ratio of sixteen to one between silver and gold were established, the production of silver for coinage would be greatly stimulated.

To press for the free coinage of silver at a ratio of sixteen to one with gold seemed less radical or dangerous than to demand direct inflation of the currency through the printing of greenbacks. Silver, after all, was a precious metal: coining it could not possibly lead to the sort of ''runaway'' inflation that had helped ruin the South during the Civil War. Debtors and other friends of inflation could also count on the powerful support of silver-mine interests. The free-coinage issue thus had a powerful political appeal. Despite the opposition of most conservative businessmen, the silverites were able, in 1878 and again in 1890, to obtain legislation providing for the coinage of *some* silver, although not enough to check the downward trend of prices.

Within a month after his tariff speech Bryan was calling for free coinage, and he stressed the issue in his successful campaign for re-election in 1892. But the new President, Democrat Grover Cleveland, was an ardent gold-standard man, and when a severe depression struck the country early in 1893, he demanded that the Silver Purchase Act of 1890, which had raised the specter of inflation in the minds of many businessmen, be repealed by Congress at once. In this way he committed his party to the resumption of the single gold standard.

Bryan refused to go along with this policy. Threatening to ''serve my country and my God under some other name'' than ''Democrat'' unless the Administration changed its mind, he resisted the repeal of the silver act in a brilliant extemporaneous speech. Cleveland carried the day for repeal, but Bryan emerged as a potential leader of the silver wing of the Democrats.

In 1894 he sought a wider influence by running for the United States Senate. In those days senators were still chosen by the state legislatures: to be elected Bryan would need the support of Nebraska's Populists as well as of his own party. He worked hard for fusion, but Populist support was not forthcoming. Though the Democrats backed Populist candidate Silas A. Holcomb for the governorship, the Populists refused to reciprocate and ran their own man for the Senate seat. The Republican candidate therefore won easily.

At this stage the Populists were trying hard to become a truly national party. Their program, besides demanding the free coinage of silver and various land reforms desired by farmers, called for government ownership of railroads, a graduated income tax, the direct election of U.S. senators, the eight-hour day, and a number of additional reforms designed to appeal to eastern workingmen and other dissatisfied groups. As early as 1892 their presidential candidate, James B. Weaver, had polled over a million votes; in 1894 the party won six seats in the Senate and seven in the House of Representatives. At least in Nebraska, the Populists were not yet ready to merge with the ''conservative'' Democratic organization.

Defeat for the Senate did not harm Bryan politically. He was still in his early thirties; to one so young, merely having run for the Senate brought considerable prestige. Also, he had conducted an intelligent and forceful campaign. Even so it was a defeat, certainly not calculated to lead him to the remarkable decision that he made after the Nebraska legislature had turned him down. This decision was to seek nomination for the Presidency of the United States itself!

The young man's "superlative self-assurance" (one might call it effrontery but for the fact that his daring plan succeeded) staggers the imagination. Many men within his party were far better known than he, and his state, Nebraska, was without major influence in Democratic affairs. With Cleveland and the national organization dead-set against free coinage and other inflationary schemes, Bryan's chances of capturing the nomination seemed infinitesimal. But if bold, his action was by no means foolish. Democratic voters were becoming more and more restive under Cleveland's conservative leadership. At least in Bryan's part of the nation, many thoughtful members of the party were beginning to feel that they must look in new directions and find new leaders if they were not to be replaced by the Populists as the country's second major party. Recognizing this situation before most politicians did, Bryan proceeded to act upon his insight with determination and dispatch.

First of all, he set out to make himself known beyond his own locality. Accepting the editorship of the Omaha *World-Herald* at a tiny salary in order to obtain a forum, he turned out a stream of editorials on the silver question, which he sent to influential politicians all over the country. He toured the South and West with his message, speaking everywhere and under all sorts of conditions: to close-packed, cheering throngs and to tiny groups of quiet listeners. His argument was simple but forceful, his oratory magnetic and compelling. Always he made sure to meet local leaders and to subject them to his genial smile, his youthful vigor, his charm, his sincerity. He did not push himself forward; indeed, he claimed to be ready to support any honest man whose program was sound. But he lost no chance to point out to all concerned his own availability. "I don't suppose your delegation is committed to any candidate," he wrote to a prominent Colorado Democrat in April of 1896. "Our delegation may present my name." When the Democratic convention finally met in Chicago, Bryan believed that he was known personally to more of the delegates than any other candidate.

Few delegates took his campaign seriously, however. At the convention, one senator asked Bryan who he thought would win out. Bryan replied characteristically that he believed he himself "had as good a chance to be nominated as anyone," and proceeded to tick off the sources of his strength: Nebraska, "half of the Indian Territory, ..." but before Bryan could mention his other backers the senator lost interest and walked off with some of his cronies. The candidate, amiable and serene, took no offense. A majority of the delegates favored his position on silver. No one had a clear lead in the race. All he needed was a chance to plead his case.

The opportunity—Bryan called it an "unexpected stroke of luck," although he planned for it brilliantly—came when he was asked to close the debate on the platform's silver plank. When he came forward to address the jam-packed mob in the Chicago auditorium he was tense, but there was a smile on his face, and to observers he seemed the picture of calm self-confidence. He began quietly, but his voice resounded in the farthest corners of the great hall and commanded the attention of every delegate. He was conscious of his own humble position, he told the throng, but he was "clad in the armor of a righteous cause" and this entitled him to speak. As he went on, his tension evaporated and his voice rose. When he recounted the recent history of the struggle between the forces of gold and silver, the audience responded eagerly. "At the close of a sentence," he wrote later, "it would rise and shout, and when I began upon another sentence, the room was still as a church."

He spoke for silver as against gold, for the West over the East, for "the hardy pioneers who have braved all the dangers of the wilderness" as against "the few financial magnates who, in a back room, corner the money of the world."

> We have petitioned, and our petitions have been scorned; we have entreated, and our entreaties have been disregarded; we have begged, and they have mocked when our calamity came. We beg no longer; we entreat no more; we petition no more. *We defy them!*

The crowd thundered its agreement. Bryan proceeded. One after another he met the arguments of the party's Cleveland wing head on. Free silver would disturb the business interests? "Gold bugs" were defining the term too narrowly. Remember that wage earners, crossroads merchants, and farmers were also businessmen. The cities favored the gold standard? Their prosperity really depended upon the prosperity of the great agricultural regions of the land, which favored bimetallism. "Burn down your cities and leave our farms," he said, "and your cities will spring up again as if by magic; but destroy our farms and the grass will grow in the streets of every city in the country."

Now Bryan was absolute master of the delegates. "I thought of a choir," he recalled afterward, "as I noted how instantaneously and in unison they responded to each point made." The crowd cheered because he was reflecting its sentiments, but also because it recognized, suddenly, its leader—handsome, confident, righteously indignant, yet also calm, restrained, and ready for responsibility. His mission accomplished, it was time to close, and Bryan had saved a marvelous figure of speech, tested in many an earlier oration, for his climax. "You shall not press down upon the brow of labor this crown of thorns," he warned, bringing his hands down suggestively to his temples; "you shall not crucify mankind upon a cross of gold." Dramatically he extended his arms to the side, the very figure of the crucified Christ.

The Controversial Commoner

When McKeighan died [William McKeighan, Nebraska free-silverite], Bryan came down to the sun-scorched, dried-up, blown-away little village of Red Cloud to speak at his funeral. There, with an audience of some few hundreds of bronzed farmers who believed in him as their deliverer, the man who could lead them out of the bondage of debt, who could stay the drought and strike water from the rock, I heard him make the greatest speech of his life. Surely that was eloquence of the old stamp that ws accounted divine, eloquence that reached through the callus of ignorance and toil and found and awoke the stunted souls of men. I saw those rugged men of the soil weep like children. Six months later, at Chicago, when Bryan stampeded a convention, appropriated a party, electrified a nation . . . one of those ragged farmers sat beside me in the gallery, and at the close of that never-to-be-forgotten speech, he leaned over the rail, the tears on his furrowed cheeks, and shouted, "The sweet singer of Israel."

—*Willa Cather, in* Round-up:
A Nebraska Reader

What a disgusting, dishonest fakir Bryan is! When I see so many Americans running after him, I feel very much as I do when a really lovely woman falls in love with a cad.

*Elihu Root to William M. Laffan,
October 31, 1900*

As for Bryan, though he has many kindly and amiable traits, what a shallow demogogue he is! I do not believe he is a bit worse than Thomas Jefferson, and I do not think that if elected President he will be a worse President. The country would survive, but it would suffer just as the country suffered for at least two generations because of its folly in following Jefferson's lead.

—*Theodore Roosevelt to Henry
Cabot Lodge, August 6, 1906*

It has become the custom nowadays, among supercillious people, to depict Bryan as a clown, or a fool, or a mountebank. He was nothing of the kind. In many respects, he was one of the shrewdest men I have ever known. In him, unsophistication and sagacity were strangely blended. Along with this he was truthful and square. His friendships were sincere; one could depend implicitly on his word. . . . He turned every public question into a moral issue. He was by nature a crusader, a reformer. . . . But anyone who pictures him as a grumpy, sour, muddled fanatic is wholly wrong. . . .

As I think of him there comes into my mind what somebody said of Gladstone—that to keep hating him, one had to avoid meeting him. I cannot say if this was true of Gladstone, but it was certainly true of William Jennings Bryan.

—*William G. McAdoo, in* Crowded Years

Amid the hysterical demonstration that followed, it was clear that Bryan had accomplished his miracle. The next day, July 9, he was nominated for the Presidency on the fifth ballot.

The issue was clear-cut, for the Republicans had already declared for the gold standard and nominated the handsome, genial, and thoroughly conservative William McKinley. As a result, the Populists were under great pressure to go along with Bryan. While the Democrats had not adopted all the radical Populist demands, their platform contained a number of liberal planks in addition to that on free silver, including one calling for a federal income tax and another for stiffer controls of the railroad network. For the Populists to insist on nominating a third candidate would simply insure the election of the "gold bug" McKinley. Not every important Populist favored fusion; some were ready to concede defeat in 1896 and build their party for the future on broadly radical lines. "The Democratic idea of fusion," said Tom Watson of Georgia angrily, is "that we play Jonah while they play whale." But the rich scent of victory in the air was too much for the majority to resist. "I care not for party names," said "Sockless Jerry" Simpson bluntly; "it is the substance we are after, and we have it in William J. Bryan." Indeed, Bryan's friendly association with the Populists in earlier campaigns and his essentially Populistic views on most questions made it difficult for the party to oppose him. "We put him to school," one anti-Bryan Populist later remarked, "and he wound up by stealing the school-books." In any case, the Populist convention endorsed him; thus the silver forces united to do battle with the Republicans.

Both Bryan and McKinley men realized at once that this was to be a close and crucial contest. Seldom have the two great parties divided so clearly on fundamental issues; a showdown was inevitable; a major turning point in American history had been reached. Silver against gold was but the surface manifestation of the struggle. City against countryside, industry against agriculture, East against South and West, the nineteenth century against the twentieth—these were the real contestants in 1896.

After Bryan's nomination McKinley's manager, Mark Hanna, abandoned plans for a vacation cruise in New England waters and plunged into the work of the campaign. The situation was "alarming," he told McKinley. A "communistic spirit" was abroad, business was "all going to pieces." A mighty effort was called for. Hanna raised huge sums by "assessing" the great bankers, oil refiners, insurance men, and meat packers, using the threat of impending business chaos and wild inflation to loosen the purse strings of the tycoons. While McKinley, "the advance agent of prosperity," conducted a dignified and carefully organized campaign from his front porch in Canton, Ohio (*see* "The Front Porch Campaign," AMERICAN HERITAGE, December, 1959), 1,400 paid speakers beat the bushes for votes in every doubtful district. The Republican campaign committee distributed more than 120,000,000 pieces of literature printed in ten languages to carry its message to the voters. Boiler-plate editorials and other releases were sent free to hundreds of small-town newspapers. Hanna, Theodore Roosevelt said, "has advertised McKinley as if he were a patent medicine!" The Republican organization reached a peak of efficiency and thoroughness never before approached in a political contest; the campaign marked a methodological revolution that has profoundly affected every presidential contest since.

Bryan had little money, and no organizational genius like Hanna to direct his drive. But he too effected a revolution that has left its mark on modern campaigning. McKinley's front porch technique was novel only in the huge number of visiting delegations that Hanna paraded across his man's lawn and the exaggerated care that the candidate took to avoid saying anything impolitic. It has always been considered undignified for a presidential nominee to go out and hunt for votes on his own. Bryan cast off this essentially hypocritical tradition at the very start. He realized that the concerted power of business and the press were aligned against him, and that his own greatest assets were his magnificent ability as a political orator and his personal sincerity and charm. His opponent could afford to sit tight; *he* must seek out the people everywhere if they were to receive his message. Between summer and November he traveled a precedent-shattering 18,000 miles, making more than 600 speeches and addressing directly an estimated 5,000,000 Americans. His secretary estimated that he uttered between 60,000 and 100,000 words every day during the campaign.

On the stump he was superb. Without straining his voice he could make himself heard to a restless open-air throng numbered in the tens of thousands. He was equally effective at the whistle stops, outlining his case from the rear platform of his train while a handful of country people gazed earnestly upward from the roadbed. He was unfailingly pleasant and unpretentious. At one stop, while he was shaving in his compartment, a small group outside the train began clamoring for a glimpse of him. Flinging open the window and beaming through the lather, he cheerfully shook hands with each of these admirers. Neither he nor they, according to the recorder of this incident, saw anything unusual or undignified in the performance. Thousands of well-wishers sent him good luck charms and messages of encouragement. "If the people who have given me rabbits' feet in this campaign will vote for me, there is no possible doubt of my election," he said in one speech. It was because of this simple friendliness that he became known as "the Great Commoner."

Bryan was also unfailingly interesting. Even his most unsympathetic biographer admits that he spoke so well that at every stop the baggagemen from the campaign train would run back to listen to his talk—and this despite a schedule that called for as many as thirty speeches a day.

Such a campaign is an effective means of projecting an image of a candidate and his general point of view. It is not well suited for the making of complicated arguments and finely drawn distinctions; for that the McKinley approach was far superior. Wisely, for it was clearly the issue uppermost in the minds of most voters, Bryan hammered repeatedly at the currency question. He did not avoid talking about other matters: he attacked the railroads and the great business monopolists and the "tyranny" of the eastern bankers. He deplored the use of militia in labor disputes and of the injunction as a means of breaking strikes. He spoke in favor of income taxes, higher wages, and relief for hard-pressed mortgagees. But the silver issue was symbolic, and the Democratic position sound. There *was* a currency shortage; deflation *was* injuring millions of debtors and pouring a rich unearned increment into the pockets of bondholders. To say, as Henry Demarest Lloyd did at the time and as many liberal historians have since, that Bryan made free silver the "cowbird" of the reform movement, pushing out all other issues from the reform nest and thus destroying them, is an exaggeration and a distortion. All effective politicians stick to a small number of simple issues while on the stump; otherwise, in the hectic conflict of a hot campaign, they project no message at all. There is no reason to suspect that, if elected, Bryan would have forgotten about other reform measures and concentrated only on the currency.

For a time Bryan's gallant, singlehanded battle seemed to be having an effect on public opinion, and Republican leaders became thoroughly frightened. In addition to money, threats and imprecations now became weapons in the campaign. A rumor was circulated that Bryan was insane. The *New York Times* devoted columns to the possibility, and printed a letter from a supposed psychologist charging that he was suffering from "paranoia querulenta," "graphomania," and "oratorical monomania." "Men," one manufacturer told his workers, "vote as you please, but if Bryan is elected . . . the whistle will not blow Wednesday morning." According to the *Nation,* which was supporting McKinley, many companies placed orders with their suppliers "to be executed in case Mr. Bryan is defeated, and not otherwise." A Chicago company that held thousands of farm mortgages politely asked all its "customers" to indicate their presidential preferences—a not very subtle form of coercion but probably an effective one. In some cases men were actually fired because of their political opinions.

By the time election day arrived the McKinley managers were so confident of victory that Hanna began returning new contributions as no longer necessary. Nevertheless, a final monumental effort was made to get out the vote. Free transportation was provided to carry citizens to and from the polls, men were paid for time lost in voting, and in doubtful districts floaters and other disreputables were rounded up and paraded to the ballot boxes. Everywhere in the crucial North Central states the Hanna machine expended enormous efforts, and in these states the decision was made. McKinley carried them all and with them the nation. In the electoral college McKinley won by 271 to 176, but the popular vote was close— 7,036,000 to 6,468,000. The change of a relative handful of votes in half a dozen key states would have swung the election to Bryan.

The victory, however, was McKinley's, and conservatives all over America— and the world—echoed the sentiment of Hanna's happy telegram to the President-elect: GOD'S IN HIS HEAVEN, ALL'S RIGHT WITH THE WORLD! A watershed in the economic and social history of the United States had been crossed. The rural America of the nineteenth century was making way for the industrial America of the twentieth. Soon business conditions began to improve, agricultural prices inched upward, new discoveries of gold relieved the pressure on the money supply. While McKinley and Hanna (now senator from Ohio) ruled in Washington, the era of complacent materialism and easy political virtue that had entered American politics on the coattails of General Grant seemed destined to continue indefinitely. Reform, it appeared, was dead.

That these appearances were deceiving was due in considerable measure to William Jennings Bryan. Unchastened by defeat and always cheerful ("It is better to have run and lost than never to have run at all," he said), he maintained the leadership of his party. Consistently he took the liberal position on important issues. Despite his strong pacifism he approved of fighting Spain in 1898 in order to free Cuba. "Humanity demands that we should act," he said simply. He enlisted in the Army and rose to be a colonel, although he saw no action during the brief conflict. The sincerity of his motives was proved when the war ended, for he then fought against the plan to annex former Spanish colonies. Running for President a second time in 1900, he made resistance to imperialism an issue in the campaign along with free silver. If both of these were poorly calculated to win votes in 1900, they were nonetheless solidly in the liberal tradition. Bryan lost to McKinley again, this time by 861,459 votes, and leadership of the reform movement passed, after McKinley's assassination, to Theodore Roosevelt. But Bryan continued the fight. In 1904, battling almost alone against conservatives in his own party, he forced the adoption of a fairly liberal platform (including strong antitrust, pro-labor, and anti-tariff planks), and when the conservative Judge Alton B. Parker was nonetheless nominated for President, Bryan kept up his outspoken criticism. While remaining loyal to the Democratic party he announced boldly: "The fight on economic questions . . . is not abandoned. As soon as the election is over I shall . . . organize for the campaign of 1908."

In that campaign Bryan, once more the Democratic nominee, was once more defeated in his personal quest of the Presidency, this time by Roosevelt's hand-picked successor, William Howard Taft. Immediately he announced that he would not seek the office again, thus throwing the field open to other liberals.

Although he thus abandoned formal leadership of the Democrats, Bryan continued to advocate reform. Throughout the Taft administration he campaigned up and down the country to bolster the liberal wing of his party. When the 1912 nominating convention met in Baltimore, he introduced and won approval of a highly controversial resolution denouncing Wall Street influence, and he stated repeatedly that he would not support any candidate who was under the slightest obligation to Tammany Hall. The platform, as one historian says, "was a progressive document, in the best Bryan tradition." In the end Bryan threw his support to

Woodrow Wilson. While this alone did not account for Wilson's nomination, it was very important in his election, for it assured him the enthusiastic backing of millions of loyal Bryanites.

Nothing reveals Bryan's fine personal qualities better than his support for Wilson, for the former Princeton professor had opposed the Great Commoner since 1896, when he had called the Cross of Gold speech "ridiculous." In 1904 he had publicly demanded that the Bryan wing be "utterly and once and for all driven from Democratic counsels." As late as 1908 he had refused to appear on the same platform with Bryan. Mr. Bryan, he said, "is the most charming and lovable of men personally, but foolish and dangerous in his theoretical beliefs." During the campaign of that year he refused to allow Bryan to deliver a campaign speech on the Princeton campus.

By 1912 Wilson had become far more liberal and no longer opposed most of Bryan's policies; even so, had Bryan been a lesser man he would not have forgiven these repeated criticisms. But he was more concerned with Wilson's 1912 liberalism than with personal matters, despite the publication of an old letter in which Wilson had expressed the wish to "knock Mr. Bryan once and for all into a cocked hat!" He shrugged off the "cocked hat" letter, and when Wilson paid him a handsome public tribute they became good friends. Furthermore, during the 1912 campaign, Bryan campaigned vigorously for Wilson, making well over four hundred speeches within a period of seven weeks. When Wilson won an easy victory in November, Bryan reacted without a trace of envy or bitterness. "It is a great triumph," he declared, "Let every Democratic heart rejoice." A few months later he said in a speech in Chicago:

> Sometimes I have had over-sanguine friends express regret that I did not reach the presidency. . . . But I have an answer ready for them. I have told them that they need not weep for me. . . . I have been so much more interested in the securing of the things for which we have been fighting than I have been in the name of the man who held the office, that I am happy in the thought that this government, through these reforms, will be made so good that a citizen will not miss a little thing like the presidency.

Wilson made Bryan Secretary of State. He was needed in the administration to help manage his many friends in Congress. The strategy worked well, for Bryan used his influence effectively. His role was particularly crucial in the hard fight over the Federal Reserve bill, but his loyal aid was also important in passing income tax legislation and a new antitrust law and in other matters as well.

In managing foreign affairs Bryan was less successful, for in this field he was ill-prepared. Because of his frank belief in the spoils system, he dismissed dozens of key professional diplomats, replacing them with untrained political hacks. Naturally the Foreign Service was badly injured. His policy of not serving alcoholic beverages at official functions because of his personal convictions caused much criticism at home and abroad. "W. J. Bryan not only suffers for his principles and mortifies his flesh, as he has every right to do,'' the London *Daily Express* complained, ''but he insists that others should suffer and be mortified.'' The Secretary's continuing Chautauqua lectures, at which he sometimes appeared on the same platform with vaudeville entertainers and freaks, were attacked by many as undignified for one who occupied such a high official position.

Bryan had answers to all these criticisms: the State Department had been overly snobbish and undemocratic; Wilson had agreed to his ''grape juice'' policy before appointing him; no one should be ashamed of speaking to the American people. He could also point to his ''cooling-off treaties'' with some twenty nations, which provided machinery for avoiding blow-ups over minor diplomatic imbroglios.

Unfortunately Bryan had but a dim understanding of Latin American problems and unwittingly fostered American imperialism on many occasions. His narrow-minded belief that he knew better than local leaders what was ''good'' for these small countries showed that he had no comprehension of cultural and nationalistic elements in other lands. Although well intended, his policies produced much bad feeling in South and Central America. Bryan did suggest lending Latin American nations money ''for education, sanitation and internal development,'' a policy that anticipated our modern Point Four approach to underdeveloped areas. Wilson, however, dismissed the idea because he thought it ''would strike the whole country . . . as a novel and radical proposal.''

When the World War broke out in 1914, Bryan, like his chief, adopted a policy of strict neutrality. America, he said, should attempt to mediate between the belligerents by suggesting ''a more rational basis of peace.'' Bryan believed in real neutrality far more deeply than Wilson, who was not ready to face the possibility of a German victory. ''We cannot have in mind the wishes of one side more than the wishes of the other side,'' Bryan warned the President after the latter had prepared a stiff note of protest against German submarine warfare. And when, after the sinking of the *Lusitania,* Wilson sent a series of threatening messages to Germany, Bryan resigned as Secretary of State. He never again held public office.

It would have been better for Bryan's reputation if he had died in 1915; instead he lived on for another decade, as amiable and well-intentioned as ever but increasingly out of touch with the rapidly changing times. He made no effect to keep up with the abrupt intellectual developments of the twentieth century, yet he was accustomed to speak his mind on current issues and continued to do so. There had always been those who had considered his uncomplicated faith in time-tested moral principles and in popular rule rather naïve; in the cynical, scientific, and amoral twenties only a relative handful of rural oldtimers saw much virtue in his homilies on the people's unfailing instinct to do always what was ''right'' and ''good.'' In the world of Calvin Coolidge the old Populist fires no longer burned very brightly, and Bryan's anti-business bias seemed terribly old-fashioned. Many had considered him an anachronism even in Wilson's day; by Harding's he had simply ceased to count in politics. More and more he confined himself to religious questions. His ardent piety was heartwarming, but he was a smug and intolerant Fundamentalist whose ignorance of modern science and ethics did not prevent him from expounding his "views" on these subjects at length. The honest opinions of "the people," he believed, could "settle" scientific and philosophical questions as easily as political ones.

Advancing age, as well as increasing preoccupation with revealed religion, was making Bryan less tolerant. Never one to give much thought to reasoned counterarguments, he became, in the twenties, an outspoken foe of many aspects of human freedom. He defended prohibition, refused to condemn the Ku Klux Klan, and participated eagerly in the notorious Scopes anti-evolution trial in Dayton, Tennessee, with all its overtones of censorship and self-satisfied ignorance. The final great drama of Bryan's life occurred when Clarence Darrow mercilessly exposed his simple prejudices on the witness stand. Bryan complacently maintained, among other things, that Eve was actually made from Adam's rib and that Jonah had really been swallowed by the whale. The rural audience cheered, but educated men all over the world were appalled.

Throughout his lifetime, Bryan was subject to harsh and almost continual criticism, and at least superficially he failed in nearly everything he attempted. But he was too secure in his faith to be injured by criticism, and he knew that for over two decades his influence was greater than any of his contemporaries save Theodore Roosevelt and Wilson. His life was useful and happy, for he rightly believed that he had made a lasting contribution to his country's development. Nor is it fair to condemn him for his limited intelligence and superficial understanding of his times. Other political leaders of at best ordinary intellect have done great deeds, sometimes without appreciating the meaning of events they have helped to shape. Still, there was tragedy in Bryan's career—he was unable to grow.

In 1896 he was indeed the peerless leader, vital, energetic, dedicated, and, in a measure, imaginative. He saw the problems of Nebraska farmers, realized their wider implications, and outlined a reasonable program designed to deal with them. He was almost elected President as a result, despite his youth and inexperience. Suddenly he was a celebrity; thereafter he moved into a wider world and lived there at his ease. He did not abandon his principles, and he helped achieve many important reforms, for which we must always honor him, but he soon ceased to feed upon new ideas. In a sense, despite the defeats, life's rewards came to him too easily. His magnetic voice, his charm, his patent sincerity, the memory of the heroic fight of '96—these things secured his place and relieved him of the need to grapple with new concepts.

Although he was a man of courage, strength, and endurance, Bryan was essentially lax and complacent. He preferred baggy clothes, a full stomach, the easy, undemanding companionship of small minds. For years the momentum of 1896 carried him on, but eventually the speeding world left him far behind. Fortunately for his inner well-being, he never realized what had happened. A few days after Darrow had exposed his shallowness before the world, he died peacefully in his sleep, as serene and unruffled by events as ever.

———————

John A. Garraty is a professor of history at Columbia University and a frequent contributor to AMERICAN HERITAGE.

For further reading: The Memoirs of William Jennings Bryan by Himself and His Wife, Mary Baird Bryan *(John C. Winston, 1925);* The Trumpet Soundeth, *by Paul W. Glad (University of Nebraska Press, 1960);* The Peerless Leader, William Jennings Bryan, *by Paxton Hibben (Farrar & Rinehart, 1929).*

The Mosher Report

Kathryn Allamong Jacob

The nineteenth century was, according to the stereotype, ashamed and fearful of all things sexual. It was an era when, as one visitor to America swore, teachers put "modest little trousers with frills at the bottom" over the "limbs" of their pianos. The Victorian woman's lack of passion was proverbial, her frigidity extolled by the popular hygiene books and marriage manuals of the day.

But were Victorian women in fact passionless? In a remarkable survey that historian Carl Degler found in the Stanford University Archives, it appears that at least one group of Victorian women defied the stereotype: they approached sex with gusto. This survey, though very small, appears to be the earliest systematic study of the sexual habits and attitudes of American women, including information on sexual desire, frequency of intercourse, and orgasm.

Other studies, such as those of Alfred Kinsey and Shere Hite, deal almost exclusively with women born in the twentieth century; this survey contains responses of women born at the time of the Civil War. It was a study made years ahead of its time, but only part of the memorable career of the researcher, Clelia Duel Mosher, a physician who devoted her life to destroying the notions of physical inferiority that had stigmatized women.

She was born on December 16, 1863, in Albany, New York. Her father, Cornelius, and four uncles were physicians. Cornelius Mosher married Sarah Burritt and settled in Albany where he became an authority on insanity, a member of the Board of Education, and the father of two girls.

In 1931 Clelia Mosher dedicated her unfinished autobiography ''to my father, who believed in women when most men classified them with children and imbeciles.''

When Mosher was eleven, her father sent her to the Albany Female Academy, from which she graduated in 1881, apparently planning to go to college. But Dr. Mosher forbade it, believing that his daughter, who had been a tubercular child, was much too delicate for college work. Moreover, her sister, Esther, had just died, and he wanted his remaining child at home. In order to keep her there, he converted the little greenhouse attached to their home into an educational laboratory where he taught her botany, and he hired a florist to give her lessons in horticulture. Gradually Dr. Mosher allowed her to expand the greenhouse and launch a business career as a florist. But his bid to keep his daughter at home backfired; in 1889 Mosher announced that she had earned and saved two thousand dollars—enough for four years' tuition at Wellesley College, to which she had just been accepted.

This self-reliant young woman became a twenty-five-year-old freshman in the fall of 1889. For a time it looked as though her father's fears for her health had been justified. Ill-prepared for college, she was overworked. By the end of her first year, she was near collapse. Over the summer, however, she recuperated and returned to Wellesley in the fall. For her junior year she transferred to the University of Wisconsin, and in the fall of 1892, she moved once more—to the newly opened Stanford University, where she graduated as a zoology major in the spring of 1893.

Mosher's westward migration is intriguing. California was about as far away from home as she could get, but by 1892 her parents were both encouraging her to work. Perhaps it was the very newness of Stanford and California's persisting image as frontier that drew her west. During her time at Wisconsin, Mosher had begun to think of her own interests as being on the frontiers of science. By the time she arrived at Stanford she had decided on her mission—she was determined to challenge every existing stereotype about the physical incapacities of women. Her journals give no clues as to how she arrived at this decision. Except for the novels of George Sand, she never mentioned reading feminist literature or being formally involved in the growing feminist movement. She was certainly aware, however, that she herself had discredited her doctor-father's dire predictions of her physical and mental collapse. She also may have been as startled as current readers by the response to her survey of women's sexual habits, which she had begun at Wisconsin.

After graduation Mosher remained at Stanford as an assistant in hygiene, a position that required her to take measurements of all incoming female freshmen. Her observations suggested a myth ripe for debunking: nearly every physiology text claimed that women breathed costally (using only the upper chest) because of the physiological requirements of pregnancy, while men breathed diaphragmatically (using the diaphragm). While admitting that most women did breathe costally,

Mosher denied that physiology demanded it. She was certain that constrictive clothing and sedentary living were responsible. Setting up elaborate measuring devices in the gymnasium, she examined Stanford co-eds as well as unmarried, pregnant girls from the Pacific Rescue Home. Mosher concluded that the only differences between the sexes in breathing were those imposed by fashion and habit. In 1894 she presented these findings for her master's degree from Stanford. Two years later, her thesis was corroborated by G. W. Fitz at Harvard.

Having vanquished one myth, Mosher turned to "functional periodicity," the allegedly insurmountable barrier that excluded women from the working world. The bias she was working against was formidable; one writer of the time described menstruation as "a constantly recurring infirmity that occupies seven years out of thirty of a woman's adult life." That view was a common one, but Mosher noted that most of the grim literature on female physiology sprang from male experience with pathological female patients. She decided to study *healthy* women, in order to determine what normal menstruation was, what factors made it abnormal, and whether these factors could be modified. She devised a detailed questionnaire that she gave to her women students, who began to keep careful monthly records.

Mosher soon realized that she was in over her head. If her work was to have credibility, and if she was to interpret her vast mass of data accurately, she would need training in medicine. In the spring of 1896, at age thirty-two, she applied to and was accepted by the recently opened Johns Hopkins School of Medicine. Borrowing money from her widowed mother, Mosher headed for Baltimore in the fall of 1896 to become one of the thirteen women in a class of forty-one.

At Hopkins, Mosher later wrote, she found both sympathy for her interest in women's physiology and respect for the women students. She also found a female support network in operation. Gertrude Stein, who entered the medical school the year after Mosher (but never graduated), recalled that such formidable women as M. Carey Thomas, the president of Bryn Mawr, and other members of the Women's Medical Fund, which had been instrumental in opening the school to women, would visit the women students over tea, urging them to study hard and not to disgrace themselves, their gender, or the fund.

The faculty evidently thought well of Mosher, and upon graduation, at age thirty-six, she was selected for a one-year externship in the dispensary at the Hopkins Hospital. Dr. Howard Kelly also selected her to serve as gynecological assistant in his sanitorium. Mosher thought she knew what had brought her to the administration's attention. Early in 1900 George Engleman, a Boston gynecologist, learned of the menstrual records she had collected at Stanford. He wanted the data and tried through a colleague at Hopkins "to put the screws on Miss Mosher" so he could get her records. The colleague ignored him. Finally Engleman wrote directly to Mosher, asking to have the records but adding, "If you wish to utilize your observations for any special purpose, I should ask at least to give me general results.'' Mosher certainly did wish to utilize her observations; she held her ground and refused to relinquish her data. The incident may have prompted her lifelong protectiveness of her research, but it also brought her work to the attention of the Hopkins authorities and, she believed, resulted in the appointments.

During her additional year at Hopkins, Clelia Mosher began to analyze the data that Engleman had sought, which included menstrual records of over four hundred healthy women, plus physical examinations. Her preliminary findings led to her first scientific publication, "Normal Menstruation and Some of the Factors Modifying It," in the *Johns Hopkins Hospital Bulletin*. In this paper she tentatively identified four factors contributing to monthly disability: constricting clothing, inactivity, chronic constipation, and the general expectation that discomfort was inevitable. Each of these, she noted severely, was reversible and not physiological.

At the end of the year Kelly offered Mosher a permanent position in the gynecology department. Would she, she asked, be trained as a gynecological surgeon? Kelly said he would train her, but he doubted whether any man would be willing to work under a woman. Mosher declined the offer. Instead, she returned to California, taking her mother with her, and opened a private practice in Palo Alto. Once settled, she took up gardening with a passion. The skill that had paid her way to college now became her chief recreation. From her lush descriptions of each new leaf, bulging seed pod, and vanquished fungus, it is clear that the emotional investment in her garden was enormous. Outside her work, her garden was to become her chief solace.

After opening her practice, Mosher embarked on a long round of grant applications, seeking funds for her menstruation studies. All the institutions to which she applied rejected her. Her research stood still for nearly a decade, to her intense frustration. So when an opportunity arose in 1910 to return to Stanford as assistant professor of personal hygiene and medical adviser for women, she jumped at it. Back in a university, with well-equipped laboratories and an abundant supply of subjects, Mosher resumed her studies and, within the year, published her first major article on menstruation. Further research had confirmed her earlier findings; there was no physiological reason why most normal, healthy women should be incapacitated by menstruation.

She urged women to shed their constricting clothing, to breathe deeply using all their abdominal muscles, to eat sensibly, and above all to cast aside the debilitating myth that menstruation was synonymous with pain and depression. She preached this message to every woman who passed through her classroom.

Mosher took her own admonitions about sensible dress to heart. Hoping to educate by example, she adopted a simple compromise between fashion and comfort: shirtwaist dress, starched collar, four-in-hand tie, and untrimmed round hat. For the next thirty-five years, styles came and went, but Mosher's outfit never varied. She was, recalls a former student, "quite a sight," marching across the campus, always erect, breathing diaphragmatically.

By 1914 Mosher was prepared to offer a practical physiological solution to the problem of painful menstruation. She proposed a simple deep-breathing exercise which, she claimed would build up weak abdominal muscles and make menstruation less painful. Every Stanford woman was taught the exercise and urged to do it daily. Sixty years later one Stanford student still vividly recalls learning her "Moshers." Her roommate swore by them; this student believed them to be nonsense. Though many were skeptical, letters from students and gym teachers across the country assured Mosher that "Moshering" worked. Whether or not "Moshers" worked, students testified that much of what they learned in Mosher's classes profoundly affected their lives. She saw herself as a force for the physical emancipation of women and urged students to understand and appreciate their bodies. Her hygiene classes were spent studying skeletons and anatomical drawings. A colleague said, "[Students] were not sent to bed during the menstrual period but were given gentle, corrective exercises in the mat room of the gymnasium, looked at pictures of Greek women's statues, read clippings and articles on modern women's achievements and books on feminism."

To convince her students that bad posture could create internal problems, and to monitor progress on improving it, Mosher and E. P. Lesley of the engineering department developed a device called a Schematograph. It consisted of a reflecting camera that reduced a person's shadow and cast it onto graph paper, where it could be traced; this device caught the "posture pictures" of Stanford co-eds each year.

In the spring of 1915 the YWCA invited Mosher to address a national convention of its officers, and the speech was published shortly afterward in book form. In *The Relation of Health to the Woman Movement,* Mosher combined her growing feminism with her medical research. If women would only liberate themselves from the fickle dictates of fashion, she felt, if they would appreciate and care for their bodies and throw off the hobbling myths of physiological inferiority, theirs would be a glorious future. She concluded, "What we need are women no less fine and womanly, but with beautiful, perfect bodies, a suitable receptacle for their equally beautiful souls, who look sanely out on life with steady nerves and clear vision."

During the spring of 1917 references to the escalating war in Europe begin to creep into Mosher's journals. Though fifty-three years old, she was determined to serve. That fall, when a former Hopkins professor visited Stanford, she cornered him and told him of her plan. He passed the word on to a colleague at the Red Cross, and a few days later the reply arrived. Could Mosher be ready to sail in two weeks?

By November 23 she was aboard the Pacific Limited bound for New York. En route she mused in her journal: "The going to France is like the irristable [sic] marching of fate. . . . Everything in me cried out to do its part in this world catastrophe. I wonder how much the long line of Puritan ancestors who fought for

American independence, how much the double strain of Alsatian French counts in this irristable [sic] force, driving me on. . . .''

Once in France, Mosher became associate medical director of the Bureau of Refugees and Relief, her primary responsibility being to evacuate children from Paris. On one occasion she led a caravan of sixty anemic children from Paris to Evian, a two-day journey. Mosher was deeply moved by the devastation she witnessed, but did not fail to notice that French women were capably replacing their husbands, sons, and brothers in the fields and factories.

One of the loose ends Mosher had tied up before leaving for France was an article on the muscular strength of women. Of this research, she enthusiastically noted: ''It looks as though we have proved that there is no inherent difference in muscular strength between men and women due to differences in sex. Another tradition destroyed, and new freedom for women—.'' The article, published jointly with Ernest Martin, a Stanford physiologist, appeared while Mosher was in Paris. In it she pointed out that, because of the war, women everywhere were performing tasks previously believed unsuitable for creatures of their delicacy. Clearly these beliefs needed re-examination. Their own research, the authors claimed—overconfidently—proved that there were no physiological differences in the strength of women and men. Rather, they said, existing differences resulted from the different ways in which boys and girls were raised.

Returning to Stanford after the Armistice, Mosher was promoted to associate professor of hygiene but went through a rather difficult period. Her mother was failing, she had disagreements with a new administration, and she found her life monotonous and harassed: ''The fates are still throwing dice for my future. . . . My garden cries aloud for care and I long with unutterable longing to dig and trim in it and then to come to my study and dig and work on my problem while my soul as well as my body grows strong and quiet and all the turmoil of these over busy years quiets down and I get perspective in regard to it all. . . .

''I must reap my intellectual harvest, now ripe and waiting. I have something to contribute and the time is ripe for its reception. Something to give to the question of woman.''

In 1923 her second book, *Woman's Physical Freedom,* appeared. This time she dealt not only with young women but also with middle-aged women who approached menopause with terror, anticipating incapacity and even insanity. Much of the problem with menopause, Mosher suggested, was not physiological but psychological, rooted in the social changes that accompany middle life (such as children leaving home, which might make a wife and mother feel superfluous). Professional women, she believed, suffered far less. As an antidote, she prescribed political, church, and community work for the woman whose child-rearing days were ending.

With *Woman's Physical Freedom* Mosher began to enjoy a much wider audience. After the book went into its sixth printing and clippings began to come in from all over the world, Stanford promoted her to full professor, a position that she held for one year. She retired in 1929, after two fruitful decades of research and teaching, to a ''dream house'' of her own design. The door to her new home, she assured her students, was always open.

Her papers indicate that many of them accepted this invitation. Until her death in 1940 students often returned to thank her for her advice and to tell her that they were sharing her ideals with their friends and daughters.

Clelia Mosher died without publishing what will undoubtedly be remembered as her most innovative and interesting work—the remarkable sex survey that caused a furor among historians and psychologists when Carl Degler introduced it in his 1974 article for *The American Historical Review*.

This survey, bound into volume ten of her unpublished works and entitled ''Statistical Survey of the Marriages of Forty-Seven Women,'' is important because it is the only such survey known to exist. While dozens of popular authors claimed to be experts on women and sex, no one had studied the subject in a systematic and objective way. Mosher did. Certainly her subjects do not represent a statistically significant sample of Victorian women. But their responses are often quite detailed and thus shed light on the question of how one group of women, in the face of conflicting and repressive notions about female sexuality, actually thought and acted.

The first data go back to 1892. In her brief introduction to the survey, Mosher explained that she designed the questionnaire when, as a junior at the University of Wisconsin, she was asked to discuss the ''marital relation'' before the Mothers Club. Her lecture was based on forms returned by the club members, who were mostly faculty wives. (That these women agreed to fill out such a revealing questionnaire is intriguing, but no more so than the puzzle of why they asked an unmarried college girl, even one of twenty-eight, to address them about marriage in the first place.) Mosher continued the survey sporadically for nearly thirty years after leaving Wisconsin, adding the responses of women from her private practice and from Stanford.

She sought the information so that she could better advise young women who came to her for help. Unmarried herself, but justifiably suspicious of material in marriage manuals written mostly by men, she was certain that married women themselves would be the best source of accurate information. In the brief introduction she says the survey gave ''the investigator a priceless knowledge for the practicing physician and teacher; a background sufficiently broad to avoid prejudice in her work with woman.''

The material gives no clues as to who these women were or how she chose them. Undoubtedly some simply refused to answer such personal questions, so in this sense Mosher's subjects, like Kinsey's and Hite's, were self-selected. Not all of them answered the questionnaires at the same time. Of the thirty-six which are dated, seventeen were completed prior to 1900, fourteen between 1913 and 1917, and five in 1920. Only one respondent was born after 1890. Thirty-three were, like Mosher, born before 1870, and of these seventeen were born before the Civil War. These, then, were largely women who grew up, married, and raised children in the nineteenth century.

Fortunately Mosher asked her subjects enough questions about place of birth and education to permit speculation about their social origins. Geographically, the women were fairly representative of late-nineteenth-century America. Educationally, they decidedly were not. Eighty-one per cent of those whose education is given had attended college or normal school, and the remainder had attended at least secondary school—this at a time when most people, male or female, did not even attend secondary school. Their alma maters included Cornell, Smith, Wellesley, Vassar, Radcliffe, Stanford, and the University of California. Most of the women were married to college graduates.

When asked about their work experience before marriage (Mosher assumed none worked after), thirty of the thirty-eight women who responded had worked. Not surprisingly, in view of the limited job opportunities open to women at that time, twenty-seven had been teachers. (The other three were a librarian, an accountant, and a bookbinder.) These women were principally daughters of the upper-middle class.

The nine-page questionnaire that confronted Mosher's subjects contained twenty-five multi-part questions, many of which sought genealogical and medical information, such as whether the respondent's husband smoked, whether her mother found menopause difficult, and whether her grandparents were native-born. The second half of the survey, however, turned to matters of sex. Many questions required only a simple yes or no, but many women were moved to add comments providing detailed glimpses into their intimate lives—and what emerges is a study of the Victorian "marriage relation." Mosher was no doubt correct in claiming that such detail could only have been elicited by another woman.

The first of the sex questions asked, "What knowledge of sexual physiology had you before marriage? How did you obtain it?" Eleven women claimed they knew a great deal about sex before marriage. They had learned it, they wrote, from books, courses, friends, and relatives. One woman learned the facts of life from "medical texts, watching farm animals, and also from very frank talks with my mother." Thirteen said they had some knowledge of sex. Declining to give her sources, one woman added defensively, "learned everything I knew from good sources and in a pure and sacred way." The majority, however, said that they had known little or nothing: "Not one thing," said one woman emphatically. Another admitted, "I was so innocent of the matter that until I was 18, I did not know the origin of babies."

How did these naive Victorians fare in marriage? Mosher began her probe by asking them whether they "habitually" shared a bed with their husbands. About two-thirds of these women, some married as long as twenty-eight years, did sleep with their spouses. Some did so enthusiastically: "The first year I had separate beds, believing that was the right thing. I abandoned it entirely before the end of the year." One wife did so "because I like to be near him," and, she added, for "economic reasons." Some did so reluctantly: "Personally, I prefer to sleep alone always." The remainder slept alone. One woman listed three reasons why she preferred that arrangement: "1. more comfortable, 2. more wholesome, 3. to avoid temptation of too frequent intercourse."

Temptation? The stereotype of the Victorian woman leaves no room for sexual desire. Yet thirty-five of the forty-four women who answered the question said they felt desire for sexual intercourse. Asked at what time of month she most desired intercourse, one woman chided: "It has no *time* regulation any more than kissing my husband or baby has." Another woman wrote that sex was not only agreeable to her but "usually quite delightful."

Even more surprising is these women's testimony to orgasmic experience. Mosher did not ask whether they ever had an orgasm but "Do you always have a venereal orgasm?"—thus assuming that orgasm was to be expected. While a few women did not answer and five wrote only "no," leaving open the possibility that they occasionally experienced orgasm, thirty-four women indicated that they did experience it.

From these answers, Mosher concluded that one source of sexual maladjustment in marriage might occur at first intercourse. Coming to marriage so innocent of sexual matters, misunderstandings were bound to occur. One problem, she believed, might be "physical terror though mental consent." Indeed, one woman reported that the sudden introduction to sex was such a shock that she "ran away after one month of marriage. [Was] sent back by parents and told to behave." Apparently as an afterthought, Mosher asked twelve women how many days after their wedding ceremony had first intercourse taken place. Six women said the first intercourse took place within the first three days; one said "immediately." Six said from ten days to one year after the ceremony.

Mosher also recognized that women's slower sexual reaction time could lead to maladjustment if not understood. Some of her subjects recognized it, too. One woman reported that for years sex had been distasteful to her because of her "slow reaction," but "orgasm [occurs] if time is taken." Another, referring to differences in reaction time, complained, "Men have not been properly trained." For some, failure to reach orgasm was devastating. The woman cognizant of her "slow reaction" reported, "When no orgasm, takes days to recover." Another described the absence of orgasm as "bad, even disastrous, nervewracking,—unbalancing, if such conditions continued for any length of time." One woman said its absence was "depressing and revolting," and described orgasm, which she almost always reached, as a "sense of absolute physical harmony." Others spoke of the "quiet" and "calmness" which followed. One woman described it as a "general sense of well being, contentment, and regard for husband." "This is true, Doctor," she added earnestly.

The most detailed and personal responses were elicited by a series of questions on the "true purpose of intercourse." Mosher asked whether intercourse was a necessity, or whether its purpose was pleasure, reproduction, or "other." (Under "other," one woman claimed, "I have taken it as a sedative.") Of those who responded, nine believed that intercourse was a necessity for men; thirteen claimed it was a necessity for both sexes; and the remaining fifteen believed it was a necessity to neither. Though a few women felt that reproduction was the *only* acceptable reason for intercourse, and thirty marked reproduction as the primary purpose, twenty-four women believed firmly that the pleasure exchanged was a worthy purpose in itself. One young wife who checked both pleasure and reproduction said, "It sweeps you out of everything that is everyday." Another woman, married thirty years, claimed it "makes more normal people." This woman wasn't even sure that children were necessary to justify intercourse: "Even if there are no children, men love their wives more if they continue this relation, and the highest devotion is based upon it, a very beautiful thing, and I am glad nature gave it to us." Still another woman argued that intercourse should be indulged in for more than offspring: "The act is frequently simply the extreme caress of love's passion, which it would be a pity to limit . . . to once in two or three years."

Since so many women believed that pleasure alone was a legitimate reason for intercourse, Mosher suspected that they must use some sort of contraceptive and she included a question on this subject. At least thirty women used some method of birth control. Even a mother who declared that marriage without desire for children amounted to legalized prostitution practiced withdrawal. Still, she probably would have disapproved strongly of the young wife, married one year, who had not children and, by using "clear water in a syringe," obviously hoped to remain childless, at least for a while. Withdrawal and "timing" ranked high as methods of birth control, but most women preferred douching. Hot water, ice water, tepid water, alcohol, sulphate of zinc, and carbonated water had their adherents. Several women's husbands used a "male sheath." Two women used a "rubber cap over the uterus," and one woman used cocoa butter—for what, she didn't say.

While most of the women Mosher surveyed found sexual expression to be normal and natural, sometimes even a joy, not all were free of guilt. One woman, who admitted she desired intercourse and experienced orgasm, noted that sexual relations were "apparently a necessity for the *average* person"; and "superior individuals," with whom she felt she could not be classed, could be "independent of sex relations with no evident ill results." Even more revealing was the young woman, married only a year, who wrote, "As I personally see it, I think a habit of intercourse once a month if both desire would be as much of an ideal as I now have." She crossed this out, however, and wrote beneath it, "Since writing the above, I have become convinced that the ideal would be to have no intercourse except for reproduction, but it is often hard to live up to such an ideal.''

Mosher's own views on the matter of guilt are suggested in her brief conclusions. She was convinced that women had every right to experience and expect pleasure from sex, and she had little patience with marital guides that advised them otherwise. Blaming such misinformation for some women's failure to adjust to marriage, she charged that ''too often her training has instilled the idea that any physical response is coarse, common and immodest. . . .''

The final question which faced each subject asked, ''What, to you, would be the ideal habit?'' Mosher had asked earlier about their actual habits of intercourse, so any discrepancies are visible. One woman's ideal was ''once a month, when both are well . . . and in the day light.'' In reality, this woman reported having intercourse three or four times a week and found it ''delightful.'' One forty-seven-year-old woman said that her ideal was: ''Now, at my time of life, never. In the prime of life, for a man twice a week, for a woman twice a month.'' How a husband and wife were to resolve this discrepancy wasn't stated. Another older woman also said that her ideal was no intercourse at all, and claimed that even as a young woman she tried to avoid it. She was, perhaps understandably, hostile to intercourse: early in her marriage, her doctor husband had become addicted to morphine and, when under its influence, had forced her to have intercourse at least once a night.

Several postmenopausal women still enjoyed and desired intercourse. The only respondent who was divorced and remarried testified in 1913, at age fifty-three, four years after menopause, that ''although my passionate feeling has declined somewhat and the orgasm does not always occur, intercourse is still agreeable to me.'' Remarried at age forty-six to an ''unusually considerate man,'' this very happy, childless woman advocated an ideal habit of ''perhaps twice a month.''

Clelia Mosher demonstrated in her small, pioneering survey that despite the conflicting warnings of the marriage manuals of the Victorian age, most of the women she studied engaged in sex with neither reluctance nor distaste. Indeed, many of them frankly acknowledged their desire for intercourse and orgasm. In the face of their disregard of the repressive sexual code of their era, as Degler noted, these women offer encouraging proof of humankind's essential common sense.

For her own part Clelia Mosher paid a price for her advanced views. That price was intense loneliness, particularly after her mother died. The personal papers that exist from her years of middle age reveal an introspective and pathetically lonely woman. She was caught between the practical nature of her work and an extreme romanticism that she carefully concealed. The same woman who marched resolutely across the Stanford campus, with perfect posture and sensible clothing, had sentimental dreams and fears that she poured out into a notebook. She wrote longingly of the friendships which sustained other women. There was a type of platonic friendship, she believed, that "supplies the working woman and compensates her for what she has missed in not marrying but cannot make up for her lost motherhood." Perhaps because of the intensity of her late-blooming career, Mosher had no such friend, and as she grew older she felt this lack more keenly.

At age fifty-two she wrote poignantly: "I am finding out gradually why I am so lonely. The only things I care about are things which use my brain. The women I meet are not much interested and I do not meet many men, so there is an intellectual solitude which is like the solitude of the desert—dangerous to one's sanity."

Her yearning becomes increasingly forlorn: "I think sometimes of some particular friend and I feel she understands as no one else does what is in my mind . . . then some day comes when I realize that what this friend is, does, feels is utterly foreign. I have imbued her with thoughts that have been in my mind, not hers, sympathies which have grown out of my desire for understanding . . . and with deep depression I realize she is the outward semblance of a creature of my imagination."

A series of increasingly intimate letters suggests that Mosher finally discovered the friend she longed for. The painful truth, however, slowly dawns—these letters were written to no one. All doubts disappear in March, 1919, when Mosher begins to address them "To you, my friend who does not exist."

Over the next few years, this invented companion became the only ear for Mosher's troubles. The letters are filled with her quotidian difficulties, as well as her meditations and imaginative—and sensual—descriptions of nature. The letters make it clear that Mosher knew what she was doing. She even admitted to feeling self-conscious about the "correspondence," but stated frankly, "I get a sense of companionship and you are spared the boredom of reading them."

On April 16, 1926, she wrote her "friend": "I have given up ever finding you. I have tried out all my friends and they have not measured up to my dreams. They still are friends, and their friendships give joy and richness to my life but I cannot share my dreamland with them. I wander alone there and show the world my prose, my common sense. But I keep normal and wholesome by going ever alone in this land of dreams. It would not take long to be as drab as most of my contemporaries were it not for this land of dreams."

By 1926 Mosher seems to have resolved many of her problems. As retirement approached, she threw herself into the project of her dream house, which was a "thrill and joy" for her. She had hopes that its peace and beauty, and her happiness there, would inspire young women who needed help in holding on to their intellectual aspirations.

In October of 1926, contemplating moving in, she looked forward with hope: "Can one go on being a balanced, sane person with only the casual companionship of one's acquaintances, or is a certain give and take of daily companionship necessary to keep one at one's best: Who knows? Anyway, I am going to try it. . . . I look forward joyously to my solitary future, rich in the beauty of my surroundings.''

On the whole, Mosher seems to have resolved her problems. Her papers from 1932 include the beginning of an autobiography to be called *The Autobiography of a Happy Old Woman.* In that year, too, she wrote a joyful and lyrical description of the special beauty of that California spring.

The wide gulf between Clelia Mosher's inner self and the face she presented to the world is striking. The lonely romantic of these letters is the same efficient, dedicated woman who, as doctor and researcher, pioneered the destruction of sexual myths, celebrated the emotional and physical strength of women, and left us with a remarkable survey of Victorian sexuality.

Kathryn Allamong Jacob, who is assistant historian in the U.S. Senate Historical Office, wrote an account for the Lizzie Borden murder case for us in February/March 1978.

Part Two

Rise to World Power

Adventures Abroad

A significant result of United States industrial development and general economic growth in the late 19th and early 20th centuries was the collapse of the nation's traditional commitment to an isolationist foreign policy. American economic expansion accentuated the nation's long-standing concern with international commerce by generating larger agricultural surpluses as well as new needs for resources and markets affiliated with its burgeoning new industries. Industrial advances, furthermore, made it possible for the United States to construct a modern navy with which to project power overseas to support its economic pursuits.

In the decades following the Civil War, naval construction and U.S. activities in Latin America, among the Pacific islands and in China, Japan and Korea revealed the gradual shift toward an active international, interventionist foreign policy. The dramatic shift was to come in the 1890s and early 1900s, however. William Leuchtenburg's account of the causes of the United States' war with Spain aptly captures the spirit of adventurism and prideful nationalism, as well as the bungling of diplomacy, characteristic of our entry onto the world scene. Here, indeed, was a war (potentially major) into which the American government more or less meandered, haphazardly and unthinkingly, and out of which the nation emerged as a recognized world power and in possession of an overseas empire, the security and exploitation of which dictated more vigorous pursuit of foreign relations.

Among the direct consequences of the victory over Spain was a very significant increase in the projection of United States power throughout Latin America. Bernard Weisberger describes one postwar adventure of the fledgling new world power. For Americans concerned with overseas commerce and naval power the war had underscored the desirability of the long-contemplated canal across Central America. Weisberger ably traces the ''strange affair'' whereby the United States was to gain possession of the Panama Canal Zone. Construction of the canal led, in turn, to a broadening of U.S. concerns with respect to the security of the entire surrounding area and to the transformation of the Caribbean into an 'American lake.' Under presidents Roosevelt, Taft and Wilson policies signalling U.S. domination of the Western Hemisphere began in earnest. Richard O'Connor's treatment of the Sandino guerilla activity in Nicaragua, and the U.S. inteventionist efforts to suppress it, indicates the continuation of essentially the same policies into the 1920s and 1930s.

The Needless War with Spain

William E. Leuchtenburg

The United States in the 1890's became aggressive, expansionist, and jingoistic as it had not been since the 1850's. In less than five years, we came to the brink of war with Italy, Chile, and Great Britain over three minor incidents in which no American national interest of major importance was involved. In each of these incidents, our secretary of state was highly aggressive, and the American people applauded. During these years, we completely overhauled our decrepit Navy, building fine new warships like the *Maine*. The martial virtues of Napoleon, the imperial doctrines of Rudyard Kipling, and the naval theories of Captain Alfred T. Mahan all enjoyed a considerable vogue.

There was an apparently insatiable hunger for foreign conquest. Senator Shelby M. Cullom declared in 1895: "It is time that some one woke up and realized the necessity of annexing some property. We want all this northern hemisphere, and when we begin to reach out to secure these advantages we will begin to have a nation and our lawmakers will rise above the grade of politicians and become true statesmen." When, in 1895, the United States almost became involved in a war with Great Britain over the Venezuelan boundary, Theodore Roosevelt observed: "The antics of the bankers, brokers and anglo-maniacs generally are humiliating to a degree. . . . Personally I rather hope the fight will come soon. The clamor of the peace faction has convinced me that this country needs a war." The Washington *Post* concluded: "The taste of Empire is in the mouth of the people. . . ."

In the early Nineteenth Century, under the leadership of men like Simon Bolivar, Spain's colonies in the New World had launched a series of successful revolutions; of the great Spanish empire that Cortes and Pizarro had built, the island of Cuba, "the Ever Faithful Isle," was the only important Spanish possession to stay loyal to the Crown. Spain exploited the economy of the island mercilessly, forcing Cubans to buy Spanish goods at prices far above the world market, and Madrid sent to Cuba as colonial officials younger sons who had no interest in the island other than making a quick killing and returning to Spain. High taxes to support Spanish officialdom crippled the island; arbitrary arrests and arbitrary trials made a mockery of justice; and every attempt at public education was stifled.

The island of Cuba had been in a state of political turbulence for years when in 1894 the American Wilson-Gorman Tariff placed duties on Cuban sugar which, coupled with a world-wide depression, brought ruin to the economy of the island. The terrible hardship of the winter was the signal for revolution; on February 24, 1895, under the leadership of a junta in New York City headed by José Martí, rebels once more took the field against Spain. At first, the American people were too absorbed with the Venezuelan crisis to pay much attention to another revolt in Cuba. Then, in September, 1895, came the event which changed the course of the Cuban rebellion: William Randolph Hearst, a young man of 32 who had been operating the San Francisco *Examiner* in a sensational fashion, purchased the New York *Morning Journal,* and immediately locked horns with Joseph Pulitzer and the *World* in a circulation war that was to make newspaper history.

Hearst capitalized on the fact that the American people had only the most romantic notions of the nature of the Cuban conflict. The rebels under General Máximo Gómez, a tough Santo Domingan guerrilla fighter, embarked on a program of burning the cane fields in the hope not only of depriving the government of revenue but also of so disrupting the life of the island that the government would be forced to submit. Although there were some noble spirits in the group, much of the rebellion had an unsavory odor; one of the main financial supports for the uprising came from American property owners who feared that their sugar fields would be burned unless protection money was paid.

While Gómez was putting Cuba to the torch, American newsmen were filing reports describing the war in terms of nonexistent pitched battles between the liberty-loving Cubans and the cruel Spaniards. The war was presented, in short, as a Byronic conflict between the forces of freedom and the forces of tyranny, and the American people ate it up. When Hearst bought the *Journal* in late 1895, it had a circulation of 30,000; by 1897 it had bounded to over 400,000 daily, and during the Spanish-American War it was to go well over a million.

The sensational newspapers had influence, yet they represented no more than a minority of the press of the country; and the South and the Middle West, where anti-Spanish feeling became most intense, the representative newspaper was much more conservative. Certainly the yellow press played a tremendous part in whipping up sentiment for intervention in Cuba, but these feelings could not be carried into action unless American political leaders of both parties were willing to assume the terrible responsibility of war.

By the beginning of 1896 the rebels had achieved such success in their guerrilla tactics that Madrid decided on firmer steps and sent General Don Valeriano Weyler y Nicolau to Cuba. When Weyler arrived in February, he found the sugar industry severely disrupted and the military at a loss to meet the rebel tactic of setting fire to the cane fields. Weyler declared martial law and announced that men guilty of incendiarism would be dealt with summarily; he was promptly dubbed "The Butcher" by American newspapermen.

By late 1896 Weyler still had not succeeded in crushing the insurrection, and his measures became more severe. On October 21 he issued his famous *reconcentrado* order, directing the "reconcentration" of the people of Pinar del Rio in the garrison towns, and forbidding the export of supplies from the towns to the countryside. Reasoning that he could never suppress the rebellion so long as the rebels could draw secret assistance from people in the fields, Weyler moved the people from the estates into the towns and stripped the countryside of supplies to starve out the rebellion. Since many of the people had already fled to the towns, the *reconcentrado* policy was not as drastic as it appeared; yet the suffering produced by the policy was undeniable. Lacking proper hygienic care, thousands of Cubans, especially women and children, died like flies.

When William McKinley entered the White House in 1897, he had no intention of joining the War Hawks. "If I can only go out of office . . . with the knowledge that I have done what lay in my power to avert this terrible calamity," McKinley told Grover Cleveland on the eve of his inauguration, "I shall be the happiest man in the world. McKinley came to power as the "advance agent of prosperity," and business interests were almost unanimous in opposing any agitation of the Cuban question that might lead to war. Contrary to the assumptions of Leninist historians, it was Wall Street which, first and last, resisted a war which was to bring America its overseas empire.

The country had been gripped since 1893 by the deepest industrial depression in its history, a depression that was to persist until the beginning of 1897. Each time it appeared recovery might be on its way, a national crisis had cut it off: first the Venezuelan boundary war scare of December, 1895, then the bitter free silver campaign of 1896. What business groups feared more than anything else was a new crisis. As Julius Pratt writes: "To this fair prospect of a great business revival the threat of war was like a specter at the feast."

McKinley was not a strong President, and he had no intention of being one. Of all the political figures of his day, he was the man most responsive to the popular will. It was his great virtue and, his critics declared, his great weakness. Uncle Joe Cannon once remarked: "McKinley keeps his ear to the ground so close that he gets it full of grasshoppers much of the time." If McKinley was not one of our greatest Presidents, he was certainly the most representative and the most responsive. Anyone who knew the man knew that, although he was strongly opposed to war, he would not hold out against, war if the popular demand for war became unmistakable. "Let the voice of the people rule"—this was McKinley's credo, and he meant every word of it.

The threat to peace came from a new quarter, from the South and West, the strongholds of Democracy and free silver. Many Bryanite leaders were convinced that a war would create such a strain on the currency system that the opposition to free silver would collapse. Moreover, with the opposition to war strongest in Wall Street, they found it easy to believe that Administration policy was the product of a conspiracy of bankers who would deny silver to the American people, who would deny liberty to the people of Cuba, who were concerned only with the morality of the countinghouse. Moreover, Bryan was the spokesman for rural Protestantism, which was already speaking in terms of a righteous war against Spain to free the Cubans from bondage. These were forces too powerful for McKinley to ignore. McKinley desired peace, but he was, above all, a Republican partisan, and he had no intention of handing the Democrats in 1900 the campaign cry of Free Cuba and Free Silver.

While McKinley attempted to search out a policy that would preserve peace without bringing disaster to the Republican party, the yellow press made his job all the more difficult by whipping up popular anger against Spain. On February 12 the *Journal* published a dispatch from Richard Harding Davis, reporting that as the American steamship *Olivette* was about to leave Havana Harbor for the United States, it was boarded by Spanish police officers who searched three young Cuban women, one of whom was suspected of carrying messages from the rebels. The *Journal* ran the story under the headline, "Does Our Flag Protect Women?" with a vivid drawing by Frederic Remington across one half a page showing Spanish plainclothes men searching a wholly nude woman. War, declared the *Journal*, "is a dreadful thing, but there are things more dreadful than even war, and one of them is dishonor." It shocked the country, and Congressman Amos Cummings immediately resolved to launch a congressional inquiry into the *Olivette* outrage. Before any steps could be taken, the true story was revealed. The *World* produced one of the young women who indignantly protested the *Journal's* version of the incident. Pressured by the *World,* the *Journal* was forced to print a letter from Davis explaining that his article had not said that male policemen had searched the women and that, in fact, the search had been conducted quite properly by a police matron with no men present.

The *Olivette* incident was manufactured by Hearst, but by the spring of 1897, the American press had a new horror to report which was all too true. Famine was stalking the island. Cuba had been in a serious economic state when the rebellion broke out in 1895; two years of war would, under any circumstances, have been disastrous, but the deliberate policies pursued both by the insurgents and by the government forces made the situation desperate. It was a simple matter for Hearst and Pulitzer reporters to pin the full responsibility on Weyler.

By the middle of July, McKinley had formulated a policy which he set down in a letter of instructions to our new American minister to Spain, General Stewart L. Woodford. The letter emphasized the need of bringing the Cuban war to an end and said that this could be done to the mutual advantage of both Spain and the Cubans by granting some kind of autonomy to Cuba. If Spain did not make an offer to the rebels and if the "measures of unparalleled severity" were not ended, the United States threatened to intervene.

On August 8 an Italian anarchist assassinated the Spanish premier; and when Woodford reached Madrid in September, a new government was about to take over headed by Señor Sagasta and the Liberals, who had repeatedly denounced the "barbarity" of the previous government's policy in Cuba. Sagasta immediately removed General Weyler, and the prospects for an agreement between the United States and Spain took a decided turn for the better.

While Woodford was carrying on skillful diplomatic negotiations for peace in Madrid, the Hearst press was creating a new sensation in this country with the Cisneros affair. Evangelina Cisneros was a young Cuban woman who had been arrested and imprisoned in the Rocojidas in Havana, guilty, according to the American press, of no other crime than protecting her virtue from an unscrupulous Spanish colonel, an aide to Butcher Weyler. The Rocojidas, Hearst's reporter told American readers, was a cage where the innocent beauty was herded with women criminals of every type, subject to the taunts and vile invitations of men who gathered outside.

When it was reported that Señorita Cisneros, whose father was a rebel leader, was to be sent for a long term to a Spanish penal colony in Africa or in the Canaries, the *Journal* launched one of the most fabulous campaigns in newspaper history. "Enlist the women of America!" was the Hearst war cry, and the women of America proved willing recruits. Mrs. Julia Ward Howe signed an appeal to Pope Leo XIII, and Mrs. Jefferson Davis, the widow of the president of the Confederacy, appealed to the queen regent of Spain to "give Evangelina Cisneros to the women of America to save her from a fate worse than death." When the *Journal* prepared a petition on behalf of Señorita Cisneros, it obtained the names of Mrs. Nancy McKinley, the mother of the President, and Mrs. John Sherman, the wife of the secretary of state, as well as such other prominent ladies as Julia Dent Grant and Mrs. Mark Hanna.

It was a startling coup for Mr. Hearst, but he had not yet even begun to display his ingenuity. On October 10, 1897, the *Journal* erupted across its front page with the banner headline: "An American Newspaper Accomplishes at a Single Stroke What the Best Efforts of Diplomacy Failed Utterly to Bring About in Many Months." Hearst had sent Karl Decker, one of his most reliable correspondents, to Havana in late August with orders to rescue the Cuban Girl Martyr "at any hazard''; and Decker had climbed to the roof of a house near the prison, broken the bar of a window of the jail, lifted Evangelina out, and, after hiding her for a few days in Havana, smuggled her onto an American steamer. Decker, signing his dispatch to the *Journal* ''Charles Duval,'' wrote: ''I have broken the bars of Rocojidas and have set free the beautiful captive of monster Weyler. Weyler could blind the Queen to the real character of Evangelina, but he could not build a jail that would hold against *Journal* enterprise when properly set to work.'' The Cuban Girl Martyr was met at the pier by a great throng, led up Broadway in a triumphal procession, taken to a reception at Delmonico's where 120,000 people milled about the streets surrounding the restaurant, and hailed at a monster reception in Madison Square Garden. The Bishop of London cabled his congratulations to the *Journal,* while Governor Sadler of Missouri proposed that the *Journal* send down 500 of its reporters to free the entire island.

On October 23 Sagasta announced a ''total change of immense scope'' in Spanish policy in Cuba. He promised to grant local autonomy to the Cubans immediately, reserving justice, and armed forces, and foreign relations to Spain. On November 13 Weyler's successor, Captain-General Blanco, issued a decree modifying considerably the *reconcentrado* policy, and on November 25 the queen regent signed the edicts creating, an autonomous government for the island. In essence, Madrid had acceded to the American demands.

While Woodford was conducting negotiations with a conciliatory Liberal government in Madrid and while there was still hope for peace, the fatal incident occurred which made war virtually inevitable. On January 12, 1898, a riot broke out in Havana, and Spanish officers attacked newspaper offices. The nature of the riot is still not clear; it was over in an hour, and it had no anti-American aspects. If the United States now sent a naval vessel to Havana, it might be buying trouble with Spain. Yet if a riot did break out and Americans were killed, the Administration would be stoned for not having a ship there to protect them. For several days McKinley wavered; then he ordered the *Maine* to Havana, but with the explanation that this was a courtesy visit demonstrating that so nonsensical were the rumors of danger to American citizens that our ships could again resume their visits to the island.

As the *Maine* lay at anchor in Havana Harbor, the rebels, with a perfect sense of timing, released a new propaganda bombshell. In December, 1897, in a private letter, Señor Enrique Dupuy de Lôme, the Spanish minister at Washington, had set down his opinions of President McKinley's annual message to Congress: ''Besides the ingrained and inevitable bluntness *(groseria)* with which it repeated all that the press and public opinion in Spain have said about Weyler,'' De Lôme wrote, ''it once more shows what McKinley is, weak and a bidder for the admiration of the crowd, besides being a would-be politician *(politicastro)* who tries to leave a door open behind himself while keeping on good terms with the jingoes of his party.'' De Lôme added: ''It would be very advantageous to take up, even if only for effect, the question of commercial relations, and to have a man of some prominence sent here in order that I may make use of him to carry on a propaganda among the Senators and others in opposition to the junta.''

De Lôme had, to be sure, written all this in a private letter (which was stolen by an insurgent spy in the Havana post office), not in his official capacity, and his characterization of McKinley was not wholly without merit, but it was a blunder of the highest magnitude. Not only had De Lôme attacked the President, but he had gone on to suggest that the negotiations then going on over a commercial treaty were not being conducted in good faith. Throughout the letter ran precisely the tone which Hearst had been arguing expressed the Spanish temper—a cold, arrogant contempt for democratic institutions. The State Department immediately cabled Woodford to demand the recall of the Spanish minister, but Madrid had the good fortune of being able to tell Woodford that De Lôme, informed of the disaster the night before, had already resigned.

A week after the publication of the De Lôme indiscretion, at 9:40 on the night of February 15, 1898, came the terrible blow which ended all real hope for peace. In the harbor of Havana, the *Maine* was blown up by an explosion of unknown origin. In an instant, the ship was filled with the sounds of shrieking men and rushing water. The blast occurred in the forward part of the ship where, a half hour before, most of the men had turned in for the night; they were killed in their hammocks. Of the 350 officers and men on board, 260 were killed. By morning the proud *Maine* had sunk into the mud of Havana Harbor.

"Public opinion should be suspended until further report," Captain Sigsbee cabled to Washington, but even Sigsbee could not down his suspicions. The *Maine* had gone to a Spanish possession on a courtesy call, and the *Maine* now lay at the bottom of Havana Harbor. What could it mean but war? "I would give anything if President McKinley would order the fleet to Havana tomorrow," wrote Theodore Roosevelt. "The *Maine* was sunk by an act of dirty treachery on the part of the Spaniards." Volunteers lined up for war service, even though there was no one to enlist them; in New York 500 sharpshooting Westchester businessmen volunteered as a unit for the colors. The *Journal* reported: "The Whole Country Thrills With War Fever."

The cause of the explosion of the *Maine* has never been finally established. That Spain deliberately decided to blow up the *Maine* is inconceivable, although it is possible that it might have been the work of unauthorized Spanish extremists. The one group which had everything to gain from such an episode was the rebels; yet it seems unlikely that either they or Spanish hotheads could have carried out such an act and remained undetected. The most likely explanation is that it was caused by an explosion of internal origin; yet the evidence for this is not conclusive. In any event, this was the explanation that the Navy in 1898 was least willing to consider since it would reflect seriously on the care with which the Navy was operating the *Maine*.

The move toward war seemed relentless. On March 9 Congress unanimously voted $50,000,000 for war preparations. Yet the days went by and there was no war, in part because important sectors of American opinion viewed Hearst's stories of the atrocious conditions on the island with profound skepticism. Senator Redfield Proctor of Vermont decided to launch his own investigation into conditions on the island. On March 17, after a tour of Cuba, Proctor made one of the most influential speeches in the history of the United States Senate.

Proctor, who Roosevelt reported was "very ardent for the war," had not generally been regarded as a jingo, and no man in the Senate commanded greater respect for personal integrity. Proctor declared that he had gone to Cuba skeptical of reports of suffering there, and he had come back convinced. "Torn from their homes, with foul earth, foul air, foul water, and foul food or none, what wonder that one-half have died and that one-quarter of the living are so diseased that they can not be saved?" Proctor asked. "Little children are still walking about with arms and chest terribly emaciated, eyes swollen, and abdomen bloated to three times the natural size. . . . I was told by one of our consuls that they have been found dead about the markets in the morning, where they had crawled, hoping to get some stray bits of food from the early hucksters."

The question of peace or war now lay with McKinley. The Spaniards, Woodford had conceded, had gone about as far as they could go; but with the *Maine* in the mud of Havana Harbor, with the country, following Proctor's speech, crying for war, how much longer could McKinley hold out? The jingoes were treating his attempt to preserve peace with outright contempt; McKinley, Roosevelt told his friends, "has no more backbone than a chocolate éclair."

"We will have this war for the freedom of Cuba," Roosevelt shouted at a Gridiron Dinner on March 26, shaking his fist at Senator Hanna, "in spite of the timidity of the commercial interests." Nor was McKinley permitted to forget the political consequences. The Chicago *Times-Herald* warned: "Intervention in Cuba, peacefully if we can, forcibly if we must, is immediately inevitable. Our own internal political conditions will not permit its postponement. . . . Let President McKinley hesitate to rise to the just expectations of the American people, and who can doubt that 'war for Cuban liberty' will be the crown of thorns the free silver Democrats and Populists will adopt at the elections this fall?"

On March 28 the President released the report of the naval court of inquiry on the *Maine* disaster. "In the opinion of the court the *Maine* was destroyed by the explosion of a submarine mine, which caused the partial explosion of two or more of the forward magazines," the report concluded. Although no one was singled out for blame, the conclusion was inescapable that if Spain had not willfully done it, Spain had failed to provide proper protection to a friendly vessel on a courtesy visit in its waters. Overnight a slogan with the ring of a child's street chant caught the fancy of the country:

"I have no more doubt than that I am now standing in the Senate of the United States," declared Henry Cabot Lodge, "that that ship was blown up by a government mine, fired by, or with the connivance of, Spanish officials."

Desiring peace yet afraid of its consequences, McKinley embarked on a policy of attempting to gain the fruits of war without fighting. On March 29 Woodford demanded that Spain agree to an immediate armistice, revoke the reconcentration order, and co-operate with the United States to provide relief; Spain was given 48 hours to reply. On March 31 Spain replied that it had finally revoked the reconcentration orders in the western provinces; that it had made available a credit of three million pesetas to resettle the natives; that it was willing to submit the *Maine* controversy to arbitration; and that it would grant a truce if the insurgents would ask for it. In short, Spain would yield everything we demanded, except that it would not concede defeat; the appeal for a truce would have to come from the rebels. Since the rebels would not make such an appeal, since they were confident of ultimate American intervention, the situation was hopeless; yet Spain had come a long way. Woodford cabled to Washington: "The ministry have gone as far as they dare go to-day. . . . No Spanish ministry would have dared to do one month ago what this ministry has proposed to-day."

For a week the Spaniards attempted to cling to their last shreds of dignity. On Saturday, April 9, Madrid surrendered. Driven to the wall by the American demands, the Spanish foreign minister informed Woodford that the government had decided to grant an armistice in Cuba immediately. Gratified at achieving the final concession, Woodford cabled McKinley: "I hope that nothing will now be done to humiliate Spain, as I am satisfied that the present Government is going, and is loyally ready to go, as fast and as far as it can."

It was too late. McKinley had decided on war. Spain had conceded everything, but Spain had waited too long. Up until the very last moment, Spanish officials had feared that if they yielded to American demands in Cuba, it might mean the overturn of the dynasty, and they preferred even a disastrous war to that. Proud but helpless in the face of American might, many Spanish officials appeared to prefer the dignity of being driven from the island in a heroic defensive war to meek surrender to an American ultimatum. In the end they surrendered and promised reforms. But they had promised reforms before—after the Ten Years' War which ended in 1878—and they had not kept these promises. Throughout the Nineteenth Century, constitutions had been made and remade, but nothing had changed. Even in the last hours of negotiations with the American minister, they had told Woodford that the President had asked the Pope to intervene, when the President had done nothing of the sort. Even if their intentions were of the best, could they carry them out? Spain had had three full years to end the war in Cuba and, with vastly superior numbers of troops, had not been able to do it. And the insurgents would accept nothing from Madrid, not even peace.

On Monday, April 11, McKinley sent his message to Congress, declaring that "the forcible intervention of the United States as a neutral to stop the war, according to the large dictates of humanity and following many historical precedents" was "justifiable on rational grounds." The fact that Spain had met everything we had asked was buried in two paragraphs of a long plea for war. It took Congress a full week to act. On Monday night, April 18, while the resolution shuttled back and forth between the two chambers and the conference room, congressmen sang "The Battle Hymn of the Republic" and "Dixie" and shook the chamber with the refrain of "Hang General Weyler to a Sour Apple Tree." At three o'clock the next morning the two houses reached an agreement—the United States recognized the independence of Cuba, asserted that we would not acquire Cuba for ourselves, and issued an ultimatum to Spain to withdraw within three days. On April 20 President McKinley signed the resolution. War had come at last. But not quite. Although hostilities had begun, not until four days later did Congress declare war. When it did declare war, it dated it from McKinley's action in establishing a blockade four days before. To the every end, we protested our peaceful intentions as we stumbled headlong into war.

We entered a war in which no vital American interest was involved, and without any concept of its consequences. Although McKinley declared that to enter such a war for high purposes, and then annex territory, would be "criminal aggression," we acquired as a result of the war the Philippines and other parts of an overseas empire we had not intended to get and had no idea how to defend. Although we roundly attacked Spain for not recognizing the rebel government, we, in our turn, refused to recognize the rebels. Although we were shocked by Weyler's policies in Cuba, we were soon in the unhappy position of using savage methods to put down a rebel uprising in the Philippines, employing violence in a measure that easily matched what Weyler had done.

It would be easy to condemn McKinley for not holding out against war, but McKinley showed considerable courage in bucking the tide. McKinley's personal sympathy for the Cubans was sincere; only after his death was it revealed that he had contributed $5,000 anonymously for Cuban relief. It would be even easier to blame it all on Hearst; yet no newspaper can arouse a people that is not willing to be aroused. At root lay the American gullibility about foreign affairs, with the penchant for viewing politics in terms of a simple morality play; equally important were the contempt of the American people for Spain as a cruel but weak Latin nation and the desire for war and expansion which permeated the decade. The American people were not led into war; they got the war they wanted. "I think," observed Senator J. C. Spooner, "possibly the President could have worked out the business without war, but the current was too strong, the demagogues too numerous, the fall elections too near."

William E. Leuchtenburg has contributed articles and reviews to numerous scholarly journals and wrote Flood Control Politics. *An associate professor of American history at Columbia, he is now writing a history of the New Deal.*

The Strange Affair of the Taking of the Panama Canal Zone

Bernard A. Weisberger

PROLOGUE: *Washington,
November 18, 1903*

As John Hay, Secretary of State of the United States Of America, prepared for bed in his comfortable home just across Lafayette Park from the White House, it must certainly have struck him that the day just concluded had been altogether one of the most curious in his four-year tenure in office—or, in fact, in a long diplomatic career that had taken him as a representative of his country to London, Paris, Vienna, and Madrid.

The hands of the clock had stood at twenty before seven when he signed a treaty with the Envoy Extraordinary and Minister Plenipotentiary of the Republic of Panama. And extraordinary was assuredly the word. The minister, a small man with fierce mustaches and an outthrust chin, was one who spoke not in sentences but in proclamations. Hay had asked him if he had a choice between two drafts of the treaty, which would permit the construction of an interoceanic canal by the United States. "I am at the orders of Your Excellency," came the reply, "to sign either of the two projects which, in Your Excellency's judgment, appears best adapted to the realization of that grand work." And when it turned out that the minister had no signet ring to seal the document, Hay had proffered two, one of them bearing his own family arms. "the share which Your Excellency has in the accomplishment of this great act determines my choice," said the minister as he reached for Hay's ring. "I shall be happy that the Treaty, due to your generous policy, should bear at the same time your personal seal and that of your family."

Such nobility of style was modestly ironic under the circumstances, a point not lost to the writer's eye of Hay, who had occasionally composed novels, humorous poetry, and editorials. For one thing, the Napoleonic little minister represented a country that was only about the size of South Carolina. Of its jungle-covered and mountainous terrain only a strip of the serpentine isthmus between North and South America was basically habitable—and the treaty had just handed over most of that region to the absolute and sovereign control of the United States forever.

In addition, the Republic of Panama had existed among the family of nations for precisely twelve days—brought into being by a revolt that was foreseen, aided, and just possibly arranged by the United States. Finally, in the most bizarre touch of all, the minister was not a Panamanian, or even a citizen of Colombia, from which Panama had been detached. He was a French engineer named Philippe Bunau-Varilla, whose diplomatic career was beginning and ending with this single episode.

All in all, a most unusual international pact. It would undoubtedly get through the Senate, for the canal that it would make possible was a universally popular project. But it would always remain tainted with suspicion and resentment among Panamanians, Colombians, and some Americans as well. It was not, in fact, the treaty that Secretary Hay himself had wanted. What was more, no knowledgeable observer would have predicted its achievement five years earlier. Time after time in Hay's administration of the Department of State the Panama Canal had appeared to be doomed. Yet at each point of crisis it had been rescued and put back on the long road to realization. Its history seemed to prove that despite the complexity of the world and the domination of chance and error in human affairs, a man with energy and enormous fixity of purpose could now and then shape the course of history.

ACT ONE: The Course of Empire
Scene I. *Washington, December, 1898*

One of the many callers on President William McKinley in the crowded days just before the opening of the Fifty-fifth Congress was a partner in the New York firm of Sullivan and Cromwell. Though only forty-four, William Nelson Cromwell already had silvery white hair and mustaches, surprising complements to his smooth complexion and baby-blue eyes. These features could mask, for the unwary, certain other assets—a salesman's rapid tongue, a wizardry with figures, and, in one reporter's observation, "an intellect that works like a flash of lightning, and . . . swings about with the agility of an acrobat."

Cromwell's specialty was corporate reorganization, and it was on behalf of a corporate client that he had presented his card at the White House. Ostensibly he merely wished to present to the President the report of an international technical commission which declared that the most practicable route for a canal linking the Atlantic and Pacific oceans—from an engineering point of view—lay through the

89

Isthmus of Panama. But both Cromwell and McKinley knew that there was already a partially dug canal in Panama; that its right of way, equipment, concessions from Colombia, and other assets were the property of the New Panama Canal Company of Paris; and that Cromwell had recently been hired to represent that company.

The concern had called him in for what was essentially a salvage job. The original French Panama Canal Company (or Compagne Universelle du Canal Interocéanique) had been organized nearly twenty years earlier under the leadership of Ferdinand de Lesseps, who had won world acclaim by creating the Suez Canal. In seven years the company, sometimes using as many as 14,000 workers, had managed to gouge out some eleven miles of canal in Panama, less than half of the total length necessary. Heartbreaking difficulties had been encountered—swift floods on the isthmian rivers and landslides that wiped out months of work. In addition, yellow fever and malaria, which the medical technology of the eighties could not control, were claiming over a thousand lives a year by 1885. Valor was not enough to beat these odds. More capital was required, and there was a desperate struggle for fresh money, some of it through lotteries. But in 1894 it was revealed that in the fund-raising campaign certain politicians and journalists had been bribed. The grand design collapsed in scandal, investors shut their pocketbooks, and de Lesseps died brokenhearted.

The New Panama Canal Company was created to inherit and liquidate the machinery, buildings, contracts, and good will (such as it was) of the old. Its directors correctly despaired of reawakening French interest in another long, expensive struggle with the elements. But they knew that the United States was eager to have the oceans joined, and they conceived the idea of selling their properties to the Americans. To that end they had hired Cromwell.

The conversation between the lobbyist and the President went unrecorded, but there is little doubt about the prevailing sentiment of the day, which the President probably articulated. He would shortly be pointing out, in his State of the Union message, that stunning events had taken place in the preceding twelve months. As a result of the brief war with Spain the United States would shortly acquire a protectorate over Cuba and absolute control of Puerto Rico and the Philippine Islands. She had also, in that summer of empire, annexed the Hawaiian Islands. The United States was now a colonial power with holdings in two oceans, and undoubtedly desired, needed, and planned a canal to shorten the travel time between them.

Furthermore, the entire Western world would smile on such a canal. A great seaborne traffic was in motion, carrying to the factories of the United States and of Europe the crude ores, rubber, petroleum, lumber, fibers, and foodstuffs of a colonized Africa and Asia and a weak Latin America, and returning to them manufactured goods ranging from rails and locomotives to kerosene and calico. The whole fabric of civilization would benefit from speeding up this interchange.

But, the President might have gone on, the great interoceanic highway would not necessarily go through Panama. The American Congress had, in fact, long been considering a route through Nicaragua. Mr. Cromwell might learn more about that subject from one of the Nicaraguan canal's most ardent supporters, Senator John T. Morgan of Alabama, ranking Democratic member of the Committee on Foreign Relations and that on Interoceanic Canals.

All of this was surely already known to Cromwell. His first task for his clients, therefore, in pursuit of which he had called on McKinley, was in some way to forestall a sudden, enthusiastic rush by Congress to embrace Nicaragua.

SCENE II. *Washington, March 3, 1899*

As the Fifty-fifth Congress worked its way through final business in the closing hours of its life Senator Morgan was furious. It was more than thirty-three years since he had been Brigadier General Morgan, Cavalry, Confederate States of America, but he remembered enough to know that he had been outflanked.

During the winter months the aging but vigorous senator had steadily nursed along a bill for a Nicaraguan canal. Behind it he had put parliamentary and oratorical skills acquired in a classical education in Tennessee. Morgan's measure would instruct the President to open negotiations with Nicaragua to secure the right of way for such a canal, and would have the effect of giving financial support to an American organization, the Maritime Canal Company. Like the Compagnie Universelle du Canal Interocéanique, the Maritime Company had begun its canal, dug a few miles, and then succumbed to the financial panic of 1893. Senator Morgan held stock in it.

Yet it was not merely for himself that Morgan was working. Though he had fought for the Old South of cotton and slavery, he represented a new South of coal and iron and shipping and banking. He was eager to see New Orleans and Mobile and perhaps other southern ports become the centers of a lusty interhemispheric trade that would stimulate the struggling southern economy. To enhance that traffic a canal was an absolute necessity, and Nicaragua seemed, to Morgan, a logical location. It was two days closer in sailing time to American ports. It could be built so as to utilize natural watercourses, including the great expanse of Lake Nicaragua, and would therefore be cheaper and quicker to finish. Nicaragua's government, unlike that of Colombia, indicated a strong interest in dealing with Washington for the canal; so did that of neighboring Costa Rica, which would be involved for part of the route. And Nicaragua's high plateaus would be free of the pestilences that lurked in the sinister Panamanian jungles.

As the session neared an end Morgan had won Senate passage of his bill. But then something had happened. The burden of getting a Nicaraguan canal law through the House fell on Iowa's William P. Hepburn, a Republican regular serving his sixth term and elevated by seniority to the chair of the Committee on Interstate and Foreign Commerce. Hepburn was in favor of Nicaragua, too. But someone had played upon his vanity in such a way as to induce him to introduce a bill of his own rather than simply sponsoring Morgan's in the lower chamber. Because the bill contained some provisions differing from Morgan's, when it passed the House a conference committee had to be created to reconcile the discrepancies.

As the hours ticked away someone got an amendment tacked on to the committee's revised bill providing for that favorite device of compromisers, a study commission to look into all the feasible routes for a canal, Panama included. Someone got Hepburn to accept it. After a brief deadlock someone persuaded the Republican senators on the conference panel to go along, abandoning their Senate colleague Morgan for their party brother Hepburn and accepting a new canal commission.

Someone had dealt Senator Morgan a defeat and bought time for pro-Panama forces to plan and to organize. The senator was perfectly sure that the someone was William N. Cromwell. And while the attorney kept discreetly silent about it at the time, he was not choked by modesty when, much later, he submitted his firm's thumping bill (for over $800,000) to his clients. At that time he declared: "We think we are justified in stating that without our efforts the new commission would not have been created."

Whether that boast was valid or not, Cromwell's efforts continued as the on-coming Presidential election approach. They included a campaign contribution of sixty thousand dollars to the Republicans. When that party's national convention met in Philadelphia in June of 1900 to tender the garland of renomination to McKinley, it raised Cromwell's hopes by calling, in its platform, for an isthmian—not a Nicaraguan, note, but an isthmian—canal. Cynics might assume a direct connection between the gift and the declarations, but in fact, until the route-investigating commission made its final recommendation, it was a natural political act for the Republicans to hedge their bets on the canal's location.

On November 30, 1900, however, just after McKinley's re-election, Panama's prospects appeared to plummet. The investigating panel—two colonels, two professors, a lawyer, and three civil engineers, chaired by retired Admiral John G. Walker and generally known by his name—issued a preliminary report favoring the Nicaraguan route. But if, in the popular view, the Walker Commission had thereby doomed Panama, the popular view was unaware of the persistence of Mr. Cromwell or the astonishing energies of Reserve Captain Philippe Bunau-Varilla, graduate of France's Ecole Polytechnique, class of 1879.

Act Two: The Downfall of Nicaragua
Scene I. New York, February–March, 1901

On a brisk midwinter evening a coach with several occupants in evening dress drew up before New York's Waldorf Astoria Hotel just as a small, dapper man emerged from its front door. He and one of the men in the carriage exchanged cries of mutual recognition. "What luck to find you here!" exclaimed the passenger, who was Myron T. Herrick, a prominent Ohio Republican. "I am going to introduce you to Senator Hanna."

Thus did Philippe Bunau-Varilla get an introduction for which he had long been hoping. A consuming passion had brought him to America, and he knew that the influential Hanna, if won over, could help him realize it. The goal of Bunau-Varilla's quest was neither power, nor money, nor a woman, nor even fame for himself. It was an idea: the idea of the Panama Canal.

A Parisian, born in 1859, Bunau-Varilla grew up believing that "the greatest virtue in a Frenchman is to cultivate truth and to serve France." For him cultivating truth meant sharing in the stupendous triumphs over nature achieved by nineteenth-century engineers. When, at the age of twenty-five, he joined a contracting firm that sent him to Panama to work on the French canal, his two loyalties became fused. To join mighty oceans had been a dream of humanity for centuries. French genius had fulfilled the dream in Suez and would do so in Panama. Bunau-Varilla flung himself zealously into the work, undaunted by a bout of yellow fever in 1886. By 1889 he had risen to the superintendency of a major part of the work in the so-called Culegra Cut and had worked out what was, in his own mind, a brilliant plan of lock building that would have the waterway ready for use in a few years.

The collapse of the Compagnie Universelle du Canal Interocéanic was, for the young technician, a social, moral, and political catastrophe. The canal must be finished! As tides of scandal eddied around the project he became increasingly monomaniacal. The great work must not end in the verdict that Panama had been a swindle; history would record that to France's everlasting shame. But despite articles, interviews, letters, and petitions arranged by a nearly frantic Bunau-Varilla, France's interest in the canal had waned and died by 1900. "From that moment on," he wrote later, "I devoted myself to the single idea of saving the honour of this great creation by preserving its life." To save its life—for France's sake-Bunau-Varilla gave up on France and began to campaign for the completion of a Panama canal by the United States.

Bunau-Varilla made it his business to meet any and all Americans with an interest in isthmian affairs and canal construction. By chance he encountered two of them in Paris at a restaurant one night in 1900. Over the wine and the sauces, the voluble Frenchman poured out his usual stream of pro-Panama propaganda, with that zeal achieved only by those to whom the truth is never in doubt. Soon after, an invitation was arranged for him to come and lecture on the subject in the United States.

Arriving in Cincinnati on January 17, 1901, Bunau-Varilla lectured before that city's Commercial Club. Then a luncheon for prominent businessmen of Cleveland was set up by his friends, and it was there that he met Herrick. Back in New York,, he dashed off a booklet, "Panama or Nicaragua," personally paying for the printing and distribution of fifteen thousand copies. And then more lectures—in Chicago, New York, and Princeton.

The meeting with Hanna capped these weeks of effort, especially when the Ohio senator made a date with Bunau-Varilla for an interview in Washington. Hanna was a portly Cleveland businessman, and though he was sixty-four years old, his wide eyes and slightly protuberant ears gave him something of the expression of a perpetually attentive adolescent. In 1896, as McKinley's campaign manager and fund raiser, he had been cruelly caricatured by opposition cartoonists as a fat plutocrat. But by 1901 he was committed to such modern viewpoints as accepting and recognizing labor unions—and empire. And he was one of the undisputed powers in Republican circles.

Therefore, at the interview Bunau-Varilla bombarded him hard. Did the senator know that the Panama route was shorter? Healthier? Easier to complete than Nicaragua, thanks to France's head start? Above all, safer. Nicaragua (said Bunau-Varilla, brandishing statistics) was notoriously susceptible to earthquakes and volcanic eruptions. Panama was the obvious route of choice, of necessity, of wisdom, of destiny.

Senator Hanna had no doubt heard it before, from pro-Panama members of the Walker Commission and from Cromwell. But what mattered was not who convinced Hanna but rather that, by April of 1901, he was converted. The friends of Panama had made an impressive gain.

SCENE II. *Washington, July, 1901*

Dr. Carlos Martinez Silva looked briefly out of the window of the Colombian embassy, then turned back to his half-packed suitcases. He would soon be off to the high, thin air of Mexico City as a delegate to the second Pan-American Congress. It would be more pleasant there than in the sultry heat of Washington, and he would escape that undercurrent of patronizing that any cultivated Latin-American diplomat sensed in the capital of the Colossus of the North. No matter how formal the courtesies, one was considered a "dago" ambassador from a powerless and insignificant state.

Nonetheless, Dr. Silva was not happy with his government for removing him from Washington at a crucial stage in his negotiations. It was undoubtedly because he had been telling them things they did not wish to hear—a classic case of punishing the messenger with bad news.

But Silva was no ordinary envoy. A former minister of foreign relations, he was a close friend of Colombia's president, José Marroquin. Both of them were academics: Silva held a doctorate in political science, while Marroquin, who wrote satire and poetry, was a university professor of literature who had turned to politics late in life. Both men represented a Colombian elite, supported by fortunes earned through ownership (or inheritance) of Colombian coffee plantations and cattle ranches.

Marroquin had been vice president but had taken power in a coup in July, 1900. Though he was automatically assumed by the Americans to be a dictator, he was actually in a precarious position. He took office after two years of a civil war between Colombia's political parties (one episode in a long history of constitutional turmoil). which had shattered the economy and cost a toll in human life estimated at something between 100,000 and 250,000. With revenues down and costs up, huge deficits had been incurred, leading to the usual inflationary devices that had rapidly made the peso all but worthless. To heal these wounds and ensure tranquillity money was needed. And if the United States would pay for the privilege of completing the canal through Panama, it was urgent to find out how much and set the wheels in motion. To do these things Marroquin had sent Silva to Washington early in 1901.

Silva soon found, in his talks, that he faced most delicate and difficult problems. The United States might in the end close with Nicaragua and offer nothing to the Republic of Colombia or the New Panama Canal Company. Indeed, one argument for Nicaragua was that it was free of the added complication of negotiation with a private concern. Secondly, if the United States did in fact elect to build a Panama canal, it would want a degree of control over the right of way that could be humiliating to Colombia. And thirdly, the United States, in the end, had the power to take what it wanted; making it an offer was something like holding out a morsel to a tiger. The tiger might merely shake its head in the negative, or it might snap off the entire hand.

Silva's task was made harder by the fact that, figuratively and literally, his principals were hard to reach. Bogotá was an inland capital, several thousand feet above sea level. It had telegraphic communication with Colón and Panama City, and from there by underwater cable to the United States. But wire service was often interrupted, and all steamer mail had to be unloaded and brought by mule over tortuous, weather-vulnerable trails, a trip of several days to several weeks.

Hence the politicians in Bogotá heard little from the outside world and suffered from a kind of parochialism that made them refer to their city—which had poorly paved streets and almost no telephones but had an auditorium for plays and operas—as the Athens of South America. In "Athens," in the spring of 1901, the feeling was that there was plenty of time to negotiate with the United States. To begin with, the United States had a half-century-old agreement with Great Britain, known as the Clayton-Bulwer Treaty. Under it the two nations had cooled a long rivalry in Central America by agreeing that neither would seize exclusive control of, or fortify, any trans-isthmian canal or land route; that both would support the neutrality of any such route; and that neither would "occupy, fortify, colonize or exercise dominion over" any part of Central America. That agreement would hold things up for some time. Moreover, in 1904 the New Panama Canal Company's rights would expire and remove that distraction from the picture. The Americans might make better terms then.

Dr. Silva had labored in vain to correct these impressions. He had written dispatches pointing out that Secretary Hay was making excellent progress with the

British ambassador on a new agreement that would abrogate Clayton-Bulwer and allow for an American-defended canal. (The result, the Hay-Pauncefote Treaty, was, in fact, signed in December of 1901 and soon ratified.) He had also read American journals of opinion carefully and knew the "tiger" was not very patient. The only result of all this caution was to provoke messages from Bogotá telling him to go slowly, make no price concessions, and yield as little sovereignty as possible. And finally, Bogotá was sending him on another mission. though only temporarily, quite possibly to silence his negativism.

SCENE III. *Washington, January 20, 1902*

William Nelson Cromwell had a lawyer's familiarity with (and distaste for) sudden and unexpected strokes of fortune that totally reversed the direction a case was taking. Yet even he could scarcely believe what he had read in the newspapers for the preceding two days. President Roosevelt was forwarding to Congress the final recommendation of the Walker Commission. It was that "the most practicable and feasible route" for an isthmian canal was "that known as the Panama route." And yet just one month earlier, to the very day, the battle had seemed hopelessly lost to Nicaragua, and Cromwell himself had been fired by the New Panama Canal Company.

The first bombshell had burst on November 16, but the fuse had been lit in the middle of the preceding month. In answer to repeated proddings from the Walker Commission, the New Panama Canal Company finally put a price tag on its properties. The sum read $109,141,500 for everything, from maps and blueprints and the forty-seven-mile-long Panama Railroad that crossed the isthmus to prospects of future profits. Admiral Walker was a New Hampshire Yankee with at least seven generations of merchants and traders behind him, and he had no difficulty in recognizing an inflated figure when he saw one. Whatever the French stockholders might think, their holdings were only, in the estimates of his experts, worth forty million dollars. His official answer to the French was in the commission's final report of mid-November. the cost of digging the Nicaragua canal was estimated at about $190,000,000. That of a Panama canal would be, to the last penny of the estimate, $144,233,358. But to go through Panama the United States would have to add the purchase price of the New Panama Company's holdings, and anything much over forty million would not only be a bad bargain but would push the Panama Canal's price beyond that of a Nicaraguan cut. Therefore it was eminently clear: the "practical and feasible route" would be through Nicaragua.

Two days later the Hay-Pauncefote Treaty was signed. With the verdict in from the commission and the green light flashing from London, Nicaragua seemed inevitable, and Panama doomed.

Swiftly, somehow, the directors of the New Panama Canal Company came to terms with the reality that they had one and only one potential customer. They wired Secretary Hay that forty million was an acceptable price to them. The news came too late to head off House passage of a new Hepburn bill for a Nicaragua canal on January 9—but not too late for Theodore Roosevelt to call the Walker Commission back into session on January 16.

Cromwell's last-minute reprieve from disaster owed much to Leon Czolgosz, who, on September 6, 1901, had fired a mortal gunshot wound into the belly of President McKinley. McKinley's death brought Theodore Roosevelt to the Presidency and changed the terms of the Panama equation. The country had never had such a President. He was only forty-three. He was well-read, knowledgeable about world affairs, a splendid if dominating conversationalist, and a supple writer of history, biography, nature lore, essays, and letters.

But there was another side to him. He was an relentlessly single-minded about some things as Bunau-Varilla (whom he later came to admire). He was restless and impulsive. A friendly observer described him as "pure act." A less flattering description came from a member of the diplomatic colony, who wrote to an acquaintance: "Always remember that the President is about six years old." And so it sometimes seemed.

With Roosevelt the canal was a top-priority item. He wanted to set the dirt flying. And, possibly through Hanna, he came into office ready to see it fly in Panama. This was worth an incalculable amount to Bunau-Varilla, Cromwell, the New Panama Canal Company, and all pro-Panama forces. He reconvened Walker's consultants on January 16, 1902; on the eighteenth they reversed their decision in the light of the new offer from the Paris directors. On the twentieth Congress was informed of their action. And on the twenty-seventh William Nelson Cromwell was rehired. Finally, on the twenty-eighth, when the Hepburn bill was brought up for consideration in the Senate, it was freighted with an amendment added by Senator John C. Spooner, an expert in business and constitutional law from Wisconsin and a most regular Republican. The Spooner Amendment directed the President to buy the properties of the New Panama Canal Company for forty million and to treat with Colombia for "perpetual control" of a canal zone in Panama, to be secured within a "reasonable" time. The final battle would turn on substituting this amendment for the original pro-Nicaragua wording. Experts believed that though Spooner's name might earn immortality through being on the amendment, the actual impetus had come from the White House and from Mark Hanna.

SCENE IV. *Washington, June 19, 1902*

The newspapers agreed that there had been no such debate in the Senate since the oral pyrotechnics of the pre-Civil War giants. It was a warm June Friday, and the ninety members of the upper chamber (minus a few absentees) were moving, after two weeks of discussion, to decide on the route of the interoceanic canal. The parliamentary convolutions, as always, were confusing to the uninitiated but clear enough to the reporters and the senators themselves. The motion was to adopt a minority report of Senator Morgan's Canal Committee—one that favored Panama. If that were done, it would show that the pro-Panama group had the votes to add the Spooner Amendment to the Hepburn bill, the subject of the Canal Committee's report. And the final "Panamized" bill would automatically go through as laggards switched and jumped aboard the bandwagon. For fall elections were coming, and no one wanted to be caught without a recorded favorable vote for the "right" canal bill.

Senator Hanna watched with his usual calm. On the fifth and sixth of the month, at the start of the two-week debate, he had given what some regarded as the most impressive speech of his career. Meticulously, calmly, now and then accepting a page of figures or a chart from a secretary seated behind him, Hanna had made the Panama case: the shorter route, the fewer locks, the already existing harbors and railroad, the backlog of French experience, the lower maintenance costs. So effective was it that at least one senator, announcing that it had changed his opinion, would for the rest of his life think of the canal as the "Hannama Canal." Now Hanna sat easily, joking, awaiting the verdict.

Philippe Bunau-Varilla, back in the United States, was following the struggle and waiting for the result, too. In his mind he had furnished unanswerable arguments in response to the pro-Nicaragua case being made on the floor by Senator Morgan and others. The country was in the midst of what might have been called a volcano scare. On May 8 Mount Pelée, an active crater on the West Indian island of Martinique, had erupted, wiping out the port of St. Pierre and forty thousand lives. To Bunau-Varilla even adversity on this gargantuan scale had its uses. In a philatelic store in Washington he picked up ninety copies of a stamp issued by Nicaragua, showing a smoking volcanic peak that could have been Mount Monotombo, only a few miles from the line of the proposed canal. He affixed each one to a sheet of paper and nearly typed underneath: "An official witness of the volcanic activity of the isthmus of Nicaragua." Then he mailed one to each senator. He counted on these "bombs, loaded with explosive truth," which arrived on the legislators' desks June 16, to do their work.

The new Colombian minister to Washington was also following the arguments intently, waiting to learn if the negotiations he had begun with Hay would reach completion. His name was Dr. Vicente Concha. He had taken over from Dr. Silva in February, and faced the same difficulties of communication. But he labored on valiantly to get a good treaty from the United States while the United States remained in a treaty-making mood.

Colombia wanted the canal zone to be ten kilometers, or about six miles, wide. She wanted to lease the zone to the United States for one hundred years and to keep a specific acknowledgement of her sovereignty. She wanted a flat payment on signing the treaty—a first suggested figure was $7.5 million—and $600,000 annually at some point after the canal had paid off its costs and was earning money from tolls, say, fifteen years after completion. She wanted the zone to be neutralized, with Colombia responsible for its defense but with the United States having the power to land troops (at Colombia's request) in emergencies. Finally, she wanted mixed Colombian and American tribunals to deal with Colombians in the zone who ran afoul of American laws.

None of this, Dr. Concha knew, would matter if Nicaragua won. All of it would be crucial if Panama prevailed. And so, like the others, he waited tensely for the results of the roll call on the minority report. Late in the day the word finally burst out of the chamber and was rushed to the wires. Enough votes had been switched from Nicaragua to carry the day for Hanna. It had been a close thing.

From there it was anticlimax. The expected rush to share credit for the amended bill took place, and Roosevelt signed the measure with a flourish of satisfaction on June 28. Only one morsel of hope had been salvaged by the Morgan-Hepburn bloc. The President was directed to pay the forty million dollars for the company's rights, to deal with Colombia for a canal zone at least six miles wide, and to build a canal usable by "vessels of the largest tonnage and greatest draft now in use, and such as may be reasonably anticipated." But if he could not achieve the first two steps in a "reasonable time," he was to proceed to build a canal in Nicaragua.

SCENE V. *Panama, November, 1902*

The final act of the drama in 1902 belonged to Admiral Silas Casey, commander in chief of the United States Pacific Fleet, a Civil War veteran nearing retirement in that busy year. On November 19, bluejackets aboard his flagship, the Wisconsin, stood to attention, pipes shrilled, and salutes snapped as two Colombian generals, with escorts, and a cluster of high civil officials came aboard and made their way to the admiral's cabin for a conference he had arranged. The *Wisconsin's* guns overlooked the white walls, tiled roofs, piers, railroad yards, palm clusters, donkey-filled streets, and waterfront bars of Panama City, the Pacific port of the isthmus.

Some weeks earlier, in mid-September, one of the two generals, Benjamin Herrera, leading an insurgency against the government in Bogotá, had been on the verge of capturing the port with his troops. Rebellions in Panama were an old story in Colombian's short history. This one, like all the others, automatically became a trigger for American military and diplomatic action under a treaty more than a half century old.

In 1846 the United States, already at war with Mexico and about to seize California, had been concerned enough about coast-to-coast communications in the future to negotiate a pact with Colombia, then known as New Granada. A pack-mule route wound its tormented way between Panama City and Colón, on the Atlantic side, and many travelers used it as a desirable if dangerous shortcut. The United States therefore agreed with New Granada-Colombia to guarantee the neutrality of the route and Colombian sovereignty over it, by force if necessary. Bogotá, in short, traded permission to the Americans to land troops in Panama to protect isthmian travelers in return for America's protection against having the province snatched away by foreign invaders or domestic rebels.

Domestic insurrection was a perennial problem. Panama was relatively isolated from the rest of the nation and as inclined to secession as the cotton states of America had once been. Early versions of Colombian constitutions even allowed Panama the privilege of peaceful separation, though the last of these escape clauses was abrogated in 1868. But there were literally dozens of outbreaks of discontent, and seven of them, between 1865 and 1901, had interrupted the "freedom of transit" seriously enough to warrant American landings, always with Bogotá's full consent.

From 1855 on the mode of transit had been a railroad, built under harrowing conditions by American engineers. It had enhanced Panamanian separatism, and it also dominated the military geography of the region. Panamanian prosperity had come to depend on the road and the business life it sustained. By 1900 all of the province's leading citizens were connected, in one way or another, with the company that owned and administered the line. They included such men as Manuel Amador Guerrero, the company's doctor; Pablo Arosemena, its legal counsel; and friends of theirs like Federico Boyd, José Arango, and Ricardo Arias, landowners and businessmen who filled contracts for the line in its various activities. All of these men were intensely eager to have a canal built through Panama, of course, for it would guarantee a virtually permanent boom during and after its construction, as it brought thousands of jobs in its train.

Any attempt to win control of Panama depended entirely upon the railroad, the only possible method of moving troops and material between Colón and Panama City. Accordingly, when General Herrera's vanguard approached Panama City, the American government, following precedent, ordered a cruiser, the *Cincinnati,* to Colón and the *Wisconsin* to Panama City, and directed Admiral Casey to take charge of the railroad and deny it to military traffic. The first reaction of Colombian government officials was favorable. They assumed that the Americans intended to protect their control of the area.

But Admiral Casey acted with vigor and license. He refused to permit *any* troops carrying arms or munitions—loyal or rebellious—to travel on the line. Colombian commanders thought of themselves as policemen, calling in outside help to enforce the law. Instead Casey's marine guards put them on an equal footing with the "criminals" and impartially kept both from acting. Bogotá's mood turned black, and in Washington, Dr. Concha was so outraged that he lost the capacity to deal at all with the Americans and soon had to resign.

Eventually a pragmatic Colombian general, Nicolas Perdomo, persuaded the admiral to permit a modest build-up of Colombian strength. Then a change in the political situation made it possible for Perdomo and Herrera to attend the peace conference aboard Casey's ship. A truce agreement was signed calling for a general amnesty and leaving outstanding problems to a meeting of the Colombian congress the following year.

The admiral had thus ended as a peacemaker. But he had demonstrated what had long been a half-formed thought in the minds of many advocates of the Panama Canal. If there was a revolt in Panama, Colombia could do nothing about it without the consent of the United States. The fact became a time bomb which began to tick away on November 19, 1902.

Act Three: The Misjudgments of Colombia
Scene I. *Bogotá, August, 1903*

Arthur Beaupré, minister of the United States of America to the Republic of Colombia, sat with pencil in hand, thinking of the best possible outline for the note he was about to draft to the Colombian government. He was by now an experienced Latin-American diplomat, having gone from a law practice in Illinois to a consulship in Guatemala in 1897, a reward for Republican faithfulness. He had also been in Honduras before being assigned to Bogotá as secretary of legation. On February 12 of this year, 1903, his friend Theodore Roosevelt had boosted him to ministerial honors. Undoubtedly it was because Roosevelt wanted someone who knew how to deal politely but firmly with temperamental Latins. Talking to them was, as Secretary Hay had once remarked, "like holding a squirrel in your lap." Beaupré was prepared to hold the squirrel tightly.

The preceding six months had been crowded ones. After the resignation of Dr. Concha the new Colombian minister in Washington, Tomas Herrán, had moved briskly. He was the son of a diplomat and had grown up, in part, in Washington and attended Georgetown University; he understood the American mentality and American politics. He knew that there was pressure from Roosevelt upon Hay to get moving and that his own room for maneuver was limited. He sparred briefly for a $600,000 annuity, but when, on January 21, Hay offered him "final" terms of a flat $10,000,000 payment and $250,000 annually thereafter, Herrán settled. The zone was to be leased for a century, was to be six miles wide, and could be "defended" by the United States. Mixed tribunals were to settle conflicts between Colombian and American laws and nationals.

The treaty was signed on January 22, with William N. Cromwell at Hay's side. Hay ceremoniously presented the signature pen to the lawyer as a well-deserved souvenir. The Senate, with unwonted speed, overrode various objections and ratified the agreement on March 17. And the nation then sat back and waited for Colombia's congress to do likewise.

And waited. And waited. And grew impatient. In the American popular mind Marroquin was a caricature—a little man with a mustache and a sombrero, who had only to snap his fingers in order to have flunkies in the "lawmaking body" run his errands. But in point of fact Marroquin was in full control of very little, and the United States soon moved to erode even that little.

101

In April, Marroquin opened negotiations with the New Panama Canal Company, looking to get for Colombia a percentage—say, a quarter—of the forty million that would be forthcoming from the American treasury. Horrified, the company directors alerted Cromwell. Cromwell spoke to Hay. By June 10 Beaupré was handing Foreign Minister Rico a sharp protest. Bogotá (it said) did not have the right to interfere in any way with the forthcoming purchase arrangements between the company and the United States by any new demands. Colombia was, it appeared, no longer sovereign over a private business firm operating on her own soil.

News of this note sharpened a dilemma that had been gnawing at Marroquin for a year. Panamanians were absolutely insisting that he close the deal quickly-something that, despite American misconceptions on the subject, he was by this time entirely willing to do. But other Colombians, running for the congress due to meet in June, were denouncing the Hay-Herrán Treaty as a shameful sellout of Colombian rights to the encroaching Yankee monster. As Herrán sadly wrote as early as mid-1902:

> History will say of me that I ruined the Isthmus and all Colombia, by not permitting the opening of the Panama Canal, or that I permitted it to be done, scandalously injuring the rights of my country

Even in mid-April it was apparent to Beaupré, who warned Hay, that the treaty would not go through. When Colombia's congress did in fact gather, it did so among floods of antitreaty oratory that invoked national honor and denounced Marroquin in splendidly balanced phrases.

In desperation, Marroquin sent private emissaries to the American minister to see if the noose could be loosened slightly. Would Washington renegotiate the treaty to allow for a first payment of fifteen million to Colombia? And to permit her to vindicate her dignity by getting ten million from the New Panama Canal Company? Hay's answer crackled back on July 12: "Neither of the proposed amendments . . . would stand any chance of acceptance by the Senate of the United States." And two days later President Roosevelt, learning of the request, shot a note to Hay from his summer residence at Oyster Bay: "Make it as strong as you can to Beaupré. Those contemptible little creatures in Bogotá ought to understand how much they are jeopardizing things and imperilling their own future."

On the fourth of August the "contemptible little creatures" took a fatal step toward darkening their future. A study committee of the Colombian senate reported back on the Hay-Herrán Treaty, suggesting no fewer than nine amendments. All of them, in one way or another, aimed at clarifying and preserving Colombia's sovereignty over the isthmus, its residents, and its two port cities. It was in response to this development that Beaupré was composing his note. He was doing so without the benefit of fresh advice from Washington, since the telegraph company, in a dispute with Colombia's government, had shut off service to Bogotá.

Beaupré deliberated for a while and then firmly did what he knew Roosevelt and Hay unquestionably wanted him to do. His handwriting rapidly filled the blank pages that would be transcribed for delivery to the ministry of foreign affairs on the Plaza Bolivar. The very first of the proposed amendments, he scribbled, was "alone tantamount to an absolute rejection of the treaty." As for the others, they would have a hard time in the American Senate even if submitted, which was "more than doubtful." And there was a final burst of undiplomatic bluntness:

> If Colombia really desires to maintain the present friendly relations existing between the two countries . . . the pending treaty should be ratified exactly in its present form, without any modifications whatever. I say this from a deep conviction that my Government will not in any case accept amendments.

Beaupré completed his work and paused for a moment of reflection. He knew precisely what would happen. The Colombians would be outraged at his peremptory tone, but Hay's instructions, when they finally arrived, would support him to the limit. The Colombian senate would also certainly reject his virtual order to sign. (Both predictions were to prove wholly accurate.) For the moment the Panama Canal would be dead once again. The next move would be up to the United States. What resurrecting miracle would her leaders now attempt?

SCENE II. *New York, October 20, 1903*

Dr. Manuel Amador Guerrero tried to listen patiently to the instructions of the fast-talking man who sat with him in a room of the Waldorf Astoria. Since he had first become involved, in May, in planning a Panamanian revolution, some curious things had happened to him, but talking with M. Bunau-Varilla always seemed especially bizarre and taxing. Amador—who was usually called by the first of his surnames only—was due to catch a steamer in a few hours that would take him home in seven days, and Bunau-Varilla, who seemed to have materialized from nowhere, had taken charge of the revolution and was telling him that it must be accomplished within five days after Amador arrived in Colón.

Amador must have felt, like others who dealt with Bunau-Varilla, that he was simply a chip being swept along on a tide of irresistible purpose. At seventy years of age, Amador did not appreciate the ride. In the entire Panama story, in fact, it often appeared that the impetuosity of the young—Bunau-Varilla, Cromwell, and Roosevelt, all in their forties—was overriding the desire of older men to do things in orderly and seemly fashion.

Roosevelt, for example, had received the news of Colombia's rejection of the treaty on August 12 with intense anger, though not with surprise, and had immediately begun to explore his options. There was one, in fact, that was not only open to him but in fact required by the Spooner Act. He could wait a "reasonable time" and then turn to Nicaragua. He had no intention of doing that. A second alternative, odd as it sounded, was to claim a right to go ahead with the Panama Canal whatever the "catrabbits" in Bogotá might say. Roosevelt could base that claim on a "brief" prepared by Professor John Bassett Moore, of Columbia University, an expert on international law who had previously worked for the State Department, which he requested and got on the fifteenth.

The Moore Memorandum was a strange exercise in jurisprudence. In essence it said that under the 1846 treaty with New Granada the United States had the right to guarantee free transit across the isthmus. Implied in the right of maintaining that freedom was the right to provide the most up-to-date and expeditious means of travel. So long as the United States kept its part of the bargain and preserved Colombian sovereignty, as it had time and time again done under the Monroe Doctrine and during rebellions, Colombia had no right to object if the United States went ahead with the canal—or, for that matter, any other mode of "transit" that was feasible. Once the canal was built, the United States would naturally own and operate it. "The ownership and control would be in their nature perpetual."

This breathtakingly broad construction of the compact of 1846 could have afforded the President some kind of lawyerlike arguments for simply seizing the isthmus and landing the steam shovels behind the troops—although, when he later tried Moore's ideas out on the Cabinet, his Secretary of War, Elihu Root, simply laughed and said: "Mr. President, do not let so great an achievement suffer any taint of legality."

But there was another avenue that might offer fewer difficulties of a diplomatic kind. That one simply involved waiting to see what would happen to various efforts to cut the slender stem that attached Panama politically to Colombia. Officially Roosevelt knew nothing of any conspiracies against the integrity of a "friendly" state. Privately he could not have been unaware of at least some of the activities in progress since June. First there had been a New York *World* story—planted by Cromwell—about the "unrest" in Panama; then a telegram came from Bunau-Varilla, in Paris, to Marroquin, warning him of Panamanian secessionism.

A few weeks later, in July, an American superintendent of the Panama Railroad had traveled up to New York on company business, which included a call on William Nelson Cromwell. When he returned, he held a meeting with Amador, Arango, Boyd, Arosemena, and other Panamanian nationalists. After this conference Amador had booked passage to New York for early September, using the public excuse that he was visiting a sick son who was in the United States.

It was then that Amador's troubles had begun. Unknown to him, someone had tipped off the Colombian minister, Herrán, who had set private detectives on his trail. Through his Washington channels Cromwell found this out and went into a cautious, lawyerlike vanishing act. He did not want a Panamanian revolution traced directly to his office. So he bought a ticket for Paris, to confer with his clients. And when poor Amador, seeking instructions and help, called at the offices of Sullivan and Cromwell, there was no one there who would see him.

Then, by a marvelous coincidence, on the twenty-third of September he received word that M. Bunau-Varilla was in town and wished to talk with him. The meetings that followed were recorded for posterity by the Frenchman and not the doctor, but later investigations established that Bunau-Varilla was usually accurate in essential outline, despite imaginative flights of ego.

Amador confided to the engineer that he had come expecting to get help from Cromwell in a secret loan of six million to buy gunboats and arms for the Panamanians. Now he was at a loss as to what to do. Bunau-Varilla, who insisted that he, too, had come to the United States only on personal business,was sympathetic and brisk. He had no clients to worry about and was happily ready to jump in. "Let me reflect," he said. "I shall try to find a solution if it is at all possible." Leaving Amador to await word from him, he plunged into a zesty twenty days of activity.

Bunau-Varilla instantly and correctly dismissed the idea of a real armed struggle for Panamanian liberation as too costly, too drawn-out, and too likely to fail. The trick was a modest revolt—confined largely to the zone of the canal, which must be instantly recognized as a new nation and protected by the United States. For two solid weeks Bunau-Varilla made appointments, made telephone calls, wrote notes, and sat in waiting rooms, working every one of his excellent American contacts, until he got what he wanted. On Friday morning, October 9, he sat down across a desk from President Roosevelt. The two men, so close in age and temperament, hit it off well as they ranged over favorite subjects: the importance of the canal, the perfidy of Colombia, the Moore Memorandum (the substance of which had, by another odd coincidence, been contained in an article written by Bunau-Varilla for a Paris paper on September 2). What they said about United States action in case of a Panama revolution—if anything direct was said— would never emerge. But Roosevelt wrote to a friend, after it was all over, that he assumed Bunau-Varilla was telling the Panamanians that Washington would interfere. "He would have been a very dull man indeed had he been unable to forecast such interference, judging simply by what we had done the year before."

Bunau-Varilla was anything but dull. He rushed back to New York and summoned Amador to meet him in room 1162 of the Waldorf on Tuesday morning the thirteenth. He told the doctor that no subsidy was forthcoming. "It is for us to act," he announced, admitting himself to the movement. Amador then raised the key question of how they could "act" with five hundred Colombian troops on the isthmus. The answer was simple for Bunau-Varilla. He knew that the soldiers had not been paid in months. Let them be bribed with twenty dollars each. Amador countered realistically: "That is not enough." He worked the figure up to two hundred apiece—a total of a hundred thousand dollars. "Well, my dear sir," said Bunau-Varilla, "it is a relatively small sum which it will be easy to find at bankers, I suppose, and if it is not to be found there, I can provide it, myself, from my own personal fortune."

For a time Amador resisted the whirlwind of Bunau-Varilla's self-confidence, then gave in and placed himself at the Frenchman's disposal. Bunau-Varilla virtually flung himself on a train to Washington, and on Friday morning was closeted with Hay. He announced to the Secretary: "Prepare yourself for the outbreak of a revolution." So far as is known, the expression on Hay's grave, bearded face remained unchanged. He neither smiled nor winked. But he said that he, too, expected trouble and that orders were out sending cruisers toward the Gulf of Panama. That was all Bunau-Varilla wanted to know.

On Saturday morning Amador showed up again in answer to a wire that Bunau-Varilla had sent him as his train rumbled through Baltimore. This time Bunau-Varilla had an unpleasant surprise in store. Amador was assured that the revolt would be supported by the Americans. He was to show up the following Tuesday to receive a flag, a declaration of independence, a constitution, and a secret communications code. He would also get his hundred thousand dollars—half when the revolt was proclaimed and half when it was completed. But the first act of the new government must be to appoint Bunau-Varilla minister plenipotentiary.

Amador considered darkly what he was going to tell his compatriots in ten days. They were supposed to make a revolution, entirely on the assurance of an insane French civilian that the United States would safeguard them. They were to get not six million but a hundred thousand dollars from the madman, and he was to be appointed their minister plenipotentiary. Poor Amador demurred, struggled, argued feebly. Bunau-Varilla, who was at the moment Amador's only possible card to play, drew himself up. No one but he could guarantee success. "Any motive of vanity, of ambition, or even of national pride," he orated, "must yield to the imperative necessity of succeeding." Amador sighed, agreed, and made his date for the following Tuesday morning.

Bunau-Varilla, who was enjoying making revolutions as much as Theodore Roosevelt enjoyed big-game hunting, proceeded to Macy's, where he bought some colored silk. He then entrained for Highland Falls, some sixty miles up the Hudson, where he had a weekend invitation from his friend John Bigelow, former American minister to France. Ignoring the crisp outdoor delights of a pleasant fall weekend, he set to work composing his documents, assisted in English by Mr. Bigelow's secretary. The flag was sewn by Bigelow's daughter Grace and Mme. Bunau-Varilla, following an attractive design. It consisted of blue, red, and white rectangles, with a red and a blue star, presumably for the two oceans that were to be joined.

These were the creations Bunau-Varilla handed to Amador early on the twentieth as he sent him off to board the *Yucatán*. The goal was at last in sight.

SCENE III. *Colón, November 3-4-5, 1903*

The day began badly and in anxiety. Great anxiety. Early in the morning the Tiradores Battalion of the Colombian army came marching into Colón. Somehow Bogotá had become suspicious and ordered the movement. The Panamanian plotters were not entirely taken by surprise. In panic Amador, only two days back from New York, rushed to the telegraph office to send Bunau-Varilla a wire in the code they had devised, which would have delighted the hearts of a boys' club: "FATE NEWS BAD POWERFUL TIGER. SMITH." It meant: "For Bunau-Varilla. More than two hundred Colombian troops arriving on the Atlantic side within five days." "URGE VAPOR COLON," continued Amador. ("Send a steamer to Colón.")

Bunau-Varilla, who had no authority whatever over any American VAPOR, took the train to Washington once more, asked questions, predicted disasters—but, above all, read the newspapers. He noted that the U.S.S. *Nashville* was at Kingston, Jamaica, the nearest point to Colón. His sense of the situation was that U.S. action was imminent. And so he wired back: "PIZALDO PANAMA ALL RIGHT WILL REACH TON AND A HALF OBSCURE. JONES." This went to Amador in care of a bank in Panama City, and meant that help would arrive in two and a half days.

Now it was the first Tuesday in November, the slated hour for the uprising. The two and a half days were almost gone, and the Panamanian underground in Colón looked in vain for the comforting gray hull of an American battleship, full of armed men who would land and prevent the Colombians from moving on down to Panama City.

While the hours ticked away the railroad officials worked at their part of the plot. They explained that rolling stock for conveying troops and equipment was temporarily unavailable. But perhaps General Tobar, the commander, would like to go on ahead, with his staff, in a passenger car? In Panama City there were more comfortable facilities available for them. Leaving his troops in charge of Colonel Eliseo Torres, the general accepted. He reached Panama City in midafternoon and soon found himself arrested by the forces recruited by the insurgents—the Colombian garrison, which had been promised its back pay, and the city's police and fire brigades.

With this done, a provisional revolutionary committee felt safe enough by six in the afternoon to go out to the cathedral plaza and announce to a happy crowd, which had gathered in response to rumors, that on the next day Panama would formally become independent. This news was somehow conveyed to a Colombian gunboat, the Bogotá, sitting in the harbor. Her commander loyally fired five shells into the town, then withdrew. They killed a donkey and a Chinese named Wong Kong Yee, the only two victims of the revolution.

The American consuls in Panama City and Colón knew what was happening. The former had already received a message from the State Department at 5 P.M.: "UPRISING REPORTED." Calmly, he cabled back: "NOT YET." Washington was unwontedly eager, possibly because President Roosevelt was due in from New York on an evening train, having gone home to Oyster Bay to vote in local elections.

The consul in Colón knew that the *Nashville* was en route because he had already gotten cabled orders to deliver to her captain. They were, not surprisingly,

The Treaty Provisions

November 18, 1903

ARTICLE I.

The United States guarantees and will maintain the independence of the Republic of Panama.

ARTICLE II.

The Republic of Panama grants to the United States in perpetuity the use, occupation and control of a zone of land and land under water for the construction, maintenance, operation, sanitation and protection of said Canal of the width of ten miles extending to the distance of five miles on each side of the center line of the route of the Canal to be constructed. . . . The Republic of Panama further grants to the United States in perpetuity the use, occupation and control of any other lands and waters outside of the zone above described which may be necessary and convenient for the construction, maintenance, operation, sanitation and protection of the said Canal or of any auxiliary canals or other works necessary and convenient for the constuction, maintenance, operation, sanitation and protection of the said enterprise.

The Republic of Panama further grants in like manner to the United States in perpetuity all islands within the limits of the zone above described and in addition thereto the group of small islands in the Bay of Panama, named Perico, Naos, Culebra and Flamenco.

ARTICLE III.

The Repulblic of Panama grants to the United States all the rights, power and authority within the zone mentioned and described in Article II of this agreement and within the limits of all auxiliary lands and water mentioned and described in said Article II which the United States would possess and exercise if it were the sovereign of the territory within which said lands and waters are located to the entire exclusion of the exercise by the Republic of Panama of any such sovereign rights, power or authority.

ARTICLE XXIII.

If it should become necessary at any time to employ armed forces for the safety or proteciton of the Canal, or of the ships that make use of the same, or the railways and auxiliary works, the United States shall have the right, at all times and in its discretion, to use its police and its land and naval forces or to establish fortifications for these purposes.

ARTICLE XXIV.

If the Repulblic of Panama shall hereafter enter as an constituent into any other Government or into any union or confederation of states, so as to merge her sovereignty or independence in such Government, union or confederation, the rights of the United States under this convention shall not be in any respect lessened or impaired.

to bar the railroad to all troops. Late in the afternoon the American vessel arrived. After some confusion Commander Hubbard got his directive and by 10:30 had acknowledged and executed it.

Wednesday, nonetheless, found the revolution only half completed. Hearing of its proclamation in Panama, Bunau-Varilla had sent his first cash installment. But in Colón, Colonel Torres remained stubbornly waiting for his trains. Finally one of the local revolutionary committee members took him to a hotel barroom and gently broke the news to him over a drink. Perhaps more than one drink. The colonel was outraged at the arrest of his superior and ready to do his duty as a soldier. He sent word to the American consul. Either they would get a train for his men or he would kill every American in town.

Commander Hubbard, confronted with this news at midday, sent boats out to evacuate U.S. nationals to ships in the harbor, deployed an armed landing party, and swung his cannon in a deadly arc aimed at the Colombian position. Before any shooting started, cool heads reached Colonel Torres. His patriotism was admirable, but he could not fight the United States Navy. Honor was satisfied by his gesture. It would now be the better part of wisdom, as well as valor, to withdraw to a waiting steamer in the harbor—troops and all—and leave. A night of meditation helped Torres to see the essential logic of this view, particularly when it was reinforced by a gift of two cases of champagne and eight thousand gold dollars for himself and his men.

And so, on Thursday afternoon, the fifth of November, the Colombian troops left, and Panama was free. The New York papers had the story now, including an interview with Bunau-Varilla, who opined:

> It is a spontaneous combustion, due to the accumulation of injured feelings, and
> the result of the Spanish colonial system, for Panama was as much a colony of
> the Bogotá government as Cuba was of the grandees at Madrid.

But the more important statement was yet to come. At 10 A.M. on Friday the sixth, in Colón, in the presence of a gathering of all the foreign and local officials who could be mustered, the steering committee of the revolution announced that Panama had joined the family of nations. A United States Army officer on hand was given the honor of raising the Panamanian flag over the city hall. No sooner had he finished than official cables notified the American State Department. And at 12:51 the consuls on the isthmus had the equally official response. The people of Panama having ''resumed'' their independence, the United States representatives were told, and a new government having been established, ''you will enter into relations with it as the responsible government of the territory.''

Panama was made and recognized. That night Bunau-Varilla, after some telegraphic dickering, got his official appointment as minister plenipotentiary and sent off the final fifty thousand dollars. He had given Amador instructions on October 20. It has taken just seventeen days to carry them out.

Wearing a uniform came naturally to Bunau-Varilla, and he looked formidably official in the one he had quickly ordered for his presentation to President Roosevelt as the official spokesman for Panama. As he waited for Secretary Hay to take him in and present him, thus converting the de facto recognition of November 6 to a de jure one, his mind was busy as always. And as always it lingered over possible plots against the future of the dream of four centuries, the Panama Canal.

Bunau-Varilla had experienced some difficult moments since assuming his new office. On November 7 he received a wire sent by the revolutionists prior to his being named minister plenipotentiary. It declared that the provisional government appointed him a confidential agent to negotiate a loan from the United States. Confidential agent indeed! The minister bristled at the very thought of the implied demotion. Fortunately, he could disregard this piece of conspiratorial "impertinence" because the higher appointment had subsequently come through.

But on Monday the ninth Hay had stunned him by asking: "What is this commission coming from Panama?" Rushing to the wires, Bunau-Varilla learned that Amador and Federico Boyd would be leaving Panama the next day to come to Washington, carrying his instructions. For Bunau-Varilla any instructions from Panama were incompatible with his dignity. He had spun his webs with an utter and delicious freedom up to then. Hay, after all, had been answerable to Roosevelt and the Senate, Cromwell to the New Panama Canal Company. Bunau-Varilla had bowed to no one, and he was not of a mind to spend a fruitless period of time in Washington rushing back and forth between Hay on the one hand and Amador and Boyd on the other. But he had only a week of freedom left. After that he would be the captive of Panamanian pride. And the Panamanians were capable of the unthinkable crime of delaying the canal by insisting on their narrow and selfish interests.

He must work fast for humanity. And he did. As he and Hay left the White House after the official reception he turned to the Secretary and delivered a tactful, almost gossamer but recognizable ultimatum:

> For two years you have had difficulties in negotiating the Canal Treaty with the Colombians. Remember that ten days ago the Panamans were still Colombians and brought up to use the hair-splitting dialectic of Bogotá. You have now before you a Frenchman. If you wish to take advantage of a period of clearness, in Panaman diplomacy, do it now! When I go out, the spirit of Bogotá will return.

Hay understood. "You are right," he said. "I wish to put the finishing touches to the project of the treaty. I shall send it to you as soon as possible."

Bunau-Varilla went back to his hotel to wait out the weekend. He was not kept in suspense for too long. On Sunday the fifteenth a messenger delivered

Hay's draft to him. It was basically the old Hay-Herrán Treaty, with blanks left for possible insertion of new figures. The envoy extraordinary had perhaps three days left to retain his extraordinary liberty of maneuver.

SCENE II. *Washington, November 18, 1903*

Wednesday morning in Washington. Cool weather, the town preparing for the approaching slack weekend of Thanksgiving, followed by the bustle of the opening of Congress the first week in December. Bunau-Varilla sat waiting for his telephone to ring and counting minutes.

He had worked relentlessly and purposefully, reading and rereading the treaty draft on Sunday. During the night he had slept only two hours, which he described as a "complete rest." By the time dawn was silhouetting the Capitol dome, he had worked out the problem. The prime objective was to win the approval of the Senate by making the treaty irresistible. Every American objection raised during passage of the Hay-Herrán ratification must be satisfied.

At 6 A.M. Bunau-Varilla began to scribble. The money would remain the same—a $10,000,000 flat sum, plus $250,000 per year. But the Canal Zone would be, not ten kilometers, but ten miles wide—a 60 per cent increase. And it would not be leased but "granted" to the United States "in perpetuity." Naturally the United States could place its armed forces as and where it wished to defend both the canal and the independence of Panama. And as for the question of jurisdiction in the zone, Bunau-Varilla cut through all that by a simple formula:

> The Republic of Panama grants to the United States all the rights, power and authority within the zone mentioned . . . which the United States would possess and exercise if it were the sovereign of the territory . . . to the entire exclusion of the exercise by the Republic of Panama of any such sovereign rights, power or authority.

There would be no question of whose laws would be obeyed. The United States would be—save only in a technical sense—sovereign. It was fortunate that the Panamanian commissioners, on the high seas, were unaware of the conception of the national interest entertained by their envoy extraordinary. In a prewireless age disaster did not descend so peremptorily upon statesmen.

Bunau-Varilla had asked Frank D. Pavey, an American friend and attorney, to come down and help him with the wording of the treaty. Pavey arrived, and he, Bunau-Varilla, and a stenographer labored through the day. At ten o'clock that night the Frenchman drove up to Hay's home but found it darkened. Next morning, Tuesday the seventeenth, he got his draft delivered, and then was condemned to wait for a response. Unfortunately, Amador and Boyd were due in New York that morning. By nightfall they would be on hand, and Bunau-Varilla's wings would be clipped.

But then came one of those lucky accidents that had a way of befalling Bunau-Varilla. Amador and Boyd did indeed debark in New York Tuesday morning. They immediately and naturally went to make contact with Sullivan and Cromwell. And there they learned that Mr. Cromwell himself was due, late in the afternoon or early the next morning, on his return ship from France. The two Panamanians wanted to talk to Cromwell about the future dealings of their country with his client. So they sent a cordial note to Bunau-Varilla that they would be along the next afternoon and settled into a New York hotel, still enjoying the tranquillity of ignorance as they awaited Cromwell.

Bunau-Varilla thus had a twenty-four-hour reprieve. Meantime Hay himself was not dawdling. He was sensitive to the Frenchman's time problem and eager to have the treaty wrapped up so that it might be reported in the President's State of the Union message of December, which would, as usual, become a campaign document for 1904. Roosevelt himself, that Sunday evening, had written to his son in characteristic fighting fettle:

> I have had a most interesting time about Panama and Colombia. My experiences in all these matters give me an idea of the fearful times Lincoln must have had in dealing with the great crisis he had to face. . . . Why, even in this Panama business the *Evening Post* and the entire fool Mugwump crowd have fairly suffered from hysterics; and a goodly number of the Senators even of my own party have shown about as much backbone as so many angle worms. However, I have kept things moving just right so far.

Late Tuesday, Hay did call in Bunau-Varilla for a conference. He had busily gone over technical points with his specialists and with other members of the Cabinet, working right through lunch and, as he wrote somewhat complainingly to his daughter a day or so later, "putting on all steam." If either he or Bunau-Varilla were concerned with possible Panamanian rejection of the pact, they did not express their doubts. Both knew that the new government had little choice in the matter and had gotten at least one sop—an enlargement of their boundaries beyond the narrow strip of isthmus first envisioned. Incredible as it may seem, Bunau-Varilla may even have believed what he afterward wrote. When he thought about presenting the finished work to the Panamanians, he declared: "I did not doubt it would be received with pleasure."

At approximately 4:30 Wednesday afternoon Amador and Boyd boarded a Pennsylvania Railroad express to Washington. And sometime around that moment the long crusade of Philippe Bunau-Varilla, begun when the old French canal died in 1889, ended. He was called to come to Secretary Hay's home. There the drafts were matched. The one Hay chose was essentially Bunau-Varilla's, with minor changes in wording. Seated at a desk in a blue drawing room, Hay took a pen from an inkstand that had belonged to Abraham Lincoln. When they had finished, he handed the "precious souvenir" to Bunau-Varilla. The task was achieved. At that moment Amador and Boyd were somewhere on the track between Philadelphia and Baltimore, rolling southward.

Hay went on to supper, presumably, and Bunau-Varilla, in glow of self-satisfaction, made his way to the railroad station. When the train carrying the Panamanians groaned to a stop, he rushed up to greet Amador, who was the first of the two commissioners to emerge.

"The Republic of Panama is henceforth under the protection of the United States," Bunau-Varilla shouted. "The Canal treaty has just been signed." To the Frenchman's surprise, the elderly physician's reaction was not joyful. "He nearly fainted upon the platform," recollected the envoy.

Dr. Amador was overwhelmed by emotion and by history—by the events that had whirled him about and perhaps by his awareness that the stream of world commerce would one day flow through his nation, even though it was to be, in effect, a country partially occupied by a greater power.

Mr. Coolidge's Jungle War

Richard O'Connor

The United States was first introduced to the vexations of large-scale guerrilla warfare forty years ago in the mountain jungles of Nicaragua. There for the first time Americans were confronted by an elusive partisan leader of a type to become bitterly familiar not only in the Caribbean but in Southeast Asia, a man who pioneered techniques of warfare when Che Guevara and Fidel Castro were in rompers and Mao Tse-tung was an obscure revolutionary. "Mr. Coolidge's War," the affair has been called. More formally, it was the American intervention in Nicaragua of 1927–28—and though it was not one of the thunderclaps of history, its significance is evident.

For well over a year a particularly agile and mischievous guerrilla chieftain name Sandino—the name became almost a household word in the late twenties-campaigned successfully against the elite battalions of the United States Marine Corps. In giving them so much trouble, he unintentionally made his country a proving ground for U.S. weapons and tactics. In Nicaragua the Marine Corps began to formulate the doctrine that would guide the jungle campaigns against the Japanese in World War II and against the Viet Cong in South Vietnam; it tried out such novelties as dive-bombing, aerial support of ground forces, search-and-destroy missions, and the counter-ambush. It would not be appropriate to belabor the point, but with a change of dateline many of the dispatches from Vietnamese battlefields read like the afteraction reports of the Marine's provisional brigade in Nicaragua.

Similarly interchangeable would be the protests of liberal and pacifist elements in the United States. President Coolidge had his Senator Fulbright in the liberal Republican William E. Borah of Idaho, who kept demanding to know the true casualty figures of the U.S. force and of those opposed to it. Another senator introduced a resolution that would have forbidden the President to employ military forces when "Congress has not declared a state of war to exist." Hundreds of ordinary citizens picketed the White House with signs reading "Wall Street and not Sandino is the Real Bandit," and Marines bound for Nicaraguan duty received letters urging them to desert when they landed and join Sandino in his "war for freedom."

It was not primarily Wall Street's interests, nor any fervor for foreign ventures on the part of the lackadaisical Coolidge, nor even an ironclad interpretation of the Monroe Doctrine that propelled the intervention. For almost a century the United States had considered Nicaragua strategic to the national interest: it offered the best alternative route for a trans-Isthmus canal—a route that is still a matter of consideration in the event that political upheaval, or the need for a larger canal, should make an alternative to the Panama Canal necessary.*

This continuing strategic interest, plus the concessions obtained by American companies for the exploitation of Nicaragua's bananas, mahogany, and gold, made the country almost an American protectorate. Between 1912 and 1925, Marines were landed several times to restore order after political disturbances. The closely drawn struggle between the Liberal and the Conservative parties in Nicaragua, which had been going on since early on the nineteenth century, erupted with even greater violence late in 1926 when a Conservative, Adolfo Díaz, was elected to the presidency by the Nicaraguan congress and recognized by the United States and most of the other great powers. The Liberal leader, Dr. Juan Sacasa, then proclaimed himself president, with the support of revolutionary forces under General José Maria Moncada. Mexico recognized Sacasa and sent him four shiploads of arms and supplies. Before long, his forces had occupied large sections of the country.

Once again the U.S. government felt it was necessary to intervene. The 5th Marine Regiment was landed on the Atlantic coast, and a shore party from the cruiser *Galveston* on the Pacific. The State Department gave the Associated Press a story pointing to the "spectre of a Mexican-fostered Bolshevistic hegemony intervening between the United States and the Panama Canal." By March of 1927 the U.S. Navy reported that 5,414 men were on duty in or en route to Nicaragua. However, President Coolidge decided to make a last try at a political solution. He rushed former Secretary of War Henry L. Stimson to the embattled country aboard a cruiser just as General Moncada's revolutionary forces advanced to within forty miles of Managua, the capital.

---

*A survey of the Nicaraguan route, undertaken by a commission set up by the U.S. Congress in 1938, estimated that such a canal would cost almost $1,500,000,000, against the $375,000,000 spent in Panama. Today, of course, it would cost much more.

Colonel Stimson briskly set about negotiating a truce between the contending factions. He persuaded President Díaz to offer the rebels a general amnesty, the return of confiscated property, and participation of the Díaz cabinet by Liberal leaders. Then Stimson arranged a meeting with General Moncada, which was held on May 4, 1927, under a large blackthorn tree just outside the village of Tipitapa. A week later they met there again. As a result, Moncada agreed to allow Díaz to stay in the presidency provided that the United States would supervise the election the following year.

The various rebel commanders, as requested, signed an agreement with General Moncada that they would surrender their arms—all but one, namely Augusto Sandino. The only word from Sandino was a note saying that he was going north to collect arms from his dissident followers and would "remain there awaiting your (Moncada's) orders." No one paid much attention to Sandino's absence as the various revolutionary battalions and the government forces surrendered their arms to officers of the 5th Marine regiment. The job of policing the country was assumed by the Marine's provisional brigade and the Nicaraguan constabulary, which was to be commanded by Marine officers.

On May 15, Stimson confidently telegraphed the State Department: "The civil war in Nicaragua is now definitely ended. . . . I believe that the way is now open for the development of Nicaragua along the lines of peace, order, and ultimate self government."

The next day two Marines, Captain Richard B. Buchanan and Private Marvin A. Jackson, were killed when a guerrilla band attacked their post guarding the railroad near León.

Sandino had spoken. It was the starting gun of a long and bitter struggle to pacify the country. Stimson later recorded that General Moncada had told him that Sandino, "having promised to join in the settlement, afterward broke his word and with about 150 followers, most of whom he said were Honduran mercenaries, had secretly left his army and started northward toward the Honduras border."

Stimson left Managua that day, May 16, to return to Washington, convinced that Sandino and his band would soon be tracked down and captured. Instead, the Marine Corps, along with the Nicaraguan constabulary, found itself plunged into a guerrilla war with few guidelines and even fewer omens of success.

There were, to be sure, certain precedents. The Marines themselves had been engaged in police actions in Haiti. The U.S. Army, confronted on several occasions by guerrillas of various types, had learned and then forgotten the lesson that it takes a vast preponderance of men and materials to hunt down determined bands of partisans operating in rough country, among people friendly to the quarry but hostile to the hunters. During the Civil War the Union Army had been bedevilled by the irregular forces of Mosby, Quantrill, and others. In 1886 the regular Army had turned out 5,000 of its best troops to run down the Apache leader Geronimo and his followers, whose strength was approximately one percent of their own. In the southern Philippines after the Spanish-American War, it had taken the army fourteen years to pacify the Moro *insurrectos*. An even more frustrating experience was General John J. Pershing's futile expedition into Mexico in 1916, chasing after Pancho Villa with the best of the U.S. Cavalry and coming back with an empty cage.

Sandino, as Marine intelligence officers quickly learned, meant to stir up as much trouble as possible. He had taken his hard-core followers up into the heavily forested mountains of Nueva Segovia and Jinotega provinces near the Honduras border and was recruiting what became a striking force estimated at one thousand men. He had even designed a battle flag of red and black emblazoned with a death's-head. It was also observed that he was adept at rousing the patriotic emotions of the people in the back country by playing on resentment of foreign violations of their native soil, an emotion stronger in the mountains than in the more sophisticated cities to the south.

Augusto Sandino was a mestizo, not much over five feet tall, with a striking look of self-confidence in his intense black eyes. In 1927 he was thirty-four years old. The son of the owner of a small coffee plantation, he was educated at the Eastern Institute in Granada, worked on his father's *finca,* and then left his native Niquinohomo after a violent dispute with a prominent man in the vicinity. For a time he worked in mines and on banana plantations in Nicaragua, and then he went to Mexico and was employed by an American oil company in Tampico. He returned to his father's home in 1926, laden with books on sociology and syndicalism—and, oddly enough, a bulky missionary tract, which he frequently consulted, published by the Seventh-day Adventists.

He loved to coin heroic slogans and hurl them at his followers on all suitable occasions ("Death is but one little moment of discomfort; it is not to be taken too seriously . . . God and our mountains fight for us"). But Sandino also had a sense of humor. Whenever he "requisitioned" supplies for his forces from the merchants, plantations, or mining companies on which he periodically depended, he insisted with sardonic punctilio on leaving nicely printed certificates: "The Honorable Calvin Coolidge, President of the United States of North America, will pay the bearer $______."

Sandino's objectives were succinctly stated in a message he left at the La Luz mines after levelling the American-owned property there: "The most honorable resolution which your government could adopt in the conflict with Nicaragua is to retire its forces from our territory, thus permitting us, the Nicaraguans, to elect our national government, which is the only means of pacifying the country. With your government rests the conservation of good or bad relations with our government and you, the capitalists, will be appreciated and respected by us according as you treat us as equals and not in the mistaken manner which now obtains, believing yourselves lords and masters of our lives and property."

The mordant edge of Sandino's humor was soon felt by Marine Captain G. Hatfield, whose force of thirty-seven Marines and forty Nicaraguan constables occupied Ocotal, the largest town in the province of Nueva Segovia, and formed the spearhead of the forces charged with running down the rebel. Captain Hatfield and Sandino exchanged a number of letters inviting each other to surrender or, failing that, to "come out and fight." Sandino easily outdid the Marine commander in bravura. One of his messages was decorated with a drawing of a guerrilla brandishing a machete over the prostrate form of a Marine; it was signed, "Your obedient servant, who wished to put you in a handsome tomb with flowers." Meanwhile, Sandino was striking hard at foreign-owned mining properties in the northern mountains. The managers of French and German mines near Ocotal were kidnapped and held for $5,000 ransom. Sandino and his followers also wrecked the gold mine operated by Charles Butters, an American, at San Albino where Sandino had worked as a clerk just before joining the Liberal revolution.

On July 15, on orders from his superiors, Captain Hatfield sent Sandino an ultimatum demanding that he surrender within twenty-four hours or be wiped out. "I will not surrender," Sandino replied, "and will await you here. I want a free country or death."

Actually he had already decided against "awaiting" the Marines in the mountains above Ocotal and had begun deploying for an attack. One day after receiving the ultimatum, at 1 A.M. on July 16, he launched a furious assault on the garrison at Ocotal with an estimated six hundred followers. Only luck saved Captain Hatfield and his men from destruction. A Marine sentry patrolling one hundred yards from the city hall sighted a shadow moving along a line of bushes. The shadow, startled, fired on him. The Marine raced to the city hall, where Hatfield's headquarters were located, and the town's defenders were alerted just before Sandino struck in force. The Sandinistas had infiltrated the town and were closing in on the main defense positions around the city hall.

Outnumbered by almost ten to one, the Marines and the constables reacted with admirable discipline and poured rifle, grenade, and machine-gun fire on the attackers from the rooftops, courtyards, and windows. One group of Sandino's men charged into the courtyard behind the city hall and killed a Marine but was forced to withdraw. In the square fronting on Hatfield's command post, the partisans were caught in a crossfire between Marines in the city hall and the Guardia (constabulary) in the nearby tower. Thomas G. Bruce, a Marine first sergeant commissioned as a lieutenant in the Guardia, lay in the street behind a heavy machine gun and accounted for many of the Sandinistas trying to cross the square.

At dawn, Sandino realized his surprise attack had failed, and he withdrew his followers from the center of town. The garrison, he decided, would have to be starved out. A heavy fire was poured at long range into the two buildings held by Hatfield and his men.

Two Marine reconnaissance planes, part of the nine-plane unit of World War I de Havillands based in a cow pasture outside Managua, happened to fly over Ocotal late that morning on a routine patrol. On glimpsing the battle below they streaked for their base. At three o'clock that afternoon a flight of five planes led by Major Ross E. Rowell swooped out of rainy skies and proceeded to demonstrate what air support could accomplish even in what the Marines called a "bamboo war." Major Rowell and his flight loosed small bombs and strafed Sandino's positions for a half hour before running out of ammunition.

At nightfall, Captain Hatfield was able to report that Ocotal's defenders had given Sandino a sharp setback. His own casualties included one Marine killed and two wounded and four members of the Guardia wounded, against reports from residents of the town that forty of Sandino's followers had been killed and an unknown number wounded.

Sandino, at any rate, was forced to lift the siege and pull back into the mountains to the east when a column of Marine reinforcements arrived. Several days later he issued a proclamation that he had attacked Ocotal to "prove that we prefer death to slavery" and added that "whoever believes we are downcast by the heavy casualties misjudges my army. . . ." Another column of Marines and Guardia was sent into the mountainous heart of guerrilla country and occupied the village of Jícaro, which Sandino had renamed Sandino City and designated as his "capital."

The guerrillas had scattered in the mountains in what would become known as a classic pattern of dispersal following an engagement. At the time, however, the American authorities simply took the dispersal as sign that they were giving up the fight. So convinced were the Americans that Sandino was beaten that they ordered a withdrawal of part of the provisional brigade to Guantánamo in Cuba and to other bases. General Logan Ferland also left, after handing over command of the Nicaragua field force to Colonel Louis Mason Gulick. Meanwhile an Army general, Frank R. McCoy, arrived with orders from President Coolidge to supervise the coming election.

The countryside was fairly quiet that summer, and by the end of July there were only 1,700 Marines still stationed in Nicaragua. But the lull was deceptive. Actually Sandino was quietly building up his forces for renewed and heavier fighting. A Marine Corps historian wrote later:

> He was a master of propaganda and managed to use the Ocotal affair to his advantage: it served to attract the attention of communistic and other radical elements in Central America, Mexico and even in the United States; and it made Sandino a central figure to rally around. Considerable sums of money were raised, some even in the United States, and turned over to him for the purpose of providing military equipment and maintaining an armed force. Within a few months Sandino had several thousand followers and an actual armed force of almost a thousand. All this went on, however, without the knowledge of any responsible American official.

Harold Denny, the *New York Time's* capable young man on the scene, agreed that Sandino may have become a hero abroad through "extravagantly false" propaganda, but in Denny's view "he did not represent public opinion in Nicaragua." His countrymen sympathized with Sandino but seldom offered their voluntary support. Many foreigners in Nicaragua, not including Americans, also sympathized with him because

> he was an under dog making a terrific fight. I have heard foreigners in fear of an imminent attack on their plantations discuss him with something akin to admiration. But few people in Nicaragua were really interested in throwing the Americans out of the country, even though they might not love them. To the more intelligent persons of both parties, Sandino was a lively danger to Nicaragua's hard won opportunity for a just peace. Toward the last even some of his supporters outside the country urged him to cease fighting because his warfare, instead of driving the marines from the country, was insuring that they would remain.

The only American to wangle a personal interview with Sandino during the year of his intense activity as a guerrilla chieftain was Carleton Beals, a correspondent for the *Nation,* one of the most eloquent of the defenders of Sandino's right to foment a rebellion against the American presence. Beals made a long and perilous journey through Honduras and across the northern border of Nicaragua, entering Sandino country through the back door. Through his well-advertised sympathies Beals was enabled to "make the proper connections in Mexico and Guatemala" and follow "the thread of Sandino's underground with the outside world," through El Salvador and then Honduras. While travelling that clandestine route, guided by Sandino sympathizers, Beals was shown a photograph of the town of Chinandega after it was bombed by U.S. planes, and in his report there are foreshadowings of Harrison Salisbury's dispatches from Vietnam. "An entire street laid in ruins and sprinkled with mangled bodies," Beals wrote; "the tumbled walls of the hospital, broken bodies of patients flung about. . . . Was it so long ago that we called the Germans Huns for destroying civilian populations without mercy?"

Beal's interview with Sandino demonstrated to Americans that he was no mere adventurer but a man of intensely idealistic convictions. Sandino attacked the Díaz government as an American puppet, blamed American financial interests for all the troubles visited upon his country, inveighed against Nicaragua's sale of its canal rights to the United States, and blamed the country's economic plight on eighteen years of American intervention. Only in relating his military successes, Beals thought, was Sandino "quite too flamboyant and boastful."

One myth exploded by Beals was the much repeated charge that Sandino was being equipped with Russian arms. Beals examined some of the rifles carried by the Sandinistas and found that they did indeed bear Russian markings. Investigation showed, however, that they had been manufactured in the United States for export to the Kerensky regime, which gave way to the Bolsheviks before the weapons could be employed against the Germans; subsequently they were sold as army surplus to Mexico, and were among the four boatloads of arms that Mexico sent to the Liberal revolutionaries just before the Nicaraguan revolution broke out. Beals was not impressed with their quality, observing that some of them ''exploded in the hands of the users.''

It was Marine air reconnaissance that finally tipped off the American authorities that a new Sandino build-up was in process. The ''squadron'' in the Managua cow pasture had been reinforced with new Corsair fighter planes, forerunners of the Navy's World War II carrier planes, and they kept a close surveillance over the mountains of Nueva Segovia province where Sandino was presumed to be hiding. In mid-October it finally became apparent to the Marine headquarters in Managua that their field commanders were right: Sandino was about to stir up trouble again.

The Marine aviators flying over the mountains of Nueva Segovia observed much activity on the trails. In October a plane piloted by Lieutenant Earl A. Thomas, with Sergeant Frank E. Dowdell as his observer, crashed near Quilali in the heart of Sandino country. The pilot of another plane in the same flight saw the two men crash-land and escape from the wreckage. A patrol was sent out to rescue them but became engaged in a heavy fire fight with an estimated three hundred guerrillas; the patrol was forced to withdraw after three of its men were killed. Marine intelligence officers later learned that Thomas and Dowdell were killed by Sandinistas after they took refuge in a cave.

About that time the Marines managed, from aerial reconnaissance and other reports, to pinpoint the center of Sandino activity. It was a mile-high, heavily forested mountain named El Chipote—meaning in Spanish slang ''back-handed slap''—in southeastern Nueva Segovia. The mountain was fifteen miles long and shaped like a battleship. On its prow Sandino had established a fortified camp scored with trenches and pitted with foxholes and machine-gun nests. The Coco River flowed down just to the south of the summit of El Chipote, the Jícaro through a valley on its western flank.

Rooting Sandino out of that stronghold became the Marines' immediate objective. On December 21, 1927, two columns set out on converging marches toward the fortified hogback of El Chipote. They were curiously undermanned, considering the fact that Marine intelligence credited Sandino with having close to a thousand men under his command. One column—one hundred fifty Marines, seven members of the Guardia, and a long pack train, commanded by Captain Richard Livingston—marched from Jinotega; another column, commanded by First Lieutenant Merton A. Richal and consisting of sixty Marines and constabulary, set out from Pueblo Nuevo. They were to meet at Quilali on the Jícaro River and join forces for the climb up El Chipote.

By the morning of December 30, both columns were within a few miles of Quilali. Suddenly Sandino's followers, awaiting their foe's slow and ponderous approach, sprang a double ambush. Less than a mile south of Quilali, as it proceeded along a narrow trail clinging to the flank of El Chipote, Captain Livingston's column was attacked by a large force of Sandinistas from concealed positions above the trail. The guerrillas rained down fire from automatic rifles and trench mortars. (The mortars, homemade, had been produced by Sandino's armory at the Butters mine a few miles up the Jícaro. They were fashioned from lengths of iron pipe, and the missiles they fired were rawhide pouches packed with scraps of iron, stones, and glass fragments; the pouches were tamped into the pipes with charges of dynamite.) Before the column could fight its way out of the trap five Marines were killed and twenty-three others wounded, six of them, including Captain Livingston, seriously. Their pack train was scattered and most of their supplies lost. Livingston's second-in-command, Lieutenant Moses J. Gould, took over the job of leading the detachment to the village of Quilali through snipers' fire on both sides of the trail.

A short time later the other column was similarly surprised a few miles west of Quilali. It took that detachment two days to fight its way out of a succession of ambushes; Lieutenant Richal himself was seriously wounded and three other Marines were also hit before they reached Quilali. Lieutenant Bruce, the machine gunner who had fought so valiantly at Ocotal, now commanded Richal's Guardia detachment; he was killed in one of the running battles.

The remains of the two columns barricaded themselves in the score of stone-walled and tile-roofed houses of Quilali; between them they could muster less than two hundred men able to shoulder arms. Against them were an estimated seven hundred guerrillas who had obviously been trained to a pitch far above that of the usual Central American bush army. The village was under constant fire. Its defenders would be starved out unless relief arrived in a hurry.

Once again it was the fledgling Marine air power, represented by the two-seater Corsairs and obsolescent de Havillands under Major Rowell's command at Managua, that was called upon to balance the odds. Planes on constant reconnaissance over rebel territory spotted the fighting at Quilali. Lieutenant Gould, now in command of the combined ground force, strung messages on wires stretched between two poles, which the pilots picked off with grappling hooks. Among other things, Gould asked if his wounded could be evacuated.

A dashing and skillful pilot, Lieutenant Christian F. Schilt, volunteered to fly out from Managua, land at Quilali, and remove the wounded—or at least try to. Meanwhile Gould and his men hacked out a landing strip. The only possible place where Schilt could land his Corsair was on the three-hundred-foot stretch of the road that ran through the village. Houses on both sides of the road were demolished and cleared away. Then, with picks and shovels dropped by other planes, Gould and his men widened the strip to seventy feet. Lieutenant Schilt would have to land on and take off from a rough patch of ground about the size of a football field.

Somehow Schilt managed to pull off the evacuation despite intense harassing fire from Sandino's men in the surrounding hills. Another Marine pilot circled overhead and poured machine-gun fire into Sandino's positions while Schilt made ten nerve-shredding landings in the besieged village, took out ten of the most seriously wounded, and brought in supplies and a relief officer; it was one of the greatest flying feats of all time. Schilt was awarded the Congressional Medal of Honor.

The Marine air unit continued to support the detachment at Quilali by dropping ammunition and supplies, and by strafing the enemy positions. Captain R. W. Peard, the officer flown in by Lieutenant Schilt, took over the command and moved it to the San Albino mine, a more suitable base for operations against Sandino's camp on the mountain towering over them. Two relief columns under Major Archibald Young also arrived, by truck and on foot. On January 14, 1928, Captain Peard led his command up the trails leading to the summit of El Chipote, supported by a flight of dive-bombing planes, and captured one of Sandino's outposts. The guerrillas' camp itself was repeatedly bombed and strafed. On January 26, Major Young's reinforcements joined them and the combined force attacked Sandino's headquarters—and found it empty.

The moment that news of the heavy fighting at the base of El Chipote was received at Washington, orders were given for a heavy reinforcement of the Marine units in Nicaragua. General Feland was restored to command there, and rifle battalions sailed once again from Guantánamo and other bases until there were 5,700 Marines on the scene. The build-up came at an embarrassing time for the United States. It was the eve of the Pan-American Congress at Havana, and many Latin-American nations were restive over the American intervention. The State Department defended the increase of troops in Nicaragua by declaring that Sandino's guerrillas were "regarded as ordinary bandits, not only by the Government of Nicaragua, but by both political parties in that country," and that American forces would stay only long enough to make certain that a free and fair election would be held. At the conference the delegates of Mexico and El Salvador tried to bring the Nicaraguan question to the floor but were outmaneuvered by the U.S. delegate, former Secretary of State Charles Evans Hughes.

Meanwhile, the Marines and their Guardia allies were launching intensive efforts to catch Sandino and stamp out his rebellion. The northern area, comprising Nueva Segovia province and the adjoining territory where Sandino's bands were operating, was declared a military zone and was handed over to Colonel Robert H. Dunlap and his 11th Marine Regiment to be pacified. His patrols moved throughout Sandino country, often supplied from the air by newly arrived Fokker transport planes. On February 27, 1928, a Marine patrol was ambushed in southern Nueva Segovia: five were killed and eight wounded before a relief column rescued them.

Several weeks later it appeared that Sandino was making a push toward Matagalpa and its coffee plantations. At the head of 150 mounted guerrillas, he occupied the large *finca* of Charles Potter, an Englishman, appropriated all the cash and supplies on the premises, enlisted a number of Potter's workers, and then amiably enough departed. Scores of refugees from the district fled to Matagalpa for protection, since it was guarded by a Marine outpost of forty-five men. Undoubtedly Sandino could have taken the town the night after he left Potter's plantation, though a battalion of Marines was being rushed there in commandeered automobiles. Instead, Sandino and his mounted force vanished in the direction of the northern mountains. Evidently he intended to employ hit-and-run tactics, in the style that would become classic when codified by Mao Tse-tung and Che Guevara. Sandino hoped to keep the country in a turmoil and prevent any American-supervised elections.

Gradually, however, the Americans succeeded in bringing most of the countryside under control, particularly in the north, where Sandino had been able to operate almost at will. Vigorous and constant patrol action, along with the systematic destruction of Sandino's supply caches, whittled down the guerrilla leader's freedom of movement. Suddenly, however, there was an outbreak of banditry on the eastern coast of Nicaragua, which had been quiet all through Sandino's activity. In April, a bandit gang raided an American-owned mine, took $12,000 in cash, and kidnapped the manager.

To combat this new menace the Coco Patrol was established under Captain Merritt A. "Red Mike" Edson, who became renowned as tactician in the jungle campaigns against the Japanese fifteen years later. The patrol, on foot and in boats, moved up and down the Coco River from the eastern lowlands to the uplands of the northwest, where it linked up with patrols from Colonel Dunlap's 11th Regiment. On several occasions Captain Edson's special force outwitted and outfought the bandits who tried to ambush it along the jungle trails. Edson developed the concept of the "fire team" to spring any traps laid for him. Specially trained, one unit of the team would build up a "base of fire" the moment the force ran into an ambush; then other elements would quickly move out to turn the enemy's flanks.

The link-up between the Coco Patrol and the 11th Regiment's patrols not only protected the mines that bandits had been raiding but reduced the guerrilla activity almost to zero. At least the country was quiet enough, by November of 1928, to hold the presidential election. An American electoral commission headed by General Frank R. McCoy and staffed by specially trained Marines supervised the voting. General Moncada, the candidate of the Liberals, won by a 20,000-vote majority over Adolfo Benard, the Conservatives' candidate. On November 5, two days after the election, *El Commercio*, the chief Liberal organ in the capital, proclaimed in its banner line: "The United States is Vindicated Before the World."

Not entirely, perhaps; but the United States did keep its promise to end the intervention as soon as it seemed feasible. The Marine contingent was gradually reduced as the Guardia was trained by American officers to take over the job of maintaining order. The 11th Marine Regiment, however, stayed at its posts in northern Nicaragua until March, 1931. The reason for its continued presence was the still intransigent Sandino. Even after the Liberal victory at the polls, he stayed in the hills and maintained his disloyal opposition. Financed from the outside, he had ''begun to carry on radical propaganda in the interior,'' as Dana Gardner Munro has written, having veered leftward of both legal political parties.

Sandino stayed on the run until 1933, when a peace agreement was worked out by Dr. Sacasa, who had succeeded to the presidency. Several months later, Sandino was engaged in disarmament talks at Managua with Sacasa and Anastasio Somoza, who was the commander of the Guardia at the time. While Sandino dined with Sacasa's family and a few other guests on the night of February 21, 1934, members of the Guardia, outraged by the leniency granted him under Sacasa's amnesty, and perhaps encouraged by the American minister, Arthur Bliss Lane, agreed that the time had come to kill Sandino. Group responsibility was assured by signing a pact that they called ''The Death of Caesar.'' When Sacasa's congenial group dispersed at about ten o'clock, their automobiles were halted as they emerged from Sacasa's grounds and the Sandinistas among them were whisked off to the Managua airfield to be executed. Somoza himself was conveniently in another part of town and, to the disbelief of the Sandinistas, refused to interpose his authority. A machine gun was positioned, a signal was given, and the prisoners were gunned down. With the Sandinista leadership went the whole movement; its remnants were wiped out within weeks.

Somoza refused to punish those responsible for the assassination. And so the theme of violence, which runs through Nicaraguan political history with the wearying persistence of a Greek tragedy, was sustained. Soon after, Somoza forced Dr. Sacasa to resign, and himself assumed the presidency. Twenty-two years later, still the dictator-president, General Somoza in his turn was assassinated. He has been succeeded in the presidency by his two sons. Early in 1967, Nicaraguan politics again figured in the news, no doubt bemusing veterans of the Marine campaigns of forty years ago who had believed they were bringing the American brand of democracy to that country. Anastasio Somoza, Jr., the younger son, was elected as expected—but only after a flare-up of street fighting in the capital.

The rebellious spirit of Augusto Sandino was not summoned up in any of the news reports of the last election. But it lives on, not only in the mountains where he fought, but as an exemplar throughout the Southern Hemisphere. He was the first to defy the armed power of the Yankee Colossus, and to show that such defiance could be relatively successful if conducted on sound guerrilla principles. Futhermore, his revolution within a revolution, tiny in geographic scope, demonstrated to all who feel that the United States is too quick to intervene in the affairs of its southern neighbors that the American hegemony is maintained by force. The lessons of his rebellion continue to be studied, if not in the U.S. staff colleges, then

in the bush camps of Colombia, Venezuela, and other disaffected areas where
guerrillas still fight.

A free-lance historian and biographer, Richard O'Connor is the author of Ambrose Bierce, *published last spring, and co-author (with Dale Walker) of* The Lost Revolutionary: A Biography of John Reed, *which appeared in the fall.*

The author found Harold Denny's Dollars for Bullets *(Dial, 1929) especially useful in preparing this article;* Banana Gold, *by Carleton Beals (Lipparing, 1932), also makes good further reading. A recent addition to the literature on the subject, and perhaps the most complete, is* The Sandino Affair, *by Neill Macaulay (Quadrangle, 1967).*

Part Three

Between Two World Wars

Discord and Prosperity, Depression and a New Deal

The diversity which has characterized American life and history was abundantly evident in the period between the two world wars. In the course of some twenty years the nation passed through a wrenching postwar economic recession and its first hysteric reaction to the threat of Communism, into the booming prosperity and carefree new freedom of the mid-1920s (disturbed, albeit, by the conformist pressures of nativist and fundamentalist revivals). Then, so suddenly and so soon, gloom, despair and poverty replaced the carefree days of prosperity in the wake of the stock market crash of 1929 and the onset of the worst economic collapse in United States history. The Great Depression posed the most serious test of the society and its institutions since the upheaval of the Civil War. Efforts of the Hoover and Roosevelt administrations to cope with the crisis fell short; it took another crisis, World War II, to pull the nation out of the depression.

Allan Damon examines the opening phase of the period in his account of the nation's first 'red scare.' The multiplicity of forces at work in the immediate post-war years—the end of the passionate wartime crusade, disillusionment over the outcome of the peace negotiations, business cutbacks and massive unemployment, a new rush of immigrants from war torn Europe—all were ingredients in this brief but significant hysteria about foreign enemies within America.

The Teapot Dome scandals of the Harding administration, detailed by Bruce Bliven, point to one aspect of the 1920's reaction to the idealistic altruism of Wilsonian, World War I progressivism. Harding's return to 'normalcy'—that is, the self-conscious effort of his administration to reestablish small scale, non-regulatory government supportive of business enterprise—produced examples of corrupt activities by public officials comparable in scope only to those of the Grant and, more recently, the Reagan administrations.

One depression era episode destined to survive in the public memory is that of the veterans' march on Washington in 1932. John Weaver describes these jobless, destitute veterans of the First World War and discusses the piteous response of the Congress and the Hoover administration to their efforts to secure federal government assistance. This episode gives one some sense of the nature of the challenges posed by the Great Depression.

Stephen Sears' account of the 1937 sit-down strike by the United Auto Workers against the General Motors Corporation demonstrates that, even after two elections and four years of Franklin Roosevelt's New Deal, the strains of the depression persisted. And yet, they were of a different sort. Some of the jobless of 1932 had found employment as a result of New Deal recovery programs, and with the legal support of the Wagner Act of 1935, many workers had once again sought strength and security through unionization. Seen from the vantage point of the 1950s and beyond, the 1937 UAW victory over GM and the subsequent rise of 'big labor' under the Congress of Industrial Organizations represented a major permanent reform achievement of the New Deal years.

The Great
Red Scare

Allan L. Damon

In November, 1919, and again in January, 1920, federal agents of the Department of Justice conducted a series of lightning-like raids on private houses and public buildings in cities across the United States and took into custody upwards of three thousand aliens suspected of plotting to overthrow the government. The mass arrests were enthusiastically acclaimed as Attorney General A. Mitchell Palmer's answer to "the sinister agitation of men and women aliens . . . either in the pay or under the criminal spell of Trotsky and Lenin." Indeed, within hours of the January roundup, William J. Flynn of the Bureau of Investigation (now the F.B.I.) told newsmen, "I believe that with these raids the backbone of the radical movement in America is broken."

If, as some have said, A. Mitchell Palmer was "a nervous man," he had a great deal of company in the spring and summer of 1919. Only a year later, William Allen White was to write a friend, "What a God-dammed world this is! . . . If anyone had told me ten years ago that our country would be what it is today . . . I should have questioned his reason." It was a sentiment that many Americans had known in the months following World War I; for amidst the normal but unsettling confusion that marked the nation's transition from war to peace, there had appeared signs of deep-seated dislocations seemingly unlike any the country had experienced before.

There was, to begin with, considerable uncertainty over the peace treaty that Wilson had brought back from Versailles. As the Senate and the nation argued over its terms, a bitter debate on the League of Nations unleashed political passions lately held in check by a wartime truce. A business recession had set in, and although it was not unexpected, its crippling effects were intensified by a series of explosive industrial disputes.

Labor and management had been uneasy partners under federal controls during the war; now they were again familiar antagonists in what, by the year's end, totalled 3,600 separate strikes. Collective bargaining, higher wages, shorter work days, and union recognition were generally the issues at stake, but as violence and instability mounted—riots were common that year—the labor unrest took on a sinister cast. Inevitably there were those who remembered the old slogan of the discredited and now nearly defunct Industrial Workers of the World: "Every strike is a little revolution and a dress rehearsal for the big one." Typical headlines of the day proclaimed: "Red Peril Here" . . . "Reds Directing Strike" . . . "Test for Revolution." By autumn, the widely respected *Literary Digest* warned, "Outside of Russia, the storm center of Bolshevism is in the United States."

There seemed to be, indeed, cause for alarm. Communism had triumphed in Russia and in Hungary; semi-anarchy reigned in postwar Germany; and there was political unrest in Poland, Italy, India, and China. The Third International had been organized in the spring of 1919 with world-wide revolution as its goal, and in the summer not one but two Communist parties were formed in the United States.

A far more frightening phenomenon had also appeared. On April 29, Mayor Ole Hanson of Seattle, Washington, had received a package containing sulphuric acid and dynamite caps. The triggering device had failed to operate, however, and Hanson, an outspoken foe of the I.W.W. and other radical groups, survived; he told reporters that the infernal machine was "big enough to blow out the side of the Country-City Building."

Hardly had the papers carried that story when a brown-paper parcel, bearing the return address of Gimbel Brothers in New York, arrived at the Atlanta, Georgia, home of Senator Thomas W. Hardwick. The Senator, chairman of the Committee on Immigration, was not in, and a maid unwrapped the package. This time the detonator functioned properly and the parcel exploded, ripping off her hands.

By nightfall, the Hardwick bombing was front-page news. Charles Kaplan, a New York postal clerk on his way home by subway, was alerted by the newspaper description of the package delivered to the Senator's home. He quickly changed trains and hurried back to the General Post Office, where he remembered having seen sixteen small, brown-paper boxes set aside on a shelf because of insufficient postage. They were there all with counterfeit Gimbel labels, and each addressed to a high-ranking government official or a well-known private citizen. Included were Attorney General Palmer, Secretary of Labor William B. Wilson, Supreme Court Justice Oliver Wendell Holmes, Jr., Judge Kenesaw Mountain Landis, John D. Rockefeller, and J. P. Morgan, Jr. Every package contained a bomb.

During the next week, watchful postal inspectors elsewhere in the country turned up sixteen more, each in its distinctive wrapper and addressed to a prominent person. The identity of the sender was never learned, but the newspapers and probably a majority of the public believed that the parcels had come from a Red bomb shop.

A month later, on June 1, seven explosions in five eastern cities ripped apart homes, public buildings, and a rectory, killing one man. In Washington that same night, an assassin came after the Attorney General again. Palmer had been reading in the first-floor library of his home in a quiet residential section of the city. At about eleven o'clock he put aside his book and went upstairs. He and Mrs. Palmer had just retired when the thump of something hitting the front porch echoed through the house and a violent explosion shattered windows throughout the neighborhood. The Palmers were unhurt, but the downstairs front of the house, including the library, was ruined. On the lawn, in the street, and on the sidewalk of Assistant Secretary of the Navy Franklin Delano Roosevelt's home opposite, "great chunks of human being" told the story. What had saved the Palmers from death was the clumsiness of the bomber, who evidently had stumbled and fallen, dropping the bomb before it could do serious damage to anyone but himself. Near the shattered body on Palmer's lawn and scattered along the street lay some fifty copies of *Plain Words,* an anarchist pamphlet that promised death to government officials ("There will have to be murder; we will kill. . . .") and proclaimed the triumph of the revolution.

Although, according to a reporter, Palmer remained "the coolest and most collected person" in the crowd that gathered to examine the wreckage, by morning he was understandably a badly frightened man. As he learned of the other bombings elsewhere on the eastern seaboard, he saw it all as part of a Red conspiracy to destroy the American way of life. He must act to save it.

The Attorney General had little difficulty persuading Congress to grant the Justice Department funds for the task. Yet as the summer of 1919 came on, Palmer appeared to be hesitating. The slowness of his preparations came as no surprise to his friends; he had always been a meticulous and somewhat cautious planner. But to many editors who daily ran stories of new Red plots, the Attorney General seemed reluctant to crush the threat the nation faced.

In truth, Palmer was at this point uncertain about the course he should follow. After the excitement of the bombings had died down, and despite the speed with which he had sought congressional aid, he became increasingly skeptical that the Reds were as active as many people claimed. Several of his close advisers predicted that the bombers would strike again and again; nothing of the kind happened. They warned that the Fourth of July would bring Bolshevik uprisings in major cities; the day passed quietly. Palmer adopted a policy of watchful waiting.

In part, his liberalism restrained him. A Wilsonian to the core, he believed strongly in the constitutional protections of the Bill of Rights, which as Attorney General he had sworn to uphold. He had been elected to Congress in 1908 with support from Pennsylvania steelworkers, coal miners, and clay-pit laborers, many of whom were recent immigrants. Now, years later, he continued to think of himself as "a radical friend of labor," and despite public pressures to the contrary, he had thus far refused to intervene in the strikes that were crippling the economy.

That kind of liberal restraint had marked his entire political career and, he was sure, had helped him move with comparative ease from the obscurity of a Pennsylvania law practice to the prominence of a Cabinet post. Given the right set of circumstances, it might conceivably carry him on to greater power and prestige in the White House itself.

Such a thought was not an idle dream, for at forty-seven the Attorney General was superbly equipped for the part. Tall, trim, and handsome, Palmer used his many talents with skill and grace. Besides his commanding physical presence, he had a quick and active mind, self-assurance in abundance, and above all, boundless energy. If—as one biographer has written—he was at times "too combative, too dogmatic, and too conceited" for his own good, he nevertheless had made more friends than enemies in high places. And if—as another has noted—his major weakness lay in his effort always "to win power by carefully attuning himself to what he felt were the strong desires of most Americans," he was no mere opportunist. He chose the issues he would support as much from deep personal belief as from political expediency.

Born of Quaker parents of moderate means, he was determined, he once wrote, "to be somebody," and his drive for power did not slacken as the years wore on. Graduating *summa cum laude* from Swarthmore before he was nineteen, he read law in the office of a former congressman, entered a lucrative practice at Stroudsburg, and soon became embroiled in the free-wheeling political life of the local scene. By 1909 he was in Washington, where he swiftly rose to a position of leadership. At the end of his first year in the House, he secured a seat on the powerful Ways and Means Committee, placed himself in the forefront of the progressive Democratic wing, and during three successive terms became identified with tariff reform and the cause of labor.

At the Baltimore convention of 1912 he delivered his state's delegation to Woodrow Wilson, hoping for the post of Attorney General as a reward. But the expected appointment fell through: instead, Wilson decided to name him Secretary of War. "I am a man of peace," Palmer said, declining the offer, and he returned to the House once more. Two years later he suffered his first major setback when, acceding to the President's blandishments, he entered a hopeless Senate race in Pennsylvania and went down to defeat.

With America's entry into World War I, Palmer was again in the national news. Despite his professed pacifism he was fiercely patriotic; "I made up my mind that I just must get into it somehow, even if I had to carry a gun as a private," he told a friend. His change of heart, however, never carried him to that extreme, and he accepted Wilson's appointment as custodian of property in the United States owned by enemy aliens. For over a year he worked with such vigor and aggressiveness that the press labelled him the "Fighting Quaker," a title he wore as a badge of honor. Some of his critics suspected that his prowar views were tied to his political hopes, but Palmer emerged from the war with his popularity intact.

In March, 1919, he claimed his long-awaited reward, appointment as Attorney General of the United States.

He had been three months on the job when the bomb burst outside his home. Despite his uncertainty about the seriousness of the Red threat, Palmer did proceed to reorganize the Department of Justice to cope with the problem. By August he had created the General Intelligence Division, a special arm within the Bureau of Investigation, to root out the Communist conspiracy if one existed. He gave charge of the new bureau to J. Edgar Hoover, a twenty-four-year-old lawyer who, in the summer of 1917, had come fresh from George Washington University Law School to serve in the Department of Justice as an aide in charge of Enemy Alien Registration. Now, as a special assistant to Palmer, Hoover with his G.I.D. put together an elaborate filing system of over 200,000 cross-indexed cards containing information on 60,000 persons, several hundred newspapers, and dozens of organizations considered dangerous to the national interest.

But this quiet, systematic preparation did nothing to allay the fears of the public, or to satisfy their panicky desire for drastic action. For if the nation had been alarmed by the riots and bombs of the spring, it was terrified by the events of late summer and early fall.

July brought race riots in Cleveland and in Washington, D.C. Labor unrest continued without letup all summer long. Then, during the first week of September, the Communist party and the Communist Labor party emerged from separate Chicago conventions. Almost immediately there were reports that their combined memberships exceeded 100,000; some accounts placed the number at six times that figure. Recent studies have shown that the most modest of these estimates was greatly exaggerated; but in the fall of 1919 it was the rumors that counted.

Already groups like the National Security League had published stories to the effect that most labor unions, the leading universities, some churches, the League of Women Voters, and a host of other organizations were under Red control or sympathetic to the cause. Some newspapers asserted that outspoken reformers like John Dewey, Roscoe Pound, Jane Addams, Robert M. La Follette, and Thorstein Veblen were linked to the growing Red menace.

In such an atmosphere and at such a time, it was difficult to know what was true and what was not. But as Bolshevism in Russia hardened into tyranny, and as magazine articles by the score rang continuous changes on the same terrifying theme of *it must not happen here,* even those who had discounted the earlier scare headlines became alarmed.

In September the Boston police went on strike. Two days of limited violence and looting followed before volunteers and some 5,000 National Guardsmen restored order. Governor Calvin Coolidge, who had done little to correct the situation, then sent his famous telegram to the A.F. of L's Samuel Gompers saying. "There is no right to strike against the public safety by anybody, anywhere, any time" (see "The Strike That Made a President" in the October, 1963, AMERICAN HERITAGE). Later in the month federal troops were sent to quiet the nation's steel towns, where a bitter dispute had just begun. When 349,000 coal miners left the pits on November 1, the public feared the beginning of a nationwide general strike, or worse.

Meanwhile, Attorney General Palmer had been suffering under a terrific barrage of public criticism. "I was shouted at from every editorial sanctum in America from sea to sea," he complained later. "I was preached upon from every pulpit; I was urged to do something and do it now, and do it quick and do it in a way that would bring results." In mid-October of 1919, the Senate took up the cry; it unanimously demanded an explanation for Palmer's inaction, and in a censure resolution implied that he might well face removal from his post.

The Senate's censure was harsh blow, especially in the light of Palmer's presidential dreams. Woodrow Wilson's debilitating stroke in mid-autumn had already awakened speculation among many men about possible successors in the election year ahead. How seriously Palmer took his own candidacy at this point is anybody's guess (he did not mention it openly until February, 1920); but he was too experienced a politician not to know that once he lost the public's favor he would be hard pressed to regain it. It is not surprising that a man of his ambition began to react profoundly to the clamor that he "do something."

Moreover, Palmer was surrounded by men who had long since become convinced that the Red menace was real. Among his Cabinet colleagues, Secretary of War Newton D. Baker, Secretary of the Navy Josephus Daniels, and Secretary of State Robert Lansing had been writing and speaking about the threat of revolution from early summer on. Even President Wilson had inserted antiradical themes in his speeches on behalf of the League a few days before he fell ill. But it was the men whom Palmer numbered among his closest advisers in the Department of Justice itself whose influence was greatest. They had taken the Reds very seriously from the start. To be sure, almost all the information they possessed had come from theoretical discussions in radical newspapers and books; there was little worthwhile evidence of active preparation for revolt. Nonetheless, to these advisers, where there was smoke there was probably fire. They were ready to act.

By November, Palmer was ready too. Now convinced by his own reading of anarchist literature that the nation was besieged by "thousands of aliens, who were the direct allies of Trotsky," he declared that the time had passed when it was possible or even desirable to draw "nice distinctions . . . between the theoretical ideals of the radicals and their actual violations of our national law."

The time for watching and waiting was over. "Like a prairie-fire," he himself wrote in *Forum* magazine the next year, "the blaze of revolution was sweeping over every institution of law and order. . . . It was eating its way into the homes of the American workman, its sharp tongues of revolutionary heat were licking the altars of the churches, leaping into the belfry of the school bell, crawling into the sacred corners of American homes, seeking to replace marriage vows with libertine law, burning up the foundations of society.'' To put out the fires, Palmer decided to enforce a part of the immigration code, introduced during the war, that outlawed anarchism in all its forms. Aliens who violated that code, even if only by reading or receiving anarchist publications, could be arrested and, if found guilty, deported.

There was a beautiful simplicity to Palmer's solution. Deportation hearings were neither lengthy nor complex. They were handled as executive functions by the immigration officers of the Department of Labor. Although the aliens were supposed to be protected by the procedural safeguards of the Bill of Rights, only minimum proof (usually a warrant of cause) was needed to show that some part of the immigration code had been violated. The rulings of the hearing officers were, in effect, arbitrary, checked only by the construction of the deportation statutes, a possible appeal to the Secretary of Labor, or, in rare instances, by a writ of habeas corpus, which led to a federal court trial. Palmer decided to test both the effectiveness of deportation as an anti-Red measure, and the public's response.

On the night of November 7, 1919, federal agents from the Bureau of Investigation and city policemen quietly surrounded the Russian People's House on East Fifteenth Street in New York. Inside the four-story brownstone that served as a meeting place and recreation center for Russian aliens, some two hundred men and boys were at work in night-school classes. That evening was the anniversary of the Bolshevik uprising in Petrograd two years before, but the directors of the school had planned no special observance, even though the school's sponsor, the Federation of Unions of Russian Workers in the United States and Canada, had been a leading publisher of anarchist tracts.

Shortly after nine o'clock the agents swarmed into the building. ''The harsh command to 'shut up, there, you,' brought silence'' in the classrooms, the *New York Times* reported next day, and in the hush that followed, the agents announced that all present were under arrest. A teacher who asked why (for no warrants had been produced) took a blow in the face that shattered his glasses. Then, while some agents searched the bewildered suspects for weapons, city policemen tore open locked files, overturned desks, pulled down pictures from the wall, and rolled up rugs in an unsuccessful hunt for incriminating evidence. At last, no weapons having been found, they herded the prisoners toward the stairs and—as an investigator from the National Council of Churches reported later—forced them to run a gantlet of officers who lined the stairwell armed with blackjacks. By the time the suspects reached the agents' headquarters, thirty-three of them required medical treatment. Their bandaged heads and blackened eyes, the *Times* remarked, were "souvenirs of the new attitude of aggressiveness which had been assumed by the Federal agents against Reds or suspected Reds."

Elsewhere in the nation that night, federal officers in nine other cities east of the Mississippi raided other Russian centers. In all, about four hundred and fifty persons were rounded up. Before the night was over, more than half of them were released as innocent, but Attorney General Palmer was distinctly pleased with the results.

For by morning he was a national hero, praised by the very press that only the week before had been railing at him and demanding his resignation. Now, as one paper put it, he was "a tower of strength to his countrymen." His new answer to the Reds, said another, was "S.O.S.—Ship or Shoot." Still another suggested that the new year might bring a three-point trade program of "import—export—deport."

By December, Palmer was riding the crest of enthusiastic public support. Working quickly now, he secured deportation orders for 199 Russians who had been found guilty under the immigration law. Taken to Ellis Island, they were joined by fifty other deportees, including Alexander Berkman, the would-be assassin of Henry Clay Frick in the Homestead Strike twenty-seven years before, and Emma Goldman, a well-known anarchist writer whose work had allegedly inspired Leon Czolgosz to murder President McKinley. All 249 aliens were to be deported to Russia by way of Finland, the Finnish government having agreed to act in this case as the agent for the United States, which had yet to recognize the Bolshevik regime.

Although immigration officials had promised that no married men would be deported and that ample time would be given the aliens to settle their affairs, neither pledge was honored. In the early hours of December 21, the aliens boarded the *Buford*, an ancient army transport now nicknamed "the Soviet Ark." Two hundred fifty armed soldiers patrolled the decks, but, with the exception of a short-lived hunger strike, the voyage passed uneventfully. In mid-January, 1920, the *Buford* docked at Hango, Finland, and under a flag of truce—the Finns were now at war with Russia—the deportees passed into Soviet hands.*

*After the furor attending their departure from the United States and the news of their arrival in Russia, the *Buford* deportees dropped out of sight. The majority apparently remained in Russia, but two, at least, did not. Berkman, ever the anarchist, was quickly disillusioned by what he found in the Communist state, and by 1925 had published two highly critical books, *The Bolshevik Myth* and *The Anticlimax*. He had, of course, left Russia by then, and he spent the remaining years of his life wandering aimlessly through Europe. He committed suicide in Nice, France, in 1936.

Following disagreements and an open break with the Bolsheviks in 1921, Emma Goldman too left the country and two years later wrote *My Disillusionment* 14
In 1924 she was permitted to re-enter the United States for a lecture tour under the terms of a curious arrangement whereby she was not permitted to discuss politics in public. She was not allowed to remain, however, and crossed the border into Canada. She died in Toronto in 1940.

Meanwhile Palmer readied a second attack on the Reds. If the November raid had netted hundreds, the new series would bring in thousands. Hoping to speed the process, Palmer asked Secretary of Labor Wilson to change that part of the deportation rules that permitted the aliens to secure counsel, and at the same time he requested a blanket deportation warrant to cover any aliens who might be arrested once the raids began. Wilson refused both requests, emphasizing that the immigrants, despite their lack of citizenship, were nonetheless entitled to the protection of the Bill of Rights. Palmer, no longer sounding like a confirmed liberal, insisted that all too often it was lawbreakers, not the innocent, who were protected by these legal safeguards, but Wilson held firm.

For the moment, the Attorney General was stymied. Then, in mid-December, Secretary Wilson went on sick leave. His duties were divided between Louis F. Post, his assistant, and John W. Abercrombie, the Labor Department's solicitor and a Palmer appointee. To Palmer's relief, Post, whom the press had labelled a "Bolshie coddler," took up the Secretary's main duties, while Abercrombie assumed control of immigration. On December 29, Abercrombie consented to a change in Rule 22 of the deportation-hearing procedure so that it no longer required the arresting officers to inform aliens of either their right to counsel or the charges against them. Two days later he issued some 3,000 mimeographed warrants for the arrest of aliens whose names were to be entered in the blanks.

The night of January 2 was chosen for a new set of raids. Agents who had infiltrated Communist cells were asked to arrange meetings for that evening "to facilitate arrests." The others were instructed to bring in as many aliens as they could find. Their orders, issued over the signature of Frank Burke, the assistant director of the Bureau of Investigation, said, in part, "I leave it entirely to your discretion as to the method by which you gain access to such places [where aliens might be]. . . . If, due to local conditions in your territory, you find that it is absolutely necessary to obtain a search warrant for the premises, you should communicate with the local authorities a few hours before the time for the arrests is set." Otherwise plans for the raids were to be kept secret. The aliens were to be held incommunicado, and the agents were urged to secure "confessions" as quickly as possible.

The all-out raid went off on schedule in thirty-three cities in twenty-three states. Palmer's men were joined by local police, and in a few instances, though Palmer had earlier refused their help, by volunteer members of patriotic societies like the National Security League. By midnight of January 2 they had collected well over 3,000 suspects from the eastern industrial states, and from California, Washington, and Oregon in the West. The true number will never be known, for the records of that evening are hopelessly confused and in some areas nonexistent. All 3,000 mimeographed warrants were used—the names in many instances being added after the arrests were made—and an estimated 2,000 other suspects were picked up and held for some time without being charged.

Whatever the number, the results were spectacular. Editorial pages swiftly echoed the praises of public officials, and Palmer's reputation was at an all-time high. The effect of the raids, said the *New York Times,* should be "far-reaching and beneficial." Even the Washington *Post,* which had called the November arrests "a serious mistake," urged that the deportation of the new suspects take place as speedily as possible. "There is not time to waste," it said, "on hairsplitting over infringement of liberty." The Philadelphia *Inquirer* ran a jovial headline: ALL ABOARD FOR THE NEXT SOVIET ARK.

It was not, however, to be all that easy. After the initial enthusiasm had died down, and as complaints of wanton disregard of the aliens' civil rights found their way into print, a number of people began to question whether Palmer had not done more harm than good. The National Council of Churches started an investigation of the events of January 2. So did the Department of Labor. In Detroit a group of businessmen that included dime-store magnate S. S. Kresge looked into the raids that had taken place in that vicinity. Elsewhere other organizations did the same.

Their combined evidence revealed some shocking particulars. One man in Newark had been apprehended simply because—as the arresting officer put it—he "looked like a radical." Boston agents with drawn pistols had broken into the bedroom of a sleeping woman at 6 A.M. and dragged her off to headquarters without a warrant, only to find that she was an American citizen with no Communist connections. Attracted by the commotion on East Fifteenth Street, where the Russian People's House had again been raided, a New Yorker questioned a policeman about what was going on and shortly found himself on his way to jail. Police in Detroit arrested every diner in one foreign restaurant, and jailed an entire orchestra. Philadelphia agents booked a choral society en masse, and in Hartford, Connecticut, sympathetic aliens who were inquiring about some imprisoned friends were themselves held as suspects for nearly a week. Of 142 persons arrested in Buffalo, thirty-one turned out to be cases of "mistaken identity." In Detroit, where nearly eight hundred were arrested, less than four hundred warrants were served; four hundred and fifty warrants arrived to cover the other suspects two weeks after the raids had taken place.

Treatment of the aliens after the roundups was in many cases harsh. Four hundred men rounded up in New England were jammed into an under-heated and overcrowded prison on Deer Island in Boston Harbor; there, in the next few weeks, one of them went insane, another jumped to his death from the fifth floor of the main cell block, and several others attempted suicide. When they were finally released, as most of them were, many were ill and a number showed signs of beatings. In Detroit, eight hundred suspects were lodged in a corridor of the United States Post Office building, without exterior ventilation, beds, or blankets. No food was distributed for twenty-four hours, and there was one toilet for the entire group. After two days of questioning, 340 of them were released, but over a hundred were imprisoned for more than a week in a detention cell 24 by 30 feet in the basement of the Municipal Building, where they lived on coffee and biscuits.

But the investigating committees discovered more than just dramatic instances of physical mistreatment. Twelve nationally known lawyers, including the Harvard Law School's Felix Frankfurter, Roscoe Pound, and Zechariah Chafee, Jr., issued at the end of May "A Report on the Illegal Practices of the United States Department of Justice." It was a sweeping indictment, solidly supported by evidence, of Palmer and his raids.

The real danger to the country, the lawyers wrote, lay not in the possibility of Red revolution, but in Palmer's obvious misuse of federal power. The Department of Justice, they said, had ignored due process of law in favor of "illegal acts," "wholesale arrests," and "wanton violence." Although the Fourth Amendment to the Consitution protects against arrest without prior warrant, Palmer's men had obtained only 3,000 writs for the more than 5,000 aliens eventually detained. Most of the warrants were defective, in any case; either they lacked substantiating proof, or they were unsworn and unsigned. All too frequently, they were unserved as well. "Instead of showing me a warrant," one suspect complained, "they showed me a gun." In the majority of cases, the federal agents carried no search warrants, either.

The twelve lawyers charged in their report that the raiders had violated the Fifth Amendment by making use of illegally obtained or hearsay evidence, or by resorting to dubious or fraudulent proof. At least two of the accused, for example, were held to be radicals on the grounds that they had been photographed reading Russian-language newspapers. Tickets to Socialist and Communist social functions, magazine subscription lists, post cards and letters from avowed Communists, and group photographs were introduced by the agents as acceptable evidence that suspected aliens belonged to revolutionary organizations. A New Jersey man was held because agents found plans for "an infernal machine" in his home; the mysterious drawings turned out to be blueprints for a phonograph. One agent turned in a stack of mock rifles from a dramatic society's prop room, but these and three 22 caliber target pistols were the only firearms Palmer's men found in any of the raids.

The lawyers' report went on to cite violations of the Sixth and Eighth Amendments. In many cases, counsel had been denied; no witnesses had been produced; interpreters had not been provided though few of the prisoners spoke fluent English; confessions had been obtained under the "third degree"; and bail had often been set at an excessively high figure.

Palmer at first refused to concede that any of this was true. But as the evidence mounted, he finally admitted that "some" illegal acts might have taken place. "Trying to protect the community against moral rats," he declared some time afterward, "you sometimes get to thinking more of your trap's effectiveness than of its lawful construction." Hearing this, Louis Post ruefully noted that whatever Palmer might think, "the traps had been wretchedly put together." Judge

George W. Anderson of the district court in Boston added, "A mob is a mob, whether made up of government officials acting under the instructions of the Justice Department, or of criminals and loafers."

By the spring of 1920, Palmer's anti-Red crusade was beginning to fall apart. In March, Abercrombie left the Department of Labor, and Post took his place. He immediately cancelled 2,000 of the original warrants as defective, and with the assistance of federal judges like Anderson, expedited hearings for those prisoners who remained in custody. Although Palmer had predicted that 2,720 aliens from the January raids would be deported, in the end only 556 were. In all, more than 4,000 suspects were released.

Shattered, the Attorney General urged Congress to impeach Post as a Communist sympathizer whose failure to press for convictions had let many dangerous radicals go free. After a month-long hearing, Post was found innocent and returned to his duties. Two months later, in June, Palmer himself was called before the House to answer charges that he had misused his office. The hearings ended inconclusively, but the charges were revived by the Senate Judiciary Committee the following year.

In a stormy committee session that began in January, 1921, Palmer stubbornly defended what his men had done. "I apologize for nothing," he told the committee. "I glory in it. I point with pride and enthusiasm to the results of that work. . . . [If my agents] were a little rough and unkind, or short and curt, with these alien agitators . . . I think it might well be overlooked in the general good to the country which has come from it."

By the time Palmer made his final statements on the raids, he was finished politically. He had flatly predicted a Communist uprising in May, 1920, and again on the Fourth of July. At first the press took him seriously, but when nothing happened the papers took to greeting his remarks with derision instead of alarm. For many people that summer, the Fighting Quaker had become a Don Quixote attacking an enemy that did not exist.

But he made one last, bold effort. In February, 1920, he had announced his candidacy for the Democratic presidential nomination, and when the convention opened in San Francisco late in June he had considerable support from the party regulars who remembered his long years of faithful service and who had benefited from his use of patronage when it was his to give. Others in the party, however, gravely doubted his ability to win, especially in the cities. It was clear to all that he had now lost the labor vote (one union magazine accused him of having used "the mailed fist of the autocratic tyrant"), and his own failure to define his stand on the League and on Prohibition worked against him. When the balloting began

on July 2, he held the lead over his closest rival, William G. McAdoo, Wilson's
Secretary of the Treasury and son-in-law, but he failed to get a majority. Thirty-
seven ballots later, Palmer conceded the nomination, released the delegates who
still supported him, and retired as the convention nominated Ohio's governor,
James M. Cox.

His presidential dreams were over, and so was the Red Scare. Had the raids
of January not fallen into disrepute by June, Palmer might have gone on to win in
San Francisco. As it was, he returned to Washington a beaten man, and when he
left the Cabinet in the spring of 1921, his departure was almost unnoticed by the
papers that only a year before had bannered his name in their headlines. With the
advent of the new administration, the Senate committee that was still investigating
Palmer's work ended its deliberations; when its report was finally published two
years later, no one much cared that the committee had passed no judgments but
had merely offered a transcript of the testimony it had heard.

By then a general calm had settled on the nation and the world. Europe was
rebuilding. Lenin had pulled back from his program of immediate world revolution
and was turning his Russian people toward the quasi-capitalism of the New
Economic Policy. The American economy was slowly coming back to normal, and
management and labor had achieved a temporary peace. The press, which had done
much to keep the public alerted to the activities of the domestic Reds, had found
other topics to pursue.

There were still to be anti-Communist crusades in the years ahead, and the
anti-alien sentiments that had led to the Palmer raids in the first place found expression in restrictive immigration laws and in the public uproar during the Sacco-
Vanzetti trial. But most Americans were content to feel that the crisis had passed,
if indeed there had been a crisis at all. In 1924 J. Edgar Hoover moved on to
become the first (and thus far, only) director of the F.B.I. and periodically issued
warnings that a Red threat was abroad in the land, but he never again resorted to
the slap-dash techniques that he and his associates had developed in the days of the
G.I.D.

In 1922 Palmer suffered the first of several heart attacks and retired from the
political scene. A decade later, in an act that some have construed as making
amends, he returned briefly to draft a Democratic program of moderate reform that
served as one basis for F.D.R.'s New Deal campaign. Four years later, A. Mitchell
Palmer was dead.

His old associates in government gathered for his funeral and paid homage
for the progressive role he had played in his congressional days. But the nation as
a whole remembered him only as the man they had goaded into a series of discred-

ited raids that struck at the heart of American freedom. Perhaps that is the way it should be. For if Palmer at times displayed the best that was in the American tradition, in 1920 he very nearly gave it all away in succumbing to the hysteria of the great Red Scare.

Mr. Damon, who for many years has worked as a researcher for AMERICAN HERITAGE, *checking articles for accuracy before publication, teaches history in Chappaqua, New York. He recommends for further reading* A. Mitchell Palmer: Politician, *by Stanley Coben (Columbia University Press, 1963);* Red Scare: a Study in National Hysteria, 1919–1920, *by Robert K. Murray (University of Minnesota Press, 1955); and* The Roots of American Communism, *by Theodore Draper (Viking, 1957).*

Tempest Over Teapot

Bruce Bliven

In the spring of 1920, very few realistic Democrats expected to win that autumn's presidential election. Their party had been in power for nearly eight years, including the World War, and had accumulated all the assorted resentments invariably incurred in wartime. Their situation was not helped by the fact that President Wilson lay ill and incapacitated in the White House while his wife and his doctor ran the Executive branch of the government.

The Republicans were correspondingly optimistic, as I knew better than most people. In that year I was managing editor of the liberal New York afternoon newspaper, *The Globe*, and naturally, as an editor who really preferred to write, I assigned myself the juicy job of interviewing all the potential presidential candidates of both parties, asking them identical questions so that their answers could be compared. I found most of the possible Democratic candidates lukewarm indeed. When I went to Miami to talk to Governor James M. Cox of Ohio, the cold-faced, weary, hard-driven man who finally got the Democratic nod, he breathed fire for public quotation; privately, he was pessimistic. He considered the nomination as hardly more than a plaque presented for meritorious past service, to be hung on the wall of his den along with the gilded golf ball with which he had once made a hole-in-one.

This impression was confirmed when I went out to San Francisco to cover the Democratic national convention. The delegates fell in love with the city—who doesn't—and they were happy with the excellent connections with bootleggers that their hosts had provided; but I found nobody who felt that the party had any real chance of winning. Having picked Cox to head the ticket, the delegates rather casually chose as his running mate a tall, athletic young unknown with a good political name—Franklin D. Roosevelt.

But there had been a very different attitude when I made my rounds among the GOP possibilities. General Leonard Wood, Governor Frank Lowden of Illinois, Herbert Hoover, and Senator Warren G. Harding of Ohio all took the hope of nomination very seriously indeed, and none more so than the last.

I interviewed him in his suite in the Senate Office Building, and like everyone else I instantly perceived that this man, who talked like somebody invented by Sinclair Lewis, looked more like a President than any President who ever lived, with the possible exception of George Washington. With his leonine head of white hair, his large, mobile, frank and friendly face, and his portly dignity, it was hard to see why Harding had not been chosen by acclamation years earlier.

Two of his remarks in that interview stand out in my memory. The first was his answer to my stock question as to what he would do, if elected, about the American tariff system that was holding back the restoration of Europe and making it harder for the Allies to pay their war debts—even if they had wanted to. His reply startled me so that I asked him to repeat it, and wrote it down verbatim.

"The United States," he said earnestly, "should adopt a protective tariff of such a character as will best help the struggling industries of Europe to get on their feet."

The other memorable remark came when he was talking about the general tendency of people to spend more money than they could afford. He lumbered from his chair, opened the door a crack, and pointed to the back of a young woman sitting at a desk twenty feet away. "That girl," he told me in a conspiratorial whisper, "owns a five-hundred-dollar fur coat. That's twice as much, by George, as I can afford to spend on a coat for Mrs. Harding." I have often wondered since if, with a touch of pixieish humor, he was pointing to Nan Britton, mother of a baby whose father, she claimed long afterward, was Harding himself.

Not long thereafter, following a deadlock between Wood and Lowden, Harding was nominated and went on to win the election handily, sixteen million votes to nine million. Then the country settled back to enjoy itself. "Normalcy," as Harding called it, with characteristic ineptitude in the use of language, was the new order of the day, but it took almost a decade for the country to learn all the chief facts of what really happened during the Harding administration. He had brought with him to Washington one of the most astonishing collections of crooks, grafters, and blackmailers ever assembled. They came to be known as "the Ohio Gang," though not all of them were from that state.

The key figure was Harry Micajah Daugherty, whom Harding made Attorney General. A corporation lawyer from Columbus who already had an unsavory reputation as a lobbyist and fixer, he had managed his friend's presidential campaign. He had come from the little Ohio crossroads of Washington Court House, where his brother was president of a bank, and had brought with him a devoted henchman, Jess (or Jesse) Smith, who had owned a dry-goods store there. Smith, though he had no title, promptly commandeered an office in the Department of Justice near that of Daugherty and began issuing orders, orally or in writing, in the Attorney General's name.

Smith and another man from Ohio rented what came to be known as "the Little Green House" at 1925 K Street, and it soon was a center of revelry almost twenty-four hours a day. For the right people, good liquor was available in unlimited amounts; much of it had been confiscated by the government, and sometimes it was delivered in official vehicles by armed guards in uniform. The Ohio Gang eagerly solicited bribes from bootleggers seeking immunity, men in jail who wanted to be released, men under indictment who wanted the proceedings dropped, and German owners of property sequestered during the war. Nobody knows what the take amounted to in the thirty months or so that the Ohio Gang was in the saddle, but it has been estimated that, in graft and waste, this group cost the country about two billion dollars.

What was the President's role in all this? At the beginning, he certainly did not know what was going on. Harding did not frequent the Little Green House on K Street, where he would have met bootleggers, dope peddlers or their agents, women of easy virtue, professional gamblers, and other sordid types. He did, however, spend much time in a similar establishment on H Street. One of his cronies was Ned Mclean, young multimillionaire playboy, whose family had come from Cincinnati; Ned obligingly rented this second refuge. If some underworld character proved hard to convince that a few hundred thousand dollars put into the right hands would give him a license to break the law, Jess Smith or one of his colleagues would take the doubting Thomas over to stand near the door of "the House on H Street," to see Daugherty or some other high-level crook emerge from a presidential limousine and enter the house arm in arm with the President and his lady. This usually worked.

Just how much Harding knew of what was going on is not certain; but it is clear that he had some information about it. In the summer of 1923, just a few weeks before his death in San Francisco of a cerebral hemorrhage, he was visibly worried and depressed; he kept asking those about him what a President should do when he was betrayed by his friends.

The most famous and in some ways the most important of the scandals that came to light after Harding's death had to do with oil, and is commonly known as "Teapot Dome," from the name of one of the naval oil reserve areas involved.

In those days before nuclear power, there was concern lest our Navy in time of emergency might run out of its precious fuel. As early as 1910, Congress began setting aside special oil fields. Two of them, Elk Hills and Buena Vista, were only a few miles apart near Bakersfield, California; the third, Teapot Dome, was not far from Casper, Wyoming. (Geologists speak of a "dome" when the earth strata curve upward and then down again, a situation that may bring oil close to the surface.)

There were commercial fields nearby, and supposedly there was some danger that the government oil might be drained off. Accordingly, in 1920 Congress gave the Secretary of the Navy almost unlimited power to save it. He might drill new wells anywhere within any reserve, pump out the oil, and store it. He might permit private operators to drill inside these areas, but only on condition that a certain proportion of the oil be turned over to the Navy for storage.

One of Harding's best friends while in the Senate had been Senator Albert B. Fall, of Three Rivers, New Mexico. With his western clothes, his luxuriant, drooping mustache, and his weather-beaten face, he looked like a movie sheriff. Fall had a terrible temper, which he made no effort to control; there were rumors that as a youth he had "killed his man," though he denied this. He had studied law, and President Cleveland had once put him on the Supreme Court bench of New Mexico Territory. But he had to be removed when he abruptly left the courtroom one day to join the pursuit of a fleeing bandit. Harding actually wanted to make him Secretary of State—which would not have suited Fall's plans at all. He persuaded the President to make him Secretary of the Interior instead.

Three months after the Cabinet was sworn in, Fall got Harding to transfer all the oil reserves from the Navy to the Interior Department, on the grounds that they would thus be better protected from depletion through private drilling nearby. Many people thought the transfer was unwise. Senator Robert M. La Follette of Wisconsin made a vigorous objection on the floor of the Senate; though he later gave his reluctant approval, Secretary of the Navy Edwin Denby protested to the President, but his letter mysteriously disappeared in transit.

Secretary Fall—promptly, secretly, and without the competitive bidding the law required—leased two rich oil reserves to two wealthy men. Elk Hills in California went to his friend of forty years, Edward L. Doheny, who had started with nothing and had accumulated about one hundred million dollars in oil holdings in the United States and Mexico. (Oddly enough, Doheny looked like a much warmer version of Fall, with the same ragged white mustache and weather-beaten face.) Teapot Dome went to Harry Sinclair, reputed to be more than three times as rich as Doheny. The Sinclair lease was for a minimum of twenty years and was to continue indefinitely as long as oil and gas could be produced at a profit. The government was to get a royalty of around sixteen per cent, and Sinclair was required to build some storage tanks and a pipeline. Doheny's lease required him to build, without profit to himself, a pipeline and a refinery in California and storage tanks at Pearl Harbor. Doheny and Sinclair expected to make at least one hundred million dollars each; since there was much more oil in the ground than anyone then knew, their profits might have been larger still. If the oil lands had been leased under competitive bidding, the government's share would have been much more than sixteen per cent; M. R. Werner and John Starr, in their book, *Teapot Dome,* estimate that it might have been worth as much as fifty million dollars.

News of the secret leases leaked out in a few days, and the Senate Committee on Public Lands and Surveys attempted to investigate. Fall brushed its members off contemptuously, saying that he had taken his action in the interest of national security, which required him to suppress all the details. But the Senate was not satisfied, and in the fall of 1923 there began the long series of investigations and civil and criminal court actions that was to last almost a decade and to reveal the most shocking state of corruption since the Grant administration.

I spent a good deal of time in Washington during these investigations, writing a series of articles on the Ohio Gang for *The New Republic,* of which I was then managing editor. The reek of corruption hung over the city, apparent to anybody whose nostrils were reasonably sensitive. The spearheads of the Senate investigations were the two able senators from Montana, Thomas J. Walsh and Burton K. Wheeler. I sat in the committee rooms day after day and saw these men put together a jigsaw puzzle, many of whose pieces had been hidden by others with ingenuity and foresight.

Walsh was austere and carefully groomed, impeccable, soft-voiced, polite; he carried a formidable amount of information in his head. Wheeler was more the rough frontier type, with tousled hair and a truculent attitude toward a squirming witness. Both of them had superlative abilities as detective-prosecutors. On the theory that the investigations were just a Democratic plot, Republican members of the committees did what they could to impede proceedings. The small importance that Washington attached to the investigations in the beginning is shown by the fact that the senators were unceremoniously thrown out of an excellent room into an inferior one because the ladies of the Senate wanted the good one for a tea party.

The members of the Ohio Gang closed ranks against the attack and tried hard to thwart the investigation, in spite of the fact that Fall had repeatedly refused to let Attorney General Daugherty give an official ruling that his actions were legal; Fall had a well-founded fear that Daugherty would want a big share of the loot.

William J. Burns had been brought from New York, where he was head of the Burns Detective Agency (today thoroughly respectable), to head the Bureau of Investigation, which was wholeheartedly on the side of the Ohio Gang. Any member of Congress who expressed public criticism was subject to harassment. Senator La Follette's office was rifled; a detective went to Montana to investigate Senator Wheeler with the hope, as he openly admitted to one or two people, of finding something there that could be used to black-mail him. Senator Walsh was called a scandalmonger and a character assassin; his past life was investigated, his phones tapped, his mail opened; and anonymous letters threatened his life. His daughter, wheeling his three-year-old granddaughter along the street, was intercepted by a stranger who threatened her with harm if she did not force her father to drop the investigation. Female detectives hung around the ladies' room used by Senator Walsh's secretaries, hoping to pick up some valuable gossip.

The members of the Senate who were engaged in the investigation refused to be intimidated and went ahead with their work. Their first big break came with news from New Mexico that Secretary Fall's cattle ranch was showing remarkable prosperity, though his neighbors, because of depression and drought, were turning their cattle loose to survive as best they could.

There was a crusading journalist in New Mexico, Carl Magee, owner of the Albuquerque *Journal,* who had been having trouble with Secretary Fall for some time. Magee had exposed various ways in which the power of the Department of the Interior was being used for the benefit of private interests in New Mexico, which enjoyed such privileges as the improper use of public land. Secretary Fall responded by trying to ruin Magee, and he almost succeeded. Banks, under Fall's influence, called Magee's loans without warning; he was harassed with successive suits for criminal libel; people who feared Fall's power were afraid to entertain Magee and his wife socially, or to be entertained by them. In one of the criminal-libel cases, Magee was sentenced to a year in jail, though he was pardoned by the Governor of New Mexico, a Democrat.

Magee now came to Washington and told his story. In 1920, he reported, Fall had been practically bankrupt and thinking of resigning from the Senate for that reason. He had paid no taxes on his property for the past eight years. Yet now, only a few months later, he was buying additional land worth $124,000, paying his debts (often with $100 bills), building new fences, pouring expensive concrete gutters.

Senator Walsh was interested in where the money had come from. Fall, pleading illness, did not appear on the witness stand, but sent a sworn statement that gave a ready explanation: He had with some difficulty persuaded Ned McLean to lend him $100,000. Senator Walsh decided to check this statement.

McLean was in a dilemma. He didn't want to lie, but he didn't want to tell the truth either. He was in Palm Beach, trying desperately to avoid returning to Washington and sending back coded messages to his aides. Finally, he sent Walsh a report saying that he had indeed lent $100,000 to his dear friend, Secretary Fall.

Walsh came near to accepting his word, but then the touch of the bloodhound in him made him decide to go to Palm Beach and see McLean. Face to face, the young playboy wilted and told the truth. At Fall's request he had in fact written checks totalling $100,000, but it was understood that these were never to be cashed and they had actually been returned to him uncancelled. Fall could not have paid for his new land with them; where did the money come from?

It came from me, said Doheny, hurrying across the country to save Fall's neck. He had loaned his old friend $100,000 in cash. He had sent the money by his son, Edward L. Doheny, Jr., who had carried a small black satchel full of greenbacks from New York to Washington. Was this not a large amount to be handled

so cavalierly? "Not to me," said Croesus, with a grand wave. "A bagatelle to me
. . . no more than twenty-five or fifty dollars to the ordinary individual." And had
he demanded no security? Certainly not; but after long thought he remembered that
Fall had given an unsecured note for the amount. Where was the note? Days later
it was produced, but with the signature torn off. Why no signature? Doheny explained that he feared he might die suddenly and that his hardhearted executors
might press Fall for the money at an embarrassing moment.

Doheny might have been able to bribe Fall out of cash on hand, but, as the
investigating committee soon discovered, Harry Sinclair's approach to this problem
was different. He had decided to raise the needed money, and a great deal more,
through a shady transaction at the expense of the stockholders in two oil companies, one of which was his own. On November 17, 1921, a group of wealthy oilmen met in a hotel room in New York City. Besides Sinclair they included Colonel
A. E. Humphreys, who owned a rich oil field of his own in East Texas; Colonel
Robert W. Stewart, chairman of the board of the Standard Oil Company of Indiana; James E. O'Neil of the Prairie Oil and Gas Company; and Henry M. Blackmer of the Mid-west Refining Company.

All except Humphreys were cronies and were in on a simple scheme. A
dummy corporation, the Continental Trading Company, Ltd., had been set up in
Canada for the sole purpose of buying 33,333,333 1/3 barrels of oil from Colonel
Humphreys at the going rate of $1.50 a barrel, and instantly reselling it at an un-
warranted profit of twenty-five cents a barrel to the companies of Sinclair and
O'Neil. It was Colonel Humphreys who had decided upon the unusual number of
barrels; the reason, he later sheepishly explained, was that this made the transaction come to a round fifty million dollars, the largest in his career.

With a profit of twenty-five cents a barrel, Continental stood to make over
eight million dollars, which was more than ample for the illicit purposes for which
the company had been formed. It actually did collect somewhat more than three
million dollars. Then the Senate investigators began to get too hot on the trail: the
company was liquidated, and all its records were destroyed. This money was
turned into Liberty Bonds—an incredible blunder, since the bonds and their coupons were numbered, and the latter could be traced after they had been cashed.
The law said that the Treasury Department must destroy these coupons after holding them a specified length of time; some of those that figured in the oil scandals
were actually rescued by investigators only forty-eight hours before this would
have been done.

The illicit profit was divided among the four oil men: Sinclair took about
$750,000, Stewart $760,000, Blackmer $763,000, and O'Neil $800,000. (Humphreys got no cut, but of course he had made a neat—and legitimate—profit on the
oil he sold to Continental.) At the time, none of them told the directors of their
respective companies what was going on. Blackmer put his bonds into a safe-de-
posit vault; O'Neil kept his for four years and then turned them over to his com-

pany. In strict secrecy Stewart handed over his share to an employee of his firm, who hid the bonds in a far corner of a company safe. Sinclair took his money home. it was finally proved that he had given Fall a total of $304,000.

When the heat was really on, all these men left the country. Blackmer and O'Neil went to Europe and stayed there. Steward went to Cuba, but finally came back to bully and berate the Senate committee investigators, refusing to answer their questions. In 1928 he was tried for contempt of the Senate and for perjury and was acquitted both times.

The Rockefeller family, of which John D. Rockefeller, Jr., was now the active head, owned nearly fifteen per cent of the stock of the Standard Oil Company of Indiana. John D., Jr., had tried unsuccessfully to get Stewart to make a clean breast of everything, and after his refusal, managed to get the stockholders to oust him at the next annual meeting. Stewart lost his job, with its $125,000 annual salary, and was forced thenceforth to scrape along on a pension of $75,000.

In January, 1924, after inconclusive testimony before the Senate committee, Sinclair had hurried off to Europe under an assumed name. But he came back some months later, for several reasons. His far-flung business enterprises demanded his presence; he believed his tracks had been well covered; and finally, he thought with some reason that he was too important an individual to be made to suffer seriously at the hands of the law.

In the meantime, the Senate committee had dug up some interesting evidence. Sinclair's secretary had remarked casually to Archie Roosevelt, who was then a Sinclair employee, that Sinclair had turned over $68,000 to the manager of Fall's ranch. Archie, after resigning his position, told the Senate committee about the money, and the secretary was summoned. All a mistake, this gentleman explained. He had not said "sixty-eight thou'." He had said "six or eight cows"—which anyone knows sounds much the same. Sinclair had in fact given Fall six heifers and a bull, and thrown in a horse and six hogs for good measure.

Since the committee still seemed skeptical, the secretary tried a new tack. He had indeed mentioned $68,000, but it was not money intended for the manager of Fall's ranch. He had been talking about the transmission of money to the manager of Sinclair's own farm—his celebrated racing stable.

Fall was by now out of the Cabinet, having finally been dismissed by Harding's successor, president Coolidge. When at last they got him on the stand (over his doctor's protest), he took the Fifth Amendment.

But by now too much was known to keep the story bottled up. With the utmost difficulty, Coolidge was finally persuaded to authorize court proceedings. He announced that he would appoint a prominent Republican and a prominent Democrat to act jointly in carrying through the investigation, and in prosecuting whatever cases seemed to justify it. His Republican was Owen J. Roberts, a little-known but reputable attorney from Philadelphia who had tried cases for the government during the war under the Espionage Act. Roberts' Democratic colleague was former Senator Atlee Pomerene, who was now practicing law in Cincinnati. They had two able assistants, George Chandler and Ulrich J. Mengert, and four skilled members of the Secret Service, led by William H. Moran.

Roberts and Pomerene asked the courts to appoint temporary receivers to take charge of operations at Teapot Dome and the fields in California leased to Doheny, and to impound all the oil produced, until the cases had been decided in which the government was asking cancellation of the leases. This was done.

The two presidential appointees and their staff now began a monumental task of detective work, interviewing hundreds of people and checking bank records, brokerage accounts, and other files in half a dozen states and Canada. Finally, when they thought they had airtight evidence, they brought a group of civil and criminal actions, which were prosecuted with great skill. It was not the fault of Roberts and Pomerene that the results were rather disappointing as far as sending people to jail was concerned.*

Nothing could be more characteristic of the sickly moral atmosphere of the times than what happened when the three chief figures in the oil scandals were brought into court. Fall and Doheny were tried jointly for conspiracy, and were acquitted. The Washington jury, composed of average middle-class Americans, had no intention of sending a multimillionaire and a fine gentleman like Doheny to jail. Then Fall and Sinclair were also tried jointly for conspiracy, since the two crimes were substantially identical. They were also acquitted. Doheny was tried alone for giving the satchelful of money to Fall, and acquitted. Fall was tried for accepting the satchelful of money, but he was not a multimillionaire or a fine gentleman: he was found guilty and sentenced to a year in prison.

When Sinclair came back from Europe he had refused to answer questions by the Senate, but he made the bad mistake of failing to take refuge behind the Fifth Amendment, saying only that he intended to reserve his testimony until later. He was judged to be in contempt of the Senate.

There were other charges against him. During his trial for conspiracy, it was discovered that one juror had been bribed to vote for acquittal. This man indiscreetly told a friend that he had been promised, in a phrase that became famous, "a car as long as this block." He also hinted darkly that he was to get some cash. The friend knew a reporter on one of the Washington newspapers, told him about it, and arranged a meeting between the juror and the reporter. They met in a saloon, the reporter's occupation being concealed, and the juror repeated the substance of the story. The reporter promptly informed a representative of the prosecution.

*The national attention Roberts received was to be a factor in his appointment as Associate Justice of the United States Supreme Court in 1930 by President Hoover. Pomerene was considered for the Democratic presidential nomination in 1928, and later was chairman of the Reconstruction Finance Corporation.

Roberts and Pomerene also learned that at the beginning of the trial a horde of private detectives had been sent down from New York and assigned to shadow each member of the jury to learn all that could be learned about them. These agents, employees of the Burns Detective Agency, assumed new identities and worked with military precision, turning in daily reports that were co-ordinated at a central headquarters in a Washington hotel room.

One of the detectives, William J. McMullin, was ordered to assist in a frame-up that would involve Norman Glasscock, one of the jurors, and Horace Lamb, a lawyer in the Department of Justice. The spies knew the license numbers of the automobiles of Glasscock and Lamb; McMullin was to swear that he had seen these two cars parked side by side on a given day at the Potomac Flying Field, and the occupants conferring. This was of course entirely false. The plan was that if the trial seemed likely to produce a verdict of guilty, McMullin was to come forward with the charge of improper contact between a juror and a Department of Justice lawyer, which would force a mistrial.

But Sinclair's forces had picked a poor choice for skulduggery in McMullin. A former New Jersey state trooper, he was sickened by what he had been asked to do. He made contact with former Governor Gifford Pinchot of Pennsylvania, his home state, and told him the story. Pinchot took it to representatives of the prosecution, who promptly made McMullin a double agent. He was to do everything that Sinclair's representatives told him to do, but he was to make a secret daily report to the prosecution of what was going on.

Armed with this information, representatives of Roberts and Pomerene raided the headquarters of Sinclair's detectives and seized carbon copies of a mass of field agents' reports. As a result, they were able to subpoena scores of individuals who had knowledge of, or who had participated in, the spying on the jurors.

Under orders from the prosecution, McMullin executed the false affidavit about Glasscock and Lamb. Before it could be used, however, the government men told the judge about the bribery of the juror. There was indeed a mistrial, though not under the circumstances Sinclair had anticipated.

The oilman's attorneys, seeking to turn public opinion against Roberts and Pomerene, produced McMullin's affidavit. The prosecution promptly revealed that he had been a double agent and released the evidence showing that the affidavit was false. Sinclair's attorneys now tried desperately to smear McMullin, digging up and publishing every unfavorable fact they could find about his past, but with little success. Fearing for his safety, the government gave him a bodyguard.

Some time later Sinclair was tried again, and found guilty of contempt of court. He was given six months in jail, in addition to the $500 fine and three months in jail he had received for contempt of the Senate.

But this was not the end of the tale of the Liberty Bonds, the profits from the only business deal ever made by the fabulous Continental Trading Company.

Will Hays, a smiling chipmunk of a man, had been Republican National Chairman in 1920, and had rashly promised that campaign contributions would be limited to $1,000 from any individual; the result was a deficit of $1,200,000. After he had made his deal with Fall, but before it was exposed, Sinclair felt it would be politic for him to make a substantial contribution toward erasing the deficit. Yet it was obviously undesirable for a single individual to give a large sum, especially an oilman who was in a position to get favors from Republican government officials.

Senator Walsh somehow picked up a rumor that Sinclair had made a very large contribution. Will Hays, who had been made Postmaster General by Harding, and then had become czar of movie morals, was summoned to the witness stand. Unluckily, Walsh's information was wrong in one detail. It said that Hays had been given not Liberty Bonds, which was a fact, but bonds of the Sinclair Consolidated Oil Corporation. This enabled Hays to deny the whole transaction. Asked whether Sinclair had made a private loan to Hays himself, he refused to answer on the ground that this was a personal matter.

What had happened was this: Sinclair had turned over to Hays $260,000 in bonds, part of his profits from the Continental Trading Company; $75,000 of this was supposed to be a contribution, and $185,000 (in theory) a loan. Hays had then approached several wealthy men and asked each of them to turn over a substantial sum of cash to the Republican National Committee. Each man would in turn be given Liberty Bonds in the same amount to hold as security. If and when the loan was repaid, he would give back the bonds. As far as Hays was concerned, there was of course little or no intention of every repaying the "loans"; they were simply a device to conceal the large gift from Sinclair. T. Coleman Du Pont, who had been treasurer of the national committee, received bonds worth $75,000; John T. Pratt, a wealthy New Yorker, $50,000; John W. Weeks, a millionaire Bostonian and Harding's Secretary of War, $25,000. Fred Upham of Chicago, who was treasurer of the Republican National Committee in 1923, took $60,000 worth and sold them to various rich Chicagoans for cash.

On the witness stand in 1924, Hays mentioned only the $75,000 Sinclair contribution. In 1928, when the government knew more about the transaction, he was summoned again and confessed to the $185,000. And why had he kept silent for years earlier? "Nobody," said the moralist indignantly, "asked me about any Liberty Bonds."

Another man who figured in this episode was Andrew Mellon, Secretary of the Treasury. A multimillionaire Pittsburgh banker, he had inherited a fortune, greatly expanded it, and while in office had reduced the national debt by one third, from the gigantic sum of twenty-four billion dollars to sixteen billion dollars.

An investigator for the Senate committee found in the personal files of John T. Pratt, who had died some time earlier, small slips of paper that had on them in microscopic writing the names of several wealthy men, with a sum of money written after each one. In the 1928 investigation, the cashier for Pratt's estate, V. E.

Hommel, was asked to look at these names and read them aloud to the committee. He read the first one clearly enough; it was "Weeks." The next name he professed to be unable to read. He thought it was the word "Candy." When Senator Gerald P. Nye asked whether the word might not be "Andy," Hommel admitted it might be, but had no idea who that could be. The spectators in the committee room laughed; there was only one famous Andy in the whole country. Mr. Mellon was now put on the stand and admitted that Hays had indeed sent him $50,000 in Liberty Bonds, suggesting that he regard them as security for a loan by himself of the same amount to the Republican National Committee. Mr. Mellon smelled something disreputable about this proposal, and instantly sent back the bonds, at the same time making an independent contribution of $50,000 of his own to reduce the Republican deficit. And why had he waited so long to tell about this? Like Hayes he was indignant; nobody had asked him.

Year after year, the government went on fighting to unravel the harm that Fall's greed had produced. Case after case was fought through to the Supreme Court. The oil leases were at last vacated on the ground that fraud and corruption had been employed. Sinclair had to return to the government more than twelve million dollars, and Doheny, almost thirty-five million. (Doheny had spent about eleven million on storage tanks at Pearl Harbor, for which he was not reimbursed.) Sinclair had also obligated himself to pay large sums to a group of blackmailers who had learned early in the game that there was something fishy about Teapot Dome. These blackmailers included the two notorious owners of the Denver *Post,* Frederick G. Bonfils and H. H. Tammen, who softened up Sinclair by publishing many articles raising questions about the Teapot Dome lease; after he had agreed to pay them off, the articles stopped. The blackmail, most of which was to come out of the profits of Teapot Dome, amounted in all to more than two million dollars.

Doheny died in 1935 at seventy-nine and Sinclair in 1956 at eighty; neither man ever publicly admitted his guilt, nor did Fall, who died in 1944 at eighty-three. Blackmer finally came home from Europe in 1949, at the age of eighty, to face the music; he was immediately arraigned on charges of tax evasion and perjury. He was fined $60,000, and he owed nearly $8,500,00 in unpaid back taxes, penalties, and interest. He finally settled with the government for about $3,600,000, and the charge of perjury was dropped.

O'Neil died in France in 1932 at sixty-four. Seven years earlier a doctor had told him, erroneously, that he had only a year or two to live, and he therefore made a secret trip to Canada. There he told two officials of his company about the bonds he was holding, and turned over the bulk of them; he had cashed a few—by inadvertence, so he said. Ned McLean, who became an alcoholic, was declared incompetent and was put into a mental institution, where he died in 1941 at the age of fifty-five. Colonel Stewart died in 1927 at eighty.

Little by little over the late nineteen twenties other scandals of the Harding regime became known. One of the worst of them centered around Charles R. Forbes, whom the President had made head of the Veterans' Bureau. The price of each new veterans' hospital planned under his regime was to be padded by $150,000, of which Forbes took $50,000 while the contractors split the rest. Sites were bought at four or five times their actual value, and Forbes demanded and got his cut. He also bought staggering quantities of supplies at inflated prices, with the understanding that he receive a kickback. Finally brought to trial, Forbes got two years in prison and was fined $10,000. Will Irwin, who made a careful study of the episode, said he had cost the United States not less than 200 million dollars.

Another notorious figure was Harding's brother-in-law, Heber Votaw, an ex-missionary from Burma, whom the President made Director of Federal Prisons. In his regime there was a huge increase in the bootlegging of narcotics to prisoners; Votaw's office tried to hamper efforts to investigate and remedy the situation. When the director of the Atlanta Penitentiary complained, he was fired. With the death of Harding, his protector, Votaw's days in office were numbered. There was insufficient evidence against him to impress a jury, and he was presently allowed to slip back into obscurity.

Of all the Ohio Gang, Harry Daugherty was the most brazen. With scandals exploding all around his head, he refused after the death of Harding to resign his post. Coolidge, characteristically, sent somebody else—Chief Justice William Howard Taft—to suggest this; the idea was coldly rebuffed. Finally, the odor of scandal became too strong, and Daugherty was forced out. When he came to trial at last, he refused to take the stand and invoked the Fifth Amendment.

It developed that a year earlier, Harry had gone to Washington Court House and had burned many records, some of them going back as far as 1916. The theory he circulated was that he did this to protect the good name of the dead President, since the records would tell both of financial irregularities by Harding and of his clandestine love life. Senate investigators were able, however, to discover that $75,000, its source unexplained, had been deposited to Daugherty's account at a time when he swore on his income-tax return that he had no property. Also on deposit in the bank was $63,000 for Jess Smith, $50,000 for Mal Daugherty, and smaller sums for other members of the Ohio Gang. This bank had been for them what the cave was for Ali Baba's forty thieves.

When the Senate committee tried to subpoena brother Mal, he fought all the way to the United States Supreme Court to avoid testifying. When he was cited for contempt of the Senate, an obliging judge, sitting in Ohio, set him free. His bank later failed with a loss of 2.6 million dollars, ruining a large proportion of the people around Washington Court House. (This was of course before the days of the Federal Bank Deposit Insurance Corporation.)

Harry Daugherty had been indicted with Thomas W. Miller, Alien Property Custodian, for having accepted bribes to turn back to a dummy Swiss corporation a large part of the assets of the American Metals Company, a German-owned firm in the United States, and I covered the trial for *The New Republic*. Daugherty looked, as always, shifty, squirming, and oily. Miller was thin-faced and sober, with, as I remember, a pincenez like that of Woodrow Wilson; he sat bemused, as though wondering what in the world he was doing in the prisoner's dock. Well he might: He was a Yale graduate, from a good Philadelphia family, with an impeccable record until he went to Washington and came under the evil spell of the Ohio Gang.

The dummy Swiss corporation had paid $441,000 in bribes, of which Miller got $49,000 and Daugherty at least $40,000; where the rest went was never made clear. Miller was sentenced to prison, served some time, and was pardoned. More than fifty million dollars in German assets illegally released by his office was eventually returned to the U.S. government. In Harry Daugherty's case, two successive juries disagreed, and he was able to boast that he had never been convicted. In 1924, after being forced to resign from the Cabinet, he retired to a pleasant life in Ohio and Florida. He died, unrepentant, in 1944.

Two members of the Ohio Gang had committed suicide even before Harding's death. Charles F. Cramer, legal adviser to the Veterans' Bureau, wrote a letter to the President and then shot himself. (Harding refused even to look at the letter, and it later disappeared without any revelation of its contents.) Jesse Smith, Daugherty's shadow, was found dead one day in 1923 with a revolver beside him. Though cynics argued that he had been murdered, there is no doubt that he had been deeply depressed because both Harding and Daugherty had cooled toward him, had in fact exiled him back to Ohio.

Could we have a repetition of the Harding or Grant scandals today? It seems to me unlikely. The Grant and Harding administrations had several elements in common, and I feel that all of them, in combination, are essential for wholesale corruption. First, you must have a period of moral relaxation such as is common after a big war. Second, you must have a President in the White House who is complacent, ill-informed, and a poor judge of the integrity of his close friends. Third, and perhaps most important, the country must be unaware, before electing him, of these aspects of a nominee's character.

Today, every serious candidate for the Presidency lives under intense scrutiny by magazines and newspapers, which in general do an enormously better job than they did forty-five (or ninety-seven) years ago. He also lives under the fierce white light of the television cameras, which have an uncanny way of revealing the things about a man that he would prefer to have concealed. If the media for mass communication do their work properly, we ought to be secure against the possibility of another Ohio Gang.

As an editor of The New Republic *in the Twenties, Bruce Bliven covered the workings of the Ohio Gang. He now lives in Stanford, California. His new book,* The World Changers, *consisting of biographical sketches of the eight most important men of the 1930's and 40's, will be published this October by the John Day Company.*

For further reading: Teapot Dome, by M. R. Werner and John Starr (Viking, 1959); Teapot Dome: Oil and Politics in the 1920's, by Burl Noggle (Louisiana State University, 1962).

Bonus March

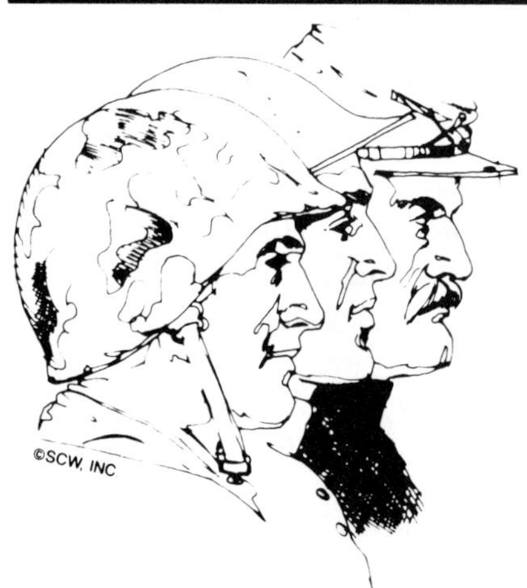

John D. Weaver

In the late spring of 1932 some 20,000 jobless World War veterans, many with their wives and children, descended on Washington, dumping the Depression on the doorstep of the Capitol and the White House. Two months later, when they had overstayed their grudging welcome, they were driven out of the city. The crimson glow of their burning camps had hardly faded from the midnight sky before a dispute arose as to who these people were, why they had come to the capital, and under what circumstances they had been expelled. After a generation of impassioned and often inaccurate oratory, the Bonus March remains one of the most controversial and grotesquely distorted episodes of recent American history.

The mood of the nation as it emerged from its third Depression winter into that sullen spring of 1932 was grim. A million or more migrants, including some 200,000 boys and girls, were roaming the country without purpose, while middle-class families—their savings, their credit, and their pride exhausted—were turning in shame to their local relief agencies, only to find that few cities and fewer towns could even begin to meet their needs.

Toledo could provide each person with a daily meal costing less than three cents. New York City averaged $2.39 a week for each family on relief. Pennsylvania miners, three or four families of them huddled together in one-room shacks, were eating wild roots, and in Chicago men were seen fighting over a barrel of garbage set outside the back door of a restaurant. It was estimated that only about one-fourth of the nation's unemployed were actually receiving relief.

Twice President Hoover had struck boldly at the world-wide catastrophe: first with the universally applauded moratorium on war debts and war reparations, and again, a few months later, with the creation of a huge federal credit agency—the Reconstruction Finance Corporation—which was given two billion dollars to lend to ailing banks, railroads, and insurance companies. Convinced that "the sole function of government is to bring about a condition of affairs favorable to the beneficial development of private enterprise," the President shrank from a federal "dole" for the unemployed, which, he believed, "would have injured the spiritual responses of the American people."

While Mr. Hoover, "so tired that every bone in my body aches," grappled with a depressed economy and a hostile Congress, an unemployed cannery superintendent named Walter W. Waters was discussing plans for a march on Washington with other jobless veterans of Portland, Oregon. An aggressive, ambitious ex-sergeant who had served overseas in the 146th Field Artillery and, once home, had drifted from job to job, always haunted by a sense of failure, Waters had read of similar marches on Washington, including one from Portland the year before.

A "bonus march" of several hundred men ("I foresaw no greater number") might, he felt, effect passage of a bill which Representative Wright Patman of Texas had introduced, calling for the immediate payment of the World War veterans' adjusted compensation certificates. These constituted the so-called Soldiers' Bonus, which Congress had approved in 1924. The money was to be paid in 1945; each veteran would receive $1 for every day he had served at home, and $1.25 for every day overseas. Although Walter Lippmann patiently explained that "to demand payment of the principal of a debt . . . before it is due is to demand money that is not owed at all now and to demand more money than is owed ultimately," the veterans felt entitled to advance payment of the few hundred dollars that might be more useful to them alive in 1932 than dead in 1945.

In May, when the Patman bill seemed to be buried in the Ways and Means Committee, Waters began for the first time to meet with real enthusiasm among the Portland veterans. More and more men signed up for the projected march on Washington, each recruit being required to show evidence of war service, take an oath of allegiance, and agree to submit himself to the military discipline of his elected officers. At the final meeting, May 10, a "commander in chief" and a "field marshal" were elected, establishing the pattern of grandiose titles which, along with rigid discipline, flag-waving, and militant anti-radicalism, was to distinguish what the men now derisively called the "Bonus Expeditionary Force."

Three hundred veterans, with less than thirty dollars among them, set off for Washington to the beat of a borrowed drum. "Not one man in twenty really expected to get the Bonus," Waters wrote in his history of the B.E.F., but after months of idleness, suffering the spiritual erosion of long unemployment, the men had finally roused themselves from the lethargy which seemed to have gripped the country. Hopping freight trains out of Portland, they eventually reached East St.

Louis, Illinois, where, to get rid of them, the authorities provided the veterans with trucks to the Indiana line. So it went, until the group finally reached their destination. As a practical fact, the men did far more riding than marching.

Toward the end of the eighteen-day trek of the Oregon bonus marchers, other jobless veterans, inspired by their example, started drifting into the capital. The difficult task of handling them fell upon the new police chief, a retired brigadier general named Pelham D. Glassford who had been the youngest general of the line in the First World War. His rangy, six-foot three-inch frame draped over his big blue motorcycle and a long-stemmed pipe in his mouth, General Glassford had become a popular and familiar figure on the streets of Washington. During his first six months on the job he had already dealt with two marches of the unemployed, the first led by Communists, the second by a Roman Catholic priest, Father James R. Cox of Pittsburgh. In both instances Glassford had received the marchers with courtesy and scrupulous attention to their constitutional rights of petition and peaceable assembly. There had been no trouble.

By May 28, when the Oregon marchers were bedding down for the night on the floor of a skating rink in Cumberland, Maryland, only a day away from the capital, the shabby vanguard of the B.E.F. had overflowed Washington missions, and Glassford was housing the men in unused government buildings, noting in his diary that night: "Bought $110 worth of food on my own financial responsibility at the Ft. Myer commissary." At the same time he was telegraphing the governors of every state, urging them to dissuade more veterans from converging on Washington, where—with 19,000 unemployed—relief resources were already overtaxed. He also buttonholed congressional leaders, pleading with them to settle the issue by bringing the bonus bill to a vote, and appealed to Secretary of War Patrick J. Hurley for army cots, bedding, and rolling kitchens.

"Mr. Hurley," Glassford noted in his private papers, which he gave to the University of California at Los Angeles before his death, "refused to be of any assistance, stating that the Federal Government could not recognize the invasion." In desperation Glassford turned to Major General Herbert B. Crosby, the District commissioner in charge of police affairs, who had originally persuaded him to take over the capital's scandal-ridden police department. Glassford suggested the organization of a welfare committee to deal with the bonus marchers. Crosby refused. His main concern, it seemed to Glassford, was to get the veterans out of Washington as soon as possible, by force if necessary.

"Is that an order?" Glassford asked.

"Oh no, it's merely a suggestion," Crosby is quoted as saying in Glassford's private memorandum of the meeting.

"Well, if you will put that in writing and publish it I will take it as an order."

"No, it's not an order and I'll not put it in writing. It's a suggestion. I don't need to remind you that in the Army a suggestion is as good as an order, do I?"

"No, but we're not in the Army now."

With no federal or District official willing to assume responsibility for either sheltering the veterans or evicting them, Glassford found himself without orders, funds, or food. "We had two alternatives," he later wrote, "feed them or fight them." He fed them. He wangled cash contributions from wealthy friends, staged a midnight show at a local burlesque house, passed the hat at boxing and wrestling matches. He also managed to cadge militia tents and rolling kitchens from the National Guard, enlist the aid of doctors and nurses, and screen freeloading impostors by the use of meal tickets which were issued only after a careful investigation of the applicant's service credentials. For a time Glassford even served as treasurer of the B.E.F., handling the donations which came in from sympathetic merchants, government clerks, and school children.

"Dangerous?" he said, echoing a reporter's question about the invading army. "No, except the danger of gradual rust and rot which attacks those with no occupation and no incentive. These are just middle-aged men out of a job."

Ex-Sergeant Waters, who had left Portland as an "assistant field marshal" of the B.E.F., had emerged from a new election en route as "regimental commander." He was in complete control of the Oregon contingent when, on the morning of May 29, he met Glassford for the first time. He was "agreeably surprised" by the ex-general. "Here," Waters wrote, "was certainly no hard-boiled disciple of the old police school. In him the human element was above the law." Glassford, for his part, took note of Waters' "blue eyes in which there sometimes burned an almost fanatic gleam."

"How many veterans will come here, do you think?" Glassford asked.

Waters, with the recklessness that marked so many of his public utterances later, predicted, "There will be twenty thousand here within the next two weeks."

When the prediction began to prove accurate, no one was more astonished than Waters—except possibly the Communist party leaders in New York City, who had been caught off guard by the spontaneous movement. They watched with increasing incredulity as reinforcements for the B.E.F. continued to pour into the capital. Fifty men from Minneapolis arrived in boxcars on the morning of June 2, followed soon after by 340 more from Pennsylvania. Nine hundred men in search of transportation had taken over a railroad yard in Cleveland, while 208 were being dumped in a Virginia pasture by a crew that cut its locomotive loose from the freight train carrying the bonus marchers. One ambitious leader of a Colorado contingent had tried to commandeer a United States tugboat on the Missouri River.

Eager to capture the runaway movement, the Communist party leaders announced a parade for June 8. Glassford suggested that the B.E.F. steal a march on them by holding a parade of its own the night before. Eight thousand veterans marched down Pennsylvania Avenue; the next day the "Red Parade" was cancelled when it was unable to muster even two hundred.

The parading veterans were coatless, freshly scrubbed and shaved, some wearing remnants of the uniforms they had been issued fourteen years before; they marched with a setting sun at their backs that seemed somehow symbolic. "There was no heart in them, no hope in them," one reporter noted, struck by the oppressive silence of the men and of the 100,000 spectators who lined the streets from, ironically enough, the Treasury Building to the Peace Monument. There were lumberjacks from Oregon, ranch hands from North Dakota and Utah, coal miners from Pennsylvania, skilled mechanics from Ohio, stockyard workers from Chicago, cotton pickers from the South, clerks from the Middle West. There were no cheers. It was not that kind of a parade.

"Washington watched," the *Star* reported, "sympathized and shrugged its shoulders. The watchers felt infinite pity for these men—wished they could do something for them. But the city wondered why it should be made the dumping ground of the nation's burden of misery."

The next day another thousand veterans showed up.

The bonus marchers were spread over more than twenty different camps, ranging from the primitive brick shells of a group of half-demolished buildings on lower Pennsylvania Avenue to the country club elegance of Camp Bartlett, where a tent village with a clinic had been set up on a tract of privately owned land turned over to the B.E.F. by a former governor of New Hampshire, J. H. Bartlett. The largest establishment was Camp Marks—named after a sympathetic Washington police captain—a shack city which had sprung up overnight on the mud flats of Anacostia and sheltered some 10,000 men, women, and children. The site had been selected by Glassford with a view to the strategic advantage of the Eleventh Street bridge across the Anacostia River; in case of trouble it could be raised to separate the bulk of the B.E.F. from the other camps.

"Every scrap of material which can possibly be fitted into a shelter of any kind is being dragged out of the big junk pile on the hill above the camp," Thomas R. Henry wrote in *Star* after a tour of the Anacostia hovels:

> There are shelters built of egg crates, of paper boxes, of rusty bed springs, of O.D. blankets, of newspapers, of scraps of junked automobiles, of old wallpaper, of pieces of corrugated iron roofing, of tin and bed ticking, of the rusty frames of beds, of tin cans, of rusty fence wire, of straw, of parts of baby carriages, of fence stakes, of auto seats. The man who can salvage an auto top from the dump has a mansion in this strange city.

At Anacostia, one man lived in a barrel filled with grass, another in a casket set on trestles, still another in a piano box which he labelled "Academy of Music." Some of the men dug caves in the clay embankment, and all trudged through a deep ooze of mud after the summer rains, fighting flies by day, mosquitoes by night. By the end of June there were 220 wives and children attached to the B.E.F. A month later the bonus-army records would list 700 women and 400 children, the roster sheets reporting one morning: ". . . and the O'Brien family with six children, all redheaded and mean as hell!"

One reporter found in the bonus marchers "no revolt, no fire, not even smouldering resentment." They were "an inchoate aggregation of frustrated men nursing a common grievance." Waters noted that Anacostia, "in furnishing some sense of security, even temporary, was answering the very need that had brought these thousands to Washington." No one, least of all the men themselves, seemed to know why they had come. The bonus, as most of them realized at the start, would not be paid, and even if it were, it would last only a few weeks or months.

"Their real demand was for security," a Pennsylvania welfare official reported, "and in their bewilderment and confusion they seem to have reverted to the old army ways and to the earlier institutional situation where shelter and food are provided and where leadership is given." New members lapsed so quickly into the army spirit of the B.E.F. that some asked for passes before leaving camp, and a few even inquired about payday. They griped about the chow and the foul-ups by their leaders, but when they drilled for visitors, they sucked in their paunches and tried to march with something of their old snap, recalling in their shabby middle age the proud days of their youth.

Their *ignis fatuus*, the bonus bill, had been pried out of the Ways and Means Committee, passed by the anti-administration House, and sent to the Senate where, facing certain defeat, it was brought to a vote on June 17—"the tensest day in the capital since the War," a local paper noted. Some 10,000 veterans were massed on the Capitol grounds, with another 10,000 waiting across the Anacostia River. A newspaper woman asked Waters, "What's going to happen when these men learn of the defeat of the bill? It's going to be swamped, you know."

"Nothing will happen," Waters said.

When darkness had fallen, Waters was asked to step inside the Capitol. He emerged a few minutes later and climbed up on the pedestal at the edge of the Capitol steps. "prepare yourselves for a disappointment, men," he announced. "The Bonus has been defeated, 62 to 18 . . ."

The crowd stood motionless, in stunned silence, and Waters was fearful of what they might do. Elsie Robinson, a friendly Hearst columnist, whispered to him, "Tell them to sing 'America.' "

"Sing 'America' and go back to your billets!" Waters shouted, and the men bared their heads and sang.

"These men," the *Star* editorialized next day, "wrote a new chapter on patriotism of which their countrymen may well be proud."

Once the bonus bill had been defeated, the police reported that 1,000 veterans quietly drifted away from Washington (the B.E.F. cut the estimate to 200). Contributions fell off, and the rank and file, split by internal dissension, elected two new leaders in three days, then gave dictatorial powers to Waters. Affecting whipcord breeches, riding boots, and a khaki shirt, he began to salute his men with a gesture reporters found disturbingly reminiscent of Mussolini.

Although he met with little response from the body of the B.E.F., who recoiled with equal horror from both Marx and Treasury Secretary Andrew Mellon on the same banners, Waters was beginning to talk of "a close-knit, semi-military organization"—the Khaki Shirts—who would, he announced, "stand ready to leap into the breach between American institutions and threatened anarchy." The Khaki Shirts, "100 per cent American," would be a bulwark against Communism, which Waters' self-styled "military police" had already attacked locally, pouncing on suspected reds and hauling them before kangaroo courts to be sentenced to belt-lashings and forcible expulsion from Washington.

"He saw 'red' a little too strenuously," Glassford noted privately of Waters. Yet, aware that the B.E.F. cupboard was bare, he contributed meat, sugar, salt, coffee, potatoes, onions, and bread, paying the bill—$773.40—out of his own modest resources. At the same time he jotted down a personal memorandum recording his impression that his immediate superior, District Commissioner Crosby, was "not at all in sympathy" with his handling of the bonus army and that Crosby "advocated, without assuming any responsibility therefor, the use of force."

The Congress was eager to adjourn and get on with the serious business at hand in a presidential election year (the Democrats had nominated Governor Franklin Roosevelt of New York, whom President Hoover regarded as the easiest candidate to beat). At the administration's request, therefore, they voted on July 7 an appropriation of $100,000 to transport the veterans home or, lacking a home, to wherever they came from or would agree to go—anything to get them out of Washington before the campaign began. The money—railroad fare and seventy-five cents a day to live on—was to be deducted from the bonuses due them.

Glassford climbed on his blue motorcycle and drove through the various camps, distributing copies of a letter he had written urging the bonus marchers to take advantage of the government's offer. But by midnight on July 10 only 500 veterans had left the city, and 1,000 more promptly arrived from the West, including several hundred led by Royal W. Robertson, a picturesque and cantankerous character who wore a steel neck brace and helmet with chin straps to support a broken back. He repudiated both the segregated Communist encampment and that of the rank and file commanded by Waters. "We came to Washington to petition Congress, not to a picnic," he told Waters on his arrival on July 12. It was their first and last meeting.

Robertson camped on the Capitol grounds. The following night the Capitol police turned on the lawn sprinklers. The men, by law, had to keep moving if they wanted to stay near the Capitol. Single file they began a silent "death march"—so called because of the impending adjournment. It was the most dramatic and ominous demonstration of the past six weeks. Several hundred members of the B.E.F. joined the marchers during the day of July 14. That afternoon Vice President

Charles Curtis called for the Marines to clear the Capitol grounds, then rescinded the order when he was tactfully reminded that only the President had the power to call out federal troops. The "death march" continued through the dawn of July 16, when 17,000 veterans began to assemble in front of the Capitol for the adjournment of Congress.

Around noon a delegation sent by the B.E.F. to the White House returned to the Capitol with word that the President had declined to receive them. He also cancelled his customary visit to the Capitol on the closing day of Congress, and when some fifty veterans started toward the White House, he ordered police to close the gates and clear Pennsylvania Avenue and adjacent streets of all pedestrians and vehicular traffic. The demonstrators were quickly dispersed and three of them hauled off to jail. Inspector O. T. Davis told reporters that the President had intended to call out Regular Army troops if the streets had not been cleared immediately.

As Congress headed for home to prepare for the coming campaign, the District commissioners, aware of the political embarrassment the bonus army was causing the White House, summoned General Glassford and informed him of a new "get-tough" policy. They demanded immediate evacuation of the buildings within the area of Pennsylvania Avenue, Missouri Avenue, Third Street, and Sixth Street, and the evacuation of all park areas, including the Anacostia mud flats, by August 4, at which time all National Guard tentage and rolling kitchens were to be returned.

The order was issued and then, because of legal complications, quickly withdrawn. Waters, during this brief period of grace, was working out a plan to move the shrinking remains of the B.E.F. to the privately owned land of Camp Bartlett. "I was more fully aware than ever of the desire to rid Washington of the bonus army in some way or other, even with force," Waters wrote of this period. His suspicions seemed to be confirmed by what was said on July 26 during a five-hour conference with the Secretary of War and the Army's Chief of Staff, General Douglas MacArthur; it was the one time, apparently, that representatives of the B.E.F. were received by administration officials.

"You and your bonus army have no business in Washington," Waters later quoted Hurley as saying. "We are not in sympathy with your being here. We will not co-operate in any way with your remaining here. We are interested only in getting you out of the District. At the first sign of disorder or bloodshed in the B.E.F., you will all get out. And we have plenty of troops to put you out."

At the end of the conference the ex-sergeant turned to General MacArthur, who had been pacing the floor most of the time. "If the troops should be called out against us," Waters asked, "will the B.E.F. be given the opportunity to form in columns, salvage their belongings, and retreat in orderly fashion?" According to Waters, MacArthur replied, "Yes, my friend of course!"

The next day Waters warned his 182 group commanders that one false step would bring out the federal troops. That afternoon Glassford called Waters to the commissioners' office. During his seven weeks in Washington Waters had never met the commissioners, nor did he meet them that afternoon. He sat in an ante-room while the police chief lumbered back and forth as go-between. ("It isn't every ex-sergeant that can have an ex-general for messenger boy!" Waters exulted afterward.)

Glassford first brought Waters word of the commissioners' decision to evacuate the billets in four partially demolished buildings on lower Pennsylvania Avenue by the following midnight. "Impossible," Waters said. Glassford ducked back into the commissioners' office, then returned with an extension of the deadline to Friday, July 29. Waters countered with a proposal to evacuate 200 men by 6 P.M. the following day, and to clear the entire area within two weeks. Glassford disappeared into the next room, conferred with the commissioners, and came back with the announcement, "The commissioners accept in part. They will give you until Monday to try your plan and clear the area."

At nine-thirty the following morning, Thursday July 28, Waters assembled the men bivouacked in the area designated for clearing. He had four days, he thought, to carry out the evacuation, starting with the removal of 200 men from a small building owned by the Treasury Department at Third Street and Pennsylvania Avenue. As the men prepared to gather up their belongings, Glassford's secretary appeared and handed Waters a written order from the Treasury Department, calling for complete evacuation of the building by ten o'clock that morning. This gave Waters ten minutes to evacuate the 200 men. "The forces of government were doing their best to egg on the men of the B.E.F. into some sort of riot," he later charged, recalling Secretary Hurley's warning that troops would be called out at the first sign of trouble.

Waters read the Treasury Department order aloud. "You're double-crossed," he told the men. Protests were checked by the arrival of a hundred policemen with coils of rope which they strung around the building, taking positions eight feet apart behind the barrier. While hundreds of spectators and some 1,500 bonus marchers looked on, six Treasury agents, with twelve policemen as bodyguards, proceeded to clear the building in what the *Star* described as "more or less of a good-natured affair."

The evacuation was completed without incident by noon. Ten minutes later a small group of men from the radical camp rushed police lines. A brick battle erupted. Paul Y. Anderson of the St. Louis *Post-Dispatch,* standing forty feet away, reported, "Glassford dashed into the heart of the melee, smiled when a brickbat hit him in the chest, and stopped the fighting in a few seconds." Glassford climbed to a vantage point above the veterans and called down, "Come on, boys let's call an armistice for lunch." The men laughed and cheered. The fighting, which had involved no more than fifty bonus marchers, had lasted less than five minutes.

At 1:45 P.M., after Glassford returned from a conference with the District commissioners in which, he wrote later, nothing had been said "to indicate that they intended to call upon Federal forces," a brawl broke out some fifty yards from the scene of the earlier disorder. Four policemen were involved, and two of them fired on the veterans, killing one instantly and wounding another fatally. Three of the policemen ended up in the hospital. Glassford stopped this second disturbance "almost before it commenced," and then, he continues, "I heard from a newspaperman that the troops were on the way."

And, in fact, the troops had been called out by the President at the written request of the District commissioners before the two bonus marchers had been killed. They were under the direct command of Brigadier General Perry Miles, but General MacArthur, accompanied by Major General George Van Horn Moseley, his deputy Chief of Staff, personally took the field. (Contemporary accounts virtually ignore the Army's liaison man with the police department, an amiable West Pointer named Dwight Eisenhower.) A cavalry squadron, an infantry battalion, and a platoon of tanks were to participate in the operation—General MacArthur explained in his official report that in dealing with "riotous elements" a display of "obvious strength gains a moral ascendancy."

The bonus marchers read in the early editions of the afternoon papers that the troops had been summoned. For nearly three hours they waited in the summer sun, some taking front-row seats in windows of the partly wrecked buildings to be evacuated, others napping in the shade of Pennsylvania Avenue's sycamores or hawking the B.E.F. newspaper to the gathering crowd of women shoppers, civil servants, and curious passers-by. Street vendors bobbed up with cold lemonade and frozen puddings. As the *Star* reported next day, "It might have been a crowd at a country fair."

At 4:45 P.M. four troops of cavalry appeared, sabers raised, with six tanks lumbering behind them, their machine guns hooded. Infantrymen in steel helmets, with blue tear-gas bombs dangling from their belts and bayonets drawn, trotted on the double behind the tanks. The crowd, still in a carnival mood, set up a loud cheer that was echoed from the windows of the old red-brick hulks packed with veterans. "No one in the crowd, any more than the veterans from their high perches, seemed disposed to take the cavalry seriously," the *Star* reported. The cavalry might well have been riding to the rescue of an embattled wagon train. Laughter and applause greeted an anonymous wag in one of the tanks who thrust a wire through an opening in the armor and waved a white handkerchief.

In the shadow of the Capitol the cavalry deployed along the north side of Pennsylvania Avenue, the infantry column along the south side. "As the soldiers approached more closely, a few brickbats, stones and clubs were thrown," according to the official report, but Thomas L. Stokes of the United Press saw no evidence of resistance, nor did his colleague Paul Y. Anderson, who heard a command and saw the cavalry charge the crowd with drawn sabers: "Men, women and children fled shrieking across the broken ground, falling into excavations as they strove to avoid the rearing hoofs and saber points. Meantime, infantry on the south side had adjusted gas masks and were hurling tear gas bombs into the block into which they had just driven the veterans."

Anderson saw a mother pleading with a noncommissioned officer for permission to rescue a suitcase which contained all of the spare clothing she owned, both for herself and her child. "Get out of here, lady, before you get hurt," Anderson heard the noncom say, and watched him calmly set fire to her shanty. At Third and C streets he witnessed a company of infantry tossing tear-gas bombs right and left. "Some fell in front yards jammed with Negro women and children. One appeared to land on the front porch of a residence. Two small girls fell to the sidewalk, choking and screaming. But the veterans were beyond the street intersection more than fifty yards away. This gas was intended for the spectators . . ."

By nine o'clock the Pennsylvania Avenue area had been cleared, the veterans routed, and their billets burned, some by the troops, others by the marchers themselves. An exhausted reporter, phoning from the War Department, checked in with his city desk. He said he had been assured that troops would not be sent to Anacostia that night, so he was going home to get some sleep. "You damn fool," his editor snapped, "the troops are already there!"

Another reporter, Thomas R. Henry, was more alert. He was on hand to see the police clear the road to Anacostia and the troops move in, while spectators collected at the bridge which separated the city from the camp. "A better ordered crowd never gathered to witness a battle," Henry reported. Their sympathies, he noted, were with the bonus marchers. The crowd dispersed quickly at the first whiff of tear gas. Nobody was hurt.

"The infantrymen go down into the open field," Henry wrote. "A truck of the District Fire Department goes just behind them, throwing its floodlights as far as the first row of tents and hovels. There is no sign of life in them. . . . The infantry advances cautiously. They move in single file along the river bank. There is a line of hovels which have been erected for veterans with families. They are deserted now. The soldiers apply the torch to them. They are like tinder."

The cavalry rode up behind the foot soldiers with "little relish for the job ahead of them." When a drunken veteran staggered out of the darkness and chided the men on horseback for turning against their "buddies," his taunts were taken good-naturedly. A delegation from the Anacostia camp was met with sympathy and cigarettes and, after a pleasant chat, escorted to General MacArthur, who granted the veterans time to collect their belongings.

It was nearly midnight when the women and children, evacuated to an embankment above the camp, saw flames suddenly burst from the center of the ebony bowl below. The platform where they had gathered with their men for vaudeville shows and the windy oratory of visiting spellbinders had been put to the torch. The flames, fed by fires the marchers began to set themselves, spread slowly, engulfing the big gospel tent, the packing boxes, egg crates, automobile bodies, and pup tents.

Silhouetted in the flickering shadows of the burning camp, the routed army began to regroup, stunned families reunited, fathers taking the smaller children into their arms as they drifted off. Some stumbled toward the Virginia border, only to find it blocked by soldiers. The Maryland line was guarded by state troopers. Some of the veterans wandered aimlessly; others dropped to the roadside, dabbing their eyes with damp handkerchiefs to ease the sting, while the children coughed and whimpered from the tear gas they had drawn into their lungs.

It was nearly four o'clock in the morning when, as rain began to fall, they were permitted to enter Maryland on the condition they keep moving toward Pennsylvania, where Johnstown's Mayor Eddie McCloskey, in a speech delivered at Anacostia only a few days earlier, had offered them sanctuary if they were ever driven out of Washington. Transportation to Johnstown was cheerfully provided by Maryland authorities eager to rid the state of this human refuse.

Driven out of Washington, herded across Maryland, the dazed men, women, and children of the B.E.F. huddled in trucks, clutching the sideboards, staring blankly at the Pennsylvania countryside. State troopers were waiting for them at a Jennerstown traffic signal nineteen miles from Johnstown. The trucks were directed west over Laurel Hill and Chestnut Ridge instead of north toward the abandoned amusement park on the outskirts of Johnstown, where stragglers were already being sheltered by Mayor McCloskey. Once the men in the trucks realized they had been duped, they stopped the trucks, clambered down, and headed back toward Johnstown. Malcolm Cowley of the *New Republic* gave two of them a lift in his car:

> One was a man gassed in the Argonne and tear-gassed at Anacostia; he breathed with an effort, as if each breath would be his last. The other was a man with family troubles; he had lost his wife and six children during the retreat from Camp Marks and hoped to find them in Johnstown. He talked about his service in France, his three medals, which he refused to wear, his wounds, his five years in a government hospital. "If they gave me a job," he said, "I wouldn't care about the bonus."

While the remnants of his routed army were converging on Johnstown's Ideal Amusement Park, a filthy, fly-ridden weed patch suddenly burgeoning with lean-tos, bough huts, and pup tents, Commander Waters was frantically trying to establish "some sort of semipermanent shelter for those in the B.E.F. who were completely homeless." A woman in Catonsville, Maryland, offered him twenty-five to fifty acres as a camp site, but the state's attorney general warned Waters that no such encampment could be established without the approval of the Board of Health. And no such approval would be given.

The Governor of Pennsylvania dispatched a committee of trained social workers to the Johnstown camp. They found the men well-disciplined ("no begging or panhandling"), and their leaders "courteous and considerate." In the teeth of intemperate new charges that most of the B.E.F. had never served in the United States Army or Navy, the Pennsylvania report stated, "There can be no question whatever that almost all of them were war veterans." This jibed with the statement just issued by the Veterans' Administrator that ninety-four per cent of the members of the B.E.F. had seen military service, two-thirds of them overseas.

The squatters shoring up their makeshift shelters in the Ideal Amusement Park were the depressed country's poor relations, no more welcome in Johnstown—despite the Mayor's invitation—than in Washington. The president of the Baltimore & Ohio Railroad, out of sympathy for the administration's embarrassment, offered to disperse this symbol of the nation's distress. A committee of Johnstown's leading citizens carried the transportation offer to His Honor the Mayor. The redheaded former prize fighter was impressed by the wisdom of accepting the generosity of the B.&O. He marched into the camp and announced, "God sent you to Johnstown. Now I am going to send you home." He smashed a heckler's jaw and shouted, "I can lick anybody in this damned outfit," but when the trains pulled out next day, the Mayor was on hand to kiss the babies good-by and speed his parting guests with a brass band.

Some 500 men, women and children were dumped in Chicago, spent two days in a condemned building, then were hustled out of the city. When the city manager of Kansas City got word that a trainload was heading his way, he scraped up $1,500 to keep the train moving. Little Joe Maida, a four-foot six-inch dynamo, organized a camp in Denver, where sixty-four families with ninety-eight children had access to a hospital, a diet kitchen for undernourished youngsters, and an entertainment center, but most of the refugees drifted back into the shifting ranks of the unemployed disappearing into shack cities, railroad jungles, and overcrowded missions.

When a convention of the B.E.F. was called in Uniontown, Pennsylvania, only 600 men remained of the 20,000 to 30,000 who had poured into Washington early that summer. The men, shivering in the autumn rain, filed into a gloomy warehouse, shouted themselves hoarse, then shuffled away. Their leaders, quarrelling among themselves, split into various groups—the Khaki Shirts, the Rank and File, the Blue Shirts and assorted local organizations, each claiming to be the real B.E.F.

". . . I was heartsick at the number of Americans who were using 'Help the B.E.F.' as a means of making a living," Waters later wrote of this confused post-eviction period. He pictured himself as fed up with "selfish attempts within the B.E.F. to seize power in the hope of acquiring a following that could be sold out to some cause or other." Waters disbanded the B.E.F. and severed his ties with the

Khaki Shirts and the Rank and File. He soon sank back into the obscurity from which he had sprung, and the B.E.F. faded away with him.

The B.E.F. leaders, with no political background, no real program, and no discernible flair for leadership, had contrived to hold their ragged ranks together with only the adhesive of a common grudge. Anyone to the left of Andrew Mellon was suspect in their eyes, and for inspiration they turned not to Stalin but to Mussolini and Hitler. In trying to rally the unemployed to the ranks of the Khaki Shirts, *The B.E.F. News* had declared, "Inevitably such an organization brings up comparison with the Fascisti of Italy and the Nazi [*sic*] of Germany. For five years Hitler was lampooned and derided. But today he controls Germany. Mussolini before the war was a tramp printer, driven from Italy because of his political views. But today he is a world figure."

The American press was too busy defending or attacking the administration's efforts to pin the Communist label on the B.E.F. to take notice of its flirtation with fascism, but Malcolm Cowley remarked on it in the *New Republic* and refused to take it seriously; as he pointed out, "a Fascist movement, to succeed in this country, must come from the middle classes and be respectable."

The bonus marchers, plunged by circumstances into a potentially revolutionary movement, had been the despair of the Communists tugging from the left and the Khaki Shirts from the right. They had marched on Washington not with the clenched fists of revolt, but with the slumped shoulders of helpless acquiescence. They were the kind of men to be found in bread lines, not at barricades.

"The spontaneous outburst of the bonus march created a crisis in the central committee of the Communist party," one of its reformed members testified in 1951, "because the party, although working for the creation of such a movement, had, as it were, missed the boat in getting it started; so it started by itself and the problem then arose as to what could be done to get hold of this runaway movement and catch up with it." The party's lack of success was attested by another ex-Communist, Benjamin Gitlow, who wrote that Earl Browder was "held responsible for the Party's failure to gain leadership and control of the movement."

Mr. Hoover, writing nearly twenty years after the event, described the evicted remnants of the B.E.F. as "mixed hoodlums, ex-convicts, Communists and a minority of veterans." The same charges had been made in September, 1932, by his Attorney General.

A copy of the Attorney General's report has been preserved in General Glassford's private papers. In the margin, alongside the Attorney General's contention that the B.E.F. had probably "brought into the City of Washington the largest aggregation of criminals that had ever been assembled in the city at any one time," Glassford jotted the question: "Why crime below normal?" Of the 362 arrests of bonus marchers, only twelve had been for criminal offenses. Crime had actually decreased in the capital during the invasion.

"You'll be made the goat," an acquaintance had warned Glassford when he stepped into the local leadership vacuum and assumed responsibility for feeding and housing the bonus marchers. "I suppose I will," he replied. "But if I'm to be the goat, I prefer it to be with my conscience clear."

A few months after the eviction of the B.E.F., he was hounded out of his job over an administrative dispute, but there could be little doubt of the real cause. Glassford conducted a survey of conditions among young transients of the Depression, turning in a report which contributed to the establishment of the Civilian Conservation Corps. He retired to a ranch in Arizona, ran unsuccessfully for Congress, returned to Washington in World War II to serve as internal security director for the Army Provost Marshal General, and, after the war, settled down in Laguna Beach, California, where he devoted his last years to his life-long hobby, painting. He died in August, 1959, at the age of seventy-six.

Glassford went to his grave denying that he had asked for military assistance or had needed it after having put down the first two disturbances in less than ten minutes, but once the District commissioners had submitted their written request to the White House, President Hoover had no choice but to comply. It was a tragic circumstance that the name of a President who had first captured the imagination of the American electorate as a humanitarian should be forever linked with the specter of federal troops driving unarmed men, women, and children from the nation's capital.

It was no less unfortunate for General MacArthur, who was called upon to carry out what he has always regarded as the most distasteful order ever given him. Admonished to "use all humanity consistent with the execution of the order," he brought it off without gunfire and with remarkably few casualties. When it was all over, the Secretary of War was quoted as saying, "It was a great victory. MacArthur is the Man of the Hour." Later Mr. Hurley denied the statement and ruefully delivered what well may be the historian's final judgment on the Bonus March: "There is no glory in this terrible episode—no hero."

"I was graduated from college in June, 1932," John D. Weaver writes, "and came home to Washington, D.C., to find the shabby environs of the Capitol swarming with jobless men in frayed shirts, faded jeans, and overseas caps half-covering their thinning hair." He talked to men and women of the bonus army and visited their camps; later this experience became the basis of a novel, Another Such Victory (Viking).

For further reading: B.E.F., *by Walter W. Waters, as told to William C. White (John Day, 1933);* The Crisis of the Old Order, *by Arthur Schlesinger, Jr. (Houghton Mifflin, 1957);* The Lean Years, *by Irving Bernstein (Houghton Mifflin, 1960).*

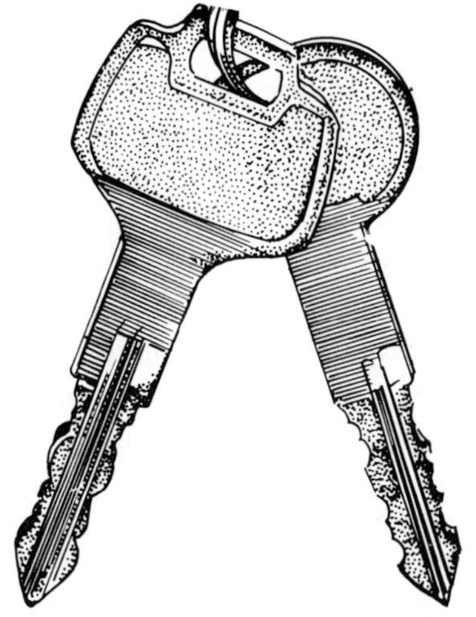

"Shut the Goddam Plant!"

Stephen W. Sears

At General Motors' Flint, Michigan, Fisher Body Number One, the largest auto-body factory in the world, it was early evening of a chilly winter day. Suddenly a bright red light began flashing in the window of the United Automobile Workers union hall across the street from the plant's main gate. It was the signal for an emergency union meeting.

When the swing shift took its dinner break at 8:00 P.M., excited workers crowded into the hall. UAW organizer Robert C. Travis confirmed the rumor crackling through the huge plant: dies for the presses that stamped out car body panels were being loaded into freight cars on a Fisher One spur track. Two days earlier, he reminded the men, fellow unionists had struck the Fisher Body plant in Cleveland; now, fearing Flint would be next, General Motors was trying to transfer the vital stamping dies to its other plants. "Well, what are we going to do about it?" Travis asked.

"Well, them's our jobs," a man said. "We want them left right here in Flint." There was chorus of agreement. "What do you want to do?" Travis asked.

"Shut her down! Shut the goddam plant!" In a moment the hall was a bedlam of cheering.

As the dinner break ended, the men streamed back into Fisher One. Travis was watching anxiously in front of the union hall when the starting whistle blew. Instead of the usual answering pound of machinery, there was only silence. For long minutes nothing seemed to be happening. Then a third-floor window swung open and a worker leaned out, waving exultantly to Travis. "She's ours!" he shouted.

Thus began, on December 30, 1936, the great Flint sit-down strike, the most momentous confrontation between American labor and management in this century. For the next six weeks Flint would be a lead story in newspapers, newsreels, and radio newscasts. Events there dramatized the new militancy of the American worker, a mass movement that was to produce basic changes in the relationship of capital and labor. To those in sympathy with labor's goal of unionizing the auto industry, the rambunctious young United Automobile Workers union was David challenging the General Motors Goliath. To those dedicated to the sanctity of property, the UAW and its methods posed a radical, revolutionary threat to industrial capitalism. Few observers were neutral about the Flint sit-down.

There was no disputing the fact that the UAW faced a giant. Auto making was America's number-one industry, and General Motors was the number-one auto maker. Indeed, it was the largest manufacturing concern in the world. GM's 1936 sales of 1,500,000 Chevrolets, Pontiacs, Buicks, Oldsmobiles, La Salles, and Cadillacs represented better than 43 per cent of the domestic passenger-car market. It had sixty-nine auto plants in thirty-five cities. Business analysts regarded GM President Alfred P. Sloan, Jr., as a genius and his company as the best managed in America. It was unquestionably the most profitable—$284,000,000 in 1936 pretax profits on $1,400,000,000 in sales. This was a matter of great satisfaction to its 342,384 stockholders, and to one in particular. E. I. Du Pont de Nemours & Company owned nearly one-quarter of GM's common stock, good that year for nearly $45,000,000 in dividends. In short, General Motors was the paragon of industrial capitalism, and there was heavy pressure, both from within and without, to maintain the *status quo* that produced so many golden eggs.

One fundamental tenet of the *status quo* was a fiercely anti-union stance. In this General Motors acted in perfect unanimity with its competitors. Nineteen thirty-six marked the fortieth anniversary of the American automobile industry, and never in those four decades had the open shop seriously been threatened. The very notion of unionism was anathema to captains of the auto industry. "As a businessman, I was unaccustomed to the whole idea," Alfred Sloan wrote blandly in his memoirs.

Before the Great Depression, unionism was in truth not much of an issue in Detroit. The vast labor army recruited during the auto boom of the twenties—white dirt farmers, poor city dwellers, southern blacks, recent immigrants—was docile and innocent of trade-union experience. Any labor grievances were defused by pay scales higher than those in most other industries and by a system of "welfare capitalism" (group insurance, savings programs, housing subsidies, recreational facilities, and the like) in which General Motors was a pioneer. Open-shop Detroit had little to fear from the nation's largest union, the American Federation of Labor. The craft-minded AFL devoted itself to horizontal unionism—organizing all the machinists, for example, regardless of industry. It studiously ignored industrial un-ionism, the vertical organization of the unskilled or semiskilled workers within a particular industry such as autos, steel, or rubber.

Then the Depression knocked everything haywire. In the early 1930's Detroit auto workers found themselves powerless as the industry collapsed like a punctured balloon. Welfare capitalism was silent on job security. Wages and work time were slashed. As layoffs mounted, workers with ten or twenty years' experience discovered that their seniority counted for nothing; it counted for nothing, either, in the call-backs that marked an upturn in auto sales beginning in 1933. Assembly lines were speeded up mercilessly to raise productivity and restore profit levels. Bitter men protested. "You might call yourself a man if you was on the street," a Fisher Body worker recalled, "but as soon as you went through the door and punched your card, you was nothing more or less than a robot." "It takes your guts out, that line. The speed-up, that's the trouble," another said. "You should see him come home at night, him and the rest of the men . . .," A Flint auto worker's wife testified. "So tired like they was dead. . . . And then at night in bed, he shakes, his whole body, he shakes. . . ."

More and more auto workers began to see unionism as their only hope to redress the balance. In this they detected an ally in the New Deal. The National Industrial Recovery Act (1933) recognized labor's right to organize and bargain collectively. The NIRA, however, was too weak a reed to support labor's aspirations, for it was largely unenforceable and easily evaded by management; and in any event, the Supreme Court knocked it down in 1935. But labor's hopes were raised anew by the passage of the National Labor Relations Act—the so-called Wagner Act, named for its chief sponsor, New York Senator Robert F. Wagner. The act established a National Labor Relations Board and gave it teeth to enforce collective bargaining and permit unionization efforts without interference by management.

The auto companies ignored the Wagner Act, confidently expecting the Supreme Court to do its duty. While they waited, they turned increasingly to labor spies to quash unionizing efforts. The most notorious spy system flourished at Ford, where goon squads instituted a bloody reign of terror in the massive River Rouge complex in Dearborn, outside Detroit. The General Motors espionage network was nonviolent but no less widespread. Evidence gathered by a Senate investigating committee chaired by Wisconsin's Robert M. La Follette, Jr., revealed that from 1934 to mid-1936 GM hired no fewer than fourteen private detective and security agencies, at a cost of $994,000, to ferret out and fire employees with union sympathies. This "most colossal super-system of spies yet devised an any American corporation," the La Follette committee charged, enveloped the worker in a web of fear. "Fear harries his every footstep, caution muffles his words. He is in no sense any longer a free American."

Launching an effective union in such turbulent waters would be difficult enough, and it was made no easier by an upheaval in labor's ranks. In 1933, prodded into action by the collective bargaining section of the NIRA, the American Federation of Labor had made a cautious stab at organizing Detroit's work force by chartering the United Automobile Workers union. However, leadership in the AFL-affiliated UAW was far too conservative to suit the rank and file. Three years' work produced a few toeholds among independent auto makers but barely a dent in the Big Three. In GM's Flint factories, for example, there was a grand total of 150 paid-up UAW members in June, 1936, just six months before the great sit-down.

This stumbling effort to organize the auto workers reflected the fratricidal conflict within the AFL. Advocates of industrial unionism, led by John L. Lewis of the United Mine Workers, David Dubinsky of the International Ladies' Garment Workers, and Sidney Hillman of the Amalgamated Clothing Workers, formed a rump group, the Committee (later Congress) of Industrial Organization. In the summer of 1936 the CIO seceded from the AFL ranks, taking with it the United Automobile Workers locals. Marching under the new CIO banner, the UAW prepared to do battle with the auto industry. It would be the first modern test of the theory of industrial unionism.

The revitalized UAW settled on General Motors as its first target. Chrysler's Walter Chrysler, who had climbed Horatio Alger-like up through the ranks, was considered the auto magnate most sympathetic to labor; if number-one GM could be conquered, number-two Chrysler might follow along. Ford was simply too tough a nut to crack yet. In addition, General Motors was particularly vulnerable. All bodies for the low-priced Chevrolet and the medium-priced Pontiac, Buick, and Oldsmobile were built by its Fisher Body division. If it came down to a strike—and no labor leader doubted that it would—the closing of only a few selected Fisher Body plants would immediately cripple the company.

And when the strike came, there was no doubt it would focus on Flint, the General Motors citadel. William C. Durant founded the company there in 1908, and it had remained the center of GM auto production. The Flint of 1936 was a drab gray industrial city of 160,000, some sixty miles northwest of Detroit, ringed by GM installations. Fisher Body One was to the south, a huge Buick assembly plant to the north, Fisher Body Two and a Chevrolet complex to the west, AC Spark Plug to the east. Two out of three of the city's breadwinners—more than 47,000 of them—worked for GM. Four out of five families, directly or indirectly, lived off the company payroll. Virtually every aspect of economic, social, and cultural life revolved around GM. Flint was very much a company town.

The union's first job was what a later generation would call consciousness raising. Wyndham Mortimer, a veteran trade unionist, began this task even before the UAW defected to the CIO, combining the five weak Flint locals into one, Local 156, and planting the seeds of unionism. In October, 1936, however, the quiet, hard-working Mortimer was replaced by twenty-seven-year-old Bob Travis, a more personable and energetic organizer. At Travis' side was Roy Reuther, who, with his brothers Victor and Walter, would become a dominant force in the UAW. The sons of a German immigrant, the Reuthers were, in Victor's words, "born into the labor movement." Eloquent, ambitious, and like his brothers deeply committed to trade unionism, Roy Reuther formed a strong partnership with Travis.

Facing a hostile management with a fearful company town infested with labor spies (the only safe topics of conversation in Flint, according to Mortimer, were "sports, women, dirty stories, and the weather"), UAW organizers did the bulk of their recruiting in workers' homes and at clandestine meetings. The labor journalist Henry Kraus was brought in to edit the *Flint Auto Worker,* an important vehicle for airing worker grievances and spreading the UAW gospel. Much effort was devoted to involving workers' wives in the movement. And rather than spreading themselves thin proselytizing the entire Flint GM work force, Travis and Reuther focused on the men in the city's two key Fisher body plants. Their efforts were made easier by Franklin D. Roosevelt's overwhelming victory in the November elections, which labor took as a good omen for support from Washington.

By late December, Flint Local 156 had signed up 10 per cent of the city's GM workers, largely in secret to foil the spies and mostly in Fisher One and Fisher Two. On December 22, GM Executive Vice-President William S. Knudsen, meeting with UAW President Homer Martin, denied that issues such as union recognition, job security, pay rates, seniority rights, and the speed-up were "national in scope." Corporate headquarters had no say in such matters, he piously declared: they must be settled on the local level with individual plant managers. Martin recognized this account of the working of the General Motors Corporation for what it was—pure fiction. it was clear that the company had no intention of obeying the Wagner Act and seriously bargaining with any independent union. The stage was set for a strike.

But what kind of strike? Veteran Flint workers remembered an attempt to close Fisher One in 1930 that had been smashed by local lawmen abetted by the Michigan state police. Pickets were scattered and ridden down by mounted officers, and strike leaders were arrested and subsequently fired. Few UAW officials in Flint had any illusions that their forty-five hundred or so members could long sustain a conventional picket-line strike in the heart of General Motors country. The solution might lie in an entirely different kind of strike—a sit-down.

The tactic was ingeniously simple. Instead of walking off the job, strikers stopped work but stayed at their machines, holding valuable company property hostage to enforce their demands. A sit-down was far less vulnerable to police action than outside picketing, and it neutralized a primary weapon in management's arsenal, the use of strikebreakers to resume production. Even more than a conventional striker, the sit-downer was taking his fight directly to management.

The sit-down was not new—some claimed to have traced its origins back to stone masons in ancient Egypt—but its baptism by fire took place in Europe in the twenties and thirties. Italian metal workers, Welsh coal miners, Spanish copper miners, and Greek rubber workers sat down at their jobs, and in the spring of 1936 mass sit-downs in France took on the proportions of a nationwide general strike. In the United States in 1936 the Bureau of Labor Statistics reported forty-eight sit-down strikes. The ones most closely watched by auto workers took place at Bendix Products (owned in part by GM) in South Bend, Indiana, and at two Detroit parts makers, Midland Steel Products and Kelsey-Hayes Wheel. All three won limited worker gains and deeply impressed UAW militants. Thus far, however, no American sit-down had been played for truly high stakes.

In the midst of the feverish unionizing efforts in Flint's Fisher One, a shop steward named Bud Simons was asked if his men were ready to strike. "Ready?" Simons exclaimed. "They're like a pregnant woman in her tenth month!" Flint's militants, however, were upstaged by militants in the Fisher Body plant in Cleveland. On December 28, 1936, Fisher Cleveland was shut tight by a sit-down. In Flint Bob Travis and his UAW organizers cast about desperately for some excuse to initiate a strike.

The report on December 30 that the company was moving the stamping dies out of Fisher One was the *casus belli* Travis needed. "Okay!" he said happily, "they're asking for it!" By midnight that day the swing shift's capture of the huge plant was complete. Two miles away the smaller Fisher Two was also taken over by sit-downers. As the new year began, production of Chevrolets and Buicks, General Motors' bread-and-butter cars, ground to a halt. Soon other GM marques were effected, for the occupation of the two Fisher Body plants in Flint and the one in Cleveland had the potential for halting fully 75 per cent of the company's passenger-car production. The sit-down gave David the weapon to use against Goliath.

Over the next few weeks, strikes would shut down more than a dozen other GM plants. Parts shortages forced many additional plant closings. The total number of idled men would reach 136,000. Yet from first to last, the spotlight remained on Flint. The strike's success or failure—and to the strikers, success meant nothing less than management's recognition of the UAW as exclusive bargaining agent— would be decided at the center of the General Motors empire.

The sit-downers began to organize themselves with military precision. Once all nonstrikers (and all female employees) left, the two plants were barricaded and patrolled. "It was like we were soldiers holding the fort," one of them said. "It was like war. The guys with me became my buddies." Everyone served a regular daily shift on a committee to manage such functions as defense, food supply, sanitation, and recreation. Discipline was strict: the strike leaders were determined to show the public that this was no rabble-in-arms take-over. News reporters and other observers who toured the seized factories remarked on the organization and on the absence of wild-eyed fanatics. "We're just here protecting our jobs," a

Fisher Two striker told *The New York Times.* "We don't aim to keep the plants or try to run them, but we want to see that nobody takes our jobs. . . ." Petty violations of strike committee rules meant extra cleanup or K.P. duty, serious offenses (possession of guns or liquor, the sabotaging of company property) meant expulsion. Round-the-clock dining halls were established in the plant cafeterias, and sleeping quarters were improvised from car seats and bodies.

Keeping the men occupied during their new six-hour "work shifts" was not difficult, but it required more ingenuity to fill the off-duty periods and keep morale high. Defense committees set up production lines for the making of blackjacks and billy clubs. Many hours were devoted to cards, checkers, and dominoes, and there was a steady flow of newspapers and magazines into the plants. UAW lecturers spoke on parliamentary procedures, collective bargaining, and labor history. There were improvised games of volleyball and Ping-pong, and here and there men could be seen roller skating between the long rows of idle machinery. Amateur theatricals, in which enthusiasm and raucous humor were more evident than acting skill, played to cheering, jeering audiences. A showing of Charlie Chaplin's satire on assembly-line mass production, *Modern Times,* was greeted enthusiastically. Those who played banjos, mandolins, or harmonicas put on impromptu concerts and almost everyone took up community singing, sometimes writing their own lyrics; to the tune of "Gallagher and Shean," for example, they belted out:

> *Oh! Mr. Sloan! Mr. Sloan!*
> *Everyone knows your heart was made of stone.*
> *But the Union is so strong*
> *That we'll always carry on.*
> *Absolutely, Mr. Travis!*
> *Positively, Mr. Sloan!*

The population in Fisher One and Fisher Two varied widely during the six-weeks strike. Local 156 set up outside picket lines as an aid to maintaining traffic into and out of the plants, which enabled sit-downers to take leave and visit friends and families. The number of men in Fisher One varied from a high of something over one thousand to a low of ninety, in Fisher Two from upwards of four hundred and fifty to as few as seventeen. The problem for the Fisher Two strike leaders was the large number of married men in their ranks; concern for the welfare of families eroded their staying power as the strike dragged on. Fisher One had a higher percentage of single men of the "hard, reckless type" (in the words of a *New York Times* reporter) and who were better able to endure the strike's pressures. Population fluctuated as hopes for a settlement waxed and waned, and when the number of sit-downers fell dangerously low, the UAW called on militant locals from Detroit and Toledo for reinforcements. The arrival of one such group moved

Bud Simons to remark, ''I have never seen a bunch of guys that were so ready for blood in my life.''

On the whole, however, the sit-downers maintained a remarkably strong sense of community. In a letter to his wife, one of them wrote, ''I could of came out when they went on strike But hunny I just thought I join the union and I look pretty yellow if I dident stick with them. . . .'' A growing self-esteem strengthened the workers' commitment. As labor historian Sidney Fine writes, they were ''transformed from badge numbers and easily replaceable cogs in an impersonal industrial machine into heroes of American labor.'' A striker remembered that ''it started out kinda ugly because the guys were afraid they put their foot in it and all they was gonna do is lose their jobs. But as time went on, they begin to realize they could win this darn thing, 'cause we had a lot of outside people comin' in showin' their sympathy.''

Meanwhile, on the outside, Bob Travis and Roy Reuther set up strike headquarters in the Pengelly Building, a down-at-the-heels firetrap in downtown Flint. The place was a beehive, with strikers and volunteer helpers cranking out publicity releases, raising money, mobilizing support, planning strategy. The most immediate problem was food. Dorothy Kraus, wife of the *Flint Auto Worker* editor Henry Kraus, directed a strike kitchen set up in a restaurant near Fisher One that was turned over to the union by its owner. Meals were prepared there three times a day and delivered to the plants in large kettles under heavy union guard. (The menus were the work of Max Gazan, former chef of the Detroit Athletic Club, a favorite haunt of the GM Establishment.) Food stocks were purchased or donated by sympathizers or by Flint merchants pressured to do so by the threat of boycott. As many as two hundred people took part in running the strike kitchen, many of them sit-downers' wives. Wives also formed a Women's Auxiliary and a Women's Emergency Brigade. Kraus's newspaper and the mimeographed *Punch Press,* put out by student volunteers from the University of Michigan, kept the men informed. Cars equipped with loudspeakers allowed instant communication with the sit-downers, and outside picket lines lent moral support.

Despite its espionage network, General Motors was caught flat-footed by the sit-down tactic. At first management tried harassment by sporadically cutting back heat and light to the two plants, but it was feared that any serious attempt to starve out or freeze out the strikers would result in violence—and they were right. Groping for a policy to deal with the crisis, the company discovered that nothing in the Michigan statute books forbade the peaceful occupation of a company's property by its employees. Nor were the trespass laws much help: since the workers had entered the plants at management's ''invitation,'' trespass presented a legal thicket. Nevertheless, GM quickly turned to the courts, petitioning on January 2, 1937, for an injunction to ''restrain'' the strikers from occupying Fisher One and Fisher Two. County Circuit Court Judge Edward D. Black, an eighty-three-year-old lifelong resident of Flint, granted it the same day.

To its subsequent great embarrassment, the corporation in its haste had failed to do its homework on Judge Black. On January 5 the UAW called a press conference to charge that in issuing the injunction Black was guilty of "unethical conduct," for he owned 3,665 shares of GM stock with a market value of almost $220,000. In the ensuing uproar, the Black injunction became a dead letter.

Round One to the UAW.

Round Two, if General Motors had its way, would find the sit-downers under irresistible pressure from the community. On January 5, GM President Alfred Sloan published an open letter to all employees. "Will a labor organization run the plants of General Motors . . . or will the Management continue to do so?" he asked. "You are being forced out of your jobs by sit-down strikes, by widespread intimidation. . . . You are being told that to bargain collectively you must be a member of a labor organization. . . . Do not be misled. Have no fear that any union or any labor dictator will dominate the plants of General Motors Corporation. No General Motors worker need join any organization to get a job or to keep a job. . . ." A campaign of mass meetings, balloting, and petitions"I Love My Boss" petitions as strikers derisively tagged them—indicated that by company count four out of five Flint workers wanted to return to their jobs. (Only AC Spark Plug among GM's Flint plants was still operating at full capacity.) The UAW charged the coercion and intimidation produced this outpouring of company loyalty. The truth lay somewhere in between. As Sidney Fine points out, there was in Flint "a large middle group of workers, who, although preferring work to idleness, were uncommitted to either side in the dispute and were awaiting its outcome to determine where their best interests lay."

Two days after Sloan's open letter, a local businessman and former mayor named George E. Boysen announced the formation of the Flint Alliance "for the Security of Our Jobs, Our Homes, and Our Community." Membership was open to all Flint citizens, and within a week Boysen claimed that almost twenty-six thousand had signed up. Evidence that GM sponsored the alliance is sketchy, but it clearly had the company's blessing. The UAW viewed the alliance with concern, seeing it as a possible umbrella group for organizing strikebreakers or triggering violence against the occupied plants.

Several main themes marked this campaign to turn public opinion against the strikers—the oppression of the majority by a militant minority; the presence of "outside agitators" disrupting the General Motors family; and the insistence that the sit-down was a "Red Plot" threatening the capitalist system. This last was one of the most persistent charges. It was pointed out that the seizure of private property was a favorite communist tactic, and that the auto workers' union was honeycombed with Red radicals.

Hindsight has magnified this communist conspiracy theory, for such prominent UAW leaders as Wyndham Mortimer, Bob Travis, and Bud Simons, head of the strike committee in Fisher One, were in fact later involved in various communist or communist front activities. Indeed, the UAW itself, for a decade after 1937, was in constant fratricidal turmoil over the issue of communists within its ranks. It is clear, however, that the Flint sit-down strike was a grass-roots revolt owing no allegiance to communist ideology or conspiracy. The sit-downers were men driven to desperation by oppressive working conditions, men convinced that management's attitude toward labor held no hope for improvement. "So I'm a Red?" a worker summed it up for a reporter. "I suppose it makes me a Red because I don't like making time so hard on these goddamned machines. When I get home I'm so tired I can't sleep with my wife."

Tension continued to build in Flint. On January 11, 1937, the thirteenth day of the strike, it exploded into violence. The incident that triggered it was carefully staged. About noon that day General Motors abruptly cut off heat to the Fisher Two plant, where about one hundred sit-downers were holding the second floor. (Unlike more strongly fortified Fisher One two miles away, Fisher Two's first floor and main gate were controlled by company security men.) It was a cold, raw day, with temperatures around sixteen degrees. During the afternoon an unusual number of police cars was seen in the neighborhood. At 6:00 P.M., when the strikers' evening meal was delivered to the Fisher Two main gate, guards refused to let it through. By 8:30, when Victor Reuther drove up in a union sound car to investigate, he found the cold and hungry strikers "in no pleasant mood." It was decided to take over the main gate to link the sit-downers with the pickets outside.

A squad of strikers, armed with homemade billy clubs, marched up to the company guards blocking the gate and demanded the key. When they were refused, a striker yelled, "Get the hell out of there!" and the guards fled to the plant ladies room, locking themselves in. The head of the security detail telephoned Flint police headquarters to report that his men had been threatened and "captured." Right on cue, squad cars arrived, carrying some thirty riot-equipped city policemen. The police stormed the plant entrance, smashing windows and firing tear gas into the interior. The strikers fought back with a drumfire of bottles, rocks, nuts and bolts, heavy steel car-door hinges, and cascades of water from the plant's fire hoses. Under this barrage, the attackers withdrew to rearm and wait reinforcements. The sit-downers put the lull to good use, tossing door hinges and other stocks of "popular ammunition" to pickets outside and rushing a squad to vantage points on the roof.

Soon the police charged a second time, firing their gas guns and hurling gas grenades through the plant windows and among the pickets outside. But now the defensive firepower was doubled as the pickets joined the battle. Fire hoses sent policemen sprawling. Others were felled by hinges, milk bottles, bricks, and pieces of roof coping. The county sheriff's car was tipped over; as he crawled out, a hinge struck him on the head. Tear gas took a toll among the defenders, who were left choking and vomiting and half-blinded. Finally, drenched and bloodied, sliding on pavement icing over from the fire-hose torrents, the attack force fled once more. Watching the "bulls" scramble away, someone gave the struggle a derisive name that stuck—the Battle of the Running Bulls.

Frustrated and humiliated, the police suddenly stopped, turned on a band of strikers pursuing them, and opened fire with pistols and riot guns loaded with buckshot. Then it was the strikers' turn to retreat, dragging their casualties with them. Thirteen suffered gunshot wounds, a dozen struck by buckshot and one hit seriously in the stomach by a pistol bullet. Eleven of the attackers also were hurt, most suffering from gashed heads but one having been hit in the leg by an errant police bullet. Retreating up a hill out of missile range, the police began sniping at the strikers in the plant, their bullets splattering against the walls and shattering windows. Clouds of acrid tear gas drifted across the icy battlefield, and above the shouting and the shooting could be heard the thundering amplified voice of Victor Reuther in the union sound car, directing the defenses and exhorting the men to stand fast. At last it was clear that the recapture effort had failed. Ambulances arrived to carry off the wounded and the injured. About midnight the sniping ceased.

But the battle had turned the sit-down onto a new course.

Hurrying to Flint from the state capital in Lansing, Michigan Governor Frank Murphy ordered in the National Guard troops and the state police. "It won't happen again," Murphy vowed. "Peace and order will prevail. The people of Flint are not going to be terrorized." By January 13 there were almost thirteen hundred Guardsmen in the city; before the strike ended, the number would rise by another two thousand. Whether General Motors had orchestrated every detail of the attempted recapture of Fisher Two, as the UAW charged, remained a matter of heated debate, but Murphy's action ensured that police violence would not "settle" the sit-down.

Organized labor had reason to fear National Guard and state police forces, which in the past had often been used to break strikes. In this instance, however, the union cheered their arrival, for it trusted the man who sent them. Indeed, the timing of the sit-down had been pegged to Democrat Murphy's taking office on January 1, 1937. He had run for governor with strong labor support. "I am heart and soul in the labor movement," he had declared during the campaign. As Wyndham Mortimer later said, "We felt that while he may or may not have been on our side, he at least would not be against us."

It was an accurate assessment. While Murphy disapproved of the sit-down tactic as an invasion of property rights, he strongly approved of the right to organize. Above all, he was determined to defuse the explosive atmosphere in Flint and get the two parties to the bargaining table. At first it appeared he would be quickly and brilliantly successful. On January 15, just four days after the Battle of the Running Bulls, Murphy announced a truce: the union agreed to evacuate Fisher One and Fisher Two, and GM agreed not to resume production while bargaining "in good faith." Then a report leaked out that GM had invited the Flint Alliance, which claimed to speak for the "greatest majority" of the city's idled workers, to attend the talks as a third party. Strike leaders saw this as fatal to their goal of winning exclusive UAW recognition; crying double-cross, they renounced the truce.

As the stalemate continued and positions hardened, new figures joined Frank Murphy in the limelight. On the GM side, Executive Vice President William Knudsen, a bluff, rough-and-ready production genius less concerned with how the strike was settled than when, was joined by two tougher-minded negotiators, Du Pont-trained financial expert Donaldson Brown and company attorney John T. Smith. On the union side, UAW President Homer Martin, an evangelical speaker but a poor negotiator, was eclipsed when the best-known figure in American labor strode onto the scene. John L. Lewis, head of the CIO, was determined to make the Flint sit-down the opening wedge in his crusade for industrial unionism. Supreme orator ("The economic royalists of General Motors—the Du Ponts and Sloans and others—" he thundered, ". . . have their fangs in labor") and a master press agent ("Seeing John Lewis," said journalist Heywood Broun, "is about as easy as seeing the Washington Monument"), Lewis was a figure to reckon with.

Just how potent a publicist he could be was evident when the spotlight shifted from Flint to Washington. The Roosevelt administration, led by Secretary of Labor Frances Perkins, tried to get the strike off dead center by bringing together Lewis and Alfred Sloan, whom Miss Perkins described as "the real principals." For all his brilliance as an administrator, the GM president was saddled with a colorless personality and did not relish taking on the theatrical Lewis. Furthermore, the intense loathing he felt for the New Deal made any dealings with the administration difficult for him. In the end he called off the talks, angering both the President and Miss Perkins. For Sloan the sticking point was bargaining with "a group that holds our plants for ransom without regard to law or justice." Lewis announced to the nation that the GM high command had "run away" to New York "to consult with their allies [a barb at the GM-Du Pont connection] to determine how far they can go in their organized defiance of labor and the law." GM gained no friends in the exchange.

General Motors, in fact, was not doing as well mustering support as might have been expected of the world's largest corporation. Its disdain for the Wagner Act, the fiasco of the Black injunction, and the violence of the Battle of the Running Bulls did little for its corporate image. Despite strong and widespread public concern over the sit-down's threat to cherished property rights, the company's position won only a fifty-three to forty-seven edge in a Gallup poll published on January 31; apparently there was considerable sympathy for the union's stated—and lawful—goal of organizing and bargaining collectively without management interference. *Business Week* analyzed the public's view as "it's 'not right' for the strikers to stay in or for the company to throw them out."

There is little doubt that the union would have done less well on any poll taken in Flint. The city's blue-collar workers were suffering intensely now. By January 20, a full 88 per cent of the city's GM work force was unemployed. The percentage on the relief rolls was greater than it had been during the depths of the Depression. General Motors also was suffering: its January output was just 60,000 cars, instead of a projected figure of 224,000. Yet neither side would budge. Tension began again to build, fueled by violent incidents at GM plants in Anderson, Indiana, on January 25 and in Saginaw, Michigan, two days later. Then two events occurred that would push the sit-down to its climax.

On January 28 General Motors turned once more to the courts, applying for a second injunction to compel the strikers to leave. This time the company first checked out the circuit court judge, Paul V. Gadola, to be sure he was clean. Flint's strike leaders, meanwhile, planned a move of their own, one considerably more dramatic.

To regain the initiative and to demonstrate to General Motors that none of its properties was safe from seizure by sit-down, Travis, Roy Reuther, and other UAW strategists plotted the capture of Chevrolet engines. Their plan had to be a daring one, for the engine plant was heavily guarded by GM police. Within hearing of auto workers whom their counterintelligence had identified as company spies, the strike leaders ''secretly'' revealed their next target to be a bearings plant, Chevrolet Nine. Company security snapped up the bait. On February 1, when the diversionary attempt was made on Chevrolet Nine, it was met by every Chevrolet guard the company could muster. After tear gas and wild, club-swinging melees, the unionists were driven out in apparent defeat. While the battle was raging inside Chevrolet Nine, however, three hundred yards away other strikers had swept through unguarded Chevrolet Four and secured the huge plant. ''We have the key plant of the GM . . .,'' one of the sit-downers would write to his wife. ''We shure done a thing that GM said never could be done. . . .'' He was right; the brilliantly executed capture of Chevrolet Four was the turning point.

Events now swiftly combined to bring the United Automobile Workers and General Motors to the negotiating table. On February 2 Judge Gadola issued a sweeping injunction that called for evacuation of the Flint Fisher Body plants within twenty-four hours, and the imposition of a $15,000,000 fine if the UAW did not comply. Although there was nothing like that sum to collect from the union treasury—''If the judge can get fifteen million bucks from us, he's welcome to it,'' a striker scoffed—the injunction did pressure the UAW to bargain. It also pressured Governor Murphy to find a quick strike-ending formula; as chief executive of the state of Michigan, he was obliged to decide how and when to enforce the injunction and uphold the law. As for GM, a massive demonstration of support by unionists outside Fisher One on February 3 seemed proof enough that any attempt to drive out the sit-downers would produce certain bloodshed and probable destruction of three of its most important plants. Reluctantly, like "a skittish virgin" in *Fortune's* irreverent phrase, the company surrendered to collective bargaining.

The talks were held in Detroit. On the GM side were Knudsen, Donaldson Brown, and John T. Smith. John L. Lewis headed the union delegation, seconded by CIO counsel Lee Pressman and UAW President Homer Martin. (The bumbling Martin was soon dispatched on a tour of faraway union locals to get him out of the way.) Murphy acted as chief negotiator, jumping back and forth between the parties "like a jack rabbit," seeking leverage for a settlement. Machinery was agreed to for later bargaining on such specific issues as wages and working conditions, and the union agreed to give up the plants and return to work while those issues were hammered out. GM agreed to take the sit-downers back without penalty or prejudice. The stiffest battle was fought over GM's recognition of the UAW as exclusive bargaining agent.

Hanging threateningly over the talks was the Gadola injunction. The very mention of using the National Guard to enforce the injunction provoked Lewis to one of his characteristic oratorical flights. According to his later recollection (perhaps embellished), he announced to Murphy: "Tomorrow morning, I shall personally enter General Motors plant Chevrolet Number Four. I shall order the men to disregard your order, to stand fast. I shall then walk up to the largest window in the plant, open it, divest myself of my outer raiment, remove my shirt, and bare my bosom. Then when you order your troops to fire, mine will be the first breast those bullets will strike!" In fact, the governor never had any notion of carrying out Judge Gadola's ruling with National Guard arms: "I'm not going down in history as 'Bloody Murphy'!" He did hint, however, at sealing off the captured plants with Guardsmen to prevent food deliveries unless the union made concessions. GM was pushed into concessions of its own by a painful economic fact. In the first ten days of February, the nation's largest auto maker produced exactly 151 cars.

Finally, at 2:35 on the morning of February 11, after sixteen grueling hours of final negotiating, the forty-four-day Flint sit-down strike came to an end. The agreement applied only to the seventeen plants that had gone out on strike, but they were GM's most important plants. As a face-saving gesture, the company did not have to state categorically that it was recognizing the union. But in fact it was: the UAW had six months to sign up auto workers before a representational election, during which time management could not interfere or deal with any other workers' body. "Well, Mr. Lewis," GM negotiator Smith said, "you beat us, but I'm not going to forget it." Production man Knudsen was not one to hold grudges. "Let us have peace and make automobiles," he proclaimed.

Late on the afternoon of February 11 the sit-downers came out. Carrying American flags, surrounded by throngs of cheering, horn-tooting supporters, the men of Fisher One marched the two miles across town to collect their compatriots in Fisher Two and Chevrolet Four. Then, thousands strong, they held a spectacular torchlight parade through downtown Flint. As they tramped along, they sang what had become their anthem:

Solidarity forever!
Solidarity forever!
Solidarity forever!
For the Union makes us strong!

They had every reason to sing and celebrate; they had won a major victory. UAW locals throughout the auto industry were promptly flooded with workers clamoring to sign up; just eight months after the sit-down settlement, the UAW could count nearly four hundred thousand dues-paying members, a five-fold increase. It easily won the representational elections in plants throughout the GM empire. Independents—Packard, Studebaker, Hudson—soon recognized the union, as did leading parts makers. In April, 1937, after a sit-down, Chrysler also succumbed. Ford held out the longest, but in 1941 it too acknowledged the UAW as exclusive bargaining agent. An important factor in all this was the Supreme Court decision, in April, 1937, upholding the Wagner Act. Unionization without interference by management was confirmed as the law of the land.

The United Automobile Workers failed to handle its success gracefully, however. From the moment of its birth, the union's high command had been rent with problems; its most decisive leaders, like those of Flint Local 156, came from the bottom. Rifts at the top were papered over during the sit-down by the overriding need for a united front, but with victory came chaos. Not until after World War II would the UAW, under the strong hand of Walter Reuther, finally put its house in order, purge itself of communists, and reach stable maturity. As for the CIO, the Flint victory, as John L. Lewis predicted, was industrial unionism's foot in the door. Beginning with Big Steel in March, 1937, the CIO successfully organized one basic industry after another. Union membership in the United States spurted 156 per cent between 1936 and 1941, most of it CIO gains.

The Flint sit-down inspired a rash of imitators. In the early months of 1937 workers of every stripe, from garbage men and dogcatchers to rug weavers and pie bakers, tried the tactic. Public irritation mounted swiftly. Many Americans had accepted the UAW's argument that the sit-down was the sole weapon it possessed to force intransigent General Motors to obey the law and permit union organizing and collective bargaining. Such an argument lost force after the Supreme Court upheld the Wagner Act; now, with both government and law behind it, organized labor was seen as achieving parity with management. Increasingly, the sit down was condemned as an irresponsible act, and by 1939, when the Supreme Court outlawed the practice as a violation of property rights, it had long since gone out of vogue.

Victory in the Flint sit-down by no means ended the discontents of the auto worker. Yet now, for the first time, he could envision himself as something more than simply an insignificant part of a great impersonal machine; as "Solidarity" phrased it, the union had made him strong. "Even if we got not one damn thing out of it other than that," a Fisher Body worker said, "we at least had a right to open our mouths without fear."

Stephen W. Sears, a frequent contributor to our pages, is a former editor with the American Heritage book division and author of The Automobile in America.

Part Four

World War II

The Nation at War—''the big one''

World War II had a pervasive and powerful impact on the United States and its people. Virtually all Americans who were adults at the time, if asked to reflect upon their personal histories, will single out aspects of the war period as among the most important and significant to themselves and their families. Any serious study of the period should include an examination of such personal memoir accounts as Studs Terkel's *The Good War* (1984) and Mark J. Harris, et al, *The Homefront: America during World War II* (1984). The articles which follow concentrate on the military and diplomatic aspects, rather than the social history, of the war. These were, after all, the matters of preeminent national concern.

One seldom finds a finer piece of historical sleuthing than that offered by William Honan. His is a fascinating account of the origin and development of the Japanese strategy for the conduct of their war in the Pacific against the United States. Honan documents how the Japanese used a theoretical war plan first formulated in the 1920s by a British journalist and naval intelligence expert.

Charles Cawthon offers us an excellent personal account of the battle for St. Lô, as the Allied forces, having successfully established a beachhead at Normandy, sought to press forward against the Nazi troops opposing them. Cawthon's narrative reveals what were to become some of the common elements of the ground war in Western Europe as experienced by American infantry units.

The tangled course of Allied diplomacy in World War II is the subject of William Hale's "Road to Yalta." Hale's article is particularly valuable for its exploration of the background of United States-Soviet Union relations dating back to 1917 and 1918. His article also serves to introduce the recent period of United States history by pointing to the collapse of Allied cooperativeness as the Second World War came to an end and the subsequent revival of the kind of fears and suspicions which had characterized international relations during the interwar period.

Japan Strikes: 1941

William H. Honan

As soon as Imperial Japan destroyed the Russian Navy in a spectacular sea battle at the Straits of Tsushima in 1905, a rash of would-be Cassandras began to foretell the day when the rays of the Rising Sun would spread eastward across the Pacific, bringing Japan head-on into conflict with the United States. These early prophets of the great war to come were not cautious theorists but, rather, a wildly imaginative, zany lot—characters such as Homer Lea, a hunchback who served as a general under Sun Yat-sen and delighted in terrifying his contemporaries with sanguinary tales of Japanese bounding across the Pacific to lay waste to California, Oregon, and Washington, and men like Ernest Hugh Fitzpatrick, a walrus-mustachioed poet who took time out from confecting elegant rhymes to picture the Japanese subjugating not only the United States but Mexico, too.

Occasionally in *les guerres imaginaires,* as this literary genre is known, one comes across a bewitching stroke of prophecy. For example, in *Banzai!,* an imaginary account of a Japanese-American war written in 1908 by German novelist Ferdinand H. Grautoff, Japanese forces deal a stunning defeat to unprepared American troops, who happen to be under the command of a ''General MacArthur.'' In time, as Grautoff relates the story, MacArthur returns to the fray, rallies his men, and drives the Japanese into the sea.

As a long-time collector of novels and stories prophesying the war in the Pacific, I was more delighted than surprised not long ago when in a secondhand bookstore in Manhattan I picked up a copy of *The Great Pacific War* by Hector C. Bywater. The book had been published in 1925 by Constable & Company of London, and it contained—I discovered as I glanced through the first few pages—a prediction that the war between Japan and the United States would commence with a sneak attack by the Japanese. When I got the book home and examined it carefully, my sense of delight slowly gave way to amazement.

The narrative of the "tremendous conflict" that Bywater described begins with Japan's seizure of strategic points in Manchuria, Formosa, and Korea. Her motive for war is the Asian mainland's rich supply of raw materials, which are necessary to support Japan's burgeoning industrial plants. "But in thus pursuing a policy which aimed at the virtual enslavement of China," Bywater wrote, "[Japan] had inevitably drawn upon herself the hostility of the Powers." Accordingly, a series of diplomatic notes are exchanged between Japan and the United States "bellicose" and "truculent" on the part of the Japanese and "courteously worded" by the Americans, who are "determined to prevent the catastrophe of war." It is in the midst of these negotiations that Japan strikes by surprise.

According to Bywater's account the Japanese catch the American Asiatic Squadron cruising off Manila Bay, not Pearl Harbor, but the result is the same—the complete destruction of the American warships as a fighting force. Bywater recognized that the attack would be heralded by the approach of carrier-based airplanes, although he expected the greatest destruction to be wrought by naval gunnery. In any event it is a one-sided contest, both because the Japanese have the advantage of surprise and because the relatively obsolete American warships are no match for the powerful, modern Japanese armada.

Bywater did not foresee the Japanese strikes against Malaya, Burma, and Hong Kong that followed the Pearl Harbor attack—perhaps because, being an Englishman, it was too much for him to conceive of Japan's taking on the United States and Great Britain, too. Nevertheless, his description of the assaults on Guam and the Philippines is truly astonishing. He predicted that Guam would come under attack from "a flight of Japanese war planes, evidently from Saipan"—which had been secretly developed by the Japanese as a major air base—and that the principal target of this initial assault would be the vital radio tower at Machanao. The air attack, he went on to say, would be followed a few days later by a terrific naval bombardment, including the use of gas shells (his single miscalculation in this campaign), and then the landing of troops on the east and west shores of the island. Bywater even foresaw the use of specially designed landing craft: "Large motor-propelled barges or pontoons were carried on board the [Japanese] transports for landing tanks and artillery. . . . [The infantry made for the shore in] motor barges . . . [riding] until the keels grounded on the beach, when the little men in khaki tumbled over the side and came plunging through the surf, holding rifles and cartridge pouches above their heads, and uttering staccato war cries." After fitful skirmishes, Bywater concluded, the American Marines would be compelled to surrender, as was the case on December 10, 1941.

Simultaneously with the destruction of the U.S. fleet and the invasion of Guam—in Bywater's projection as in actual history—the Philippines come under siege. With the United States Navy out of commission, "the chief danger, the [Japanese] perceived," said Bywater, "would come from the American aircraft." Moreover, "thirty machines of a new and powerful type," he declared, would just have arrived from the United States (in reality thirty-five new B-17 Flying Fortresses did arrive by late November, 1941). Consequently, Bywater prophesied, hostilities in the Philippines would commence when Japanese planes "heavily bombed the aerodrome at Dagupan." (Actually Clark Field, which had replaced nearby Dagupan, was attacked.) Bywater further predicted that the Japanese would have long scrutinized the topography of the Philippines. Provided with complete intelligence about the defenses of the islands, he reasoned, the Japanese invasion plan would give a wide berth to the fortress at Corregidor guarding Manila Bay as well as to the other heavily fortified base not far to the north at Olongapo guarding Subic Bay, both of which, in fact, the Japanese did avoid.

To confuse the island's defenders, Bywater went on, the Japanese would try a diversionary bombardment at Santa Cruz on the west coast of Luzon. However, this stratagem was "so obviously a ruse to draw the [Americans] away from other parts of the coast that it failed in its purpose." Here, the historical parallel is the actual diversionary Japanese landings on Luzon at Aparri and Vigan in the north and at Legaspi in the south, which General Jonathan M. Wainwright, the Northern Luzon Force commander, who was not fooled, believed to be feints. The major landings, Bywater wrote, would take place at Lingayen Gulf, northwest of Manila, and in "Lamon Bay between Cabalete and Alabat Islands," southeast of Manila. The two forces would then converge on Manila "simultaneously from north and south." The second largest island of the Philippine archipelago, Mindanao, would be invaded with a landing at Sindangan Bay, Bywater declared. The total invading force, he estimated, would consist of "an approximate strength of 100,000 men."

Here again it was almost as if Lieutenant General Masaharu Harma, who commanded the Fourteenth Army, which invaded the Philippines in December, 1941, had done so with a copy of Bywater tucked in his pocket. Homma's forces consisted of one hundred thousand men. Moreover, there were two main landings on the island of Luzon—one at Lingayen Gulf and the other at Lamon Bay, precisely between Cabalete and Alabat islands. Finally, a third major landing party attacked the island of Mindanao, also as Bywater foretold, although coming ashore at Davao Gulf on the southeast coast rather than at Sindangan on the northwest. Given the fact that there are over seven thousand islands in the Philippines and innumerable invasion routes with an almost infinite variety of combinations for simultaneous diversions and landings, the coincidences between Bywater's book and the course of history are startling.

The first American attempt to carry the war into Japanese waters, Bywater imagined, would consist of a bold, indeed a reckless, stab at the Bonin or

Ogasawara islands, which lie some five hundred miles southeast of Yokohama, not far from Iwo Jima, and which, if captured, might lead to a speedy conclusion of the war. In the attempt, however, United States forces would over-extend themselves and be beaten back with heavy losses. It would then become apparent to the American commanders that the only practicable way to strike at Japan would be by means of cautious and deliberate pouncing from island to island all the way across the Pacific, carefully retrenching at each new base and pausing to bring up the rear. Three such routes across the ocean vastness are considered, and Bywater has the Americans select the same course that would actually be travelled by U.S. forces in the early 1940's—across the stepping stones of the South Pacific—although the zigzag path of island hops that he described is slightly to the north of that actually followed, since Bywater did not expect the British Solomons or Dutch New Guinea to be included in the war zone. Nevertheless, there is a remarkable correspondence between Bywater's campaign and the one later fought by General Douglas MacArthur. Moreover, once the Americans are within striking distance of the Philippines, the Imperial Navy is brought to bear en masse, and there follows a tremendous naval engagement destined, like the Battle of Midway, to become the turning point of the war.

It is at the Battle of Yap, as Bywater called it, that his account contains its most serious lapse: Bywater failed to foresee great naval duels, such as those later to be fought at the Coral Sea and Midway, in which the opposing surface vessels never fired a shot at each other, while trading devastating blows by means of their aircraft. Writing two years before Lindbergh's flight across the Atlantic, Bywater understandably did not appreciate the might of air power.

Nevertheless, he did make a few redeemingly accurate prophecies about the war in the air. First, he anticipated the kamikazes. The desperation of the Japanese after having seen their defensive rings of islands smashed, combined with their fanatical Emperor-worship, he said, would result in Japanese aviators "never hesitating to ram when otherwise balked of their prey, preferring to immolate themselves. . . ." Second, Bywater foresaw that the torpedo plane would demonstrate its "complete superiority" over the bomber as an instrument of naval combat, since the six-hundred-pounders, which he judged to be the heaviest bombs that planes would be able to lift in the short take-off space provided by carriers, were simply not big enough—barring a down-the-stack freak hit—to sink a modern warship. As it turned out, except at the Battle of Midway, the Douglass "Dountless" dive bomber, which carried a five-hundred-pound bomb, could not compare in effectiveness with the Grumman "Avenger" torpedo plane; the huge "tin fish" accounted for the great majority of heavy Japanese ships sent to the bottom by aircraft during the war. The rule was borne out by Japanese experience, too; enemy successes at Pearl Harbor as well as a few days later off the east coast of Malaya against the British dreadnoughts *Repulse* and *Prince of Wales* were the work of torpedo planes.

Bywater did not foresee the atomic bomb. And yet, curiously, he did perceive that something out of the ordinary would be attempted by the United States to spare both itself and its adversaries the horror of an invasion of the Japanese home islands. This *coup de grâce,* he guessed, would be a "demonstration" air raid on Tokyo in which the "bombs" contain leaflets urging the Japanese to petition their government to come to terms rather than "waste more lives." American planes did indeed drop millions of leaflets over Japan urging the citizenry to petition Emperor Hirohito to end the war. In Bywater's account the surrender is duly arranged after the "demonstration," a treaty of peace is signed, and the former German islands mandated to Japan by the League of Nations are turned over to the United States "for their future administration."

Needless to say, Hector Bywater was no ordinary fabricator of *les guerres imaginaires;* he was right much too often. Not only did he predict a great many details of the coming war, but, more significantly, he spelled out in advance the daring, unorthodox strategy with which Japan would burst her confines in the Pacific. This strategy, based on the concept of the surprise destruction of the American fleet and simultaneous invasions throughout the southwestern Pacific, was novel; it leaned heavily on the elements of surprise and exact timing, which are always difficult to achieve in a tactical situation. It also violated the cardinal military rule of the concentration of an overwhelming force at a single point, positing instead the dispersion of already fairly weak forces throughout a far-flung theater of operations. Furthermore, the Bywater plan ran counter to the accepted war-contingency strategy that had been rehearsed at the Imperial Staff College in Tokyo since at least 1918. In the event of war with the United States, this rather conventional battle plan called for employment of the full might of the Imperial Navy in a crushing attack to capture the Dutch East Indies, on which Japan would depend for oil in time of war. Once these oil-producing islands were safely under Japanese control, the fleet was to be redeployed to lie in wait for the expected American counterattack somewhere in Japanese waters, against which the Imperial Navy would fight a defensive war. The majority of top Japanese Navy officials, led by Admiral Osami Nagano, chief of the Naval General Staff, favored this strategy until the very outbreak of war. Even Captain W. D. Puleston, the foremost American naval strategist of the period, wrote in 1941 that the American commander in the Pacific ought to be "grateful" if, in the event of war, "Japan should obligingly scatter her light [naval] forces, submarine and aircraft." Influenced by this line of thinking, American planners did not take Bywater's prophecies seriously.

However, Fleet Admiral Isoroku Yamamoto, the supreme commander of Japanese forces in the Pacific, harkened to a different drummer. It was Yamamoto who devised the plan for the surprise attack on Pearl harbor together with simultaneous invasions throughout the southwestern Pacific—in essence the Bywater plan—and he was so ardent in his commitment to this strategy that he once threatened to resign unless it was adopted and put to the test. But how did Yamamoto come upon this remarkable plan for conquest? Could it be that he was influenced by Bywater? Could it be that in writing *The Great Pacific War* Hector Bywater had unwittingly composed the *Mein Kampf* of Imperial Japan?

Yamamoto was killed in 1943 when the plane in which he was travelling was shot down by an American fighter. Unfortunately he left no memoirs, and there is no mention of Bywater's name in his biography. Most of Yamamoto's colleagues are today no longer living, and the memories of the few still alive have been dimmed by the years. I wrote, for example, to Vice Admiral Shigeru Fukudome, who was Yamamoto's chief of staff at the time he conceived of the Pearl Harbor attack, to ask if he knew whether the Admiral had been influenced by Bywater. Fukudome replied that although he recalled Bywater's name as a "world-renowned naval journalist," he could not say if my suspicions were correct.

It seemed I had run into a blank wall, so I tried to learn what I could about Bywater himself. The British *Who's Who* listed Bywater as having been naval correspondent for the London *Daily Telegraph*. The librarian of that newspaper informed me that Bywater had died in August, 1940—only sixteen months before his imaginings were confirmed by world events. Just two weeks after the Japanese attack at Pearl Harbor, an abridged version of *The Great Pacific War* was published in *Life* magazine, billed as "the most current book of the week." Soon after, the complete text was republished as a hard-cover book with the subtitle "A Historic Prophecy Now Being Fulfilled" and an introduction by Hanson W. Baldwin, military editor of the *New York Times*, who described the book as "deeply prophetic."

Despite this flurry of interest in his work when the war in the Pacific broke out, Bywater remained a prophet without due honor, for his name is otherwise ignored in the literature of the Japanese-American war. Indeed, because both the *Life* condensation and Baldwin's introduction to *The Great Pacific War* went to press so soon (Baldwin was writing just six days after the attack at Pearl Harbor), all either could say about Bywater was that he appeared to have been correct in guessing that the Japanese would strike without warning. Even after Japanese records became available, no one checked to see how prophetic many of his other guesses were.

Bywater had shipped around the world in his youth, visiting ports of call throughout Europe, Africa, and the United States. His ramblings, however, were not so romantically aimless as were those of some of the other journalists of the time, for between about 1909 and the end of World War I he was an undercover agent for British naval intelligence—at first posing as a young blade seeking his fortune in distant lands and later carrying out his missions while doubling as a naval correspondent for the *British Naval and Military Record*, the *Pall Mall Gazette*, and the London *Daily Graphic*. He probably became engaged in intelligence work through the connections of his father, a Welshman who had immigrated to

the United States a few years before the Civil War and become a federal secret
agent, rising to the rank of colonel in the U.S. Army. (The elder Bywater later
returned to England, where his son was born in the Chelsea section of London.)
Young Bywater's experience and contacts gained while sleuthing abut foreign ship-
yards and anchorages for the Royal Navy (and also, briefly, for the United States
just prior to this nation's entry into World War I) doubtless stood him in good
stead when he became a full-time naval reporter after the war.

It was in 1921, shortly after the United States acquiesced in the League of
Nations' mandating to Japan the Carolines, the Marianas, and the Marshalls—formerly German islands—that Bywater turned his attention to the Pacific, recognizing that the balance of power in this quarter of the globe had suddenly shifted. In
that year he wrote an exhaustive strategic study called *Sea Power in the Pacific*, in
which he described and analyzed the relative strengths and weaknesses of the Japanese and American positions. Bywater pointed out that Guam, which he regarded
as the Malta of the Pacific, had been effectively "surround[ed] . . . with a cordon
of potential Japanese strongholds and naval bases," adding that the notion that
Japan "would forego the use of such invaluable bases in case of emergency is not
to be believed." At the end of the book he appended a twenty-eight-page chapter
entitled "Possible Features of a War in the Pacific," in which he groped over the
chart of the ocean in an effort to foresee the shape that a future conflict in this vast
area might take. Over the next four years he expanded this chapter to book length
and finally published it in 1925 as *The Great Pacific War*. His purpose, as he explained in the preface, was "to develop the theme . . . in a previous volume . . .
further," not because he wished to usher that theme into reality but because he
hoped to demonstrate in graphic detail the truth of the statement that "war is never
a paying proposition from any national point of view." To accomplish this task, he
wrote, "it was necessary to have recourse to the medium of fiction."

Evidence that Bywater's strategic plans had been taken to heart by Japanese war
lords still seemed agonizingly out of reach, until one day I happened to be in
the Library of Congress in Washington and looked up Bywater's name in the card
catalogue. I caught my breath suddenly when I came upon two entries under his
name in Japanese. Quickly I copied down the Arabic numerals on the cards and
rushed over to the Orientalia Division, asked for the books, and then begged a
young Japanese-American librarian to translate the titles for me. When he did, I
had my first important clue that Japanese military thinking had been influenced by
Bywater. During the next few months I began to correspond with both military and
academic scholars in Japan and began to piece together impressive evidence that
hector Bywater had, in effect, originated the plans for Japanese conquest in the
Pacific.

Hardly had a month gone by after the publication in 1921 of Bywater's *Sea
Power in the Pacific*—the book containing the twenty-eight-page chapter that later

became *The Great Pacific War*—when the Office of the Naval General Staff in Tokyo translated it into Japanese and distributed mimeographed copies to top naval officers as "material for strategic studies." Because of "numerous demands" for additional copies, according to a publication of Suikō Sha, the quasi-official naval officers' association, Suikō Sha was granted permission by the Imperial government to have *Taiheiyō kaiken ron,* as *Sea Power in the Pacific* was titled in Japanese, printed and distributed to a still wider circle of naval officers, although not to the general public.

By the time *The Great Pacific War* appeared in 1925, Bywater evidently had a wide enough following in Japan so that Hakuhō Sha, a regular commercial publisher, had the book translated and offered for sale as *Taiheiyō no Soha-sen.* The following year *The Great Pacific War* was again translated and published by Bunmei Kyokai, the Waseda University Press, under the title *Taiheiyō Senso to sono Hihan* ("The Pacific War and Comment") with an introduction by Tota Ishimaru, a lieutenant commander in the Imperial Navy. Apparently the Japanese government did not wish to have these translations known about in the West and thus intervened with the publishers so that, contrary to the usual practice, Bywater never received a royalty or learned of the pirated editions. Copies of both books are today in the National Diet Library in Tokyo and the library of the Japanese Defense Academy, formerly the Imperial War College, at Yokosuka.

Such widespread publication naturally stirred up a good deal of discussion. In his introduction to *The Great Pacific War* Commander Ishimaru said that the book possessed "a certain degree of rational probability and practicability" and that while Bywater's conclusion that Japan would necessarily lose the war was "slander," it was nevertheless possible that "by making good use of this publication the people of our country may turn a misfortune into a blessing."

Also illustrative of the impact of *The Great Pacific War* on Japanese military thought are the many references to Bywater in a book called *The Three-Power Alliance and a United States-Japanese War,* which was written in 1940 by Kinoaki Matsuo, an intelligence officer in the Imperial Navy and a high official of the influential politico-religious Black Dragon Society. Matsuo began by arguing that war with the United States was "inevitable." Proceeding from that premise, he suggested that the best place for the "Japanese surprise-attack fleet" to strike would be at Pearl Harbor, that "simultaneous" attacks should be launched against Guam and the Philippines, and that the actual landings on the latter, preceded by a "diversion," should come ashore on Luzon at Lingayen Gulf and Lamon Bay, precisely according to Bywater's plan, which the author acknowledged having studied. Indeed, Matsuo took courage from Bywater's conclusion that Japan could achieve a great strategic advantage by striking first and driving American forces from the southwestern Pacific. "As Bywater has pointed out," Matsuo declared, "if Guam and the Philippines fall into [Japanese] hands, the United States will be confronted with a serious problem, the solution of which will be almost impossible." But

Matsuo was more a polemicist than a student of strategy, for he seized upon those elements in Bywater's analysis useful to his thesis—namely, that Japan might hold off the United States indefinitely—while dismissing other considerations that he found distasteful. Bywater's prophecies that the Imperial Navy would be shattered, the Philippines retaken, and Tokyo bombed were all brushed aside by Matsuo with the argument that Japan would display "a courage a hundred times higher than ordinary," being possessed of "a burning determination to win."

There is no doubt that Bywater's plans were studied and debated at the Imperial War College, too. Mitsuo Fuchida, a leading Japanese military historian, reported to me that as a lieutenant commander in the Imperial Navy in 1936 he attended the Japanese Naval War College, the highest school for strategic studies in Japan at the time, and there studied both *Taiheiyō kaiken ron* and *Taiheiyō Senso to sono Hihan*. Fuchida said that Bywater's name was "well-known" among top naval officers, that he presumed that the Englishman's book must have had "a great influence" on Japanese strategy.

The key question, of course, is whether or not Bywater influenced the man responsible for Japan's strategy—Yamamoto. Like a great many other officers, the admiral probably encountered at least the rudiments of the Bywater plan as early as 1921, when the Office of the Naval General Staff first distributed *Taiheiyō kaiken ron*. He could have easily read *Taiheiyō no Soha-sen* or *Taiheiyō Senso to sono Hihan* after they were published several years later. The chances are, however, that Yamamoto's first exposure to *The Great Pacific War* was to the American edition of the book. After two years as a graduate student at Harvard, Yamamoto could read English perfectly, and in 1925—the year *The Great Pacific War* was published in the United States as well as in Great Britain—he was serving as the Japanese naval attaché in Washington. That September *The Great Pacific War* was discussed on the front page of the *New York Times Book Review* under a one-inch-high banner headline—"IF WAR COMES IN THE PACIFIC"—and a large, spectacular photograph of destroyers laying a smoke screen on maneuvers off Hawaii. Indeed, the Japanese government registered an official protest in Washington, denouncing Bywater's book as provocative and destined to arouse ill feeling between the two countries.

It should not be surprising to think that a Japanese naval officer would be strongly influenced by the work of a British naval authority, since the Japanese Navy was, from its infancy, virtually a creation of Great Britain. When the Japanese decided to build a modern navy in the 1860's, replacing their old coast-defense ironclads with modern ocean-going warships, they purchased British ships and sent their most promising young officers to train aboard British men-of-war. By the time Japan was ready to deal a resounding naval defeat to Czarist Russia at the Straits of Tsushima in 1905, the majority of her ships were of British construction, and many of her commanders, including the famous Admiral Togo, had tied their first clove hitches aboard British warships. It would therefore be natural for

In 1924, three years after Hector Bywater's Sea Power in the Pacific appeared, the air-power enthusiast General Bill Mitchell returned from a tour of the Far East with a report predicting the possibility of a Japanese air attack against Pearl Harbor itself. Bywater also ultimately took cognizance of the increasing role of air power, and in a revised edition of Sea Power in the Pacific published in 1934 he noted the "marked superiority of the United States Navy over the Japanese in numbers of ship-borne aircraft." In a few years, he continued, "the first-line aircraft at the disposal of the United States Navy will number 2000, a total which could be multiplied indefinitely in a national emergency. . . . If, then, the air weapon is to prove a preponderating element in a Far Eastern naval campaign, the dice will be loaded against Japan, whether her opponent is the United States or the British Commonwealth." In this case, also, Bywater's warning was not heeded by the Japanese.

Yamamoto—who had been with Togo at Tsushima and lost a couple of fingers in the engagement—to study the ideas promulgated by the leading British authority of his day on naval theory and practice.

On the other hand it would be reckless to conclude that the Japanese simply stole their design for conquest from a British writer. In the thirty-seven years between Tsushima and Pearl Harbor, Japan had built her own fighting ships and developed her own doctrines of naval combat. Furthermore, numerous influences must have played upon Yamamoto's mind as he created the strategy of 1941. There were, for example, the highly publicized American war games off Hawaii in 1932, in which it was demonstrated that a flight of planes, taking off in a predawn attack from aircraft carriers, was able to reach Pearl Harbor without being detected and to "sink" all of the heavy naval vessels in the harbor. There were also Yamamoto's own war games at Kagoshima Bay in May, 1940, at the conclusion of which he remarked to a colleague: "Well, it appears that a crushing blow could be struck [by torpedo planes] against an enemy surface fleet."

Bywater was merely the first to put all of the pieces together, the first to show in detail how the strategic confines that had held Japanese ambitions in check for a generation could be overcome with a daring *coup de main*.

His failing perhaps was that his narrative of the action was more compelling than the warning in his conclusion. "Unfortunately," one review of *The Great Pacific War* wrote in 1925, "the dramatic side of the tactical excitement of war so overshadows the horrors of the losses sustained on both sides that one would almost wish to see Mr. Bywater's drama acted."

William H. Honan is the travel editor of the New York Times.

July, 1944: St. Lô

Charles R. Cawthon

Three decades ago a battle was fought for St. Lô, Normandy, France, in the second of the great world wars of this century. To have been young at St. Lô and now to be old is a matter of personal amazement, for the time lapse seems instantaneous. In rank, the battle is in that heavily populated tier of major bloodlettings that have determined the course of campaigns, as opposed to the few decisive Gettysburgs and Waterloos on which history itself has turned. In keeping with this stature, St. Lô seems destined for the footnotes of history, unlikely to be remembered beyond the memory span of the First United States Army and Seventh German Army veterans who fed its flames so prodigally, of those who anxiously followed their fortunes, and of the Normans whose lives and homes were in its path. Further in perspective: St. Lô was an essential objective of the First Army's offensive launched during that fateful month of July, 1944, to gain the terrain and road net on which Operation COBRA could coil and strike to break out of the Normandy beachhead. The overall offensive involved twelve divisions in four corps attacking on a twenty-five-mile front. It was bitterly contested at every point; losses were uniformly appalling. In this general holocaust St. Lô caught the public's attention, possibly because the town had the largest population (eleven thousand) in the offensive and was a provincial seat of government. Even more, it acquired a symbol, "the Major of St. Lô," whom I knew. To the allied command the town was important as the hub of a network of seven roads and because the high ground to its east and west commanded the Vire Valley, in which tanks could operate. Both factors were essential to COBRA. The German command had an equal appreciation of road nets and terrain and, in addition, had a captured American field order designating St. Lô as a primary objective. This determined that it would be defended with all the resources that the enemy would be able to muster on its accommodating hills and ridgelines.

Presuming to speak for those who fought there but knew nothing of COBRA or of captured field orders, I recall the battle only as a boiling caldron that no man entered without dread or emerged from without being marked.

In the end, of course, St. Lô was taken. Operation COBRA was launched, and a general advance was begun that with some setbacks, notably the Battle of the Bulge, ended in less than a year with victory in Europe. The cost was high: in three weeks over forty thousand Americans killed, wounded, or missing—the same price, incidentally, as at the Bulge six months later. The Germans, who fought with courage and skill, had losses perhaps half again as heavy. St. Lô was knocked apart, and about a thousand citizens were killed before it was finally evacuated. Conservatively speaking, well over a hundred thousand human beings died or suffered wounds in the brief time and space that bounded the offensive.

My memoir is that of a foot soldier groping through this hurly-burly. Its scope is the few hundred yards' front of the 2nd Battalion, 116th Regiment (the Stonewall Brigade), 29th Infantry Division. I was aware of other mighty blows being exchanged across Normandy; but being fully occupied with my own microcosm of Armageddon, I paid them little heed.

A memoir is a public appearance, and one is inclined to stand straighter and present the best profile. Mitigating this tendency, there are no deeds of personal daring to relate, and no action of mine affected the battle one way or the other. This is personally regrettable, but it also lessens the self-consciousness of narrating in the first person. I was there; I endured, and not so well as some, also regrettable. Otherwise, I was a bookishly inclined amateur soldier with some ability at dissembling the uncertainty and irritability that the war inspired. At the battle's start I was a captain commanding the 2nd Battalion's headquarters company and battalion adjutant; during its course I became battalion executive officer and a major.

My account is not thirty years of faded memories and afterthoughts. It was originally written directly after the war, when the sights, sounds, and smells of St. Lô were sharp and clear. My aim then was a history of the battle through the 2nd Battalion's story. The result was predictably far short of the mark; I found that the great ebb and flow of St. Lô cannot be encompassed by one of its parts. Disappointed, I set it aside.

Now there is the delayed second thought that while a battalion affords a limited view of field armies locked in battle, it is unequalled for observing those who fought it personally and directly. The soldiers of the 2nd Battalion were assembled through largely random selection to perform the irrational acts of war. We were fairly representative of all battalions similarly assembled in this offensive.

As a generation we inherited a world that had blown itself up in the great war of a quarter century before. We had come of age in the vast uncertainties of the Great Depression, and we had a largely bankrupt legacy from the great illusion that America could do all to make the world right. As soldiers we were overwhelmingly amateur. We had neither revolutionary fervor nor the greed of empire building to obscure the insanity of the killing and destruction to which we were put. We accepted beyond question, however, that the threat to our country's existence was real and had to be defeated; the challenge of Pearl Harbor was unqualified. No soldier I knew was even remotely interested in dying in the process; that so many went directly into death's way as duty is a measure of the generation.

The result, I believe, was an army remarkably homogeneous in viewpoint and purpose, though wide personal and group differences existed. (In a segregated army, for example, I was unaware of the vast dissatisfaction swelling among black soldiers.) This combination of shaping factors is not likely to reappear; the army they produced is gone so completely that I must look and look again to convince myself that it ever existed. In my more somber moments I think that we may have been the last great army of the Republic—one that could truly march to "The Battle Hymn of the Republic." This is the sketchy canvas on which my memoir is superimposed. It is largely as written so long ago. Violence distorts perception, and some sights I recount may be larger than life, and others of more significance may have been missed altogether. Memories must reflect such distortions, but on the whole I believe mine to be within the scope of what really happened during the battle for St. Lô.

An infantry battalion is a closely knit little world, and recollections of it must be heavily peopled, which poses the question of who among them should be summoned by name. There is much room for error here, and as names do not particularly serve my purposes, I shall call from the shadows only one—Tom Howie, dead near the end of the battle. For quiet and enduring reasons to be recounted in turn, the twilight of St. Lô has lingered longest on him of the entire Stonewall Brigade, and under his name I gather us all. He became the nation's symbol—the "Major of St. Lô."

The XIX Corps of three infantry divisions and on occasion an armored division did battle directly for St. Lô, but for the battalion soldier a corps was a remote "they" with which he was unlikely to have contact. Not so my division. The 29th was a strong and present personality that, on the basis of its combat record, was of uncommon military merit. It was mustered for the war in 1941 and had three years of training before being committed to battle on D-day on Omaha Beach. Of its three regiments the 115th and 175th were of the Maryland National Guard, and the 116th from Virginia. All three are of long lineage; the 116th's goes back to the French and Indian War, but its proudest days were those in the years 1861–65. It entered that war as the 2nd Virginia of General Thomas J. Jackson's brigade at the

First Battle of Manassas, and both Jackson and the brigade emerged with the title "Stonewall."

A regiment, no less than an individual, is not inclined to forswear a resounding title won by an ancestor even if he fought on the "wrong" side. In 1944 the 116th's ranks held as many Yankees as Virginians, but the Stonewall Brigade we were, and to those of a historical bent this was a proud and notable thing.

On D-day the 116th had led the assault on the right sector of Omaha Beach and within a few hours lost some thousand killed or wounded. This was about one fourth of its strength and an even greater proportion of the riflemen who carried the burden of its battles. At the time this memoir begins, six days later, these losses had not been replaced, and attrition had continued, yet the regiment remained in action. Old Stonewall would probably have regarded this as no more than performance of duty. Most of us, I think, felt that others should take over the war for a while.

With this perhaps excessive amount of prior circumstance, I come down to late afternoon of June 12 and a dusty road near the gray huddle of houses of the hamlet Ste. Marguerite d'Elle. It was here that I first heard St. Lô designated as another appointed place on the Stonewall Brigade's long road of war. At the time, I and others of the battalion command post were strung out along a roadside ditch while the rifle companies, a hundred or so yards ahead, contended for a passage over the Elle River. Black smoke showed above the trees to our left front from two tanks that had been knocked out trying to cross the river.

The ditch took the menace from the bullets that cracked occasionally overhead, and I dare say my heroes and I would have been content to sit out that hot, humid afternoon of the war there. I was successfully coping with an urge of conscience to go up and see if the battalion commander had any overlooked need of our devoted efforts when the divisional chief of staff, a colonel, appeared striding toward us. Since it was obviously improper to remain in the ditch and exchange "good afternoons," I clambered onto the road and reported our identity. My lads, with a fine grasp of protocol, simply stood up in the ditch and looked vague.

The colonel, a big, square man, acknowledged my report and, looking us over thoughtfully, began a quiet talk on combat. He described a fire fight and how becoming intent on winning it made it something like a ball game. We listened respectfully, but since we had been under fire for the past six days, I doubt that he convinced anyone that this was a sporting event or obscured its terminal probabilities.

He got more attention by saying that our objective was St. Lô and that after it was taken, the division might well get a real rest, a possibility more important to us than what taking the town would do for the crusade in Europe.

The colonel wished us luck, which we returned, and continued down the road. Inspired by his presence if not by his words, we gathered map boards and field phone to move closer to the battle. Directly afterward the latest commander of

E Company—the third since D-day—limped by toward the rear, one arm hanging loosely, bright red drops dribbling slowly from the fingers onto the dusty road. We had served together for two years, but I didn't stop to inquire about his injury; death and hurt had become commonplace, and a wound with which one could with honor walk out of the war was a matter for congratulation rather than condolence.

We set up shop behind a hedgerow closer to the racket, one result of which was the shattered leg of the intelligence officer, a young lawyer from Louisiana who had performed bravely and well. In addition, the brief action cost two platoon leaders and, as always, a number of riflemen.

As the long evening of double daylight-saving time waned the Germans pulled out, and the 2nd Battalion splashed across the knee-deep, narrow river and headed across country for its objective, the village of St. Clair-sur-l'Elle, about a half mile away. Unknown to us, a German column was pulling back on a parallel route and just outside the village sideswiped our right flank company. There was a brief exchange of fire, and the two columns pulled apart, the effect on the war being a few more killed and wounded.

With daylight the battalion perimeter was pushed south of the empty village, its citizens having learned that bombs and artillery fire were the going price of liberation. The command post was set up in a vacant house, and here we stayed for several days, both sides remaining relatively quiet and killing very few of each other.

Our wounded, however, included the battalion executive officer, and as the senior surviving captain I took his place. It was an advancement about which I could have few illusions, for it had become apparent that the principal requirement was simply to stay alive and in reasonable mental health.

Other events of the stay at St. Clair were a visit by the divisional commander, a major general, and the arrival of the first replacements. The general came one afternoon by jeep, expected to the extent that he could be expected at any time or place. He was about fifty years old and conformed to General Sheridan's specifications for a cavalryman, which he had been before the war: short, wiry, daring, and quick. Everything about him was explosive: gestures, speech, action, temper. He dominated the 29th by knowing exactly what he wanted done, discarding those who didn't produce it and rewarding those who did. As with other success formulas, the trick to this one lay in its application. He tolerated only the facts of a situation, and to present him with a conjecture was fatal to a future in the division.

His rough side was reserved for commanders, and strenuous efforts were made to avoid it. His orders were simple and direct. They included the requirement that every man be able to recite verbatim a simple statement of correct sight alignment and trigger squeeze. The 29th's tradition of wearing the helmet strap bucked under the chin rather than dangling, as was the general practice, was not to be violated under any circumstance. There were many others, unremarkable except in their total enforcement.

The general's first impression of a commander was apt to be final. Fortunately my company was in the midst of one of its better days when he first came upon us during training, and I purposely avoided later exposure whenever possible. I admired and respected—as well as avoided—him, for he sounded a clear and certain trumpet in baffling and fearsome situations. It is my unsupported opinion that the number of divisional commanders of this caliber that the nation can muster in a given war is fewer than the divisions that can be mustered. The combination of courage, professional ability, imagination, and ruthlessness found in these few is rare enough to make them beyond price in war. As a matter of fact, the same applies to the exceptional enlisted infantryman, who, on a relative basis, is just as rare a bird and suffers an incomparably higher casualty rate.

In any case, this divisional commander arrived with his usual pronounced impact at our command post on a damp afternoon in mid-June. Those who had not gotten away in time stood in attentive attitudes around the stained walls of the musty parlor while he and the battalion commander sat and conversed in front of the empty hearth. I do not recall exact words, but the general indicated approval of our efforts, which was gratifying if the cost of achieving it was not considered.

That night the new adjutant and I met the trucks bringing in the first replacements and hurried the dark shapes laden with packs and weapons behind guides to their companies. We had been clamoring for men, so I was surprised at a vague sense of regret as I saw them march toward the front. Their efforts to keep their places and reach a harm beyond their conception were somehow pathetic. I felt an ancient among children, knowing and dreading what they had to endure.

The way of the replacement foot soldier in that war was hard, crowded, and dull: training camp, troopship, overseas replacement depot; then, probably leaving any friends acquired along the way, by truck and foot to join strangers in facing death or great injury. On occasion he never completed the journey. I recall the sad, brief saga of a column of replacements caught by artillery fire while toiling to the front at St. Lô, and for some ten of them this proved the end of the war.

On occasion new men were fed into units actively locked in battle. They were sent in at night and placed in among dark shapes that occupied gravelike holes scooped out behind hedgerows. The resident shapes, if they spoke at all, did not slight the dreadfulness of the situation or overestimate anyone's chances of surviving it. Sometimes a new man did die before dawn, and none around knew him by sight or name. The replacement system improved as the war wore on, but I think it remained essentially a wasteful distribution of numbers, disregarding the fact that it was dealing with the human heart.

While speaking of the emotional nature of battle one has to consider fear. I have firsthand knowledge only of my own, its chief manifestation being the stomach drawing into a cold, protective knot at the sound of shells whooping and screaming in my direction and a reluctance to leave depressions in the ground. I like to believe that I dissembled these tendencies very well; however, I knew fear intimately and believe this was a fairly general experience. When I speak of courage, I speak not of the absence of fear but of the disregard of it.

There was, come to think of it, another visit while we were at St. Clair, brief but offering a lesson to heed. I was standing in front of the command post at the time, and a jeep roared by headed for the front, a staff officer beside the driver waving as it passed. I was annoyed by the dust and noise and amazed that anyone should close with disaster with such apparent abandon. The jeep, disappearing down the road—its route traced by rising dust—halted simultaneously with a burst of machine-pistol fire just where we figured the German roadblock lay. Later I asked the Stonewallers covering the road why they hadn't stopped him. The arrival, they said, had been too sudden. One added that he didn't see why someone from the rear (as opposed to infantrymen) shouldn't have an opportunity to pinpoint roadblocks for a change.

Early on June 16 we were relieved at St. Clair and struck southwest through close, wooded terrain for St. Lô, only to be brought to a bloody halt near the hamlet of Villiers Fossard. The discovery that this was a key German position cost a staff officer and thirty-four men. The officer died literally over my head. He was in the attic of a cottage, looking out over the terrain, and I was on the ground floor, trying to locate our position on a mud-smudged map, when a sudden blast of rifle fire smacked into the cottage, and three riflemen dashed in announcing that they had shot a German directly above me. At the same moment blood began to drip through the ceiling, and in the attic we found the lifeless body. The riflemen left with stark faces, and I went to tell the battalion commander that we had lost the second operations officer since D-day.

The fight flared with noise and smoke at intervals all afternoon. I returned to the command post at dark just as a tank, sent to support our efforts, clanked up and its commander asked, in a weary Ivy League accent, in which direction he should traverse his gun. I advised him that it was more important to cut his motor before he ran over the dark bundles of headquarters men sleeping along the track whom nothing short of the Last Trumpet could rouse. As the battlefield settled into its strange nighttime mutter we all slumbered around the steel war-cart.

The next day the battalion clawed again at Villiers Fossard and lost another officer and thirty-five men, including two first sergeants. Clearly this place was not going to fall to a lone infantry battalion; a combined infantry, armor, and air attack was later required to crack it.

Early on the eighteenth the regimental commander arrived with word that we were to shift, that day, to the left flank of the division's sector in a general realignment for the push on St. Lô. Our new position lay a little over a mile south of the village of Couvains and was astride an unpaved north-south road that, at its firmly held German end, intersected the main Bayeux-St. Lô artery, one of the principal stretches of macadam for which the battle was fought. Our march to it began that humid evening, and it was in the cold damp of early morning that the companies were deployed along the new line.

There was much starting and stopping. At one halt I sat down on what I thought was a boulder, but I found it soft and yielding, the flank of a dead hog or calf. Weary, I walked on without investigating. Toward the end I became so vocal about the operation that the battalion commander suggested that I do my job and complain less, and we would all benefit. I was immediately ashamed, and am now, at adding to burdens heavier than my own.

This commander is prominent among the shadowy figures I write about. He was one of the two professional soldiers in the battalion. Usually he was relaxed and easy to serve, though minor irritations could trigger an explosion. That the battalion held together through D-day and afterward was due to his courage and energy. He was wounded after St. Lô; I fell heir to command and followed his pattern to the best of my ability. He returned to command the regiment, and after the war he was one of the organizers of Special Forces.

Finally that night the rifle companies got into position, and the command post settled down along the road. An hour or so later we were up shivering in a soggy dawn to take stock of the place and the prospects for further survival. The date was June 19, and here we were to stay until July 11, either on line or in reserve, while XIX Corps gathered for the battle.

Any position that the German allows you to occupy without a fight is unlikely to be a bargain. This one was no exception. The lifting ground mist showed us deployed along an east-west elevation that was dominated by a parallel ridgeline to the south at about fifteen hundred yards' distance. This higher ridge was called Martinville after the farm hamlet on its crest; its western end sloped off into the outskirts of St. Lô. The enemy held Martinville Ridge and a line well forward of it up against our own positions. To take St. Lô, Martinville Ridge had to be taken first.

During the three weeks we stayed there I had time to note that the two ridges corresponded in relative elevation and separation to Seminary and Cemetery ridges at Gettysburg at the point of the grand assault in the center. This was not a comforting comparison for a Virginia regiment, so I didn't mention it. Martinville Ridge also culminated in a hill on its German-held right, similar to Culp's Hill, where the Stonewall Brigade had fought; it was called "192" after its meter elevation. To strain the comparison still further, St. Lô had its Roundtop, Hill 122 on the left flank of the German defenses. South of Martinville Ridge was another elevation, along which ran the Bayeux-St. Lô road; south of that was still another parallel ridge.

Hill 192, looming to our left front, was in the area of the V Corps' 2nd Infantry Division, which took it on the first day of the July 11 attack. I visited its crest after the battle and was amazed that with field glasses I could look directly into some of the fieldworks we had occupied. Why the Germans didn't use this advantage to swat us like flies on a table is a mystery.

Our first day was spent in realigning the positions that had been taken in the darkness and weariness of the night before. The command post was dug into the side of a deep depression in a field alongside the road. Covered with a camouflage net, this served very well, though the first hard rain showed that its original purpose was as a sump to drain the field.

Across the road to our left were the mortar pits of the Heavy Weapons Company, and the sharp whang of its firing was fairly constant until the late June storms damaged the artificial harbors on the invasion beaches and curtailed the ammunition supply. The reserve rifle company was also deployed along the left to cover the open flank between us and the 2nd Division. A hundred or so yards to the front, the war was fought moment by moment by the other two rifle companies. Their lines ran along a sunken farm land until it wandered off toward Martinville Ridge, and then the positions took to the fields. The battalion's eight heavy machine guns were posted at critical points, and our 57-mm. antitank guns were sited on a slope to the right of the command post, covering the road.

The terrain setting was completed by hedgerow-enclosed apply orchards and pastures. Even more than the ridgelines and streams, these centuries-old hedgerows dominated the war in Normandy. They have often been described; earthen banks four to six feet high, topped with trees and brush, needing only the addition of men and guns to become a ready-made fortified place. The Germans accomplished this with consummate skill.

The orchards bore small, tasteless apples for making cider and its dissolute cousin, the potent applejack Calvados. Much of the battle was fought under the apple trees, and the natural obscenity of the scene could have been greater only if it had been blossom time.

War had touched this fair and fruitful countryside before we moved in and had left two of its modern mementos in the form of a crashed British bomber and a wrecked German armored car. More traditional mementos were a number of the huge black-and-white Norman cattle lying in bloated final repose in the fields, contributing the chemistry of their decay to the already heavy atmosphere. After digging itself underground the battalion buried the dead cattle and performed the amazing amount of personal hygiene, including shaving, that a man can accomplish with a helmet of water. Memory is apt to idealize such points, but as I recall it, no matter how dreadful the day he faced, the Stonewaller shaved; whatever the state of his uniform, it was worn correctly; and his weapon was kept clean.

Even directly after the war I had trouble ordering the events of the three weeks preceding the July 11 attack. Individual scenes were vivid but tended to tumble together without sequence, as in a troubled dream. One persistent memory then and now is of a bone-sagging weariness, possibly a result of long-standing strain or of feeling that on the basis of having to fight for every hedgerow, the war would go on forever. Whatever the causes, it seemed to affect us all—I noted young men around me take on the look and movements of middle age. This physical weariness was accompanied by unrest that made sleep fitful. The effect was that of a motor racing to move a sluggish machine or of trying to run in a nightmare with much effort and little progress.

Also affected was my boasted ability to maintain outward emotional control. One afternoon a military policeman returned two soldiers who had hidden out on the transport on D-day to avoid Omaha Beach. The loss of friends on that day had now come truly home, and the sight of these two, who had skulked while their betters were being killed, triggered a great anger. They were short, scruffy men, obviously not cast in anything of a heroic mold, but I became excessively the Stonewall Brigade major in describing their moral deficiencies and expressed regret that they had not been shot. I terminated by asking if they had anything to say for themselves. Yes, said one, they would like a transfer. Spluttering, I waved them out of the command post. It would be gratifying to report that they went on to redemption through soldierly deeds. The truth is, I don't know their fate but suspect they found their way out of the battle, as everyone who wanted it badly enough seemed able to do at some time or other.

The high points of hazard during this period were combat patrols, artillery fire that crashed into treetops and hedgerows, and mortar rounds that showered steel fragments for yards around. The combat patrols, led by lieutenants until expended and then by sergeants, reduced drastically the life expectancy of all who took part. The patrols did little more than demonstrate the aggressive posture desired by ''them'' and proved that the German outposts were still no more than a hedgerow or so beyond our lines, which we knew in any event.

The mortars distributed their summonses throughout the battalion area and were particularly dreaded because the shells approached with a whisper in contrast to the warning banshee scream of incoming artillery fire. I recall one remarkably fine day coming upon the body of a young runner, slightly built and looking in death like a small boy tired of playing war and asleep in the meadow, face serene and fair hair stirring in the breeze. Nearby was the fin of a mortar round in a black rupture in the sod. The two-wheeled death cart came, pulled by its two attendants, who took him away. Thus casually did death arrive and a life depart—though that is not quite accurate: death did not have to arrive; it never left us.

The battalion executive officer is important primarily through being next in line for command, but in the meantime his duties are comparatively light. I took advantage of this during the static period at St. Lô to travel to the rear on missions whose principal purpose was to breath the safer air out of artillery range. One trip was to a field hospital to have some metal fragments, acquired on D-day, removed from my face. The wound was more spectacular than serious, and I had upgraded it by maintaining that the metal deflected a compass held to the eye for sighting. In truth, I never had occasion to make such a sighting.

Returning, I stopped to see a friend commanding the corps replacement depot. He was a topflight soldier whose family had long been connected with the regiment. Now he told me that his only son, a paratrooper, had been killed on the D-day drop. He said staunchly that his son's unit had accomplished its mission, but his eyes were not staunch. The depot was filling with replacements for the St. Lô attack. From a distance they also looked staunch and well turned out. Up close I noted that they were already acquiring the intent frown of the front line. The nameless regret, I had felt on seeing the new men arrive at St. Clair returned; these also seemed too young and innocent to pit against veteran German paratroopers.

Another remembered scene was on a Sunday. I was en route by jeep to the regimental command post and near the village of Couvains encountered a procession of young girls in white dresses, accompanied by their elders in Sunday black, headed for an ancient gray stone Norman church. My driver stopped to avoid dusting the procession, and a detail stringing telephone lines along the road ceased work to gape. Just at that moment a stretcher jeep from the front crept by with its bandaged, broken load. Here were all the elements of a contrived scene of a war movie, but this one was real, and its screaming incongruity etched it on my memory.

Romance did not surface at St. Lô. No girl of the French Resistance appeared to guide us by a secret route into the city. Our only connection with love was by letter, and this was avidly pursued. I thought we wrote more than we received, but this impression may have been gained from the disagreeable duty of officers to censor letters for mention of where we were and what we were doing.

Censorship in World War II must have made its soldiers' letters about the dullest on record. Some showed a knack for pornography, but the only letters I recall distinctly were those of a quiet older soldier to his wife about the home they planned to build after the war. Letter after letter went into every detail, and I gathered that most of his soldier pay and of her war-factory wages were being saved toward it. He was, of course, killed.

From this one, and others I knew of, I would judge that the dreams per capita at St. Lô were numerous. Undoubtedly many were of gossamer, but at the time they all seemed possible, for this war was the Last Judgment on an old, wrong world and the genesis of a new, better one. In the event, the good and bad parts seem to have maintained about their usual ratio, and I fear that the mortality rate of dreams at St. Lô has been high.

As time wore on, plans for the assault were refined and resources gathered. The battalions were rotated between the front and a reserve area where, in company with engineers and tanks, the tactics for attacking hedgerows were practiced. The attack was finally set for July 11. The XIX Corps designated the 29th Division to make the main effort; the 29th decided to lead with its left flank regiment, the Stonewall Brigade. The attack was to be in a column of battalions with the 2nd leading. We were to strike astride the Couvains road to the crest of Martinville Ridge, then wheel right, or west, down a farm road that ran along its crest toward St. Lô. Simultaneously, on our left, the 2nd Infantry Division was to go for Hill 192, and upon its success depended much of what we would be able to do.

As when we had been designated for the Omaha Beach assault, the news of this St. Lô assignment had a stimulating effect: it represented distinction among our peers, one to be observed with pride. Preparations were stepped up; replacements brought the battalion up to about 75 per cent of strength; rehearsal of hedgerow tactics was intensified; artillery and mortar concentrations were plotted for every possible target. The memory that even greater preparations for D-day had not prevented near disaster was still fresh, but planning acquires its own momentum, and once again we became confident of walking over a pulverized enemy.

Crowning this confidence was a massive air raid that thundered out of a clear sky late one afternoon, about a week before the attack, to dump streams of black specks on and around the town. The specks translated into a constant rolling thunder. Everyone watched as the majestic trains of bombers, trailing white contrails like cloaks, crisscrossed the target. To the soldier fighting in the dust and mud this seemed a safe and clean way to wage war until smudges of antiaircraft fire blossomed among the formations, sullying the white-on-blue patterns of contrails and sky. First one, then another, then still others of the caravans merged with the black smudges and tumbled toward earth. Still, it was all so far removed from the war we knew that I had trouble realizing that men were being burned and broken in those far-off machines. The thunder and concussion of the bombs were more familiar, and the knowledge that the enemy was caught in them gave a macabre lift to the spirits.

Altogether it was a recharged 2nd Battalion that made final preparations to jump off at 0600 hours. A forward command post was dug in behind the line of departure, which was the present front line; tanks were fitted with metal tusks to rip through hedgerows; five battalions of artillery were to lay down twenty minutes of preparatory fire before the jump-off and then lead the advancing force with a continuing barrage.

By dark on July 10 all plans were complete, all resources assembled. I was confident that a battle-proven battalion could not fail its task. German artillery had been more active than usual that day, but I gave it little thought. When I crawled into my slit trench under a hedgerow in the assembly area about midnight, my main concern was what the tanks might do to our new telephone lines laid along the ground, and I had the belated thought that the lines should have been strung overhead.

The sleep was brief, the awakening abrupt. For a source of early-morning nausea I give you an unexpected German barrage, crashing and quaking earth and air. My first resentful thought was "Where did they get all those guns?" The sound was that of ton after ton of brick being dropped from great heights, and I looked out from my hole expecting to see the assembly area erupting in fire and smoke. Instead, the tumult was all off to the right; the trees around us were carrying on their timeless dripping in the ground mist.

Regiment could tell us only that the 1st Battalion of the 115th, about a thousand yards to our right, was under attack. The artillery swelled, died, and swelled again. The lulls were filled by the tearing bursts of machine guns; tracer bullets streaked in crazy patterns across the sky.

This clangor continued at varying pitches for over three hours; except for an occasional shell our sector was never hit. Later we learned that the German attack had a local objective and was made in ignorance of our own effort. The 115th had a very bad night before containing and driving it off. Our loss was limited to the few hours of rest we might have had before what was certain to be a long stretch. Then, too, it was a sobering demonstration of the artillery the Germans could concentrate. It also cost us, indirectly, a rifle-company commander who came streaking into the command post about daylight, carrying a lightly wounded soldier on his back. This strongly built young lieutenant had been propelled by attrition to command and, I thought, had done very well. Now he insisted that he must carry the wounded man to the rear, and from his eyes it was clear that he would not command that day. We did not see him again.

Word came that the attack would go in as planned; and, bent as though under tremendous burdens, the files moved forward through the ground mist. All remained quiet until a rapid volley of thuds behind us announced the departure of the preparatory barrage. The shells sighed overhead to end their brief careers in noise, smoke, and flying fragments on the German positions. From then on, salvo after salvo crashed along the front. The tanks moved up and, sure enough, tore up the telephone lines as they went. The ear-shattering blast of high-velocity tank guns and the beat of machine guns joined in until it seemed that noise alone would destroy everything.

No so. At 0600 the artillery fire lifted to the German support positions, and the rifle companies starting forward were met by the blast of machine guns that had somehow survived the bombardment. The futility of charging machine guns had been proved often enough, so the slow process of erasing these guns began.

The telephone line to regiment was re-laid, and along it came incessant demands for reports. The lines up to the attack kept going out, and, to get away from questions to which I did not have answers, I went up to see the battalion commander, passing a swath of dead Stonewallers who had been caught by the machine guns as they topped the first hedgerow.

The attack had progressed only two or three fields. Marking its limit was the turret of a tank, and while I watched, a soldier climbed up behind it, apparently to see what lay ahead. As he raised up, a burst of fire swept the turret, knocking him backward as though jerked with a rope. A pall of smoke was over the fields, holding in it the sweet, sickening stench of high explosive, which we had come to associate with death. The green covering of Normandy was gouged by shells and tank tracks; blasted limbs hung from the trees. The attacking riflemen, visibly shrunk in numbers, crouched behind the farthermost hedgerow while volumes of artillery, mortar, and tank gunfire flailed the fields beyond.

The battalion commander told me to keep up pressure on the heavy mortars, to maintain the fire on the ridge, and to tell regiment that the advance would continue when it damn well could. I walked back to the command post heavy with the thought that this was Omaha Beach all over again in a different setting. German counterfire was hitting in considerable volume onto some empty fields to my right, and I judged that our own efforts must be just about as effective.

I had, however, misread the battle. Soon came the message that the battalion had broken into a sunken lane that was the anchor of the German position. Part of the cost also appeared: two badly wounded company commanders. One was a firebrand lieutenant of the type that made the gray-clad 1860's brigade a terror in battle, the other a captain who had joined as a replacement. Of the four company commanders at the dawn's early light there now, at high noon, remained only one. Perhaps half of the platoon leaders and sergeants were casualties. The losses in riflemen were heavy but uncounted; the battalion commander was now leading all that remained.

Whatever we had suffered, the Germans had fared worse. Once past the sunken lane, their defense crumbled, and the attack moved rapidly up the ridge. The command post gathered up map boards and radios and, trailing telephone wire like an umbilical cord, moved after it, passing through the area of the battalion's suffering and into that of the Germans'.

Advancing into territory denied you by an enemy is like setting foot on an unexplored shore; you look around, wondering at the evidence of a strange and hostile people. In the lane and beyond, all was devastation, blasted and burned. German paratroopers, whole and in parts, lay about, difficult to reconcile, in their round helmets and blood-soaked camouflage smocks, with what had a short time before been among the most dangerous fighting men of the war.

A long-barrelled assault gun on its low-slung armored chassis that had taken a heavy toll along our front was blackened and smoking. The battalion commander's orderly was nearby as we paused in the shambles of inert flesh and shattered equipment. He remarked in puzzled sadness, more to himself than to anyone around, "I don't understand it. I just don't understand what it is all about." His words must have echoed those on many a battlefield and in many a language; there could be no elation in a sight so brutal and pitiful.

We went on in the wake of the destructive force that had swept up the ridge and to the road that ran down its spine westward. The rifle companies had made their sharp right turn astride this road and in doing so exposed their flank to the two German-held parallel ridges to the south. Evidence of what this was going to mean was near the turn in the form of stinking shell craters and more dead.

Shortly after making the turn we halted to let the crews toiling under heavy reels of telephone wire catch up. While we were so disposed a tall young lieutenant in a clean uniform and the then highly sought combat boots (we still wore leggings) strode by; he was obviously a general's aide from some remote "they" area. Someone behind me muttered that there went another bastard to collect his medal. I don't know that this was his mission, but it was not uncommon for "them" to make a quick visit to the front and be decorated for "voluntary exposure to enemy fire." Medals can be acquired in ways that are passing strange. The nation recognized the majority of the dead and wounded with Purple Hearts for their hurts and with the Combat Infantryman Badge; in a postwar spasm of conscience the Bronze Star went on application to holders of the combat badge. Measured against this, I take a jaundiced view of claims of valor for fleeting visits to the front on the basis of a job that did not require exposure. That in war some should be subject constantly to death and dismemberment while others should not be—and should be rewarded if they are momentarily—is as hypocritical a form of segregation as exists.

In any event, the command post continued on down the ridge road to where the rifle companies had come up against exhaustion and a German stand, still about two miles short of St. Lô. As the long evening darkened, the command post was dug in alongside a stone wall next to the road, and here we remained for nine days as the battle reached a peak of dull red fury.

During the night the Germans dug in their new line. The next day, July 12, we made little progress. The 1st Battalion, committed in the deep draw to our left, had much the same experience, as did the 3rd Battalion attacking south against the Bayeux road ridge. On the third day the 175th Regiment attacked through our 1st and 3rd Battalions and made small gains at heavy cost.

The 2nd Battalion went nowhere at all on this third day, and it was evident that its bolt had been shot; it could only stand and bleed. Familiar enough by then with the results of men discharging projectiles at one another at close range, I was still aghast at the rate at which the corpse carts and stretcher jeeps were trundling away the Stonewall Brigade. The 2nd Battalion had started the attack of 75 per cent of its full complement of about nine hundred officers and men. By the end of that first day we were well below half strength, and by the end of the third day less than one third of the battalion remained. As always, over 90 per cent of these losses were riflemen. Instead of three rifle companies, we barely mustered the equivalent of one; heavy-machine-gunners suffered to a like degree.

Again the German losses were heavier. Their 3rd Parachute Division, which fought so nearly to the death, lost 4,064 men in three days. Their 352nd Infantry Division, perhaps not so do-or-die, recorded 984 casualties in two days.

On the third evening, July 13, the 2nd Battalion went back for rest and refit near St. André-de-l'Épine. The kitchens sent up hot rations, and replacements arrived to bring us back to just over 50 per cent strength. However, some of the replacements were patched-up wounded from D-day, and while perhaps restored physically, they were not emotionally up to rejoining the battle.

The divisional commander visited the bivouac area that evening and spoke to representatives from each company in his staccato fashion about how well we had done. Faces lit up a bit, but I don't know if it was because of the praise or because the general repeated that after taking St. Lô the division would get a real rest. We had been depending on this for some time, but it was good to hear it from this man.

Somewhat restored, the battalion trudged back up to its old position on the ridge on July 15. That afternoon word came down that we and the 1st Battalion, on our left, were to try before dark to break through. The way was to be prepared by thirteen battalions of artillery and a fighter-bomber strike, nearly three times the firepower of the first day of the assault. As with any prolonged battle, St. Lô proved a magnet attracting more and more metal from both sides.

Whether it was the tremendous weight of metal crashing down upon a narrow front or German command confusion, I do not know, but the attack broke through, and the companies took off in full career with an élan to which even Old Stonewall would have had to raise his cap. A squad or so of the reserve rifle company, the command post, and heavy mortars were en route to follow when word came down to halt. The effect was that of throwing a hard-running machine abruptly into reverse; we of the rear end skidded to a stop, while the front end broke loose and kept going right down to the crossroads hamlet of La Madeleine, less than a mile from St. Lô. The battalion commander took off on the run to catch them. Later we learned that the halt order stemmed from ''their'' not knowing or else being unable to credit our success.

Uncertainty took over while command and staff wheels ground out the decision not to withdraw from La Madeleine but for the rest of the Stonewall Brigade to fight on down and join them. In the meantime German command wheels must also have been grinding, for the gap was rapidly closed and the bulk of the 2nd Battalion was cut off.

Over the next two days the advance, won at so little cost, became progressively more ominous. The Stonewall Brigade was in a poor posture to strike effectively; instead of a clenched fist, it now had a weak finger stuck over a mile deep into hostile territory. Halfway back, well out of supporting range, was the 1st Battalion, which had been halted intact; back on the original position were the 3rd Battalion, which had been badly mauled that morning, and the remnant of the 2nd Battalion.

Compounding their hazard, the companies at La Madeleine had only the ammunition and rations that individuals had carried with them. Communication was by the artillery-liaison officer's radio, and its batteries faded more with each transmission.

Still impressed, however, by the day's success, I was confident that we would push on through the next morning. I knew my outfit, and with its commander there I would bet on its being able to survive one night anywhere.

Events didn't turn out exactly that way. The next day, July 16, instead of attacking toward La Madeleine, the 1st Battalion had to fight for its life. Its right flank company along the ridge road was blasted by a tank at pointblank range and was reduced within minutes to less than platoon size. We were caught in this hurricane of fire and noise that swept back and forth across the narrow front, hour after hour.

Late that afternoon, as the fury abated, I reached my personal depth of the war, and it has remained with me as only the ultimate depth, and height, of one's life can remain. I was alone at the time outside the now useless command post. The sun, setting behind St. Lô, glowed a dull, furious red through the smoke and dust raised by the shelling. Tall trees cast long black shadows; on the road was a smashed jeep with the flayed remains of the driver fallen half out of it. In the next field a dump of mortar ammunition burned and flared. Here the shelling had stopped, but in the distance it still rumbled like far-off summer thunder.

The scene was *Gotterdämmerung,* an effect opera-set designers strive for but can never equal. A Teutonic heart might have found it stirring grandeur. But not mine, not then. For suddenly I was convinced that my battalion was gone, irrevocably lost, destroyed. If the Germans could threaten to overrun this well-supplied position, what chance of survival had the undermanned and undersupplied companies isolated in their midst? And if the battalion that had been the boundaries of my life for three years was gone, what chance had I? At that point I was despairing of the war and uncaring of its purpose.

After dark I was called to the regimental command post with the staffs of the battalions to meet with the divisional commander. The dimly lit bunker was crowded and the air oppressive. The general reviewed the situation; he said that the 2nd Battalion had survived the day without serious trouble and that the attack to relieve it and take St. Lô would go on. He then delivered a harsh judgment on defeatism, racking a hapless captain who had expressed discouragement. He did not know that in the back of the bunker stood perhaps the most despairing major on the Normandy front.

Usually this dynamic man's statement of purpose and direction lifted my spirits. But not that night; I could not believe that the 2nd had survived such a day inside the German lines, or, perhaps to justify my own funk, I didn't choose to believe it.

The regimental commander, who had just taken over the job, assured the general that we were full of fight, and the session was over.

I stumbled back through the dark to arrive at our position just as a heavy shelling filled the night again with noise and concussion. My usually highly active sense of self-preservation was not functioning, for instead of diving into the nearest hole, I wandered aimlessly around, ears ringing from a nearby tree burst whose shower of fragments somehow missed me. My route passed the slit trench of a sergeant who had been in the first platoon of which I had taken uncertain command. He called a warning, and when I continued on, he jumped out and dumped me into the nearest hole and demanded that I stay there. So I did, and recall little of the rest of the night.

The battalion surgeon appeared at daylight to inquire about the situation but showed more interest in what he said was my loss of hearing and suggested that I go back to the division's medical clearing station for a check. What was left of the 2nd Battalion had been attached to the 1st, leaving me particularly useless, and I made no objection. At the clearing station I was given a blue capsule and sent to a nearby tent area. The capsule, reputedly capable of stupefying an elephant, was known popularly as the blue-88, in tribute to the Germans' dreaded 88-mm. gun. I barely made it to the tent and a blanket on the ground before falling off a high place into a deep, vacant sleep.

Eight or ten hours later I climbed reluctantly back to awareness and found the tent had been removed while I slept. Nearby was a line of hapless-looking soldiers carrying mess gear, though there was no kitchen in sight. While I was trying to sort all this out a lightly built, sandy-haired lieutenant came up and pointed shakily to a bombed-out railway station barely visible in the distance. This place, he said, was too close to that target and ought to be moved. Obviously he was at one with the dejected-looking soldiers seeking comfort in the familiar ritual of standing in a mess line—even one that offered no food.

It came to me then, with a jolt, that this was the trampled field of the defeated in spirit—the division's way station for the emotional wreckage of the battle, called combat-fatigue cases. Here was determined those salvageable for further war and those to be discarded into the teeming areas.

No *Gotterdämmerung* this—no twilight of the gods full of the grandeur of noble death. This was a place of whimper and cringe, the skid row of the battle zone. I had heard of it, and my offhand judgment had been that it was a mistake to so cater to weakness. Finding myself there brought on a panic akin, I imagine, to that of a minister who has walked inadvertently into a brothel. Now I can see that field as a true note in the awful clanging harmony of St. Lô. The abject spirits were counterpoint to those enduring on Martinville Ridge; their weakness accented strength as death accents life.

The answer to my shame at having slept through my battalion's agony at such a place was to flag down a ride back to the ridge. Leaving physically was a matter of minutes, but emotionally that place remains with me; I must always wonder how truly I belonged there.

Back on the ridge the battle was in a perceptibly lower key. Where salvos of shells had been crashing in, there were now only random rounds. I found my people still in place. No one mentioned my absence, and I didn't bring it up.

There was much news. That morning a 3rd Battalion attack had reached La Madeleine and found the 2nd in good shape, still unaccountably ignored by the surrounding Germans. The other news was that Major Thomas D. Howie, commanding the 3rd, had been killed shortly after reaching La Madeleine. I have said that he alone among the shadowy figures in this account is to be called forth by name, and this is because he combined to an uncommon degree the kindness and courage that would have better become us all. In mourning Tom Howie I mourn all for whom life and laughter ended at St. Lô and, by some projection, those for whom it has ended since.

The divisional commander, who was imaginative as well as arbitrary and, I suspect, compassionate in his way, had the flag-draped body taken into St. Lô when it fell two days later and placed high on a bier of rubble in front of the town's shattered Notre Dame, thus fulfilling Tom Howie's vow as he launched the attack that he would reach the city. News stories and photographs followed, and Tom Howie became the Major of St. Lô—the nation's symbol of the battle. Many who grieved for the fallen soldier at the time may now have forgotten, and the new generations may never have heard of him at all, but the story stirred America to no small degree in that July of 1944. A dramatic tribute in the classic tradition to the dead warrior rising above the murk of a long, ugly war caught the imagination and the heart. The Major of St. Lô inspired editorial tributes and one of the few poems of merit to come out of the war, unimportantly in error on some points. There is now a memorial to Tom Howie in the rebuilt St. Lô and another at Staunton Military Academy, where he coached football before the war.

Ironically, the qualities that made his death mourned and marked did not serve him well in the hard climate in which we trained before D-day. In that pre-battle period those who were most assertive and demanding by nature seemed to prosper most; those who were hard simply because the job demanded it had a degree of success; and those of a naturally kindly nature who underwent no war change had a difficult time.

When the caps began to pop on Omaha Beach, however, personal calm and courage took immediate precedence over all other leadership qualities, for those alone could cope with the supreme assertiveness of enemy bullets. It is my impression that these qualities surfaced fully as frequently among the kindly as among the harsh. They took Tom Howie to battalion command and to his final appointment at La Madeleine. In daring, unsparing demands upon himself and in thoughtfulness he resembled Turner Ashby, commander of Stonewall's cavalry in the halcyon days of the valley campaign of 1862. Stonewall was harsh in his judgment of Ashby's failure to push his troopers; but he wept, and the South wept, when Ashby was killed, as of course he was, the nature of such soldiers making death in battle almost inevitable.

Through knowing Tom Howie I feel I know Ashby and the gallant-hearted and selfless in every army in every war. They do not finally win the wars; those who are arbitrary and demanding do that. But the Howies and Ashbys add a note of grace to a generally brutish scene, and for this they are loved and remembered.

The Germans could, perhaps, not notice the fragmented 2nd Battalion at La Madeleine, but the arrival of the 3rd was large enough to attract deadly attention. The mortar round that killed Tom Howie was followed by a day of heavy shelling and attack; the last one, late in the day, was broken up by a spectacular concentration of our artillery fire and by fighter-bomber strikes. Even so, the day's end found both battalions low on ammunition and with many dead and wounded.

Now, however, the tragedy of St. Lô was moving rapidly to its close. For this final act the devastated town was the stage, with XIX Corps divisions gathered above it on the hills to the north and east. On the afternoon of the eighteenth a 29th Task Force broke into the ruins and raised the division's flag. At about the same time, the Stonewall Brigade opened a supply corridor to La Madeleine, and evacuation of wounded and dead was begun, Tom Howie's body being carried into St. Lô.

On July 20 the 29th's sector was taken over by the 35th Division, which had been heavily engaged on our right. As the 29th's units were relieved they began moving back to the promised land of corps reserve near St. Clair-sur-l'Elle, where this account started. The division had been in combat continuously for forty-five days at a price of over seven thousand casualties; in effect its nine rifle battalions had been used up about twice over.

Five days later Operation COBRA was launched with a massive aerial bombardment. The breakout from Normandy followed.

There remains a brief epilogue. The 2nd Battalion departed the battle by foot from La Madeleine to the ridge road. While waiting for it I took a last look around the now quiet field. The salvage crews were at work, and much of the wrecked equipment and weapons had been removed. But the deep wounds in the land were undressed and gave the appearance of verdant desolation. Every hedgerow was scalloped with holes, for no man had stopped without digging in. Practically every hedgerow had been fought for, plowed by shells, and gaped with raw passages for tanks. Whole trees were blasted down, and shattered limbs hung from others. The sickening smell of high explosive persisted.

While I looked and wondered at all this the battalion, in column of twos, commander leading, appeared toiling up the slope. The column was pitifully short; at first I thought that it was only one company and the other would follow. Then I realized that this was all there was, and the memory of it still dries the throat and stings the eyes.

I had seen the great, gray ships of the D-day armada stretching to the horizon in every direction, and I had often seen majestic fleets of Flying Fortress bombers returning from Germany. These were scenes awesome in power and portent. But for a sight to grasp and hold the heart forever I give you a decimated infantry battalion lurching out of battle, bowed with a mortal weariness and with all it has endured. This is not a drama of machines but of ordinary men who have achieved an extraordinary triumph over their fears and vulnerable flesh. For me all sights must pale beside it. I joined the commander and told him of arrangements for the bivouac. The column trudged on toward the Couvains road. Behind us the mists of onrushing time and events began to gather over St. Lô.

A newspaper editor before World War II, Charles R. Cawthon chose to remain on active duty after hostilities were over and later commanded a battalion in the Korean War. Now retired, he operates a tree farm in Virginia.

The Road to Yalta

William Harlan Hale

On a brisk November day in Washington in 1933, two spare, tall American officials of high rank and collected demeanor emerged from under the mansards of the old State Department building to journey to Union Station and there greet a squat, rotund, grinning foreigner who in the eyes of many of their compatriots was a dangerous revolutionary. The moment itself was revolutionary, even in a sartorial sense. Protocol prescribed that when our Secretary of State and his assistants received the visiting foreign minister of another sovereign power, formal morning dress be worn. Yet on this occasion, so Under Secretary William Phillips recorded of the trip across town that he and his chief, Secretary of State Cordell Hull, undertook that day to welcome Soviet Foreign Commissar Maxim Litvinov, "None of us wore top hats because [Litvinov] came as the representative of a government not yet officially recognized by the United States."

The affable Russian, speaking excellent English and himself wearing a snap-brim felt hat, had come here to achieve exactly that recognition, and thus to restore the American-Russian relations that had been broken off in 1918 with the United States' refusal to deal with the atheistic, debt-repudiating, proselytizing new Bolshevik regime of Lenin and Trotsky. The breach had left the world's two potentially greatest powers, after more than a century of mutual cordiality, not speaking to each other for the next fifteen years (*see* "When the Red Storm Broke," AMERICAN HERITAGE, February, 1961). Yet now suddenly, it seemed, America's mood had changed. On the very afternoon of his arrival, Litvinov was taken in to see President Franklin D. Roosevelt, also eager to resolve what he called "this

222

anomalous situation.'' After barely a week of discussions the United States—the one great nation still refusing to accept what Lenin had wrought—agreed to do business with his heir, Joseph Stalin.

In return, the Soviets agreed to mend some ways of theirs that had been particularly offensive to us. They promised to honor at least some of the debts Russia owed America and its citizens, to refrain from fomenting subversive agitation in our midst through their Communist International (or Comintern), and to protect the religious and other civil rights of American nationals in Russia. Ambassadors and a growing wealth of goods would be exchanged, and all or nearly all would now be well between our contrasting fellow republics.

Along this new route to reconciliation, however, traveling conditions were to be as subarctic as northern Russia itself: protracted deep freezes suddenly followed by brief, torrid summer; bright sunshine giving way to violent squalls and sudden darkness. The route, moreover, led over treacherous terrain, with every step along the way a challenge to the most sure-footed and imaginative of explorer-diplomats.

Alas! Again, as during America's most demanding previous test—the erupting Russia of the winter of 1917–18—we had painfully few men equal to the task at hand. We had floundered then in Petrograd because we had been amateurish, indecisive, and entangled in cross-purposes. What had we learned during the intervening years about how to comport ourselves when returning to the land of the Great Bear? As in 1917–18, we now proceeded to send to Russia a series of emissaries of sharply contrasting backgrounds, commitments, and beliefs. Moreover, on occasion we again sent several simultaneously, thereby further blurring our "image."

America found itself represented in Moscow first by a millionaire, William C. Bullitt, who had been greatly taken with the Soviets at the outset and ended totally at odds with them; next by a multimillionaire, Joseph E. Davies, who became greatly taken with the Soviets and remained that way for the rest of his days; later by a crusty, retired admiral, William H. Standley, who talked back firmly to the Soviets but also to President Roosevelt, and fell out with both. And these were but a few of the contrasting American visitors to face the Russian monolith.

In the Petrograd of 1917–18 our affairs had become snarled through the presence of proliferating, independent American missions—military, Red Cross, propaganda, etc.—all bypassing our ambassador and feuding with one another. In Moscow, during a second wartime, we were to enlarge upon those precedents by establishing massive lend-lease and military-aid missions also independent of our principal envoy and, moreover, headed by successive chiefs—Generals Philip R. Faymonville and John R. Deane—of wholly diverging viewpoints. The President's personal bright star, Harry L. Hopkins, flew in briefly through the early wartime Moscow sky, as did Averell Harriman, later to return as America's able regular ambassador. Ex-Ambassador Davies oddly reappeared, too, and both a would-be President, Wendell Willkie, and an itinerant Vice President, Henry Wallace, showed up. While we spoke with multiple voices, the Kremlin talked back with one.

Clearly the President was of a divided and changing mind when confronting the heirs of Marx and Lenin. He was not alone. Our whole nation was uncertain how to deal, if deal we must, with this vexing, frightening, secretive colossus. Hence we exported to Moscow during the 1930's and the war years all our own domestic ideological differences about it—every emissary representing his own faiths or fears.

In 1933, though, when the proposal to strike up official relations with the Soviet pariahs received the new President's attention, there was widespread agreement to this much at least: let's give it a try. Times had changed radically since 1918—had been changing, so far as American estimation of Russia was concerned, for quite a number of years. For one thing, the Soviet regime had proved itself stable and responsible (save when it came to that matter of debts); it had emerged far enough from its seclusion to confer with the West at Geneva about disarmament and to ring general alarms about the new menace of militarist Japan. For another, the new, industrializing Russia had become a natural American market— an increasingly desirable and important one as the onset of world-wide depression shriveled every other.

Thus encouraged—and kept up to date on Russian affairs by journalists like Walter Duranty, William Henry Chamberlin, and Vincent Sheean—Americans had become increasingly fascinated by what they called the "Soviet experiment," even while preserving varying degrees of distaste for it. No man had been more fascinated all along than the wealthy Philadelphian William C. Bullitt, who in 1919, at twenty-eight, had persuaded President Wilson to send him on an unofficial mission to the Bolsheviks to sound out possible conciliatory sentiments among them (*see* "The Wasted Mission," AMERICAN HERITAGE, April 1961). Angered by Wilson's abrupt dismissal of his hopeful report, Bullitt had denounced what he held to be American folly, and subsequently resumed his ardent advocacy of American-Soviet *rapprochement*. Intense, articulate, a polished Main Line aristocrat but also a maverick, Bullitt had at once attracted the attention of the incoming President Roosevelt—a man often drawn to such mixtures—with the result that early in 1933 he was sent to Moscow to repeat, in effect, his exploratory mission of 1919. And when this time the response brought Litvinov to Washington with powers to conclude an agreement on very broad terms, it seemed only logical to dispatch the enthusiastic Bullitt to Moscow as America's first ambassador to the Soviet Union.

He arrived there that December, bringing with him as Third Secretary a very young Foreign Service officer named George F. Kennan (soon to be joined by another named Charles E. Bohlen), and established himself across Red Square from the Kremlin in the National Hotel, the grubby capital's cavernous refuge for foreigners. Immediately Bullitt found himself receiving, over and beyond the respect due an envoy, the regime's marks of favor as a special friend. Litvinov staged for him a "tremendous" reception; and Stalin, who "until my arrival had never received any ambassador, summoned Bullitt and assured him that "At any moment day or night, if you wish to see me you have only to ask and I will see you at once."

Yet the honeymoon begun so deliriously lasted only a very few months. By March, 1934, Bullitt was sending home flustered, disappointed cables about "misunderstandings" on matters ranging from Litvinov's debt agreement (which was not being fulfilled) to Moscow's permission for an American Embassy building to be erected there (which was now being blocked). "Oral promises of members of the Soviet government are not to be taken seriously," the veteran proponent of closer ties sourly concluded. By October, infuriated by the Kremlin's default on still another promise—that of curbing the activities of the Comintern within American borders—Bullitt reached the point of cabling Washington, "I think I might go so far as to intimate to Litvinov verbally that we might sever diplomatic relations if the Comintern should be allowed to get out of hand."

The falling-out reflected underlying antagonisms between the two nations which the first genial meetings in Washington and Moscow had covered over, not resolved. It was also America's introduction to a typical Soviet tactic: demanding a foot when given an inch. Having received the accolade of recognition, the Kremlin now wanted speedy American credits and support of its drive for "collective-security" pacts against the rising threats of Nazi Germany, Fascist Italy, and Japan; America, on the other hand, insisted on settlement of at least some of Russia's debts to us before there could be talk of going further (and collective security was something that our still-isolationist republic especially did not wish to pursue). So a new freeze set in between the two capitals—coldest in Moscow as between Bullitt and Litvinov. The Kremlin had erred in assuming that its American friend Bullitt would be all-compliant. Bullitt had erred in assuming that the Russians, whom he had trusted, would live up to their word. Stalin's promised "open door" slammed shut in Bullitt's face (during a whole year, the two conferred only once), and the American who in 1933 had entered Moscow in triumph as its most favored guest quit it in 1936 in frustration as one of Soviet Russia's most embittered critics.

The Kremlin had learned a lesson too: never again an American liberal, with all the mercurial tendencies of the breed! Far better to have from America a hardheaded, stalwart capitalist—a "class enemy" to be sure, but at least one whose reactions you could predict. So the Soviets were relieved when President Roosevelt chose as his next envoy to them the prominent corporation lawyer Joseph E. Davies, financier, politician, and sharer—through his marriage to Mrs. Marjorie Post Close Hutton, the daughter of C. W. Post of Post Toasties—in an immense fortune. Yet Moscow was due for some surprises at Davies' hand. So was America.

A handsome, gregarious figure of many-sided accomplishment and charm, Davies had early begun moving in leading Democratic circles. He had turned down President Wilson's offer of the ambassadorship to czarist Russia in 1913, but later served Wilson as chairman of the Federal Trade Commission and as economic adviser at the Versailles peace conference. A close friend and political backer of Franklin D. Roosevelt since Wilsonian days, he was going forth now to Moscow as the President's immediate confidant (with the result, as Secretary of State Hull was to complain, that Davies, like Bullitt before him, frequently communicated with Roosevelt directly, "over my head").

All this was impressive. But what seemed to impress the Soviets most of all was the regal state in which Ambassador and Mrs. Davies commenced their expedition to darkest Moscow. Thirty trunks, fifty smaller pieces of luggage, and six personal servants accompanied them. ("We are going to live in Moscow very quietly, very simply," explained Davies; " 'When in Rome,' you know . . .") Mistrusting Soviet produce, they also took along some two thousand pints of frozen American cream (Birds Eye process, owned by Mrs. Davies' General Foods), together with twenty-five freezers in which to store it. "Contrary to popular belief," said a Soviet spokesman in New York, "there are cows in Russia."

Half a year later, when supplies ran low, Mrs. Davies was to order another two thousand pints, along with *two tons* of frozen meats, fruits, and vegetables from home. Yet Soviet leaders, far from being affronted by this swollen self-indulgence amid Russia's lean times, were fascinated by it. Coming from below, they had tasted enough of power to like to indulge themselves, too—and the most Lucullan table to be seen in Moscow since the revolution now beckoned them. It soon appeared that the master of Spasso House (the stately mansion of a czarist grandee acquired as the American Embassy) was surprisingly hospitable to their minds as well.

The paunchy Litvinov, restored to amiability now that the demanding Bullitt was gone and this expansive capitalist was here, flattered Davies by telling him (as Davies promptly reported to Washington) that "I had acquired more information and knowledge of Russia in the three months I was here than any other ambassador had obtained in two years." He then went on to ask the new ambassador's general impressions. "I told him briefly that I was very much impressed with what they were doing, with the strength of their leadership, the difficulties they were overcoming; that I felt they were presently sincerely devoted to peace . . ." Meanwhile the colorful Mrs. Davies, to the astonishment of the British ambassador ("I have been here seven years and haven't been able to get so much as a toe in their house!"), was invited to lunch at the country *dacha* of Mme. Molotov, the Premier's consort.

It was a new thaw, evidently—passing at once into balmy summer. Then what, amid all this sweetness and light, was a secret, nocturnal Soviet agent doing in the attic of Spasso House? We come to the incident of Second Secretary Kennan and the night the Davies' cream turned sour. It is recounted by Charles W. Thayer, a young Philadelphian who had become the assistant to the gifted, Russian-speaking Kennan-Bohlen team that often had to pull ambassadorial chestnuts out of the fire.

As Thayer tells it in *Bears in the Caviar*, they had discovered that a Soviet spy was in the process of "bugging" Mr. Davies' office with a microphone run down from the attic. After several fruitless nights of vigil up there to try to observe him, they retired to more comfortable quarters below, leaving a net of cross-wire alarms to alert them at his next visit. But when the intruder returned, he got away in the night—after knocking out the entire Spasso House electrical system. Two days later, Ambassador Davies' butler reported to Thayer: "Two of the deep-freezes seem to have failed to get back into action after we reconnected the current."

"What was in them?"

"The frozen cream, and it's passed all saving."

There were indeed several hundred pints of well-publicized Davies cream rotting in the basement, and there was only one way of getting rid of them so as not to damage the Davies prestige. Since all regular Embassy employees were under close Soviet surveillance, the only thing for Thayer to do was to round up some Russian workmen to help him quietly dump a truckload of the stuff in a deserted pine forest.

There were more hazards facing Davies than espionage and sour cream. As Kennan was to point out in a searching memorandum, "The Position of an American Ambassador in Moscow," there was Soviet evasion, double talk, secrecy, dilatoriness, and a tactic of isolating the American envoy and his staff from all but the most superficial contacts with Russians. But greatest of all (though Kennan did not bring this up) was the danger of impressionable and gullible thinking on the part of the envoy himself—and of this, Davies is one of diplomacy's classic exhibits.

In setting out, as he tells us in *Mission to Moscow* (the best-selling memoir that was to be made into one of the most debated movies of the war years), his verbal instructions from the President were to seek to persuade the Soviets to break the debt and trade impasse, meanwhile assuming a posture of "dignified friendliness" qualified by "definite reserve." Reserve, however, flew out the window at his first meeting with Soviet President Kalinin. "A fine type," Davies called him, "a kind, good man." But this was nothing compared to the Ambassador's enthusiasm on meeting Stalin himself: "His brown eye is exceedingly kindly and gentle. A child would like to sit in his lap and a dog would sidle up to him. . . . Throughout [the interview] he joked and laughed at times. He has a sly humor."

Yet there was little to laugh about during Davies' first year in Moscow. For his arrival there coincided with the start of the second and greatest of the series of "purge" trials that bewildered the world and bitterly divided those until then inclined to befriend the "Soviet experiment." A long procession of hitherto high-ranking Communist ministers, intellectuals, ideologues, and generals were quickly tried for counter-revolutionary conspiracy and duly led off to execution. Were the trials a frame-up? Had the accused been tortured in some mysterious fashion, and was this Stalin's Oriental way of disposing of his rivals?

Many observers of the macabre spectacle were torn by doubt, but Davies, watching from one of the best diplomatic seats in the Soviet Supreme Court as the "Old Bolshevik" editor Karl Radek and nearly a score of others went under, seemed untroubled. He wrote home that he accepted at face value Public Prosecutor Andrei Vishinsky's thesis of a dark terrorist plot and blandly concluded after the prisoners had been condemned: "The purge . . . cleansed the country and rid it of treason." This view he also maintained when visiting London. Dining in company with Winston Churchill, Davies was chagrined to find that it did not go down well there, "so violent is the prejudice. . . . I gave the facts as interpreted from the Soviet viewpoint."

An American ambassador handing out in London the "facts" as interpreted by Stalin: What next?

Early in 1938 President Roosevelt realized that his man in Moscow was a liability—for all his popularity there, he still had not achieved that debt settlement—and withdrew him to the safer post of Brussels. Litvinov threw Davies a great farewell dinner, and the amiable visitor left trailing such pronouncements as "I do not think that the world is in any real danger from communism for many years to come," and, later, "It is not [the Soviets'] intent to seek to project communism in the United States."

The Soviet Union was, however, embarking on a course that would once more lead to a freeze in Russo-American relations. For fully three years we would again be barely on speaking terms; for many months on end—particularly those of the Munich crisis, the height of Western humiliation and distress—we were to be without an ambassador in Moscow at all.

For while the Soviets had been clamoring for joint opposition to Hitler, Mussolini, the aggressive Japanese, and then Franco, America (like its old European partners, Britain and France) had avoided doing anything effective about it—a fact that had enormously increased Communist prestige among all those aroused to resistance. Roosevelt in the fall of 1937 had tried to reverse America's position by his historic "quarantine-the-aggressors" speech, but when he was unable to prevail, it next became the turn of the Soviets to reverse their own: by the next summer they were threatening to retreat into isolation unless we came out of ours, and by the spring of 1939, in the aftermath of Munich, they did precisely that, furthermore denouncing the Western allies as "warmongers" just when these at last were arming against the general danger.

In August came Russia's second turnabout—alliance with the former enemy, in the pact that helped unleash Hitler's forces and win for Russia a share of Poland.

This was followed by Russia's "dreadful rape of Finland," as Roosevelt termed it, which led us to place an embargo on many exports to this latest aggressor, while at home sentiment was rising in favor of aiding embattled France and Britain. In Moscow an appropriately chilly Foreign Service professional, Ambassador Laurence A. Steinhardt, represented us, engaged largely in delivering messages of protest over such incidents as the Soviet detention of the American freighter *City of Flint.*

Then on June 22, 1941, Hitler performed *his* fateful turnabout: he invaded Russia with 175 divisions. Overnight the whole configuration of affairs changed again: the Western "warmongers" of yesterday became in Russia's eye partners in her "Great Patriotic War," while a hitherto lonely Britain and a defensive America set out to build with Russia the Grand Alliance. In barely a month, the President's personal adviser, Harry L. Hopkins, was on the Moscow scene with an introduction from Roosevelt asking Stalin to treat Hopkins with "the identical confidence you would feel if you were talking directly to me." Cordially welcomed at the Kremlin, he declared to Stalin "the determination of the President and our government to extend all possible aid to the Soviet Union at the earliest possible time."

It was characteristic of Roosevelt under pressure that he conveyed this vital message not through his regular ambassador on the ground or through a visit by Secretary of State Hull (with whom his own relations had become distant) but by a special emissary. Hopkins, for his part, hastened to point out to Stalin that his mission was "not a diplomatic one" in the usual sense, In title, Hopkins was Roosevelt's administrator of lend lease. In fact, he was his Colonel House and closest friend; and the skill of this extraordinary expediter, sensitive yet durable, often ill and nerve-racked yet searching and thorough, was never greater than during the crucial sessions—lasting only two days—in which he won the inscrutable Stalin's confidence, gained from him a complete picture of Soviet military strengths and weaknesses, placed Soviet-American relations upon an entirely new footing, and did all this so circumspectly as to draw from the sidetracked Hull and Steinhardt no audible murmur of criticism. As Hopkins' biographer, Robert E. Sherwood, remarks: "This was indeed the turning point in the wartime relations of Britain and the United States with the Soviet Union."

It also marked a point from which there was to be no turning back. Stalin, whose armies were reeling under German impact across the Ukraine toward Moscow, needed immediately great supplies of guns and aircraft metal. Many expert Western observers on and around the scene were pessimistic; why, asked Major Ivan Yeaton, the American military attaché at Moscow, lend aid to a doomed cause? Yet when Hopkins reported to Roosevelt, "I feel ever so confident about this front. . . . There is unbounded determination to win," his word tilted the scales. Within a few days, at their seaborne conference in Newfoundland's Argentia Bay at which the Atlantic Charter was framed, Roosevelt and Churchill determined to rush all possible equipment to Stalin even at some risk to their own arsenals, and to send at once a joint supply mission to explore his needs. This was the occasion that brought Averell Harriman for the first time to Moscow, along with England's Lord Beaverbrook. Two weeks after they arrived, German spearheads had pushed to within thirty miles of the capital, government offices were being evacuated to Kuibyshev in the rear, and Major Yeaton was reporting that the end of Russian resistance might not be far away.

Yet while Americans were concentrating on first things first—to help Russia stave off defeat—Stalin was already thinking far ahead to the shape that Europe should take after the victory. Here was the great misstep on our road to Yalta: not only did Western leaders seem to fail to realize how large the Soviets might loom in the event of victory, but they refused to discuss the future with Stalin at a time advantageous to themselves, when he was so hard-pressed and weak. Thus it happened that soon after Pearl Harbor, Roosevelt, though aware of Soviet territorial demands in Poland and the Baltic area, specifically asked Stalin to omit such questions from the treaty of alliance then being negotiated. The absence of territorial discussion now left the new alliance a one-way street—we were giving the Russians more and more aid against Hitler's onslaught, without pressing them to surrender some of their aspirations in return.

How much aid—and when? How soon are you going to open a "second front" to relieve us? When are you going to recognize our just claims in eastern Europe? These were the constant calls from Moscow, and each brought new East-West collisions. Only a few months after Hopkins' warm reception at the Kremlin, the visiting Harriman was given a brusque one: Stalin showed impatience at the slowness of Western aid and warmed only when Harriman promised him five thousand jeeps. The President, aware how tough a customer we were dealing with, now thought we had better send him as resident ambassador a markedly tough personality of our own, and so Stalin got a battleship admiral.

The President had a particular fondness for the Navy and its proven leaders—and William H. Standley had served him outstandingly as Chief of Naval Operations. A square-jawed, sharp-spoken quarter-deck disciplinarian with forty-five years in the service, Standley had no experience of Russia except for a brief ceremonial visit to Vladivostok in 1896 as a midshipman. But upon retirement he had become one of Roosevelt's staunchest supporters in the long domestic battle for aid to the Allies before Pearl Harbor; such a man might serve with insight and muscle.

His first reaction to Stalin differed noticeably from that of Davies. Standley found the Soviet dictator "a cocky, healthy-looking individual, with swarthy complexion and an Oriental cast of countenance . . ." A man of stalwart build himself, Standley carried chips on both broad shoulders: he was easily offended when Stalin kept him waiting or when Washington failed to brief him fully or when visiting firemen from home intruded. He wanted to run his Embassy as a "taut ship" in perilous waters with himself in sole command—a logical aspiration, but quixotic in view of the Rooseveltian way of conducting wartime affairs abroad. Messages passed directly between Roosevelt and Stalin, "leapfrogging over my tophatted head," Standley complained; summit conferences were arranged and second-front commitments entered into without his being the wiser; and Hopkins' and Harriman's lend-lease man on the spot, Colonel (later Brigadier General) Faymonville, pursued his own quite independent course. The old admiral finally exploded when two further visiting emissaries, Wendell Willkie and the familiar Joe Davies, arrived on the scene with powers to go over his head to the Kremlin.

Willkie, the President's 1940 electoral opponent who had subsequently been enlisted into the bipartisan war effort, touched down in Moscow during his globegirding "One World" tour in the fall of 1942. He delivered himself of statements declaring America's unqualified friendship for Soviet Russia, and after closeting himself alone with Stalin went so far as to remark to Standley that some of the things he had learned there were too secret for even the ambassador to know. As if this were not galling enough, Willkie made a point of telling the world that Soviet Russia had been misrepresented in the United States and that he wished to "put over a more favorable picture" of it. "Many among the democracies fear and mistrust Soviet Russia . . ." he wrote. "Such fear is weakness . . ." He issued in Moscow a call, echoing Stalin's, for the early opening of a second front.

"Mr. Willkie, I have been very patient," Standley finally exploded. "Now I feel it my duty to remind you that there is only one United States representative in the Soviet Union, and I, the American Ambassador, am that representative."

But Standley's patience was to be tried even more by the brief return engagement of Davies, who arrived the following spring on a 10,000-mile round trip from Washington—in a special plane, with a crew of nine plus his personal staff and physician—simply to deliver a letter from Roosevelt to Stalin proposing a top-level meeting. It was a message that conceivably could have been delivered to the Kremlin by Standley himself from his office four blocks away. Welcomed at the airport by Soviet dignitaries as a returning hero, Davies insisted on delivering his letter alone. He had also brought along an advance print of the Warner Brothers movie made from his *Mission to Moscow* (Stalin was flatteringly portrayed by Manart Kippen, Davies by Walter Huston), which he prevailed upon the dictator to show after dinner in the Kremlin projection room. Stalin was visibly bored by it, and diplomatic guests went up in arms over its obvious distortions of the history of the purge trials and acceptance of the Soviet line on them. Next, Davies met the American press corps, and on hearing its complaints that the Soviets were failing to show appreciation for American aid, tongue-lashed the correspondents and accused them of "non-co-operation." "His lack of knowledge regarding Russia," wrote Quentin Reynolds, "shocked us all."

The reason behind the Willkie-Davies visits was that the President had lost confidence in his newest ambassador, while Standley had taken to grumbling about the President. Standley felt himself alone in a hostile environment and at odds with Washington, which he felt was playing the game on Stalin's terms. Our policy, he snorted, was only "Do not antagonize the Russians, give them everything they want, for, after all, they are killing Germans. . . ."

Increasingly suspicious, Standley fell out particularly with General Faymonville, the gifted, Russian-speaking Regular Army officer who was managing lend-lease from an office down the corridor, and whose predictions as to the staying power of the Red Army when others had given up hope in it had been amply borne out. Feeling that Faymonville was working too closely and enthusiastically with the Russians, Standley made direct representations to Roosevelt and Hopkins that the general be placed under Standley's orders. He got him reduced in size and then banished—though at the cost of any remaining White House good will toward himself.*

Standley had the ill fortune to represent us in Moscow during our hardest times there. During 1942 and most of 1943 the promised American aid never lived up to expectations, due first to enormous convoy losses and then to our own build-up for the second front that Stalin had demanded. But the Soviet chieftain kept upbraiding us for our delays in respect to both. When Allied armies streaked across Sicily and landed on the Italian mainland, though, the Bear warmed once more; and when in October, 1943, Standley having been retired to the shades, Secretary Hull arrived in Moscow for a four-power foreign ministers' conference accompanied by a new ambassador (Harriman) and a new military-aid chief (General Deane), Stalin was genial. With enormous forces now building up for OVERLORD (the Anglo-American descent upon Normandy) and supplies flowing to Russia over several seas, broad pledges of mutual aid and confidence were exchanged. Harriman was particularly elated when, in a daring mood, he proposed a toast at the Kremlin to the day "when we would be fighting together against the Japs," and Molotov suddenly responded: "Why not—gladly—*the time will come.*"

Yet Harriman was not so elated as to lose perspective. A shrewd observer and Presidential trouble shooter, he had known all the ups and downs of American-Soviet relations, and the reassuring atmosphere of the Moscow foreign ministers' conference had not concealed from him its lack of real achievement.

*A personal recollection: While at the Office of War Information in 1942, in charge of broadcasts to Germany, I was assigned by Robert E. Sherwood to go to Moscow on a mission arising from an offer made by Foreign Minister Vishinsky—that of my speaking nightly from there to eastern-front Germans in the name of the Voice of America. At that time, when American troops had not yet come to grips with Germans, it seemed a promising idea to convey in this fashion the message of Allied unity, and Vishinsky had promised that, apart from sheer military censorship, what I said over the Moscow radio would be subjected to no surveillance whatsoever. After I had waited several months with packed suitcases for travel orders, though, the mission was finally vetoed by Ambassador Standley on the ground that this, too, might lead to too-close collaboration with the Russians.

Now the final stage of the road led via Teheran and Moscow to Yalta—conferences marked by increasing inter-Allied warmth as the outlines of military victory became clearer, although the ultimate political consequences remained hidden in the veil. It was as if the civil plenipotentiaries, having failed to lay a basis of searching diplomacy with each other at the start, had come to feel that the soldiers would resolve their problems for them by providing a smashing triumph that would leave everyone happy—if exhausted. Stalin was enormously impressed by the prospects of OVERLORD. Churchill was equally impressed by the avenging progress of the Red armies and supported Stalin's claim for territory to protect Russia from future German invasions, even though this meant shifting Poland several hundred miles westward. Roosevelt, though he said he wanted no part of the Polish wrangle—not until after the 1944 elections, in any case—was inclined to support the Anglo-Soviet understanding reached on this point during the summit meeting at Teheran at the end of 1943.

Harriman, though a devoted admirer of Roosevelt and a believer in mobility in dealing with the Soviets, was not quite so sure. Shouldn't we, he asked, try to awaken them to the fact that we expected them to give as well as receive? In this he was supported by his top military-aid man, General Deane, a newcomer constituted very differently from his predecessor, General Faymonville. Deane demanded detailed information from the Soviets as to just what they were doing with supplies, even as Harriman kept requiring of them more specific knowledge of their political plans as Hitler's legions fell back. But then came the great convergence of Anglo-American armies upon Germany, (simultaneously with the Soviet armies' even greater one); the knowledge that the Soviets would join our hard-won march against Japan; and a profound feeling that amid so many mutual sacrifices made and joint victories won, the problems remaining between us—the fate of eastern Europe, the control of Germany, the level of reparations, the structure of the Balkans, the ratio of representation in the new United Nations—could be amicably resolved.

This was the immense agenda that faced the Big Three chiefs of government when they met at Yalta in the Crimea in February, 1945, for a week of breathless negotiating and climactic banqueting that would give new shape to the world. Time was short at Yalta—too short; the chieftains had to hurry home to direct the closing scenes of the military drama in Europe and stage its last act in Asia. Moreover, Roosevelt and Hopkins were both ailing; the new Secretary of State who accompanied them, Edward R. Stettinius, was inexperienced; and our standing representation in Russia itself had been so assorted and at times discredited that the President found himself with little in the way of a concerted body of first-hand experience there on which to draw. In our massive delegation at the Livadia Palace, the effective ''Russian experts'' were just two—the overburdened Harriman and young ''Chip'' Bohlen, serving as interpreter.

Many settlements, or what passed for settlements, were reached. The westward shift of Poland was confirmed; pledges as to the self-determination of liberated peoples were renewed; the Soviet Union, about to enter the war against Japan, was recognized as a major power in the Pacific, with legitimate aspirations there. The Soviets, in turn, recognized America's particular interest in succoring the regime of Chiang Kai-shek, gave ground on some points concerning joint occupation of Germany, and seemed willing to forego crushing reparations if it could obtain American reconstruction aid. The debate over seating at the United Nations also resulted in what both sides then regarded a fair draw; and such was Yalta's resulting mood that Prime Minister Churchill spoke in exalted terms of "the glories of future possibilities . . . before us," while Harry Hopkins reported a deep sense of accomplishment there. "We really believed in our hearts," Hopkins said, "that this was the dawn of the new day we had all been praying for. . . . We were absolutely certain that we had won the first great victory of the peace."

Perhaps, then, all—or almost all—would be well at last. Yet it was not to be so; and bitter blame has been heaped upon the Yalta Conference, as if it were the author of all our woes with Russia since. Yet perhaps it was culpable not so much for what it did as for what it did not do. Yalta left more matters unresolved than settled. In its headlong haste to catch up with the facts of military success, it was a political convocation that came too late. Moreover, it was one to which the warring partners came as unequals in the sense that they harbored very different political intentions, clothe them as they might. All spoke of liberation, but to the Soviets this meant also annexation of the liberated. On the other hand, the Western allies had no ulterior territorial motives: true, the British were willing to bargain with the Russians over spheres of influence so as to preserve their own, but the United States had no thought—and, it was agreed by all sides at home, no need—of aggrandizement at all.

America's position all along had been to avoid making postwar commitments until the war itself was nearly won. As late as October, 1944, Roosevelt had cabled Harriman (then sitting in on the Churchill-Stalin meetings at Moscow that prefaced Yalta), "It is important that I retain complete freedom of action after this conference is over." Yet the area of such freedom was narrowing fast as Red armies swarmed over southeastern and central Europe, pushing borders westward on their own. The most that could now be done about displaced Poland was an ambiguous formula calling for "reorganization" of the provisional Warsaw regime—by which the West meant a new government based on democratic elections, while Moscow meant one firmly attached to itself. The West asked for free ballot boxes all over eastern Europe; Moscow promised, but at the same time began converting once-free nations into satellites.

The ailing President, returning homeward across calm seas aboard the U.S.S. *Quincy* in the trust that Yalta's promise of freedom and equity would be fulfilled, was not to be spared disillusionment in the few weeks of life remaining to him. A mere fortnight later, Ambassador Harriman in Moscow was protesting sharply against Soviet moves to make defeated Rumania a captive state, and the West flatly refused to recognize the puppet regime set up there. More trouble was in store for our ambassador when an inter-Allied commission began to work out Yalta's indecisive plan for Poland. On April 2, after wrangling sessions in which Molotov had become more and more intransigent, Harriman reported flatly, "No agreement was reached on any point." Stalin himself, on the wire to Roosevelt, concurred. Harriman, for his part, was now reaching the point of recommending to Washington that further aid to Russia be suspended until Moscow ceased violating Yalta agreements. Then Stalin, suspicious because he had not been made party to the parleys between surrendering German commanders and advancing Anglo-American troops in Italy, cabled Roosevelt to charge deception and trickery. Roosevelt, aroused to the core, expressed "bitter resentment" at such "vile misrepresentations of my actions or those of my trusted subordinates." This and Stalin's reply were the last communications that passed between the two most powerful leaders of what had briefly been a common cause.

So the bright day dimmed even when the sun seemed to stand high. Roosevelt died, and Harriman in Moscow was alone in the gathering darkness. Once again the modern world's two titans, so different in their ways and make-up, so subject to alternating currents of mutual attraction and repulsion, drew apart. We had been by turns cordial friends over great distances (never more so than during our own Revolution and the Napoleonic wars), far-removed yet mutually amenable expansionists through the later nineteenth century, uneasy allies in two world wars, and profound ideological antagonists in the aftermath of each. Yet we had never, despite all our differences, become declared enemies on the battlefield; in fact, we were the only two great powers to have preserved peace—or what passed for it—with one another during all this long span of modern time. We did not speak one another's language; perhaps in the deepest sense we never quite would. Yet some recognition of the madness of ever making war upon one another in the name of our two immense and kindred humanities on opposite sides of the globe seemed to have been borne in upon us both. Will the time now come when, if nuclear war is unimaginable and the sheer absence of war not enough, we may proceed with firmer skill to the building of peace?

William Harlan Hale is managing editor of HORIZON. *His last contribution to* AMERICAN HERITAGE *was "When the Red Storm Broke," in the February, 1961, issue.*

For further reading: Churchill-Roosevelt-Stalin, *by Herbert Feis (Princeton University Press, 1957);* Admiral Ambassador to Russia, *by William H. Standley (Henry Regnery, 1955);* The Strange Alliance, *by John R. Deane (Viking, 1946):* Speaking Frankly, *by James F. Byrnes (Harper, 1947).*

Part Five

Contemporary America

Struggle for Democracy at Home and Abroad

Historians have had little difficulty arriving at a general consensus as to the over-arching context of recent United States history—namely, the great super power struggle between the United States and the Union of Soviet Socialist Republics. From 1945 to 1989, these two giants engaged in a world-wide contest of diplomatic, military, economic and ideological strength. For the United States, the 'cold war' against the Soviet Communist menace posed extraordinary challenges at home and abroad. On the homefront the response has led to the establishment of a national security state, operating behind the cloak of official secrecy, engaging in extensive court activities and sustaining the largest, most heavily armed peacetime military force in our history. A troublesome and often corrupt military-industrial complex has been one consequence of these developments. Abroad, the cold war has produced extensive commitments and entanglements without comparison to any previous period in the nation's history. This turbulent, difficult and lengthy period of international strife has had a profound impact on the United States. The sudden and dramatic relaxation of the East-West tensions which accompanied the rapid unraveling of the Soviet block in 1989 and 1990 is sure to mark the onset of a new period in U.S. history, the course of which remains uncertain and unpredictable.

The articles which follow are but a sampling of the many exciting developments in our history since World War II. Tom Braden's account of the creation of the Central Intelligence Agency indicates how rapidly United States relations with the Soviet Union deteriorated in the immediate postwar period and how the devious tactics employed by the Soviets led the Truman administration to embrace equally devious countermeasures. Passage of the National Security Act of 1947, which, among other things, created the independent C.I.A., has been recognized as a pivotal move toward institutionalization of the American warfare state of the cold war era.

The great civil rights crusade of recent times clearly had roots in the racial and ideological aspects of the Second World War. Even more certainly the crusade gained momentum from the ideological context of the super power struggle. Janet Stevenson's account of the Montgomery, Alabama bus boycott of 1955–56 treats one of the important phases in the evolution of the Afro-American struggle for freedom and equality in a nation portraying itself to the world as the shining light of freedom and democracy. Rosa Parks, furthermore, reminds us all that righteous indignation in the face of blatant injustice, in combination with an act of courage, is a potent force in the course of human events.

Abuses of public office and special privilege have been a persistent feature of the United States Political-economic system, as has been their exposure. Doubtless no administration in the nation's history has been free of scandal. Recent American history would suggest a connection between the size and scope of governmental activities and the frequency and degree of public scandals. Big government seems to have spawned more frequent and more extensive misconduct. Walter Karp discusses the scandal which stands as the greatest abuse of power and public trust by government officials in the course of United States history. Only the Iran-Contra scandal of the Reagan administration—the full dimensions of which remain to be plumbed—can rival the activities of the Nixon administration which have come to be referred to as the Watergate Scandal.

Many conditions and concerns of our times which have heretofore received little attention because they seemed much less important than the defense of our nation will most certainly reassert themselves onto the national agenda as the cold war winds down. Among these will be a variety of ecological issues. Kenneth Davis traces the development and use of DDT, the first of the truly powerful and seemingly miraculous synthetic pesticides produced by modern scientists. His account of the discovery and exposure of the harmful consequences of this pesticide's use documents one case of the rise of the kind of public concerns which will likely increase in the decades ahead.

The Birth
of the CIA

Tom Braden

The history of successful ideas is sometimes marked by a trade-off. In his old age General William J. Donovan, founder of the United States intelligence service, may have reflected on the phenomenon. The trade-off goes something like this:

A man has an idea and proceeds to push it. Naturally, his idea is opposed by those to whom its acceptance will mean loss of power, stability, and comfort. Often the man is termed "power-mad"; he may even be hated. But suppose the idea is a very good one. There comes a point in the battle when to those who must decide the issue, a compromise occurs. Why not accept the idea and bar the man who had it from having anything to do with carrying it out?

Some such trade-off—trade-offs are never explicitly stated—hit Donovan very hard on a day in January, 1953, when Allen W. Dulles became Director of the Central Intelligence Agency, an institution that had sprung largely out of Donovan's brain.

"Ah," the old soldier sighed when he heard the news, "a very good man, Allen. I chose him personally to be chief of OSS in Switzerland. But Allen is young and inexperienced. He's never had a large command. He ought to be number two."

The emissary from Dulles to whom Donovan made this observation was amused at hearing the sixty-year-old Dulles called "young and inexperienced." But when Donovan's remark was reported back to Dulles, he was understanding. "Poor Bill. He's never wanted anything so much in his life. And you know, if they'd bought Bill's idea in the first place, we'd be a lot better off than we are now.''

Dulles was trying to be generous, but he was not exaggerating. Anyone who looks at the early history of the United States intelligence effort must be struck by the time wasted between Donovan and Dulles, or, to put it more precisely, between 1945, when Joseph Stalin opened his cold-war offensive in Poland, and 1950, when the Soviet Union attacked through its satellite in Korea.

During that period Russia erected its iron curtain; threatened Turkey, the Balkans, West Germany, and the Middle East; fought proposals for a United Nations army, international control of atomic energy, and the Marshall Plan; and began its enormously effective hate-America campaign in western Europe. While all this was going on, what might have been a United States counterforce languished in the hands of ineffectual men, subalterns to chieftains who were carving out empires in a battle over the unification of the armed services.

It was a time when a huge defense establishment was being dismantled at a rate as alarming to the country's leaders as it was popular with the country's people, and when Americans, tired of war and trusting in peace, wanted very much to believe that the leaders of the Soviet Union felt the same way. ''Wild Bill'' Donovan, with his talk of spies and saboteurs, seemed an anachronism.

The name ''Wild Bill'' was a generational heritage—a pitcher for the Detroit Tigers named William Donovan walked six and hit one in the first three innings of the deciding game of the World Series of 1909. But it was not an inaccurate sobriquet. Donovan was a fearless soldier and a first-rate lawyer. He had a bland manner, enormous round blue eyes, and a habit of walking on the balls of his feet, like a halfback who might suddenly swerve.

But he was also a romantic, and like all romantics he could be from time to time both endearing and irritating. For example, driving across town in New York City shortly after V-J Day, Donovan suddenly ordered his chauffeur to halt, darted from the car and disappeared into the crowd. Reappearing a few moments later, with a boyish grin, he explained to a companion, ''I just remembered I ought to pay my respects to Father Duffy. Haven't talked to him for a long while.''

Father Duffy had been regimental chaplain of Donovan's Fighting 69th during World War I and had been on the field when Donovan won the Congressional Medal of Honor. But he had, at this time, been dead for many years. Only a man of endearing romanticism would have thought to confer with his statue in Times Square.

On the other hand, Donovan's romanticism led him to deeds which seemed arrogant. He had himself transported to World War II beaches during landings for no other reason than that he wanted to be there; he went over other peoples' heads; he ignored channels and organization charts. And he would try anything. The more insane the idea, the more likely it seemed that Donovan would wave his hand and say, "Let's give it a try."

To the Army's intelligence branch, G-2, to the Office of Naval Intelligence, to J. Edgar Hoover's FBI, Donovan was anathema. The bureaucracies of these organizations could not abide the thought that this freewheeling, independent, little round man who had built the Office of Strategic Services, the enormous wartime spy agency, who reported directly to his friend Franklin D. Roosevelt, and whom, throughout the war, the bureaucrats had unsuccessfully endeavored to confine would survive to threaten their responsibilities and prerogatives now that peace had returned and things were going to get back to normal. "A mad man," was the way Major General George V. Strong, chief of the Army's G-2, referred to Donovan privately. Undersecretary of State Dean Acheson expressed the general view: "Donovan would have surprised no one if . . . he left one morning and returned the previous afternoon."

The bureaucracy succeeded in stopping Donovan and in killing his beloved OSS. But history played Donovan's enemies an enormous trick. The intelligence service they created to replace OSS eventually became the Central Intelligence Agency; CIA eventually became almost as powerful as Donovan had envisioned that his OSS in peacetime would be; finally, when Allen Dulles was named Director of CIA, American secret intelligence once again had at its helm a man who had learned his trade in the OSS and would not be long in reverting to the lessons he had learned.

Was it a good thing or a bad thing that Donovan's enemies won their battle and lost their war? The question is still being argued. Is it a good thing or a bad thing that the United States owns a huge secret intelligence agency with a powerful subversive arm? It is not my intent to argue but only to set down what happened. The story begins with the defeat of Donovan.

At five o'clock on the morning of February 9, 1945, the 62-year-old Donovan picked up a copy of the Washington *Times-Herald* on his Georgetown doorstep. There on the front page was his name in headlines and under that the by-line, Walter J. Trohan! The story must have burst upon Donovan like one of those artillery barrages Father Duffy had described after the second Battle of the Marne: "No crescendo about it; just a sudden crash, like an avalanche."

"Creation of an all powerful intelligence service to spy on the postwar world and to pry into the lives of citizens at home is under consideration by the New Deal," it began. *"The Washington Times-Herald* and the *Chicago Tribune* yesterday secured exclusively a copy of highly confidential and secret memorandum from General [William J.] Donovan to President Roosevelt . . . also obtained was a copy of an equally secret suggested draft of an order setting up the general intelligence service, which would supersede all existing Federal police and intelligence units, including Army G-2, Navy ONI, the Federal Bureau of Investigation, the Internal Revenue Agency. . . .''

Trohan went on to imply that the new unit would undermine J. Edgar Hoover. It would have secret funds for spy work ''along the lines of bribery and luxury living described in the novels of E. Phillips Oppenheim. . . .''

The article, in short, was more than a leak. It was a hatchet job. Donovan finished reading it and called his executive officer, Colonel Ole Doering. Doering still remembers the soft voice on the telephone: ''Ole, I want you to find out who did this and report to me at nine.''

Doering dressed hurriedly and set about tracing the distribution of the five typed copies of Donovan's plan for peacetime intelligence. ''At 9, I was ready,'' he recalls. ''I told the General that J. Edgar Hoover had personally handed the memorandum to Trohan. Donovan never said a word.''

Roosevelt did say a word. The President called that afternoon to say that he wanted the whole thing shoved under the rug for as long as the shock waves reverberated. Seven weeks later, Roosevelt judged that the heat was off and released a letter to Donovan giving the plan his general approval and asking Donovan to get comments from members of the Cabinet and other government officials. It was too late. A week later, Roosevelt was dead.

It is important to note the outlines of Donovan's plan for a peacetime intelligence agency because it was the starting point from which the country departed and to which it eventually returned. The chief features were as follows:

First, the director of the new agency would report only to the President. Meaning: power.

Second, the new agency would ''collect'' intelligence. Meaning: it would have its own sources of information, including spies.

Third, the agency's director would make ''final evaluations of intelligence within the government,'' final ''synthesis,'' and final ''dissemination.'' Meaning: Army and Navy Intelligence and the State Department could continue to perform the work ''required by such agencies in the actual performance of their functions and duties,'' but there would be no doubt as to who was to be boss.

Fourth, the new agency was to have ''an independent budget.'' Meaning: again, power.

Fifth, the agency was to have ''no police or law enforcement functions, either at home or abroad.'' Meaning: Donovan intended no such threat to J. Edgar Hoover as the newspaper revelation implied.

Sixth, the new peacetime agency would conduct ''subversive operations abroad.'' Meaning: just that.

In summary, it was to be the wartime OSS taken from under the jealous eye of the Joint Chiefs of Staff, and given the independent power to issue orders to G-2, ONI, the intelligence branch of the Department of State—and to the extent to which J. Edgar Hoover was collecting foreign intelligence in South America, to the FBI.

Trohan had not been far wrong in calling it "all-powerful," though there was no basis in Donovan's memorandum for the suggestion that it would conduct espionage at home, supersede the FBI, or enable its employees to live luxuriously.

Still, it was pretty strong stuff. Would Roosevelt have accepted the plan if he had lived? We know only that Donovan thought so. He was in Paris the day Roosevelt died. One of his deputies, Colonel Ned Buxton, talked to him that evening. "What will happen now to OSS?" Buxton asked. "I'm afraid it's the end," was Donovan's reply.

He was, however, to make one more try. Shortly after V-J Day, Naval Commander John Shaheen walked into the general's office to bid him good-by. "You're not through yet," said Donovan, and he ordered Shaheen to stay in uniform for sixty more days. Shaheen sat down in mild shock while Donovan related a story. There had been that sensationalized prewar investigation of the munitions industry, conducted by Senator Gerald Nye of North Dakota, in which Donovan had acted as counsel for the Du Pont Company, one of the firms most heavily attacked. "You remember that, John? You know, John, I had to argue, not just the merits but against the whole propaganda campaign and that campaign was Gerald Nye's *Merchants of Death*. I tell you John, I learned something. Now let's see if you can do as well for OSS as Nye did for the isolationists."

Shaheen rose. "Could your secretary get me a list of writers in OSS who happen to be in Washington?"

For weeks, a series of sensational stories dominated the newspapers and magazines hailing the exploits of OSS's secret war. As Shaheen and his assistants scoured the files, had the facts declassified, fed them to "writers in OSS who happened to be in Washington," and as they fed them in turn to eager journalists, OSS parachutists returning from their hitherto secret war and expecting to hear the usual jibes about "Oh So Social" suddenly found themselves figures of glamor. But the new President, Harry Truman, was annoyed. On September 20, 1945, the publicity campaign was cut short. Truman signed Executive Order 9621, "Termination of the Office of Strategic Services and Disposition of Its Functions."

While the pro-OSS publicity was at its height, Donovan had written a letter announcing his wish to return to private life. "Therefore, in considering the disposition to be made of the assets created by OSS, I speak as a private citizen concerned only with the security of my country."

Thirty years later, it seems odd that this last plea for his old outfit should have been addressed not to the President of the United States but to Harold B. Smith, Director of the Bureau of the Budget. But it was, at the time, not at all an odd thing to do.

As the war ended and the mind of Harry Truman turned to problems of demobilization and reorganization for peace, Harold B. Smith became for a few weeks a very powerful man. He was the one man to whom Truman could turn who knew where everything was and where it had been before. Moreover, he had a tidy housekeeper's view about what to do with it now. OSS appalled the neat-minded Smith. Here was an agency which was part research, part spies, part propaganda, part paratroopers, part saboteurs and forgers, all mixed up together in such fashion that it was impossible to reduce it to a chart. Smith came at once to a solution:

Put the research professors and analysts under the State Department, he advised Truman; put the spies and propagandists and forgers under the War Department and let the paratroopers and saboteurs go home. For the next four months, the Smith formula of separated functions of State and War became the United States intelligence establishment. Donovan, when he heard about the new formula, called it "absurd."

In the State Department, Secretary James Byrnes, acting upon the President's written instructions to "take the lead in organizing peacetime intelligence," turned the action over to Dean Acheson, who brought in Colonel Alfred McCormack, an able lawyer from New York who had served G-2 during the war. Valiantly, McCormack tried to organize a research and analytical intelligence branch in State. Opposition came not only from G-2 and ONI but from within the State Department itself. Desk officers of the Foreign Service, certain that the idea was an assault upon their authority and an insult to their expertise, reacted vigorously. In a forecast of an era to come, they succeeded in sinking the effort in a debate about whether one of the OSS men who had been brought into the department was or was not a Communist.

In his memoirs, Dean Acheson described the rout as the story of how the Department of State "muffed the intelligence role," and placed the blame on Byrnes, for whom, he said, "ideas of organization were not congenial." Eventually, McCormack resigned, and the unit he had organized was split into seventeen committees. Gradually, it wasted away.

In the War Department, the Smith formula worked a little better. There, Colonel William Quinn, a tough, open-faced man who radiated a bustling confidence—Allen Dulles called it the Donovan spirit—kept intact the spies and forgers, grouped together now under a new name, the Strategic Services Unit, or SSU. Quinn was a rarity among regular army officers because he had worked closely with OSS during the war and had admired the job it had done for him. Quinn had been G-2 of the Seventh Army during the invasion of southern France and had made good use of the OSS agents (mostly German prisoners of war) whom OSS had infiltrated behind the German lines to pick up order of battle information.

"Preserve the assets and eliminate the liabilities," Assistant Secretary of War Howard C. Petersen had told Quinn when Quinn took over SSU from retiring Brigadier General John Magruder; and among the assets Quinn counted intelligence networks in eastern Europe, Austria, the Balkans, and China. To preserve these networks, he had to hold on to the men who ran them.

There was James Angleton; there was Hugh Cunningham; there was Frank Wisner; there was Richard Helms; there was Harry Rossitzke. These were the men who over the next fifteen years were to conceive and manage the major U.S. intelligence operations against the Soviet Union. Wisner, who as CIA's Deputy Director of Plans was destined to become their chief, was the only one Quinn could not keep happy. He quit in a huff—to return some years later—because Quinn on a particular occasion refused to provide him with an additional two hundred bicycles for the agents Wisner had hired to peddle into East Germany, take a look at the Russian occupation, and report back what they learned.

Quinn had other problems. G-2, and newspaper columnists Joseph Alsop and Harold Ickes, the former Interior Secretary, suggested that Quinn's unit harbored Communists. But Quinn quickly established good relations with J. Edgar Hoover, and Hoover, having nothing to fear now from Donovan, came forward to say that he had checked the employees of SSU and found them "clean."

Whenever Quinn felt sorely threatened, he would call David Bruce, Donovan's wartime deputy for Europe, and Bruce would invite members of the old OSS hierarchy to dinner at his Washington home. Charles Cheston would arrive from Philadelphia, Donovan and Russell Forgan from New York, and they would discuss strategy for keeping the unit intact. "Without Quinn," Allen Dulles would later remark, "our profession would have lost many of its pros."

While McCormack was losing in the State Department and Quinn was hanging on in the War Department, Truman was complaining to Admiral Leahy, his chief of staff, that too many intelligence reports from State, ONI, and G-2 were cluttering his desk, and Leahy was putting pressure on Byrnes to do something about it. It was Byrnes's failure to do something about it that led to the next move around the circle.

Even as he was ordering the dissolution of OSS in 1945, President Truman was telling intimates that we needed a peacetime intelligence agency. "I was in his office one afternoon right after the war ended—I believe it was in August," his former naval aide, Clark Clifford, recalls, "when he began to talk to me about Joe Grew's cables." (Joseph Grew had been U.S. Ambassador to Japan at the time of Pearl Harbor.) "You go back and read Joe Grew," Truman said to Clifford, "and then you come in here and tell me how anybody could have read those cables and not known there was an attack coming." He proceeded to list what he considered to have been other warnings of Japanese intent. Clifford recalls that Truman knew a lot about the amount of scrap iron the Japanese were buying before Pearl Harbor. The new President concluded his lecture, according to Clifford, as follows: "If we had had some central repository for information, and somebody to look at it and fit all the pieces together, there never would have been a Pearl Harbor."

Within a few weeks Truman decided that under the plan suggested by his budget director, Harold Smith, nobody was fitting all the pieces together. His complaint to Admiral Leahy was reflected in the note Secretary of the Navy James Forrestal placed in his diary in October, 1945:

"Mr. Byrnes next raised the question of a central intelligence agency . . . responsible to a Council of Defense which would consist of the Secretaries of State, War and Navy. . . . All of the secretaries (Robert Patterson, Secretary of War, Byrnes, and Forrestal) agreed with the principle of the proposal, that any central intelligence agency should report to the three Secretaries rather than directly to the President."

The Byrnes proposal was exactly what Forrestal wanted to hear, so much so, that one suspects he arranged with Leahy to feed the idea to Byrnes in such a way that Byrnes might project it as his own. Forrestal was then engaged in a fierce struggle with the Army over a proposal to merge the two services. Desperately, he was casting about for ways to avoid it.

As a basis for argument, he had hit upon the idea that Winston Churchill's war cabinet was the way to run things: "An inner council of the most important and trusted advisers," he put it, "to care for problems of common concern." In addition, he had asked his close friend and former partner, Ferdinand Eberstadt, to make "a thorough study of postwar organization of the military services." Not surprisingly, Eberstadt echoed the idea of coordination rather than merger. The second chapter of Eberstadt's report was entitled, simply, "Intelligence." It came out strongly for a central intelligence agency which would not attempt to direct the services of the Army and Navy but which would deal with "problems of common concern," would "coordinate" and "synthesize."

"How often," Dean Acheson later wrote, "those same dismal words . . . issued from the White House during the war in order to 'clarify' various powers, functions and responsibilities . . . a good many of us had cut our teeth and throats with this sort of nonsense. We had learned that no committee can govern and no man can administer without his own people, money and authority."

Acheson had learned. But Forrestal had not. And so, on January 22, 1946, Truman, forsaking the Smith plan, directed, by executive letter to Byrnes, the establishment of a new National Intelligence Authority. It would consist of the Secretaries of State, War, and the Navy, and would possess, as its operating arm, something called the Central Intelligence Group. The man on top would be Director of Central Intelligence. He would have no money of his own, no people of his own, and no authority except the high-sounding title.

As the first Director of Central Intelligence Truman chose Rear Admiral Sidney Souers, who in private life was a St. Louis businessman. I recall an interview with Admiral Souers shortly after he took office. "What do you want to do?" I asked the new appointee. The admiral looked up from behind Donovan's old desk and chuckled: "I want to go home," he replied.

Contrary to assumptions at the time, Souers was not a Truman crony, though he later became one. Forrestal had recommended him; he had promised to stay only six months, and at the end of that time he left. But even within that short period Souers was to find that his mandate "to correlate, evaluate and plan for the coordination of . . ." was mushy task. Just before he left, he asked for a budget of his own to be provided by the three departments he was trying to serve. He was turned down.

In June, 1946, the handsome Lieutenant General Hoyt Vandenberg, Air Force ace and nephew of the most powerful Republican in the Senate, Arthur S. Vandenberg of Michigan, succeeded to Souers' job. Vandenberg wanted very much to be the first Chief of Staff of the Air Force and was not inclined to rock any boats on the way to the job. Nevertheless, his title, his looks, and his relationship to the senator, as well as his high abilities, gave him authority Souers had lacked. Despite opposition from Byrnes and Patterson, he succeeded in getting a specific allocation of money for the CIG, in replacing the FBI as the intelligence collection agency in South America, and in winning the right to conduct research and analysis independent of the military services. Most important, Vandenberg took over Quinn's SSU, thus acquiring a clandestine collection capability and, incidentally, sending Quinn off to the Army War College for a leg up on what would be a highly successful army career.

But Vandenberg like Souers wanted to leave quickly, and when in May, 1947, he won the top Air Force job, he turned over CIG to a lackluster leader, Rear Admiral Roscoe H. Hillenkoetter.

Hillenkoetter never seemed to be quite sure whether he was more interested in foreign intelligence or domestic communism. He liked to pore over long lists of people in and out of government whom he suspected of being left-wing, and then issue memoranda forbidding CIG employees to "have any communication with the Following." Nevertheless, he holds the honor of being the only American ever to head both the Central Intelligence Group and the Central Intelligence Agency, and when he left in 1950 to assume a sea command, the groundwork for what was to become an enormous intelligence and covert-action bureaucracy had been laid.

Still, Harry Truman could not have been pleased by the change he had set in motion. Separate intelligence reports from G-2, ONI, and the State Department continued to flow across his desk. The new CIG merely added one more. But the military intelligence services had not wanted the CIG and had indeed fought hard against it. Only the agreement between Patterson and Forrestal had carried the day. Perhaps Truman thought that real change would come when the armed services unification bill was finally passed, and a more powerful intelligence agency could take its place in the new organization that would emerge.

An intelligence agency was the tail," Clark Clifford says of the establishment of CIA. "The entire defense establishment spent 1946 and part of 1947 arguing about the National Security Act. How should we merge the Army and the Navy and establish the Air Force and what should be the powers of the Secretary of Defense, and what should be the mission and the authority of each service? That was the dog. Nobody paid much attention to the intelligence part of the bill."

Indeed, the drafters of the unification act planned it that way. The GIG legislative counsel, Walter Pforzheimer, went to the White House one day with two copies of draft legislation. The first authorized a CIA. The second authorized covert and unvouchered funds for the CIA. In a meeting with Admiral Forrest Sherman, who was handling unification legislation for the Navy, General Lorris Norstadt, who was doing the same for the Army, and White House counsel Charles Murphy, Pforzheimer was told to forget about the second draft. "They thought," he recalls, "that the secret funding would open up a can of worms, and delay unification. We could come up with the house-keeping provisions later on."

And so the CIA was born. "A small but elite corps of men with a passion for anonymity and a willingness to stick to the job." That was Allen Dulles' description to Congress of what he thought the agency should be. General of the Army Dwight D. Eisenhower also testified, and some thought that his remarks pointed to Dulles.

"One of the difficulties," said Eisenhower, doubtless thinking of the military attachés of G-2 for whom he had more than once expressed contempt, "is getting a man who will understand intelligence. He must show a bent for it and be trained all the way up. If I could get the civilian I wanted, and knew he would stay for ten years, I would be content, myself."

There was almost no opposition to the intelligence portion of the act. Congressman Clare Hoffman of Michigan wanted an amendment to bar the new agency from "the collection of intelligence." Hoffman represented G-2's last stand. Congressman Walter H. Judd of Minnesota introduced an amendment that would "prevent this agency from being allowed to go in the inspect J. Edgar hoover's activities and work." Judd represented the FBI's last stand. Neither of the amendments was adopted.

When it was all over—the date was July 26, 1947—the nation's newspapers headlined the fact that Congress had passed the National Security Act. The armed services were to be "unified" under a new Department of Defense. Far down in its account of the historic event, the *New York Times* reported that "there will also be a Central Intelligence Agency." Donovan read the account and remarked to friend, "I see they finally made intelligence respectable."

The National Security Act of 1947 gave the Central Intelligence Agency power to hire its own people and to have its own budget, though it was not yet to be a secret, unvouchered budget. The legislation made the new agency responsible to a new National Security Council (Forrestal's vehicle for handling problems of "common concern"). Apart from this change, CIA was a continuation of CIG, its powers and functions recited in almost the same language in which President Truman had enumerated the posers and functions of CIG in the letter he had written to Byrnes back in 1946.

Donovan, who had not been called to testify on the act, noted this fact. "Those fellows don't know what they're doing," he remarked, "because they're not sure what they can do." It was not quite an accurate statement. "Those fellows" knew they could spy. They had been spying for CIG under the authority "to perform for the benefit of existing agencies . . . services of common concern." This language from Truman's 1946 directive was now incorporated into law, and the legislative history makes it clear that Congress knew what the language meant.

On the other hand, the question of whether Congress authorized what Donovan had once called "subversive operations abroad" is less clear. The weight of evidence suggests that it did not. But the legislation did contain the following clause, also carried over from the Truman directive that had set up CIG: ". . . perform such other functions and duties related to intelligence affecting the national security as the National Security Council may from time to time direct."

This was Donovan language—straight out of his 1945 memorandum to Roosevelt, though slightly amended by Clark Clifford, who had inserted after the word "Intelligence" the words "affecting the national security" and had thought of it at the time as "a restricting clause." But Donovan had never intended "such other functions and duties" as any more than a catchall. It was later—about a year later—before it occurred to anyone that "such other functions and duties" might be construed to mean "subversive operations abroad."

One day early in 1948, Admiral Hillenkoetter, who was still in charge, called CIA's general counsel, Lawrence Houston, into his office and asked him a question. Could CIA spend money to help defeat the Communist Party in the upcoming Italian elections? Houston remembers that Hillenkoetter said he had been talking to James Forrestal, the new Secretary of Defense. "I've looked all over the government and I can't find anybody who can do it," Forrestal had said to him. "Can you fellows do it?"

Houston told Hillenkoetter he doubted the new agency had that authority. Then he went back to his office, got out the legislation, and reread it. There it was: "such other functions and duties. . . ." He thought about it, and decided that it did not constitute congressional authorization to spend money to influence an election in a foreign country. He informed Hillenkoetter that this was his opinion.

But the point had been raised, and now it became an arguable one. Forrestal and Hillenkoetter disagreed with Houston. So did Harry Truman. The CIA decided that it would conduct the Italian operation; and it was a turning point. Suddenly, down the road—with presidential approval—the light turned green.

On a late winter's day in 1954, United States Ambassador to Thailand William J. Donovan paid his last official visit to the CIA. By that time the agency was almost precisely what Donovan had envisaged that his peacetime OSS would become. If the relatively overt intelligence and analysis side of the house was not performing as Donovan had intended, if there was still duplication in reporting and overlapping with the armed services and State, the secret side of the house had more than compensated.

All over the world there were networks and agents in place, and both at home and abroad "other functions and duties" were being carried out. Paratroopers were in training; newspapers, radio stations, magazines, airlines, ships, businesses, and voluntary organizations had been bought, subsidized, penetrated, or invented as assets for the cold war. In terms of manpower alone, the agency was already bigger than Donovan's wartime OSS had been, and it was spending more money than General Donovan, an imaginative man, may have imagined.

"The sums made available to the Agency may be expended without regard to the provision of law," said the CIA ACT of 1949. ". . . such expenditures to be accounted for solely on the certificate of the Director and every such certificate shall be deemed a sufficient voucher. . . ."

Admiral Hillenkoetter had presided over congressional approval of this language, and had then handed over his office to Lieutenant General Walter Bedell Smith, the irascible sergeant who had risen to become Eisenhower's chief of staff during World War II. Then had come war in Korea and good reason to do what Smith wanted to do, which was to centralize, expand, and bring in the promised civilian head who would stay for ten years.

Smith had had half his stomach removed, and the operation had not improved his temper. "Dulles," he would roar through the open door to his new deputy's office, "Dulles, Goddamnit, get in here." But there was never any doubt—except perhaps in the mind of Bill Donovan—that Smith respected Dulles and that Dulles would get his job.

It was an odd meeting that Donovan attended in 1954 on the occasion of his last call, partly ceremonial and partly business. Most of the deputies and division chiefs who had served under him were there, and the meeting was given additional emphasis by the presence of Frank Wisner, who supervised all covert operations from his office of Deputy Director of Plans, as well as of Dulles himself.

From a chair facing a semicircle of juniors, Donovan made his plea. He wanted money—quite a lot of money—in order to fight the Communist guerrillas in Thailand and he knew how the battle should be waged. "All I'm asking for is a bowl of rice in their bellies and a gun in their hands," he said, referring to a hoped-for army of counterinsurgents.

So there they all were—former subalterns risen to high responsibility, hearing once more from the Old Man and hating it mightily. The things he was talking about were already afoot, through the responsible government of Thailand. Each of those present had at least some small piece of the action and each dreaded the thought that the complicated work might be further complicated by having to ideal with Wild Bill Donovan as a kind of third force.

When Donovan finished, there was polite applause. Hands were shaken all round and Dulles took the visitor off for a private chat. Years later, one of those who was present thought to inquire about the outcome. "What did you ever do," he asked Dulles, "about Bill Donovan's last request?"

Dulles smiled reflectively. "I arranged for him to have a very capable assistant," he answered, "so that I knew exactly what he was doing—and then I gave him some of what he wanted."

"You know," he added, and his eyes took on that familiar "this-is-in-confidence" look, "it wouldn't have been right for us to turn Bill down altogether."

———————————

Tom Braden was for many years the editor and publisher of the Oceanside, California, Blade Tribune, *and is now active in and around Washington, D.C. With the late Stewart Alsop he was the co-author of* Sub Rosa: The OSS and American Espionage.

Rosa Parks
Wouldn't Budge

Janet Stevenson

A neatly dressed, middle-aged black woman was riding home on a Montgomery, Alabama, bus on the evening of Thursday, December 1, 1955. Her lap was full of groceries, which she was going to have to carry home from the bus stop, and her feet were tired from a long day's work.

Mrs. Rosa Parks was sitting in the first row of seats behind the section marked ''Whites Only.'' When she chose this seat, there had been plenty of empty ones both in front of and behind the ''Great Divide.'' Now they were all occupied, and black passengers were standing in the aisle at the rear.

Then two white men got aboard. They dropped their dimes into the fare box. The driver called over his shoulder, ''Niggers move back.'' Three of the passengers obediently rose from their seats in the black section and stood in the aisle. Rosa did not.

Even when the driver repeated his order and heads turned to see who was ''making trouble,'' she sat as if she hadn't heard. The driver swore under his breath, pulled over to the curb, put on the brakes, and came to stand above her.

''I said to move back. You hear?''

All conversation stopped. No one dared move. Mrs. Parks continued to stare out the window at the darkness. The driver waited. Sounds of other traffic dramatized the silence in the bus.

It was a historic moment: the birth of a movement that was to challenge and ultimately change the social patterns that had established themselves in most

Americans' minds as a way of life which was traditional and deeply rooted in the South.

Actually, that tradition of racial segregation—loosely nicknamed Jim Crow—was not as venerable as most of its adherents believed. Many segregation laws—especially those concerned with public transportation—only dated from the turn of the twentieth century, and at the start had been resisted, through boycotts, by southern blacks, sometimes successfully. But by 1906 resistance had worn itself out. And in the intervening fifty years the memory had also worn itself out. E. D. Nixon, the man who proposed the Montgomery bus boycott of 1955–56, had never heard of the successful Montgomery bus boycott of 1900–1902. In fact he did not even know that boycotts were again being tried—without much success—in a few southern cities; for example, Baton Rouge.

Nixon was a leader of the Brotherhood of Sleeping Car Porters and one of the founders of both the Alabama state and the Montgomery city branches of the National Association for the Advancement of Colored People. For almost a year before the night of Mrs. Parks's refusal to give up her seat, he had been trying to persuade Montgomery's black community that "the only way to make the power structure do away with segregation on the buses was to take some money out of their pockets."

Few aspects of Jim Crow life were as galling to Montgomery blacks as travel on the city's bus line, which most of them had to use to get to and from work, school, and the central shopping district. There were runs on which a white passenger was a curiosity. Yet the first four rows of seats (ten places) were permanently reserved for whites. And blacks sitting behind those rows could be told to vacate their seats if whites got on after the reserved section was filled.

Blacks also had to endure discourtesy and sometimes hostility from many drivers, all of whom were white. Some used insulting language; others picked quarrels and put blacks off the bus for real or imagined offenses. Some played a peculiarly tormenting practical joke. Since all fares had to be deposited in the box beside the driver, every passenger had to get on by the front door. Blacks then had to get off the bus and board from the rear. The game was to wait until a black passenger got outside, slam the two doors, and drive off, leaving him standing on the curb without his dime.

Resentment was wide and deep in the black community. Some whites, too, were known to disapprove of the bus drivers' harassments. And even among the die-hard segregationists, the mixing of races on a public bus was hardly the emotionally charged issue that integrated schools, or parks, or swimming pools, were. For all these reasons, in the months following the United States Supreme Court ruling of May, 1954, against segregated schools in *Brown v. Board of Education,* Black leaders all over the South had been arguing that city bus lines were the next appropriate target for the integration movement.

In Montgomery three individual blacks, all women, had refused to give up their seats when ordered. In each case Nixon and the Montgomery NAACP had vainly tried to rally the black community to some sort of effective protest.

The most nearly successful attempt had been organized in March, 1955, after one of these three, a fifteen-year-old high school girl named Claudette Colvin, had been arrested and removed in handcuffs. An *ad hoc* committee of prominent Negro leaders had called on the manager of the bus company and on the City Commission, which governed Montgomery, to protest the way she had been treated and the whole system that led to such acts of spontaneous defiance. Three demands had been formulated: a guarantee of courtesy by drivers; a first-come first-served seating policy; and the hiring of Negro drivers on runs predominantly in Negro areas.

The proposed seating plan would not have ended segregation on the buses. It only required that when all seats were filled (blacks having seated themselves from the back forward and whites from the front backward), the next passengers to board would have to stand, no matter what the color of their skins. Such plans were in use in other southern cities, and the manager of the Montgomery City Lines was willing to go along with the idea until he consulted the company's attorney, Jack Crenshaw, who declared that the company was obligated to abide by the law, which was "clear on the principle of segregated seating."

In fact, it was not at all clear. Alabama state law did require clearly segregated white and black sections, but the Montgomery city code had a provision that no passenger could be required to give up his seat if another was not available. And there was sound legal opinion to the effect that within the city's limits the Montgomery statute took precedence over state law.

Nevertheless, Crenshaw's ruling stiffened the company's resistance. Hope of a legal challenge died when Claudette Colvin's parents refused to let her appear in court. Then community interest cooled to such a degree that the next woman who refused to move back received no organized support at all.

No one knew this background better than Mrs. Parks, who had worked with Nixon on many projects in the NAACP. She could hardly have hoped that her gesture was going to work any profound change in the status quo. She didn't move—as she explained later—because she was "bone weary" and suddenly fed up with being imposed upon. Yet circumstances would render her arrest the spark that lit the fires of resistance.

When E. D. Nixon got home that evening, his wife told him that Mrs. Parks had called from the city jail. Nixon telephoned the desk sergeant to ask about the charges and bail, and was refused the information, as an "unauthorized person." Ordinarily his next step would have been to call a young black Montgomery lawyer named Fred Gray, with whom he had worked on some NAACP cases. But Gray happened to be out of town. So Nixon turned instead to Clifford Durr, a distinguished white Alabamian who had recently returned to private law practice after twenty years in Washington, D.C. Durr had been on the legal staff of the Reconstruction Finance Corporation in the early New Deal years; later he had served as general counsel for the Defense Plant Corporation; and finally he had been a member of the Federal Communications Commission. He and his wife Virginia were part of a small group of southern white liberals who met, with black counterparts, under the aegis of the Alabama Council on Human Relations, to find ways of improving the South's racial picture. Nixon had come to know and trust them both.

"I called Mr. Durr," Nixon remembered later, "and he called down to the jail and they told him what the charge was. Bail was about $50, so I could make that all right." Then Nixon drove the attorney and his wife (who was a friend of Rosa Parks's) down to the jail. "I made the bond," Nixon told an interviewer, "and we got Mrs. Parks out. We carried her on home, and had coffee and talked."

Over coffee, Durr explained the legal alternatives as he saw them: Mrs. Parks could be defended "on the facts." She had not violated the Montgomery city code because there was no other seat available. He thought such a case could be won, but no challenge to segregation was involved. On the other hand, her attorney could challenge the constitutionality of the Alabama state law. That would mean a protracted and expensive battle, with no possible hope of victory short of a successful appeal to the United States Supreme Court. But a victory there would strike a major blow against Jim Crow.

Such a fight would need the backing of some national organization like the NAACP. Above all, it would take all the community support that Montgomery's blacks could mobilize.

Fired by the prospect Durr outlined, Nixon went home and told his wife, "I think we got us our test case at last." As he saw it, Fred Gray would take Rosa Parks's case and "do like Mr. Durr said. Go up all the way!" Meantime, he added, "What we got to do now is see about getting folks to stay off those buses Monday when Mrs. Parks comes up in Recorder's Court."

Mrs. Nixon told her husband he was "just plain crazy." "If headaches was selling for a dollar a dozen," she said, "you'd be the guy who'd go into a drug store and ask the man to put some in a bag." She didn't believe sympathy for Mrs. Parks was going to keep people off the buses "when it's as cold as this, and Christmas coming on."

There was some cause for pessimism. Montgomery's black community of fifty thousand persons was, in one observer's phrase, "as caste-ridden as any country in the world except India." No issue and no leader had yet managed to bring anything resembling unity out of its political, religious, economic, and cultural diversity. There might be strong support for Mrs. Parks in the professional group (made up in the main of faculty members from Alabama State College), but those people did not use public transportation. The working people, who did, depended on the buses to get to their jobs and on their jobs to feed and shelter their families.

The risk of losing even a single day's pay was too much to ask of the head of a household already living on the edge of poverty.

But Nixon was determined to ask just that and more. Before he went to bed that night he planned a meeting of some forty people for the next day at the Dexter Avenue Baptist Church, a leaflet calling for a one-day bus boycott, and a Monday evening mass meeting to organize further action. He hoped to find a leader to carry on while he was out of town on his job.

Among the local blacks whom Nixon summoned was the Reverend Ralph Abernathy, a militant young Baptist preacher wholeheartedly in agreement with the plan and eager to get to work. There was also the Reverend H. H. Hubbard, head of the Baptist Ministerial Alliance. The Baptists were the largest denomination in the black community, so Hubbard's promise to cooperate in notifying his associates was crucial, and Nixon was elated to get it. Thus encouraged, he called young Dr. Martin Luther King, Jr., the new pastor of the Dexter Avenue church.

It was a fateful contact. Neither man could foresee that it would put young Dr. King on the road to national and historic importance, a Nobel Prize, and ultimately, death at an assassin's hand. The future leader was then merely a recently arrived young minister of a fashionable Negro church in a southern town, well educated in the North, with a doctorate from Boston University, but with no other distinctions or activist record. Busy with his new duties, in fact, and the responsibilities of a young baby at home, he had only recently turned down the presidency of the local NAACP, and he told Nixon that while the protest organizers were welcome to meet in his church, he was not sure of his own participation. But he soon changed his mind and, with it, his destiny.

The meeting of more than forty people that afternoon quickly agreed to a one-day boycott of the city buses on the day of Mrs. Park's trial. When it came to agreeing on demands, however, the initial unity was threatening to dissolve until someone pointed out that demands were unimportant compared to the practical problem of spreading the word quickly. There was no black "ghetto" in Montgomery. Negroes lived everywhere in and around the city. A volunteer phone committee could start work at once, but many black families were without phones—and radios or TV sets—and did not take newspapers. Leaflets, which Abernathy had wanted mimeographed immediately on hearing from Nixon, could be passed out at stores where Saturday shoppers congregated. Announcements could be made from church pulpits on Sunday, provided that every minister in town could be persuaded that the notice was important enough not to be ignored.

Transportation was a more serious problem. The first draft of the leaflet said: "*. . . take a car, or share a ride, or walk.*" But thousands lived too far from their jobs to walk, had no car, and knew no one with whom to share. For them some alternative way of getting to work on Monday had to be found, or the protest would not achieve the 50 per cent cut in company revenues that was the agreed target.

Someone suggested appealing to the Negro cab companies, asking them to pick up pedestrians and carry them to their destination for the ten-cent bus far. (Segregation was so complete in Montgomery that only cabs driven by blacks and marked "Colored" were permitted to carry black passengers. The eighteen such companies and their 210 black drivers would prove a strong help in the first days of the boycott.)

By the time the meeting adjourned, assignments for phoning, distributing leaflets, and reaching ministers and the cab companies had been handed out, and morale was high. Some optimist even suggested that the passenger load of the bus lines might be cut as much as 60 or 65 percent! Then, two events took place on Sunday that increased the chances of such success. The first was the result of a Friday encounter between E. D. Nixon and a reporter from the Montgomery *Advertiser* named Joe Azbell. The *Advertiser,* Montgomery's major journal, was seen by everyone, white and black, who read the papers in the city. It was by chance that Nixon ran into the white reporter, whom he knew to be friendly. Nixon told him he would give him a hot tip, but warned: "I don't expect to cooperate with anybody who's going to write some sort of degrading story about Negroes."

Azbell promised to write a useful story, if any. Then Nixon told him about Mrs. Parks's action and the planned boycott. Both men agreed that the story should not be attributed to Nixon, but that Azbell should "find" one of the leaflets on some city sidewalk. Sure enough, Sunday morning's *Advertiser* carried a two-column, front-page story, presumably given to the paper by an indignant white woman who had got it from her illiterate maid. The tone was properly disapproving ("Just listen to what the Negroes are up to now!"). But Azbell had kept the bargain, and as Nixon had anticipated, "every preacher in town saw it before he went into his pulpit that morning," and found it important enough to announce.

The other helpful event was a radio announcement by Montgomery's police commissioner that two motorcycle policemen would be assigned to follow every bus on Monday, "to protect anyone who wished to ride from harassment by goon squads." This, it was believed, had the effect of frightening some waverers away from the bus stops.

It was dark when the first buses began to roll on Monday, December 5. Dr. King and his wife, Coretta who lived a few yards from a stop on one of the predominantly Negro runs, were up at dawn to see how the prospects for a 60 per cent reduction looked.

The early buses were usually crowded with black domestic workers on their way to make breakfast in white kitchens. Today, the first bus was empty. The Kings stayed at the window until the next bus passed. It, too, was empty. The third had two passengers, both white.

As the sky brightened, those of the planning committee with cars cruised the streets in different parts of town. What they saw was amazing. Sidewalks were crowded with black pedestrians. College and high school students were thumbing rides. Cars driven by blacks were overloaded with ride-sharers. There were a few old-fashioned horse-drawn buggies on the street, and one man was seen riding a mule. Youngsters waved in derisive humor at motorcycle policemen behind most of the buses. Some walkers—with up to six miles to go—sang as they trudged along. As King later wrote in his book, *Stride Toward Freedom:* "A miracle had taken place. The once dormant and quiescent Negro community was now fully awake."

At 9:30 A.M. the drama shifted to the courtroom, as Mrs. Parks's case was called. Fred Gray adhered to the line Durr had suggested. He ignored the conflict of state and local laws, and argued instead that segregation on public transportation was a violation of the spirit and letter of the United States Constitution. Without comment on Gray's argument, the judge found Mrs. Parks guilty and fined her ten dollars and court costs, which brought the total to something like fourteen dollars. Gray announced that his client would appeal the verdict, and she was released on bail. Now it was time for a third act; the mass meeting scheduled for 7 P.M. at the Holt Street Baptist Church.

But first, Nixon and Abernathy talked over the needs of the future. These included long-term plans and a permanent organization to carry on the fight. Nixon proposed to call it the Montgomery Citizens' Council, but Abernathy thought that sounded like the White Citizens' Councils that were springing up in opposition to school desegregation. His own suggestion was the Montgomery Improvement Association, and Nixon agreed to go along. They also agreed to ask the meeting to approve of repeating the demands made in Claudette Colvin's case—which fell short of total integration. And then, Abernathy raised the potentially touchy issue of leadership. "Brother Nixon, you're going to serve as president, aren't you?"

"Not unless you all turn down the man I have in mind. That's this young reverend, Martin Luther King, Jr."

Abernathy was surprised. King was not only young—not quite twenty-seven years old—but very new to the area. To nominate him would be to pass over a number of other, older ministers, many of whom had good qualifications.

"I'll tell you my reasons," Nixon said. "First, there's the way he talks. Day I first heard him preach, I turned to the fellow sitting next to me and I said, 'I don't know just how I'm going to do it, but one day I'm going to hook him to the stars!' "

King's education equipped him to talk to Montgomery's white leaders in their own terms. King had a reputation for courage, too. As Nixon said, "You knew he wasn't any white man's nigger." And he had not been in Montgomery long enough to become entangled in any of the factional struggles that divided the black community.

Abernathy agreed that King was a good choice, but thought he would decline. So it was decided to nominate him without warning at a session of the "planning committee"—which would frame resolutions to present to the mass meeting. King was so astonished by the very fact of his election—it was unanimous—that he put up no resistance, confessing later that if he had had time to think, he would have almost certainly refused. Immediately afterward he received a tough assignment: presenting to the crowd not merely the routine matters of choosing a name and officers but the hard choice of whether to continue the boycott or merely threaten to renew it if demands were not met. That decision, clearly, had to be made by those who would carry it out: the thousands of humble people who had walked on this cold, gray morning. Many of them would be present at the Holt Street Baptist Church, and they would there be asked to vote on whether they could sustain their incredible initial momentum by approving a recommendation to continue.

By the seven o'clock meeting time there was not a seat empty in the Holt Street church. Loudspeakers had been installed on the roof to accommodate late-comers who might not find room inside. It took Dr. King fifteen minutes to work his way through the crowd from his car, and ten more to get to the platform after he was inside. The audience was singing "Onward, Christian Soldiers" when he joined Nixon, Abernathy, a number of other ministers, Mrs. Parks, and Fred Gray. After the ritual of prayer and scripture reading—with which all such meetings open in the South—and an ovation for Mrs. Parks, E. D. Nixon rose, glancing at Montgomery's police commissioner, whom he saw seated in one of the pews.

"Before you brothers and sisters get comfortable in your seats," Nixon began, "I want to say if anybody here is afraid, he better take his hat and go home. This is going to be a long, drawn-out affair, and before it's over, somebody's going to die."

There were loud amens, but no one reached for his hat. Nixon then delivered a rouser in favor of continuing the boycott, ending with the challenge: "We've worn aprons long enough. It's time for us to take them off!"

The next speaker was Martin Luther King, Jr. He came to the rostrum almost completely unprepared for what he knew by now would be one of the most important addresses of his life. There had hardly been time in the two hours since he had been given this task to think through the basic purpose of his speech. His analysis had gone as far as dividing it into two possibly contradictory aims: the first, to drain off the anger of those who were "tired of being kicked about by the brutal feet of oppression"—anger that might lead to violence of which he disapproved; and a second, to "keep them courageous and prepared for action." Or, as he put it in another place, the problem was to be militant and moderate at the same time. To make things more difficult, he would have to face the microphones and lights of television crews, for news of the morning's action had focussed national attention on Montgomery.

King rose to the moment. Pulpit oratory, once a typical American art, is obsolete in most parts of the country today. But it lingers on in the black South, and King's sermon was a classic production. Stating the Christian case for nonviolent protest, he said: We have been amazingly patient . . . but we come here tonight to be saved from that patience that makes us patient with anything less than freedom and justice." Though he roused his audience at first by shouting, "We are tired. Tired of being segregated and humiliated," he brought them down to calmness again by declaring, "Once again we must hear the words of Jesus. 'Love your enemies. Bless them that curse you. Pray for them that despitefully use you.' If we fail to do this, our protest will end up as a meaningless drama on the stage of history. . . . We must not become bitter and end up by hating our white brothers." And in a final chord, he wooed them to their better selves.

"If you will protest courageously, and yet with dignity and Christian love, future historians will say, 'There lived a great people—a black people—who injected new meaning and dignity into the veins of civilization.' This is our challenge and our overwhelming responsibility."

The audience rose, cheering, and one elderly woman remembered afterward the feeling that she "saw angels standing all around him when he finished, and they were lifting him up on their wings!"

Even before Ralph Abernathy read the recommendation, the verdict was in. It was, in Clifford Durr's recollection, "a grass roots verdict if there ever was one. Some of the [black] middle-class professionals were saying, "Well, we showed them this morning.' But the maids and the cooks, the ones who had done the walking, were saying, 'We haven't showed them a thing yet! But we're going to stay off those buses until they make up their minds to treat us decently.' "

For the first few days this unanimous determination created a euphoric optimism. In view of the unprecedented effectiveness of the boycott and the willingness of the Montgomery Improvement Association to settle for a partial victory such as first-come first-serve seating through separate doors, it was generally believed that there would be a negotiated settlement. But on Thursday, December 8, when Abernathy's committee met with the City Commission, the bus company attorney, Jack Crenshaw, once more insisted that the Alabama law required continued total segregation. City officials were taking a hard line, too. It was clear that they did not want a Negro victory to stimulate further challengers. And a hint was dropped of strong action to come. The city code set a minimum cab fare of forty-five cents per passenger. Negro taxi companies might soon be forbidden to take passengers at ten cents per trip. The next day that threat did materialize. But fortunately, on Thursday evening there had been one of the twice-weekly meetings planned for the boycott's duration as a way of exchanging information, squelching rumors, boosting morale, and ratifying decisions. Anticipating the city's action, the chairman had appealed for volunteer drivers. One hundred and fifty names were handed in. Next, Rufus Lewis's Transportation Committee sat up all night, working out the details of a system which utilized the whole intricate network of black institutions that had grown up under the hothouse conditions of total segregation.

On Tuesday, just a week after the first day of the boycott, thousands of leaflets were ready for distribution, showing on a map of the city the location of forty-eight dispatch and forty-two pick-up stations, with the hours at which each would be operative. There were plenty of problems still. Dispatch stations for sending people off to work were easy to locate in Negro neighborhoods, and churches could shelter riders who had to wait in bad weather. But after-hours pick-up stations had to be in less friendly territory. Without the intimate knowledge of Montgomery's white neighborhoods supplied by black mail carriers, this part of the plan would have been impossible to design. There were never quite enough volunteer dispatchers at rush hours. Cars sometimes broke down, and so, occasionally, did the tempers of passengers and drivers. But overall, the car pools worked as well as, if not better than, the old bus system. And their impact as a unifying force in the black community was incalculable.

It was expensive, but help came from two unexpected sources. As the "Montgomery Story" was spread throughout the country by the news media, contributions began coming in to the M.I.A. from cities in the North and West. Black churches took up collections to buy station wagons, which were presented to Montgomery churches of the same denominations for car-pool use.

The load was also lightened by some white Montgomery housewives, who entered into a sort of conspiracy with their black domestics. Accepting the police commissioner's fiction about "goon squads," these women began to drive their maids and cooks to and from work, "to protect them from harassment." When the mayor protested that this gave aid and comfort to the boycott, ladies wrote letters to the newspaper suggesting that he provide them with other help before telling them how to run their households.

As weeks went by without the blacks yielding, threats of violence began to be directed against the leadership of the M.I.A. King, Abernathy, Nixon, and other officers started to receive hate mail and phone calls warning them to "get out of town or else. . . ." Then, on January 30, the ugliness erupted.

On that night, while Dr. King was attending one of the regular mass meetings, a bomb tossed onto the porch of his house exploded seconds later with a shattering roar. Having heard the thud as the missile landed, Mrs. King and a visiting friend had moved quickly toward the rear of the house. They and the Kings' infant daughter escaped injury. But it looked for a time as if the chief casualty of the night would be the concept of nonviolence to which the Negroes had so far been held by their leaders.

Rushing home, King found an angry crowd milling on his lawn. As he stepped from his car, he heard one black man offer to shoot it out with a white policeman who was trying to push him back. Mayor W. A. "Jackie" Gayle and Police Commissioner Clyde Sellers were on hand, along with white reporters and the police. The mood of the crowd was so hostile that all of them later reported having felt that a race riot was distinct and immediate possibility.

Dr. King went into his house, assured himself that his family was all right, and then came back to speak to the crowd. His voice was unusually quiet, and everyone else stopped speaking or moving, to listen.

"My wife and baby are all right," he told them. "I want you to go home and put down your weapons. We cannot solve this problem through retaliatory violence. . . . We must love our white brothers no matter what they do to us. We must make them know that we love them. Jesus still cries out across the centuries, 'Love your enemies.' This is what we must live by." Then, his voice swelling with emotion, he added: "Remember, if I am stopped, this movement will not stop, because God is with this movement."

It was another miracle of oratory, in a different style from his Holt Street speech. This time there was no applause. Simply, at his request, the crowd began to melt away, and with it, the tension. King even got them to listen quietly as the mayor promised a reward for information leading to the arrest of the bombers. But it had been a close thing. A small incident could have brought bloodshed. Calm returned, although two nights later a bomb landed—harmlessly—in the Nixons' yard.

After that climactic moment, there was a year-long struggle marked by court actions, by feats of improvisation that kept the M.I.A.'s transportation system rolling, and finally by fresh bombings.

Perhaps the most significant and least publicized action on the legal front was the petition on behalf of the M.I.A. for a hearing on the constitutionality of the Alabama segregation law before a three-judge federal court. This tactic was first suggested by Clifford Durr. About mid-April he realized that something more would be needed than Mrs. Parks's appeal, which was before the Alabama court of appeals, to carry the case to the top. The Supreme Court could not render a decision "on the merits" until the Alabama court had spoken—almost certainly against Rosa Parks. Durr later related what the problem was:

We knew they [the Alabama judges] were going to hold out as long as possible, and maybe never rule on the merits at all. They could reverse the lower court on some narrow technical ground and send the matter back for a new trial, and it could just drag on forever. Meanwhile, the city authorities were getting ready to break up the car-pools. They'd found some grounds for an injunction and if it was granted, that meant the end of the boycott. People just couldn't afford to give up their pay checks—not the people who were the backbone of the movement, who had low wages and large families and no savings to live off of.

Durr therefore suggested to Fred Gray that he petition for a special three-judge federal court and ask it for an injunction against discrimination in seating, on the grounds that it was a violation of rights guaranteed in the Constitution. Such a panel was allowable in a federal action challenging a state law. And its rulings could be appealed directly to the Supreme Court.

Gray went to work at once, made contact with the New York and Washington branches of the NAACP, got some high-powered co-counsel, and filed his petition. The hearing was set for early in May. The court was composed of Richard T. Rives, at the time judge of the United States Circuit Court for the district including Alabama, who was the presiding justice; Judge Frank Johnson, an indigenous ''Andrew Jackson Republican'' (in Durr's words) from the northern part of Alabama; and Judge Seybourne Lynn of Birmingham.

Within three weeks, two of the three white southern judges—Johnson and Rives—outvoted their colleague and ruled in favor of Gray's petition. Rives, who wrote the majority opinion, was threatened, obliged to listen to sermons attacking the federal judiciary in the Montgomery church he attended, and had garbage dumped on his son's grave in a local cemetery. Johnson took similar abuse. But the stratagem was successful.

The federal question was raised at last. For the city of Montgomery appealed the ruling ''on the merits,'' and the state of Alabama joined in the appeal; the matter now went onto the Supreme Court's docket.

That made the third case arising out of the bus battle to be working its way through the judicial system. The first was Mrs. Parks's appeal. Then, in March, a second had arisen when King and other M.I.A. leaders had been found guilty of violating a state antiboycott injunction—in a trial that usefully exposed black Montgomeryites' grievances to the national public. Their conviction, likewise, was on appeal.

Montgomery authorities were meanwhile harassing the car pools. A car full of riders would be flagged down; the inspecting officer would find one or more violations of the state safety standards—weak brakes, poorly aligned headlights, or something else. The driver would be forced to abandon his vehicle, and a city wrecker would be called to tow it away (at the owner's expense) for repairs (also at his expense) in a city-approved shop. A similar tactic was the arbitrary cancellation of black auto-owners' insurance.

But all this was only prelude to the main attack. On October 30 mayor Gayle directed the city's legal department to request an injunction ''to stop the operation of the car pools or transportation systems growing out of the bus boycott,'' and to collect damages of fifteen thousand dollars for loss of tax revenues. Fred Gray's counterpetition to prevent the city's interference on behalf of the bus company was denied. A hearing was set for November 13.

There was no question in the minds of the M.I.A. leaders that this was, as King confessed to a mass meeting on the second of November, a bad moment. The city was certain to get its injunction, and to end the car pools would hopelessly undercut the boycott. He tried to rally confidence by saying, ''This may well be the darkest hour before dawn. We have moved all these months with . . . daring faith. . . . We must go on with that same faith. . . .''

November 13 found the main contestants on both sides in court for the injunction hearing. The same judge who had tried Mrs. Parks a year earlier was listening to the arguments when, some time around noon, there was an interruption.

The two attorneys for the city, the mayor, and the police commissioner were all called out of the court, and there was an excited buzzing at the press table. One of the reporters brought over to the defense table a copy of a message just received over the wire service teletype machine:

> The United States Supreme Court today affirmed a decision of a special three-judge U.S. District Court declaring Alabama's state and local laws requiring segregation on buses unconstitutional. The Supreme Court acted without listening to any argument; it simply said, "the motion to affirm is granted and the Judgment is affirmed."

Legally, the struggle was over. The black-led and black-supported boycott, rising out of Mrs. Park's spontaneous act, had resulted in the highest court's driving another nail in the coffin of legalized segregation. But life follows law slowly. It took a month more for the judicial mandate actually to reach Montgomery. In that time the injunction against the car pools was granted. So blacks, still staying off the buses, walked many extra miles when no alternative arrangements were possible.

The interval was used to prepare the black community for the first day of the new dispensation. Sheets of suggestions on how to behave "in a loving manner" were distributed. Role-playing sessions were held in black churches. Among whites reactions varied. The City Commission received front-page coverage to proclaim its "determination [to] do all in its power to oppose the integration of the Negro race with the white race in Montgomery . . . [and] stand like a rock against social equality, intermarriage and mixing of the races under God's creation and plan." But the fateful December 21, the day of official desegregation, came and went with what the Montgomery *Advertiser* called "a calm but cautious acceptance of this significant change in Montgomery's way of life." Black and white ministers sat together undisturbed in what had been the "Whites Only" section. Drivers were uniformly courteous. most white passengers chose to ignore the innovation; those who made nasty remarks were in turn ignored by the blacks.

There was a swift and violent backlash, a flurry of explosions. On the night of January 9, 1957, four Baptist churches were severely damaged by bombs. Ralph Abernathy's home was virtually destroyed; so was that of Robert Graetz, a young white Lutheran minister who served on the executive board of the M.I.A. A few nights later there was a second attempt to bomb the King home. A filling station across the street was shattered by an explosion, presumably because its owner had given the F.B.I. the license number of a suspicious car. This tip, however, finally led to the arrest of seven white men who confessed to the January 9 attacks.

Their trial marked the final immediate aftermath of the bus boycott. Their defense attorney, John Blue Hill, was paid from funds collected on Montgomery street corners in plastic buckets bearing the exhortation: SAVE OUR SOUTHERN WAY OF LIFE. His fee was rumored to be five thousand dollars in cash per defendant, and among Montgomeryites a joke circulated that he had stopped the bombings by making it too expensive to continue them. In court he summoned the black boycott leaders to the stand and focussed his questioning on their personal lives and sexual preferences. Most of the testimony was stricken, but not before it made the desired impression on the local all-white—and all-male—jury.

The jury's verdict was rendered with better than deliberate speed, and it was Not Guilty. The bombers left the courtroom with the confident carriage of folk heroes.

Nevertheless, in the long run, their triumph was overshadowed, for at the very moment when the four churches were being attacked, the M.I.A. leadership was in Nashville laying plans for a new organization: the Southern Christian Leadership Conference. Its president was Martin Luther King, Jr.; its basic philosophy was militant nonviolence. Ahead lay many events: sit-ins, freedom rides, gunfire on the campus of the University of Mississippi, the March on Washington, the Civil Rights and Voting Rights acts of 1964 and 1965, the summers of rioting in northern cities—and then, the murder of Martin Luther King, Jr., in a Memphis motel. Perhaps it would take the decade of the seventies to discover the full meaning of the record that began with the Montgomery boycott. But in that January of 1957, as integrated buses rolled down the streets of the Confederacy's first capital, over which the Stars and Bars still flew, almost everyone must have sensed that a new page in the history of black (and white) Americans had been turned.

Janet Stevenson has written an adaptation of the material in this article for young readers. It was recently published in book form by Franklin Watts, Inc., under the title The Montgomery Bus Boycott.

The Hour of
the Founders

Walter Karp

Exactly ten years ago this August, the thirty-seventh President of the United States, facing imminent impeachment, resigned his high office and passed out of our lives. "The system worked," the nation exclaimed, heaving a sigh of relief. What had brought that relief was the happy extinction of the prolonged fear that the "system" might not work at all. But what was it that had inspired such fears? When I asked myself that question recently, I found I could scarcely remember. Although I had followed the Watergate crisis with minute attention, it had grown vague and formless in my mid, like a nightmare recollected in sunshine. it was not until I began working my way through back copies of *The New York Times* that I was able to remember clearly why I used to read my morning paper with forebodings for the country's future.

The Watergate crisis had begun in June 1972 as a "third-rate burglary" of the Democratic National Committee headquarters in Washington's Watergate building complex. By late March 1973 the burglary and subsequent efforts to obstruct its investigation had been laid at the door of the White House. By late June, Americans were asking themselves whether their President had or had not ordered the payment of "hush money" to silence a Watergate burglar. Investigated by a special Senate committee headed by Sam Ervin of North Carolina, the scandal continued to deepen and ramify during the summer of 1973. By March 1974 the third-rate burglary of 1972 had grown into an unprecedented constitutional crisis.

By then it was clear beyond doubt that President Richard M. Nixon stood at the center of a junto of henchmen without parallel in our history. One of Nixon's attorneys general, John Mitchell, was indicted for obstructing justice in Washington and for impeding a Securities and Exchange Commission investigation in New York. Another, Richard Kleindienst, had criminally misled the Senate Judiciary Committee in the President's interest. The acting director of the Federal Bureau of Investigation, L. Patrick Gray, had burned incriminating White House documents at the behest of a presidential aide. Bob Haldeman, the President's chief of staff, John Ehrlichman, the President's chief domestic adviser, and Charles Colson, the President's special counsel, all had been indicted for obstructing justice in the investigation of the Watergate burglary. John Dean, the President's legal counsel and chief accuser, had already pleaded guilty to the same charge. Dwight Chapin, the President's appointments secretary, faced trial for lying to a grand jury about political sabotage carried out during the 1972 elections. Ehrlichman and two other White House aides were under indictment for conspiring to break into a psychiatrist's office and steal confidential information about one of his former patients, Daniel Ellsberg. By March 1974 some twenty-eight presidential aides or election officials had been indicted for crimes carried out in the President's interest. Never before in American history had a President so signally failed to fulfill his constitutional duty to "take care that the laws be faithfully executed."

It also had been clear for many months that the thirty-seventh President of the United States did not feel bound by his constitutional duties. He insisted that the requirements of national security, as he and he alone saw fit to define it, released him from the most fundamental legal and constitutional constraints. In the name of "national security," the president had created a secret band of private detectives, paid with private funds, to carry out political espionage at the urging of the White House. In the name of "national security," the President had approved the warrantless wiretapping of news reporters. In the name of "national security," he had approved a secret plan for massive, illegal surveillance of American citizens. He had encouraged his aides' efforts to use the Internal Revenue Service to harass political "enemies"—prominent Americans who endangered "national security" by publicly criticizing the President's Vietnam War policies.

The framers of the Constitution had provided one and only one remedy for such lawless abuse of power: impeachment in the House of Representatives and trial in the Senate for "high Crimes and Misdemeanors." There was absolutely no alternative. If Congress had not held President Nixon accountable for lawless conduct of his office, then Congress would have condoned a lawless Presidency. If Congress had not struck from the President's hands the despot's cudgel of "national security," then Congress would have condoned a despotic Presidency.

Looking through the back issues of *The New York Times,* I recollected in a flood of ten-year-old memories what it was that had filled me with such foreboding. It was the reluctance of Congress to act. I felt anew my fury when members of Congress pretended that nobody really cared about Watergate except the "media" and the "Nixon-haters." The real folks "back home," they said, cared only about inflation and the gasoline shortage. I remembered the exasperating actions of leading Democrats, such as a certain Senate leader who went around telling the country that President Nixon could not be impeached because in America a person was presumed innocent until proven guilty. Surely the senator knew that impeachment was not a verdict of guilt but a formal accusation made in the House leading to trial in the Senate. Why was he muddying the waters, I wondered, if not to protect the President?

It had taken one of the most outrageous episodes in the history of the Presidency to compel Congress to make even a pretense of action.

Back on July 16, 1973, a former White House aide named Alexander Butterfield had told the Ervin committee that President Nixon secretly tape-recorded his most intimate political conversations. On two solemn occasions that spring the President had sworn to the American people that he knew nothing of the Watergate cover-up until his counsel John Dean had told him about it on March 21, 1973. From that day forward, Nixon had said, ''I began intensive new inquiries into this whole matter.'' Now we learned that the President had kept evidence secret that would exonerate him completely—if he were telling the truth. Worse yet, he wanted it kept secret. Before Butterfield had revealed the existence of the tapes, the President had grandly announced that ''executive privilege will not be invoked as to any testimony [by my aides] concerning possible criminal conduct, in the matters under investigation. I want the public to learn the truth about Watergate. . . .'' After the existence of the tapes was revealed, however, the President showed the most ferocious resistance to disclosing the ''truth about Watergate.'' He now claimed that executive privilege—hitherto a somewhat shadowy presidential prerogative— gave a President ''absolute power'' to withhold any taped conversation he chose, even those urgently needed in the ongoing criminal investigation then being conducted by a special Watergate prosecutor. Nixon even claimed, through his lawyers, that the judicial branch of the federal government was ''absolutely without power to reweigh that choice or to make a different resolution of it.''

In the U. S. Court of Appeals the special prosecutor, a Harvard Law School professor named Archibald Cox, called the President's claim ''intolerable.'' Millions of Americans found it infuriating. The court found it groundless. On October 12, 1973, it ordered the President to surrender nine taped conversations that Cox had been fighting to obtain for nearly three months.

Determined to evade the court order, the President on October 19 announced that he had devised a ''compromise.'' Instead of handing over the recorded conversations to the court, he would submit only edited summaries. To verify their truthfulness, the President would allow Sen. John Stennis of Mississippi to listen to the tapes. As an independent verifier, the elderly senator was distinguished by his devotion to the President's own overblown conception of a ''strong'' presidency. When Nixon had ordered the secret bombing of Cambodia, he had vouchsafed the fact to Senator Stennis, who thought that concealing the President's secret war from his fellow senators was a higher duty than preserving the Senate's constitutional role in the formation of United States foreign policy.

On Saturday afternoon, October 20, I and millions of other Americans sat by our television sets while the special prosecutor explained why he could not accept "what seems to me to be non-compliance with the court's order." Then the President flashed the dagger sheathed within his "compromise." At 8:31 P.M. television viewers across the country learned that he had fired the special prosecutor; that attorney general Elliot Richardson had resigned rather than issue that order to Cox; that the deputy attorney general, William Ruckelshaus, also had refused to do so and had been fired for refusing; that it was a third acting attorney general who had finally issued the order. With trembling voices, television newscasters reported that the President had abolished the office of special prosecutor and that the FBI was standing guard over its files. Never before in our history had a President, setting law at defiance, made our government seem so tawdry and gimcrack. "It's like living in a banana republic," a friend of mine remarked.

Now the question before the country was clear. "Whether ours shall continue to be a government of laws and not of men," the ex-special prosecutor said that evening, "is now for the Congress and ultimately the American people decide."

Within ten days of the "Saturday night massacre," one million letters and telegrams rained down on Congress, almost every one of them demanding the President's impeachment. But congressional leaders dragged their feet. The House Judiciary Committee would begin an inquiry into *whether* to begin an inquiry into possible grounds for recommending impeachment to the House. With the obvious intent, it seemed to me, of waiting until the impeachment fervor had abated, the Democratic-controlled committee would consider whether to consider making a recommendation about making an accusation.

Republicans hoped to avoid upholding the rule of law by persuading the President to resign. This attempt to supply a lawless remedy for lawless power earned Republicans a memorable rebuke from one of the most venerated members of their party: eighty-one-year-old Sen. George Aiken of Vermont. The demand for Nixon's resignation, he said, "suggests that many prominent Americans who ought to know better, find the task of holding a President accountable as just too difficult. . . . To ask the President now to resign and thus relieve Congress of its clear congressional duty amounts to a declaration of incompetence on the part of Congress."

The system was manifestly not working. But neither was the President's defense. On national television Nixon bitterly assailed the press for its "outrageous, vicious distorted" reporting, but the popular outrage convinced him, nonetheless, to surrender the nine tapes to the court. Almost at once the White House tapes began their singular career of encompassing the President's ruin. On October 31 the White House disclosed that two of the taped conversations were missing, including one between the President and his campaign manager, John Mitchell, which had taken place the day after Nixon returned from a Florida vacation and three days after the Watergate break-in. Three weeks later the tapes dealt Nixon a more potent blow. There was an eighteen-and-a-half minute gap, the White House announced, in a taped conversation between the President and Haldeman, which had also taken place the day after he returned from Florida. The White House suggested first that the President's secretary, Rose Mary Woods, had accidentally erased part of the tape while transcribing it. When the loyal Miss Woods could not demonstrate in court how she could have pressed the "erase" button unwittingly for eighteen straight minutes, the White House attributed the gap to "some sinister force." On January 15, 1974, court-appointed experts provided a more humdrum explanation. The gap had been produced by at least five manual erasures. Someone in the White House had deliberately destroyed evidence that might have proved that President Nixon knew of the Watergate cover-up from the start.

At this point the Judiciary Committee was in its third month of considering whether to consider. But by now there was scarcely an American who did not think the President guilty, and on February 6, 1974, the House voted 410 to 4 to authorize the Judiciary Committee to begin investigating possible grounds for impeaching the President of the United States. It had taken ten consecutive months of the most damning revelations of criminal misconduct, a titanic outburst of public indignation, and an unbroken record of presidential deceit, defiance, and evasion in order to compel Congress to take its first real step. That long record of immobility and feigned indifference boded ill for the future.

The White House knew how to exploit congressional reluctance. One tactic involved a highly technical but momentous question: What constituted an impeachable offense? On February 21 the staff of the Judiciary Committee had issued a report. Led by two distinguished attorneys, John Doar, a fifty-two-year-old Wisconsin Independent, and Albert Jenner, a sixty-seven-year-old Chicago Republican, the staff had taken the broad view of impeachment for which Hamilton and Madison had contended in the *Federalist* papers. Despite the constitutional phrase "high Crimes and Misdemeanors," the staff report had argued that an impeachable offense did not have to be a crime. "Some of the most grievous offenses against our Constitutional form of government may not entail violations of the criminal law."

The White House launched a powerful counterattack. At a news conference on February 25, the President contended that only proven criminal misconduct supplied grounds for impeachment. On February 28, the White House drove home his point with a tightly argued legal paper: If a President could be impeached for anything other than a crime of "a very serious nature," it would expose the Presidency to "political impeachments."

The argument was plausible. But if Congress accepted it, the Watergate crisis could only end in disaster. Men of great power do not commit crimes. They procure crimes without having to issue incriminating orders. A word to the servile suffices. "Who will free me from this turbulent priest," asked Henry II, and four of his barons bashed in the skull of Thomas á Becket. The ease with which the powerful can arrange "deniability," to use the Watergate catchword, was one reason the criminal standard was so dangerous to liberty. Instead of having to take care that the laws be faithfully executed, a President, under that standard, would only have to take care to insulate himself from the criminal activities of his agents. Moreover, the standard could not reach the most dangerous offenses. There is no crime in the statute books called "attempted tyranny."

Yet the White House campaign to narrow the definition of impeachment met with immediate success. In March one of the members of the House of Representatives said that before voting to impeach Nixon, he would "want to know beyond a reasonable doubt that he was directly involved in the commission of a crime." To impeach the President for the grave abuse of his powers, lawmakers said, would be politically impossible. On the Judiciary Committee itself the senior Republican, Edward Hutchinson of Michigan, disavowed the staff's view of impeachment and adopted the President's. Until the final days of the crisis, the criminal definition of impeachment was to hang over the country's fate like the sword of Damocles.

The criminal standard buttressed the President's larger thesis: In defending himself he was fighting to protect the "Presidency" from sinister forces trying to "weaken" it. On March 12 the President's lawyer, James D. St. Clair, sounded this theme when he declared that he did not represent the President "individually" but rather the "office of the Presidency." There was even a National Citizens Committee for Fairness to the Presidency. It was America's global leadership, Nixon insisted, that made a "strong" Presidency so essential. Regardless of the opinion of some members of the Judiciary Committee, Nixon told a joint session of Congress, he would do nothing that "impairs the ability of the Presidents of the future to make the great decisions that are so essential to this nation and the world."

I used to listen to statements such as these with deep exasperation. Here was a President daring to tell Congress, in effect, that a lawless Presidency was necessary to America's safety, while a congressional attempt to reassert the rule of law undermined the nation's security.

Fortunately for constitutional government, however, Nixon's conception of a strong Presidency included one prerogative whose exercise was in itself an impeachable offense. Throughout the month of March the President insisted that the need for "confidentiality" allowed him to withhold forty-two tapes that the Judiciary Committee had asked of him. Nixon was claiming the right to limit the constitutional power of Congress to inquire into his impeachment. This was more than Republicans on the committee could afford to tolerate.

"Ambition must be made to counteract ambition," Madison had written in *The Federalist*. On April 11 the Judiciary Committee voted 33 to 3 to subpoena the forty-two tapes, the first subpoena ever issued to a President by a committee of the

House. Ambition, at last, was counteracting ambition. This set the stage for one of the most lurid moments in the entire Watergate crisis.

As the deadline for compliance drew near, tension began mounting in the country. Comply or defy? Which would the President do? Open defiance was plainly impeachable. Frank compliance was presumably ruinous. On Monday, April 29, the President went on television to give the American people his answer. Seated in the Oval Office with the American flag behind him, President Nixon calmly announced that he was going to make over to the Judiciary Committee— and the public—"edited transcripts" of the subpoenaed tapes. These transcripts "will tell it all," said the President; there was nothing more that would need to be known for an impeachment inquiry about his conduct. To sharpen the public impression of presidential candor, the transcripts had been distributed among forty-two thick, loose-leaf binders, which were stacked in two-foot-high piles by the President's desk. As if to warn the public not to trust what the newspapers would say about the transcripts, Nixon accused the media of concocting the Watergate crisis out of "rumor, gossip, innuendo," of creating a "vague, general impression of massive wrongdoing, implicating everybody, gaining credibility by its endless repetition."

The next day's *New York Times* pronounced the President's speech "his most powerful Watergate defense since the scandal broke." By May 1 James Reston, the newspaper's most eminent columnist, thought the President had "probably gained considerable support in the country." For a few days it seemed as though the President had pulled off a coup. Republicans on the Judiciary Committee acted accordingly. On the first of May, 16 of the 17 committee Republicans voted against sending the President a note advising him that self-edited transcripts punctured by hundreds upon hundreds of suspicious "inaudibles" and "unintelligibles" were not in compliance with the committee's subpoena. The President, it was said, had succeeded in making impeachment look "partisan" and consequently discreditable.

Not even bowdlerized transcripts, however, could nullify the destructive power of those tapes. They revealed a White House steeped in more sordid conniving than Nixon's worst enemies had imagined. They showed a President advising his aides on how to "stonewall" a grand jury without committing perjury: "You can say, 'I don't remember.' You can say, 'I can't recall. I can't give any answer to that, that I can recall.' " They showed a President urging his counsel to make a "complete report" about Watergate but to "make it very incomplete." They showed a President eager for vengeance against ordinary election opponents. "I want the most comprehensive notes on all those who tried to do us in. . . . They are asking for it and they are going to get it." It showed a President discussing how "national security grounds" might be invoked to justify the Ellsberg burglary should the secret ever come out. "I think we could get by on that," replies Nixon's counsel.

On May 7 Pennsylvania's Hugh Scott, Senate Republican Minority Leader, pronounced that revelations in the transcript "disgusting, shabby, immoral performances." Joseph Alsop, who had long been friendly toward the President in his column, compared the atmosphere in the Oval Office to the "back room of a second-rate advertising agency in a suburb of hell." A week after Nixon's seeming coup Republicans were once again vainly urging him to resign. On May 9 the House Judiciary Committee staff began presenting to the members its massive accumulation of Watergate material. Since the presentation was made behind closed doors, a suspenseful lull fell over the Watergate battleground.

Over the next two months it was obvious that the Judiciary Committee was growing increasingly impatient with the President, who continued to insist that, even in an impeachment proceeding, the "executive must remain the final arbiter of demands on its confidentiality." When Nixon refused to comply in any way with a second committee subpoena, the members voted 28 to 10 to warn him that "your refusals in and of themselves might constitute a ground for impeachment." The "partisanship" of May 1 had faded by May 30.

Undermining these signs of decisiveness was the continued insistence that only direct presidential involvement in a crime would be regarded as an impeachable offense in the House. Congressmen demanded to see the "smoking gun." They wanted to be shown the "hand in the cookie jar." Alexander Hamilton had called impeachment a "National Inquest." Congress seemed bent on restricting it to the purview of a local courthouse. Nobody spoke of the larger issues. As James Reston noted on May 26, one of the most disturbing aspects of Watergate was the silence of the prominent. Where, Reston asked, were the educators, the business leaders, and the elder statesmen to delineate and define the great constitutional issues at stake? When the White House began denouncing the Judiciary Committee as a "lynch mob," virtually nobody rose to the committee's defense.

On July 7 the Sunday edition of the *New York Times* made doleful reading. "The official investigations seem beset by semitropical torpor," the newspaper reported in its weekly news summary. White House attacks on the committee, said the *Times*, were proving effective in the country. In March, 60 percent of those polled by Gallup wanted the President tried in the Senate for his misdeeds. By June the figure had fallen to 50 percent. The movement for impeachment, said the *Times* was losing its momentum. Nixon, it seemed, had worn out the public capacity for righteous indignation.

Then, on July 19, John Doar, the Democrats counsel, did what nobody had done before with the enormous, confusing mass of interconnected misdeeds that we labeled "Watergate" for sheer convenience. At a meeting of the Judiciary Committee he compressed the endlessly ramified scandal into a grave and compelling case for impeaching the thirty-seventh President of the United States, He spoke of the President's "enormous crimes." He warned the committee that it dare not look indifferently upon the "terrible deed of subverting the Constitution." He urged the members to consider with favor five broad articles of impeachment, "charges with a grave historic ring," as the *Times* said of them.

In a brief statement, Albert Jenner, the Republicans' counsel, strongly endorsed Doar's recommendations. The Founding Fathers, he reminded committee members, had established a free country and a free Constitution. It was now the committee's momentous duty to determine "whether that country and that Constitution are to be preserved."

How I had yearned for those words during the long, arid months of the "smoking gun" and the "hand in the cookie jar." Members of the committee must have felt the same way, too, for Jenner's words were to leave a profound mark on their final deliberations. That I did not know yet, but what I did know was heartening. The grave maxims of liberty, once invoked, instantly took the measure of meanness and effrontery. When the President's press spokesman, Ron Ziegler, denounced the committee's proceedings as a "kangaroo court," a wave of disgust coursed through Congress. The hour of the Founders had arrived.

The final deliberations of the House Judiciary Committee began on the evening of July 24, when Chairman Peter Rodino gaveled the committee to order before some forty-five million television viewers. The committee made a curious spectacle: thirty-eight strangers strung out on a two-tiered dais, a huge piece of furniture as unfamiliar as the faces of its occupants.

Chairman Rodino made the first opening remarks. His public career had been long, unblemished, and thoroughly undistinguished. Now the representative from Newark, New Jersey, linked hands with the Founding Fathers of our government. "For more than two years, there have been serious allegations, by people of good faith and sound intelligence, that the President, Richard M. Nixon, has committed grave and systematic violations of the Constitution." The framers of our Constitution, said Rodino, had provided an exact measure of a President's responsibilities. It was by the terms of the President's oath of office, prescribed in the Constitution, that the framers intended to hold Presidents "accountable and lawful."

That was to prove the keynote. That evening and over the following days, as each committee member delivered a statement, it became increasingly clear that the broad maxims of constitutional supremacy had taken command of the impeachment inquiry. "We will by this impeachment proceeding be establishing a standard of conduct for the President of the United States which will for all time be a matter of public record," Caldwell Butler, a conservative Virginia Republican, reminded his conservative constituents. "If we fail to impeach . . . we will have left condoned and unpunished an abuse of power totally without justification."

There were still White House loyalists of course; men who kept demanding to see a presidential directive ordering a crime and a documented "tie-in" between Nixon and his henchmen. Set against the great principle of constitutional supremacy, however, this common view was now exposed for what it was: reckless trifling with our ancient liberties. Can the United States permit a President "to escape accountability because he may choose to deal behind closed doors,'' asked James Mann, a South Carolina conservative. ''Can anyone argue,'' asked George Danielson, a California liberal, ''that if a President breaches his oath of office, he should not be removed?'' In a voice of unforgettable power and richness, Barbara Jordan, a black legislator from Texas, sounded the grand theme of the committee with particular depth of feeling. Once, she said the Constitution had excluded people of her race, but that evil had been remedied. ''My faith in the Constitution is whole, it is complete, it is total and I am not going to sit here and be an idle spectator to the diminution, the subversion, the destruction of the Constitution.''

On July 27 the Judiciary Committee voted 27 to 11 (six Republicans joining all twenty-one Democrats) to impeach Richard Nixon on the grounds that he and his agents had ''prevented, obstructed, and impeded the administration of justice'' in ''violation of his constitutional oath faithfully to execute the office of President of the United States and, to the best of his ability, preserve, protect, and defend the Constitution of the United States, and in violation of this constitutional duty to take care that the laws be faithfully executed.''

On July 29 the Judiciary Committee voted 28 to 10 to impeach Richard Nixon for ''violating the constitutional rights of citizens, impairing the due and proper administration of justice and the conduct of lawful inquiries, or contravening the laws governing agencies of the executive branch. . . .'' Thus, the illegal wiretaps, the sinister White House spies, the attempted use of the IRS to punish political opponents, the abuse of the CIA, and the break-in at Ellsberg's psychiatrist's office—misconduct hitherto deemed too ''vague'' for impeachment—now became part of a President's impeachable failure to abide by his constitutional oath to carry out his constitutional duty.

Lastly, on July 30 the Judiciary Committee, hoping to protect some future impeachment inquiry from a repetition of Nixon's defiance, voted 21 to 17 to impeach him for refusing to comply with the committee's subpoenas. ''This concludes the work of the committee,'' Rodino announced at eleven o'clock that night. Armed with the wisdom of the Founders and the authority of America's republican principles, the committee had cut through the smoke screens, the lies, and the pettifogging that had muddled the Watergate crisis for so many months. It had subjected an imperious Presidency to the rule of fundamental law. It had demonstrated by resounding majorities that holding a President accountable is neither ''liberal'' nor ''conservative,'' neither ''Democratic'' nor ''Republican,'' but something far more basic to the American republic.

For months the forces of evasion had claimed that impeachment would ''tear the country apart.'' But now the country was more united than it had been in years. The impeachment inquiry had sounded the chords of deepest patriotism, and Americans responded, it seemed to me, with quiet pride in their country and themselves. On Capitol Hill, congressional leaders reported that Nixon's impeachment would command three hundred votes at a minimum. The Senate began preparing for the President's trial. Then, as countless wits remarked, a funny thing happened on the way to the forum.

Back on July 24, the day the Judiciary Committee began its televised deliberations, the Supreme Court had ordered the President to surrender sixty-four taped conversations subpoenaed by the Watergate prosecutor. At the time I had regarded the decision chiefly as an auspicious omen for the evening's proceedings. Only Richard Nixon knew that the Court had signed his death warrant. On August 5 the President announced that he was making public three tapes that "may further damage my case." In fact they destroyed what little was left of it. Recorded six days after the Watergate break-in, they showed the President discussing detailed preparations for the cover-up with his chief of staff, Bob Haldeman. They showed the President and his henchman discussing how to use the CIA to block the FBI, which was coming dangerously close to the White House. "You call them in," says the President. "Good deal," says his aide. In short, the three tapes proved that the President had told nothing but lies about Watergate for twenty-six months. Every one of Nixon's ten judiciary Committee defenders now announced that he favored Nixon's impeachment.

The President still had one last evasion: on the evening of August 8 he appeared on television to make his last important announcement. "I no longer have a strong enough political base in Congress," said Nixon, doing his best to imply that the resolution of a great constitutional crisis was mere maneuvering for political advantage. "Therefore, I shall resign the Presidency effective at noon tomorrow." He admitted to no wrongdoing. If he had made mistakes of judgment, "they were made in what I believed at the time to be in the best interests of the nation."

On the morning of August 9 the first President ever to resign from office boarded Air Force One and left town. The "system" had worked. But in the watches of the night, who has not asked himself now and then: How would it all have turned out had there been no White House tapes?

Walter Karp's account of President Truman's clash with General MacArthur appeared in the last issue.

The Deadly Dust:
The Unhappy
History of DDT

Kenneth S. Davis

Everyone knows a little about the rise and fall of DDT—how it was once hailed as a great boon to mankind; how useful it was in field and garden, house and yard; and how at last to our dismay it was unmasked as a killer, the chemical Al Capone, a threat to our environment and possibly our very existence. Everyone knows that the federal and state governments are acting to end the DDT menace, saving us, if narrowly, from disaster. We can breathe easy again. . . . Or can we?

The history of DDT is well worth pondering, for its fatal implications extend to the whole of our civilization. The central character of the story is, of course, the chemical compound itself. But there are also two human protagonists—a chemist in Switzerland and a marine biologist in the United States—and our story begins in 1936, a year of crucial career decision for each of them.

The chemist, Dr. Paul Herman Müller, was thirty-seven years old that year, an employee of the great dye-manufacturing firm of J. R. Geigy, S. A., of Basel. As a remarkably skillful and creative laboratory technologist, he had developed a number of synthetic tanning substances; by 1936 he had turned his attention to pesticide research.

Also in 1936 a short, slender, solemn-faced woman, twenty-nine years old and single, was teaching in the zoology department of the University of Maryland. In her student years she had majored in English composition as well as biology, followed by postgraduate work at the Marine Biological Laboratory in Woods Hole, Massachusetts. Now her desire to write moved her to accept a position in the U.S. Bureau of Fisheries (soon to be the Fish and Wildlife Service) offered her that year. When the school year ended, her name was listed on the U.S. civil service rolls: ''(Miss) Rachel Carson, aquatic biologist. . . .''

Meanwhile, Dr. Müller's pesticide research was leading to quick results. Within a few years he had invented two new insecticides, trade-named Gesarol and Neocid; their specific toxic ingredient, however, remained mysterious to him. In 1939, in search of this specific, he synthesized a chlorinated hydrocarbon whose unabbreviated chemical name is dichlorodiphenyltrichloroethane. Müller soon dubbed it DDT. He also soon learned that he was not the first man to make it. Back in 1874 a German student named Othmar Zeidler, working toward a doctor's degree, had synthesized it as an exercise in pure chemistry. But Zeidler had no notion how, if at all, the new compound could be used.

Not until Müller took some of it home with him one day and tried it out on houseflies did anyone realize that DDT kills insects. It was, indeed, the toxic ingredient of the two earlier insecticides Müller had compounded. And he soon found ways to make it even more potent.

By that time World War II had begun, and during its opening months Müller, having already proved DDT's effectiveness in controlling Colorado potato beetles on crops, found it equally effective in destroying lice on war refugees.

With each test, his and his firm's excitement grew. They became convinced that he had discovered the most powerful synthetic insecticide then known—fatal on contact in extremely minute quantities to an incredibly wide range of insects, yet apparently wholly nontoxic to man. Geigy quickly patented the formula (1940) as a general insecticide, and the manufacture of DDT began.

The patent descriptions were sent to Geigy's branches in Britain and the United States and, through them, made known in early 1942 to British and American entomologists, who read the patents with mingled hope and skepticism. Of immediate concern to them, because of the millions of Allied army and navy personnel spread around the world, was DDT's possible use for control of malaria (carried by anopheles mosquitoes), epidemic typhus (carried by body lice), and dysentery and typhoid fever (both carried by houseflies). With growing desperation they had been searching for a substitute for pyrethrum, a contact insecticide extracted from a flower and, before the war, imported chiefly from Japan. War with Japan cut off the major source of supply just as the demand for pyrethrum soared. Allied doctors and sanitation engineers began to have nightmares about losing the war to germs that could kill more people than all the bombs and bullets imagined in preatomic years.

Urgently needed was the kind of synthetic contact insecticide—easy and safe to handle, capable of being economically mass-produced—which DDT seemed to be. British and American scientists were quick, therefore, to begin testing. Geigy's claims, which had at first seemed wildly excessive, were soon verified. With the War Production Board encouraging its manufacture, DDT production was approaching its wartime maximum of three million pounds a month by the time it was placed on Army supply lists in May, 1943, and on Navy lists in January, 1944. All DDT was allocated to the armed services save a few hundred thousand pounds for further experiments. Among these were field tests in which DDT in powder form was successfully used, in 1943, to arrest small typhus epidemics in Mexico, Algeria, and Egypt.

The Egyptian work was done under the supervision of the American Brigadier General Leon Fox, a field director of the Typhus Commission headquartered in Cairo. It was Fox who was summoned to newly captured, refugee-swollen Naples in late 1943, where Allied medical authorities saw that a major typhus epidemic was in the making. New typhus cases in the city approached sixty a day, and people were dying by the score everywhere, even in the gutters. If the epidemic followed the age-old pattern, there would be an explosion of death, with perhaps as many as 250,000 fatalities. In mid-December, the general and his men began a systematic dusting of the entire Neopolitan population with DDT. Within a month the number of new cases per day was in sharp decline. By mid-February there were no new cases at all. For the first time in history, in winter (typhus is a winter disease), under filthy, overcrowded conditions perfectly suited to it, a well-advanced typhus epidemic was not only arrested but, in a few weeks, totally eliminated. And this was but the beginning of DDT's march to glory.

Soldiers and sailors by the million carried small cans of DDT powder to protect themselves against bedbugs, lice, and mosquitoes. They came to love the stuff, especially in the tropics. Millions of DDT aerosol bombs were used to spray the interiors of tents, barracks, and mess halls. Through European refugee camps, along the Burma Road, across jungle battlefields of Southeast Asia, on Saipan and dozens of South Sea isles infested by stinging, biting insects, DDT spread its beneficent mist.

By the war's end, DDT had become the most publicized synthetic chemical in the world. One American newspaper clipping service accumulated nearly 21,000 items about it in an eighteen-month period in 1944–45. Most were glowingly enthusiastic; only a few questioned the unmixed blessings of DDT.

It was the questions, however, that impressed Rachel Carson.

Her career had prospered since 1936. In 1941 she had published a book, *Under the Sea Wind,* a blend of science and belles-letters which had won critical acclaim, respectable sales, and its author's appointment as editor in chief of the Fish and Wildlife Service, a post in which she could happily combine her scientific and literary interests. Her required professional reading in that post naturally included a good deal about the "miracle" insecticide. What she read disturbed her.

For instance, an experiment conducted by the U.S. Department of Agriculture's Bureau of Entomology on May 23, 1945, was reported not only in scientific journals but also in general-circulation magazines. At the rate of five pounds per acre an oil solution of DDT was sprayed over a gypsy-moth-infested 1,200-acre oak forest near Moscow, Pennsylvania. It was terrifyingly effective. Every gypsy-moth caterpillar in the forest died within hours. But so did every bird—at least 4,000 of them within eight days. Nor was this the limit of DDT's mischief. Annihilation of ladybug beetles by the spraying resulted in a tremendous multiplication of aphids, which are not affected by DDT but are naturally controlled by ladybugs. The forest was on the way to being completely defoliated when rains halted the outbreak; aphids are short-lived in wet weather.

In few if any other tests was the rate of DDT application as high as in the Pennsylvania oak forest. One pound per acre was found sufficient to kill gypsy-moth caterpillars in a nearby forty-acre wood—a rate of application that seemed not to harm birds but was still disastrous for aquatic life, a point of special interest to Miss Carson. And when DDT in this lesser amount was sprayed over peach orchards to kill caterpillars of the Oriental fruit moth, it was found to be considerably more destructive of a parasite that attacked the moth than it was of the caterpillars themselves. In other instances, fruit trees were turned literally blood red with spiders, myriad upon myriad of them, after DDT killed the insects that normally fed on them.

Research reports noted the amazing persistence of DDT's effectiveness, due to its chemical stability and insolubility in water. Pyrethrum as then used in ordinary household sprays was highly poisonous to insects for the first few hours after application but gradually lost all power within a day or two. But DDT, sprayed upon an interior wall, was fatal to flies and mosquitoes for as long as three months; a treated mattress was a fatal resting place for bedbugs for as long as nine months; a DDT-sprayed blanket could be laundered a half dozen times, even dry-cleaned two or three times, and still kill every moth that touched it. This was an obvious advantage of the Army and Navy as well as to future civilian consumers, but among biological scientists it raised further questions as to the wisdom of releasing DDT for mass sprayings of fields and orchards, forests and pastures, city parks and tree-lined streets, year after year.

How could it be removed from sprayed fruits and vegetables since, unlike earlier poisons, it would not wash off? Would it persist and build up in soils to a level poisonous to warm-blooded animals? And just how toxic was it to such creatures, including man? Harmless to man when absorbed in small doses over the short run, might it not build up in fatty tissues (experiments with dogs in 1944 and '45 proved it *did* concentrate in fatty tissues) with harmful long-term effects? Would it be carried by soil erosion into streams and lakes and seas, with deadly effects on aquatic life? And, in general, what effect would its widespread use have upon the ecological balance?

These questions, discordant notes in the swelling anthem of praise for DDT, were all explicitly and repeatedly raised in the popular press as well as in special journals by concerned and knowledgeable men in 1944 and during the first nine months of 1945.

In early April, 1945, a report was released by the U.S. department of Agriculture on two years of nationwide testing of DDT by department entomologists. The report spoke of DDT as a "two-edged sword," at once the "most promising insecticide ever developed" and the most menacing. Obviously a great deal more needed to be known about it before it could be deemed "safe for general use," said *Time* magazine on April 16.

Nevertheless, DDT was released for general use barely four months later. On August 31, 1945—three days before the end of World War II—the War Production Board revoked its allocation order reserving the insecticide for military use. Certification by government agencies for almost unrestricted agricultural, household, and other uses swiftly followed. The Food and Drug Administration, for example, established as "safe" a DDT content of up to 7 p.p.m. (parts per million) in foods, though no one could possibly know at that time what, if any, level was "safe" over the long run.

Once DDT was released from wartime federal controls, the government's power over its production, distribution, and use was diminished, probably more than a trusting public was aware. The U.S.D.A.'s limited control over pesticide manufacture and marketing derived from a 1910 act of Congress primarily intended to protect the farmer against fraud; it lacked any requirement for registering a pesticide *before* marketing it. The latter was not required until 1947, when Congress, facing a flood of chemical poisons in the wake of DDT, passed an Insecticide, Fungicide, and Rodenticide Act that incorporated and strengthened major provisions of the 1910 law. Consumer protection was broadened to include regulations for proper labelling and detailed instructions for safe use. The quintessential problem of the broad environmental effects of pesticide use was not even considered in the legislation, or in the debate preceding its passage.

In 1945 the pressures of DDT's prompt release were, of course, immense. There were great immediate profits to be made from DDT's manufacture, distribution, and agricultural use; and there was an eager market for house, yard, and other domestic uses as well. Worldwide, there was a desperate need for all the food and fiber that could be produced, and DDT could do more to increase production than any other insecticide. There was an even more desperate need to bring malaria and other insect-carried diseases under control, in our own South and in many countries (Greece for one, India for another), and again DDT was the only available product up to the job.

For a number of years, the decision to release DDT seemed overwhelmingly justified by its benefits. The worldwide incidence of malaria was spectacularly reduced. In Greece, where a third of the work force had been losing two to three months of work time annually to malaria, and where malarial infant mortality in many villages approached 100 per cent, the disease was virtually eliminated from some 6,000 villages by a massive DDT-spraying campaign under the auspices of UNRRA, the United Nations Relief and Rehabilitation Agency. At the same time, through the use of DDT against insect pests, farm production was reportedly increased by as much as 40 percent. In Egypt and India, equally remarkable results were achieved. It was reliably estimated that by 1950 DDT had saved five million lives over the world through destruction of malarial mosquitoes.

Millions more were saved from starvation because of increased food production made possible by DDT. The U.S.D.A. has estimated that, without chemical pesticides, some 30 per cent of America's protein supply and 80 per cent of her high-vitamin crops would be lost to insects*—and DDT was by far the most widely and heavily used chemical pesticide through the 1950's.

Small wonder that the discoverer of DDT was honored throughout the world during the postwar years. Though he held no medical degree and had never engaged in medical research, Dr. Paul Herman Müller was awarded a Nobel Prize in Medicine for DDT in 1948. And then—at the very height of his glory Müller dropped from public view.

Three years later, Rachel Carson became famous. In 1951 her lyric yet scientifically accurate book about the sea, *The Sea Around Us,* was published to a chorus of praise; it sold so well that, abruptly, its author became financially independent. She resigned her government job the next year to devote herself to research and writing. Her third book, *The Edge of the Sea,* appeared in 1955, adding even more luster to her reputation and marking a transition point in her career. The concern she had first felt during the war, as she read about the wartime uses of DDT and about the field and forest tests of the "miracle" insecticide, had become a deeply felt anxiety by the time *The Edge of the Sea* was published.

She had been quick to grasp the significance of an announcement in early 1946 that U.S.D.A. entomologists had succeeded in producing, through selective breeding in a laboratory, a strain of housefly much more resistant to DDT than the common stock. "In view of the increasing use of DDT for housefly and mosquito control," said *Science,* cautiously, on March 12, 1946, "it seems possible that, in time, a similar increase in resistance may occur under natural conditions." It had happened before, with other insecticides. And, sure enough, DDT-resistant strains of houseflies, mosquitoes, and crop-destroying insects soon began to appear naturally—and in such numbers in some areas that ever more massive doses of insecticide were required to control them.

Miss Carson recognized the implications of this genetic evolution. What if DDT's effectiveness were so reduced, in the not-distant future, as to require extensive use of the even more toxic chlorinated hydrocarbons (dieldrin, aldrin, chlor-

---

*This estimate, one must note, is based on the assumption that present methods of single-crop farming over huge acreages would continue (strip-farming—dividing large fields among several different crops—would greatly reduce insect hazards) and that increasingly effective biological controls would not be developed.

dane, endrin) which DDT's success had inspired? Would not these in turn lose effectiveness? No doubt chemicals still more toxic would by then be available; but what consequences would follow from their use—if, indeed, they were not so lethal to men as to be unusable?

Rachel Carson, like other biologists, saw nightmare answers to these questions. The end of the process might be an environment far more hostile to man than to his insect "enemies." After all, insect generations succeed themselves hundreds of times more rapidly than human generations. If man insisted on running a genetic adaptability race with insects, he was bound to lose.

The evidence that DDT was poisoning the environment multiplied throughout the 1950's. There were increasingly frequent reports of direct poisonings of birds, of fish, of small game, sometimes after applications in excess of prescribed amounts but often, too, when the prescriptions were precisely followed.

One day in January, 1958, Olga Huckins wrote a long, eloquently angry letter to her friend Rachel Carson, describing the deadly effect of DDT spraying for mosquito control over the Huckinses' private two-acre bird sanctuary at Powder Point, in Duxbury, Massachusetts. Not long afterward Miss Carson was a house guest at Powder Point when, late in the afternoon, the spraying plane came over. The next morning she went through the estuary with the Huckinses in their boat. She was sickened by what she saw—dead and dying fish everywhere, crayfish and crabs dead or staggering as their nervous systems were destroyed. "You ought to write about this," the Huckinses kept saying. "You're *got* to. . . ."

And Rachel Carson, publicity shy, no controversialist by temperament, acutely aware of the abuse in store for anyone who dared challenge the million-dollar pesticide industry, was forced to agree—especially as she came to realize that the direct kills were by no means the worst effect of the chemical pesticides. More widespread and disastrous by far were the delayed kills, coupled with the inhibition of reproductive processes. Entire species of birds were threatened with extinction. And how could a substance so toxic to other warm-blooded animals fail to have toxic effects, in the long run, on humans?

For as the stubbornly persistent DDT enters a food chain that begins with herbivores and runs through small to large and then larger carnivores, including man, the process known as "biological magnification" occurs. An early instance was recorded on the East Lansing campus of Michigan State University. Annual spraying of elms with DDT began there in 1954 to control the beetle that spreads Dutch elm disease. For the first year or so there were no apparent side effects. But then people noticed that there were no more robins on the campus. Earthworms feeding on elm leaves with tiny amounts of DDT on them accumulated the stuff in their body fat until a level toxic to robins was reached. Robins that ate those worms died—and robins unfortunate enough to visit the campus even two years after spraying had been discontinued also died.

In other studies the magnification rate in specific food chains was measured. In the bottom of Lake Michigan's Green Bay, for example, live billions of tiny crustaceans. The mud was found to contain 0.014 p.p.m. of DDT; the crustaceans, absorbing DDT from the mud, concentrated it in their bodies to 0.41 p.p.m.; fish, feeding on the crustaceans, concentrated DDT in their bodies to from 3 to 6 p.p.m.; herring gulls feeding on the fish accumulated DDT to the level of a 9 p.p.m. This concentration, though not immediately fatal to individual gulls, reduces normal reproduction. The eggs of these herring gulls contained 227 p.p.m. of DDT, and their shells were abnormally thin.

By the late 1950's it was clear to Miss Carson, and other knowledgeable observers, that DDT's increasingly massive invasion of the food chain was largely responsible for the fact that bald eagles were ceasing to breed on the East Coast between Florida and Main (large concentrations of DDT residues were found in the brains of prematurely dead eagles); that eagles in the Great Lakes region faced extinction because their egg shells were growing too thin (the physiological mechanics by which DDT inhibits calcium production would soon be discovered); that peregrine falcons were disappearing as breeding birds in the whole eastern half of the U.S.; that ospreys would disappear from Connecticut by the early 1970's if present rates of decline continued. Nor was DDT's invasion of the food chain limited to land or to offshore waters. Oceanic food chains were being similarly contaminated, and ocean currents were spreading DDT residues to the most remote corners of the earth.

Predictable in a general way by the pattern of events was the sad case of the Bermuda petrel, a carnivorous bird that feeds solely on oceanic life far from any area where DDT is used. The bird comes to Bermuda for only a few hours, at night, to lay its eggs. It eats nothing there. Yet its eggs in the late 1960's contained 6.44 p.p.m. of DDT on the average, and its reproduction was declining at a rate which, if continued, must end in complete reproductive failure by 1978. Even Antarctica's Adélie penguins, Wedell seals, and skua gulls, carnivores all, were soon found to carry trace amounts of DDT in their fat, though they live thousands of miles from the nearest area of DDT use. Undoubtedly they ingest DDT residues in their food.

But DDT was also found, in the 1960's, in Antarctic snow,* indicating that the food chain is not the only means by which the poison spreads. Studies conducted in Maine and New Brunswick, Canada, in the 1950's showed that approximately half the DDT sprayed over forests at treetop level hung suspended in the atmosphere to be spread worldwide on the wind. DDT attached to erosion debris also travels in irrigation water, rivers, and ocean currents.

*Some 2,400 tons of it have been estimated to have accumulated by now in Antarctica's snows.

The realization that the oceans' organisms are becoming depositories for DDT has led some ecologists to premonitions of an apocalypse, based on the assumption that much of he oxygen in the atmosphere is produced through photosynthesis by marine phytoplankton (vegetable life). Hence, anything that might inhibit oceanic photosynthesis on a large scale is a threat to life on earth.

Scientists of this persuasion took little comfort in the 1968 report by Charles F. Wurster, Jr., of the State University of New York at Stony Brook; in the laboratory very low concentrations of DDT had measurably reduced photosynthesis in cultures of four species of coastal and oceanic phytoplankton representing four major classes of algae. Furthermore, the same had been found true of a natural phytoplankton community (as distinct from a laboratory culture) at Woods Hole. "I'll tell you what we worry about most," said David M. Gates, director of the Missouri Botanical Garden in St. Louis, to a reporter in 1969, "—an irreversible catastrophe. A number of pesticide spills, for example, in those areas of the ocean where . . . much of the world's oxygen [is produced]. If you plot the frequency of this kind of event, they're getting closer and closer." Much of this kind of fear has been allayed by recent scientific findings that suggest that no significant interchange of oxygen occurs between ocean and atmosphere, and, in addition, that some phytoplankton are considerably less sensitive to pesticides than others. Such findings, of course, do not alter the fact that any large-scale interference with ocean life would have serious repercussions.

Whatever its ultimate effects may be, the frightening fact is that most of the hundreds of millions of pounds of DDT sprayed over the world during the last quarter century remain in circulation—only a fraction has decayed into harmless substances—and no one can say what fatal damage it alone (apart from the DDT being constantly added) may yet do.

Credit for the fact that public, governmental, and scientific attention was focused on the threat of DDT and other chemicals in the environment must certainly go to Rachel Carson's *Silent Spring*. Researching it meticulously (her argument was sustained by no fewer than fifty pages of closely printed source notes), she wrote the book in longhand, slowly, most of it in her home in Silver Spring, Maryland, and much of it at night, over a period of nearly four years, beginning in 1958. She well knew that her warning of the threat to the environment from the indiscriminate use of ever more and stronger pesticides would provoke attacks upon her motives, professional competence, and "scientific objectivity"; and so she was not surprised by the storm of controversy her book aroused even before its formal publication date in 1962. But with scientific colleagues, with the general public, and with many governmental policy makers, *Silent Spring* was enormously persuasive.

One of Rachel Carson's central points was that man, like every living thing, is a creature of his environment, and, consequently, any chemical fatal to his environment must ultimately be fatal to him (a concept commonly understood today but new to many a decade ago). She also challenged the constantly reiterated assertion that DDT and its close chemical affiliates are not directly toxic to human beings.

True, most Americans now probably have 10 to 12 p.p.m. DDT in their body fats, which is 3 to 5 p.p.m. more than the F.D.A.-set tolerance level for human food; and we seem unharmed by it. But what of the effects that may not show up for two or three decades or generations? Is DDT damaging chromosome structure? Is it, through subtle attacks on the central nervous system, slowly impairing mental processes? Is it a carcinogen (cancer-inducing agent)? Rachel Carson cited disturbing evidence that the answer to such questions might be affirmative.

Today DDT is increasingly suspected of direct injury to man. Evidence of the carcinogenic effects of DDT have multiplied since 1962. Indeed, in the very year following publication of *Silent Spring,* Dr. William C. H. Hueper of the National Cancer Institute reported DDT to be "cancer producing according to presently available evidence" and incriminated DDT in the "production of benign and malignant tumors of the liver, cancers of the lung, and leukemias."

Two years after her best seller was published—in mid-April, 1964—Rachel Carson, aged fifty-six, died of cancer. (Dr. Paul Müller died in October of the following year, at the age of sixty-six.) But before she died she had the satisfaction of knowing that her work was influencing public policy.

In 1963, in direct response to the public concern aroused by *Silent Spring,* President Kennedy's Science Advisory Committee recommended a reduction of DDT use with a view to its total elimination as quickly as possible, along with other "hard" pesticides. Soon thereafter Secretary of the Interior Steward Udall issued an order banning the use of DDT on Interior-controlled lands "when other chemicals can do the job." Wisconsin, Michigan, California, Massachusetts, and other states began to move toward state prohibitions of DDT. Finally, in November of 1969, acting on the recommendation of a special study commission on pesticides, Robert H. Finch, Secretary of Health, Education, and Welfare, announced that the federal government would "phase out" all but "essential uses" of DDT within two years. Many Americans assumed that this phasing out means the end of DDT. But not so.

Event though, belatedly, the search has been intensified for safe alternatives to persistent pesticides, the worldwide demand for DDT increases as underdeveloped countries face the immediate desperate problems of feeding and protecting the health of exploding populations. The U.N.'s World Health Organization and the Food and Agricultural Organization have strongly opposed any prohibition or even reduction of DDT's use, arguing that it is the cheapest effective pesticide (it costs about fifteen cents a pound as compared with a dollar or more for other chemicals), that poor countries cannot afford substitutes, and that without the kinds of crop protection and disease control provided by DDT, millions must surely and quickly die. In India, for instance, U.N. consultants are now working with the government to *double* within a year the percentage of cropland sprayed by hard pesticides, chiefly DDT. Even in America the government has moved so slowly to implement its "phase out" policy that citizen conservation groups, led by the crusading Environmental Defense Fund, have taken action to stop the manufacture and use of DDT through legal suits against government agencies and the major manufacturer.

And so the use of DDT continues, even as its disastrous effects on living things are being established beyond any doubt. The need for some system of broadly assessing the likely consequences of technological innovations before they are unleashed seems all too apparent. In the case of DDT, however, we can only hope to live with our mistakes.

Mr. Davis, a frequent writer on conservation subjects, is now writing a biography of Franklin D. Roosevelt to be published by G. P. Putnam's Sons.